For my parents, Vivien and Edward Michals

Contents

Illustrations

Acknowledgments

Although a book's faults are the author's own, it owes its existence to the virtues of many other people. I want to thank Frances Ferguson, who as a teacher showed me how to make few assumptions about what a literary text may mean, and who as a mentor and friend has been equally open-minded about the directions a scholarly career may take. At George Mason University, Kristin Samuelian has been a source of infectious pleasure in the practice of literary criticism, and Amelia Rutledge has opened children's literature for me as an academic field. My colleagues Miruna Stanica, Alok Yadov, David Kaufman, and Roger Lathbury read and insightfully commented on large swathes of this book, as did Elaine Hadley at the University of Chicago. I am also grateful for George Mason University's Junior Faculty Fellowship, which provided time to write, and Jen Stevens, our library's tireless friend of research in the humanities. The scholarship of Andrea Immel, Curator of the Cotsen Children's Library at Princeton University, was a starting point for this project, and her help navigating rare books kept it from flagging. Laura Wasawicz, Curator of Children's Literature at the American Antiquarian Society, was my guide in tracking Robinson Crusoe. A portion of this book's final chapter first appeared in *NOVEL: A Forum on Fiction* as "Henry James and the Invention of Adulthood," and is now reprinted by permission of the present publisher, Duke University Press. I am grateful to my son, David, for his patience when I compared his middle-school challenges to those of eighteenth-century midshipmen over the dinner table, and to my daughter, Rachel, for all the cups of tea she kindly brought me. Robert Matz believed this was a book when it started as a conversation by the fire, and then spent years helping that belief to become reality. His insight and enthusiasm animate every page. He is my first reader, and my best. I would like to thank Lorraine Matz and the late Joseph Matz for summers of writing by the lake. Finally, I want to thank my parents, Vivien and Edward Michals, who are my model of pride and joy in family. This book is dedicated to them.

CHAPTER I

Introduction

In a 1960 trial over the British publication of *Lady Chatterley's Lover*, prosecutor Mr. Mervyn Griffith-Jones opened his case by asking the jury not only, as we might expect, "would you approve of your young sons, young daughters" reading this book, but also "is it a book you would even wish your wife or your servants to read?" Titters were heard in the courtroom. The jury, which included a dockworker, a butcher, and a dress machinist, ruled unanimously for publication. In his closing address the counsel for the defense summed up the assumptions about age and print that he believed had caused that laughter. He dismissed the prosecution's concern to protect women and the working class as "an echo" from an earlier time, leaving age as the only serious criteria for dividing up the general reading public. And important though young readers were, they were not in fact the most important age-leveled group to be considered: "Society cannot fix its standards by what is suitable for a young person of 14," he flatly declared.[1] Whether or not *Lady Chatterley's Lover* was a bad book for children, it deserved to be published because it was a good book for a new figure, one recently granted a central place in literary matters: the adult. Worrying in 1900 that being obliged to write for the multitude of "boys and girls" who read novels prevented the serious artist from producing great work, Henry James would have greeted this new deference to the adult reader with delight.[2]

How did *adult* come to matter so much as a description of literature? How did readers judge the value of a novel before they could rely on this term to mean that a piece of writing was aesthetically excellent, ethically complex, sexually explicit, or any of these? *Books for Children, Books for Adults: Age and the Novel from Defoe to James* describes the relationship between the novel and modern ideas of adulthood. Children's reading has been examined historically since the publication in 1960 of Philippe Ariès's ground-breaking work, *Centuries of Childhood*.[3] But the notion of the adult reader has not received this attention, since adulthood is usually assumed to be historically constant. This assumption is incorrect. Both who counted as an adult and the importance of any idea of adulthood varied widely through the eighteenth and nineteenth centuries – as they still do. *Books for Children, Books for Adults* helps to open a new area of inquiry: the emergence of the idea of books intended specifically for adult readers in the writing and the reception of English novels. Before this emergence, I demonstrate, the novel was written for a mixed-age audience, one that was primarily imagined not in terms of age but of social status and gender – the audience that still lived on in Mr. Griffith-Jones's imagination in 1960. At the same time, when earlier novelists and their readers considered the ideal age of the novel's audience, they tended to claim that the most important member of that audience was "the young person" rather than the adult.

As twenty-first-century readers, we may assume that there have always been adults-only novels, and that we recognize them when we see them because they have distinctive qualities: perhaps they minimize didacticism, for example, while foregrounding formal complexity, sexual content, or moral ambiguity. Rejecting this assumption, I argue that eighteenth-century novels were written not for adults but rather for a popular mixed-age audience of women, children, and servants. At that time, women and servants of all ages were routinely lumped together with children as the ideal – or the nightmare – reader of popular vernacular print. Thus, while we may imagine that children's literature was an offshoot of literary forms intended for adult readers, that is not the case. Rather, the opposite is true. The first commercially significant age-specialized publishing appeared with the rise of a distinct market for children's literature in the middle of the eighteenth century. These children's books contrasted with novels intended for a mixed-age audience – not with novels intended for adults. Specialization by age for adults occurred only much later in the history of the novel. Through most of the nineteenth century, the novel's core readership remained mixed-age. If we think of children's literature as emerging out of "adult reading," and as changing "adult" conventions of form and content to make them suitable for children, we reverse the order in which fiction was in fact age-leveled.

Books for Children, Books for Adults traces this history of adult reading from Daniel Defoe's *Robinson Crusoe* to Henry James's *The Awkward Age*. It offers a series of case studies of key eighteenth- and nineteenth-century novels, popular in their day and canonical today. While the book examines ideas of adulthood within these novels, it also aims to raise questions about reception and the history of the book. Thus it provides a wider focus on less familiar adaptations of these novels, adaptations that were designed to target readers by social status and gender as well as by age. In addition to considering the different kinds of readers that these different versions of the novels seem to imply, it considers comments made by the novelists themselves about their intended audiences, the pronouncements of professional critics, and, where possible, responses from ordinary readers of various ages. In doing so, it explores the reasons why some books originally written for a mixed-age audience, such as *Robinson Crusoe*, eventually became children's literature, while others written for this same audience, such as *Pamela*, became adult novels. Seeing literary history within the social history of age, *Books for Children, Books for Adults* also examines why, at the turn of the twentieth century, authors such as Henry James finally resolved to write for an audience of adults only. Fundamentally, it argues that in these novels and in the history of their marketing and reception, we can see how a world of masters and servants became a world of adults and children.

The amusement of children and the lower classes

It is difficult for us today to imagine a reading audience that is not age-leveled. As Mitzi Myers notes, sheer "habit makes it hard to think of earlier child and adult readers as inhabitants of one literary world, or at least of parallel reading worlds with more permeable boundaries than those we are accustomed to."[4] We work within a framework of national standards of primary and secondary education, a framework that carries with it a powerful set of working assumptions about how reading levels correlate with stages of individual development, as well as the assumption of near-universal adult literacy. These assumptions can of course still be problematic today. When we look back at earlier centuries, the equation of adulthood with literacy becomes even more misleading. To be sure, a developmental tradition linked to numerical age runs from Puritan devotional works through children's literature, the bildungsroman, and psychological realism. This tradition influences not only the thematic content of the literary canon as we know it, but also the classrooms, the databases, and the floor plans of public libraries and bookstores in which any given novel now appears, clearly identified as Adult, Young Adult, or Juvenile. In contrast, after meticulously tracking the eighteenth-century child reader through sources such as marginalia, letters, diaries, and book-sellers' records, M. O. Grenby concludes that in this earlier period, "there was seldom rigid segregation between literature for children and for adults and little stigma attached to cross-reading in either direction."[5]

Through the eighteenth century and much of the nineteenth, writers often cared more about social status than age when discussing reading. Moreover, when they refer to age, it is generally not to a sense of numerical age tightly keyed to a widely accepted developmental scale that assigns each book its appropriate place in the world. Rather, age itself appears as a kind of corollary of social status. As Andrea Immel suggests, age is often imagined through a number of other social categories: "it is usually a bundled set of associations – childishness with, say, servitude or femininity – that structures action and perception at any given time."[6] This sense of age reflects political subordination: in this context, the opposite of the child is not the adult, but rather the master. As late as 1810, referring to "those popular narratives, which are the amusement of children and the lower classes," Walter Scott invokes this older understanding of age and reading. Seeing "children and the lower classes" as a single category of readers runs counter to the idea of adulthood as a developmental category that begins for all people at, or at least around, a particular numerical age. Scott suggests an earlier and weaker sense of adulthood by conflating age and social status. For him, working people of all ages and young people of all classes are the same kind of reader. However numerically old or young they may be, what is most important about them all is that they are not gentlemen. That is, they lack both a gentleman's independent property and his education. Eighteenth-century printers often followed this set of assumptions in targeting elite readers with expensive books and poorer readers with cheap books rather than dividing up the market by numerical age.

Like social status, gender often weighed more heavily than numerical age in describing readers. Ian Watt calls attention to this way of thinking when he remarks that elite eighteenth-century writers imagined maturity through their ideas of both status and gender. He points to the literary importance of one set of norms, "the norms of the mature, rational and educated male world." This idea of maturity as equivalent to educated masculinity often leads to the confusion of gentlemen in particular with adults in general: "the Augustan stresses on masculine and adult values . . . are, of course, functionally related; as when Chesterfield told his son that 'Women . . . are only children of a larger growth' (September 5th, 1748)."[7] Such comments invoke age as a way of describing and of reinforcing social inequalities rather than age as a developmental scale that, at least in principle, cuts across both status and gender.

This older, blurry sense of age is especially important for the novel. In considering earlier eighteenth-century novels' reception, readers still can be usefully categorized not in terms of numerical age, as either adults or children, but rather in terms of status and gender, as either gentlemen or everybody else.[8] Most of the people who bought novels in the eighteenth century were educated gentry and professional men. But for most of that century, novels were also read by and strongly associated with a mixed-age audience of non-elite readers – an audience that included both "children of a larger growth" and very young people. For example, William Warner stresses the commercial importance of the novel's appeal to an unusually broad audience, in terms of age as well as status: "The novel's ability to assemble a diverse group of readers – women and men, the learned and the barely literate, the young and the old – enabled the successful novel to build a large general audience."[9] This blurry sense of age also suggests why, as Myers writes, even today, "children and the newly literate often constitute an undifferentiated audience."[10] Contemporary scholars often work against this older habit of conflating age categories with status categories. They insist that in psychological terms an illiterate or semi-literate adult is an entirely different sort of person from a child.

This modern idea of adulthood cuts across social status and gender. Although imperfectly realized, it is an egalitarian ideal, one whose influence has increased over the last two centuries. Frances Ferguson notes both the centrality and the difficulty of the distinction between adults and children in modern political thought: "The ability to treat children as different from adults is almost as fundamental to modern political thinking – of a more or less liberal cast – as any distinction we make politically . . . it is a distinction that is all the more fundamental for being extraordinarily difficult to correlate with actual empirical descriptions and a specification of one's criteria."[11] In order to weigh so heavily against older ways of describing and ranking people, this idea of adulthood requires something more specific in addition to liberal principles: a standardized, widely accepted numerical scale. "Practical tests" of age once determined what people could do on a daily basis. For example, a medieval burgess's son generally came of age whenever he could count, measure cloth, and tell a good coin from a bad one and so conduct business for his father.[12] In contrast, no matter what their level of personal maturity, gender, or property, unless barred by felony, all American citizens today become eligible to vote at the same age. Unlike the cloth measuring test and the inherited right to the family shop, this idea of adulthood is an abstraction backed by nothing more than faith in the number 18. Feminism and queer theory have made us familiar with the ways in which systems of ideas and institutions shape which human biological differences matter in terms of gender and what they mean. Age systems do similar work. As Steven Mintz argues, "age categories are not natural; rather, they are imbued with cultural assumptions, meaning, and values."[13] These assumptions, meanings, and values change over time: "Far from being static and unchanging, age categories and age consciousness have shifted profoundly in distinct historical eras."[14] Today we readily think in terms of numbers in reflecting on who we are, and routinely offer proofs of numerical age in establishing our identity to others. Perhaps the very centrality of numerical age to our ways of thinking makes this a difficult category of analysis on which to gain critical distance. The impact of educational, medical, psychological, and legal age norms on our daily lives may prompt us to take numerical age as a straightforward aspect of human identity. As Myers notes, age-leveling is a habit.

It is important to remember (as well as, perhaps, hard to imagine) that until the early eighteenth century most people in England did not know their numerical age. Keith Thomas points out that it was only then that "awareness of their numerical age came to form part of most men's basic self-consciousness."[15] Through the early eighteenth century, numerical age was something that one kept track of (or – more often – retroactively estimated, usually in good round numbers) only for special occasions, particularly in a legal context.[16] And such occasions then occurred less often for people than they do for us today. "The real pressure on men to know their ages," writes Thomas, "came from the lawyers, who constantly worked to replace practical tests of age by numerical ones, and from the bureaucrats and legislators, who specified precise numerical ages for an increasing number of civil rights and duties."[17] Mintz similarly calls our attention to the novelty of our own routine preoccupation with demarcating age by number: "Contemporary societies' fascination with age stands in stark contrast to earlier societies' rather vague and amorphous age categories."[18] Of course, these earlier societies knew that human beings change through the course of a lifetime. Mintz's point is that such change meant less than it does now, and meant different things from what it does now: "no society is unaware of age, and historians need to ask what age meant or entailed in societies that lacked the rigid age categories and the intense age consciousness of western societies in the mid-twentieth century."[19] That is, in thinking about age consciousness before the twentieth century, we should look for differences, not for an absence. The difference that this book concentrates on is the rise in importance for the novel of a numerically grounded idea of adulthood.

Serving a variety of social purposes, ways of measuring age often differ sharply from each other. Early modern writers, for example, inherited medieval schemes of the ages of man, but "could not agree about the numbers."[20] Early modern religious handbooks, literary works, and the woodcuts of popular ballads represented as few as four to as many as eleven stages. Childhood, youth, and adulthood nearly always appear in these schemes, but their numerical range varies wildly. For example, Thomas Fortescue claims youth runs from the age of twenty-two to forty-two, while Richard Mulcaster places it "from seven till one and twenty."[21] *The Office of Christian Parents* (1616) claims youth begins at fourteen and ends at twenty-eight. Aristotelian biology divided human life into the three phases that are still familiar today: growth, maturity, and decay. Also popular, however, were Galenic physiology's scheme in which the four body humors controlled human life, and Christian theology's analogy between "the ages of man and the six historical ages of the world."[22] Furthermore, Ptolemaic astrology "divided human life into seven ages, each corresponding to a planet in an order unfolding from the earth to Saturn, and each associated with specific qualities . . . There were other traditions which divided life into three, four and six ages, as well as seven and even eleven and more."[23]

When thinking about numerical age before the middle of the eighteenth century, rather than looking for one well-recognized number that correlates to our developmental sense of adulthood as the central phase of life, perhaps we should think instead of different numbers around which significance tended to cluster for different kinds of people. Some of these important numbers are quite low, and they all vary by gender as well as status. Boys' lives were often counted by sevens, while girls' lives were counted by sixes: "ancient mental habits, based on a septenary numerology . . . made twenty-one, like seven (the end of innocence) and fourteen (the age of discretion), into a point of particular significance in a boy's life. (For girls the reckoning tended to be duodecimal: six, twelve, and eighteen.)"[24] Additionally, when examining age across time, it is especially important to be conscious of terminology. Although familiar terms about age appear quite early, in context, these words may tell us only that they do not mean what we expect them to mean. For example, while we tend to take as a good marker of adulthood official acceptance into the working world in general, or the military in particular, from 1918 to 1924 "boy" was the lowest rank in the Royal Air Force.[25] Similarly, while we generally understand sexual availability as a central attribute of adulthood, the early modern term "*boy* readily elided . . . with . . . *whore*."[26] What looks like a familiar age of legal majority, twenty-one, appears reassuringly early in medieval common law – but in this context, twenty-one is rather "the knightly age." Most medieval tenants were in fact out of ward, able to inherit land, to make binding contracts, and to perform military service at fourteen or fifteen. Only those who held land by knight service gained their inheritance and the ability to contract (for things other than necessities) so late, supposedly because a medieval knight's armor was heavy and medieval combat was complex: only at twenty-one would men be strong and skillful enough to fight for their overlord carrying that much metal.[27]

The word adolescence, or "adolescency" or "adolescentia," appears as early as the 1400s, but formal descriptions of "the ages of man" tend to exclude it, as do court records. Early uses of adolescence often seem interchangeable with youth – but neither term reliably corresponds with our sense of a crucial developmental phase that begins with puberty. Sources that distinguish between the two sometimes disagree on whether adolescence precedes or follows youth.[28] Moreover, although lust is important to early descriptions of youth, puberty itself as a time of sexual development receives remarkably little attention. Extended medical descriptions of physical development related to puberty begin to appear around the middle of the seventeenth century; as Paul Griffiths explains, "there does not seem to have been any clear and considered medical opinion about sexual development in the earlier period *c.*1560 – *c.*1640."[29] And it is only in the early eighteenth century that discussions of puberty figure in a significant number of popular medical texts, the cheap and enduring "little books" described by Paul-Gabriel Boucé.[30] Most important for this study, even the term "adult" must be read with caution. In his 1656 manual on family life, Thomas Cobbett mentions "Adult persons" – but only to explain that he includes the overwhelming majority of such persons, all those who are in a subordinate position to the master of a household, "in the notion of children." He urges the reader to "remember . . . that under the notion of children, in this discourse, are understood, all such as are in the relation of children, whether Adult persons, or children in Age."[31] Such an open assertion of the permanent subordination of "Adult persons" gives us pause because, in principle, the modern idea of adulthood overrides social status and gender. This egalitarian aspect of adulthood is at times disregarded today, but it is an ideal with important cultural influence.

Even today, however, the numbers we so routinely use do not always add up to one consistent identity. What an adult is depends on why one is asking the question, now as well as in earlier centuries. Medicine offers the most definite numbers. The American Academy of Pediatrics and Infancy, for example, holds that after one's twenty-second birthday, one is for medical purposes an adult. One now has a reasonable expectation of living much longer as an adult than as a child or adolescent, and medical norms reflect this fact. In contrast, when life expectancy was shorter, adulthood may have had less prominence. In the early modern period, for example, people seem to have been more likely to live nearly half of their lives in the category of "youth."[32] Sandwiched between youth and an old age unsoftened by modern affluence, sanitation, or medicine, adulthood was only one stage of life, as fleeting as all the others.

Law defines adulthood a bit less crisply than does medicine. As Joseph Goldstein remarks, in law, "adult" remains a relatively unmarked term, a category that consists of what is left over after all the special exceptions have been made: "'Adult,' unlike 'child,' is a word infrequently used in secular law . . . law defines an adult primarily by implication: its meaning is determined by the general exceptions provided for the non-adult – the infant, the minor, the juvenile, and the unemancipated person."[33] Law relies on two different ways of conceptualizing adulthood: the age of license and the age of majority. License refers to the age at which one has one's government's permission to perform specific acts: for example, entering into legally binding contracts, purchasing and drinking alcohol, leaving school, voting, or marrying. The age of majority is a broader legal recognition that the authority and responsibilities of one's parents or guardians have ended. The age of majority varies from place to place, as does the age of license to engage in specific activities. For most US states, the age of majority is eighteen (in Mississippi it is twenty-one; in four other states it is nineteen), while the age of license can be both higher and lower. Despite its variability, the entire range of ages at which we now hold people fully accountable for crimes or allow them to form binding contracts is much higher than it was in the past, suggesting a greater commitment to some age-leveled idea of personal maturity: in sixteenth-century England, for example, four-year-olds made binding wills, seven-year-olds married, eight-year-olds were hung for felonies, and propertied teenagers "routinely" became members of Parliament.[34]

A psychological idea of adulthood as a set of internal qualities that mark the maturity and autonomy of the individual is the most resonant of all these concepts for the contemporary study of literature. This idea of age is crucial for classifying books according to their appropriate readership, as adult, young adult, or juvenile. It is also crucial for analyzing characters within such books and for judging their merit as a whole, as in the claim that a truly "adult" work shows maturity of taste and ethical judgment. The psychological idea of adulthood is also, however, the most difficult to specify in terms of numerical age: it is a vanishing point as well as an age-leveled norm. This psychological idea of adulthood is a latecomer. Psychology is of course a younger field than either medicine or law; moreover, even in terms of concentrated attention from the profession of psychology, adulthood is something of a novelty. It first appears as a kind of framing device for the study of adolescence at the opening of the twentieth century. If adolescents are people who have left childhood behind and are moving towards a new developmental goal, "adult" is what we call them once they get there.[35] In comparison to the richly charted, tumultuous development of the adolescent, however, this definition of adulthood seems fairly shadowy. It is also harder to assign it a number. Contemporary psychological studies of adolescence tend to end around the age of eighteen – but there is no consensus that nineteen-year-olds have achieved adulthood. Some psychologists suggest the term "emerging adulthood" to characterize people from eighteen to thirty;[36] others use the term "quarter-life period"; others suggest a "novice phase" stretching to the age of thirty-three.[37]

As the endpoint of adolescent development, adulthood suggests a range of highly admirable personal qualities: one fairly typical checklist includes "the attainment of cognitive self-sufficiency, emotional self-reliance, and behavioral self-control."[38] But such lists describe an ideal that many of us never attain at any age. Looking for the high standard of ethical awareness that Erik Erikson identifies with adulthood, for example, James Côté notes that it "is an ideal to which many – perhaps most – do not rise for reasons of discrimination, ignorance, and distraction."[39] Similarly, pioneering developmental psychologist Jean Piaget suggests that the use of hypothesis and deductive reasoning characterizes adulthood – but then finds himself wrestling with the failure of many adult research subjects to demonstrate these formal reasoning structures. "Can one demonstrate, at this level of development [the period from fifteen to twenty years] as at previous levels, cognitive structures common to all individuals?" he asks.[40] Other developmental psychologists answer in the negative, claiming that "most adults do not use hypotheticodeductive reasoning in all aspects of their lives and many do not use it at all," making this a "dubious criterion" for adulthood's achievement.[41] While the category of "emerging adulthood" implies that the positive personal qualities it foregrounds will indeed emerge, given enough time, here researchers are more skeptical. The psychological sense of adulthood as an age-leveled norm (even a norm defined as generously as starting anywhere between eighteen and thirty-three) is in tension with its meaning as an aspirational ideal.

Before the twentieth century, such questions about adulthood were less pressing. Less was at stake in any age-leveled norm of maturity. A major theme of this book is the historical significance of social status rather than a specific numerical age in determining when – or if – a person achieves the personal autonomy and authority that we now associate with adulthood. "The authority of fortune," writes Adam Smith in 1776, "is very great . . . much greater than that either of age or of personal qualities." In other words, when thinking about power, Smith still imagines age as quite properly coming in a distant second to social status, at least among "opulent and civilized" nations. He gives age the very limited role of deciding who has power over whom *only* "among those who are in every other respect equal and among whom, therefore, there is nothing else to regulate" rank.[42] Smith refers here to a traditional way of thinking about age and power: for example, in 1667, thirteen-year-old Christopher Monk, son of a powerful Devon family, was elected to Parliament, served on committees, and made important floor speeches. He was one of many similarly wealthy teenage MPs.[43] Pope's *Dunciad* (1743) attacks such youthful legislators: "The pale Boy-Senator yet tingling stands, / And holds his breeches close with both his hands."[44] By imagining the "Boy-Senator" still subject to a flagellating schoolmaster, Pope tries to subject the authority of status to the authority of numerical age.

For those who lacked property, adulthood could not always be reached, no matter how many years one lived: "The borders between childhood, youth, and adulthood were sometimes imprecise and blurred. They were widely observed but sometimes neglected, or in fact were unattainable for some people in tough socio-economic conditions."[45] People who could not afford to set up a household, marry, or become full members of a trade were likely to remain instead in the position of children. As Leslie Paris explains, "the meanings of adulthood and childhood are co-determined, and both are always in process of being articulated."[46] *Books for Children, Books for Adults* examines "child" and "adult" as relational terms in the eighteenth- and nineteenth-century English book market in particular. It argues that in reading, as in other kinds of human activities, it is the difference between these two terms that becomes newly important, influencing not only modern ideas about childhood and the child reader, but also modern ideas about adulthood and the adult reader.

Overview

We have excellent historical studies of children and their books, such as M. O. Grenby's *The Child Reader, 1700–1840* (2011), and a wealth of scholarship about distinct groups such as women and working-class readers. The historically variable idea of the adult reader remains largely unexamined, however. The exception to this lack of critical focus on the social construction of adulthood is Beverly Lyon Clark's *Kiddie Lit: The Cultural Construction of Children's Literature in America*. Lyon Clark calls attention to the deliberate pruning away of children from the novel's audience at the opening of the twentieth century.[47] While Lyon Clark's account starts with the pivotal figure of Henry James and is primarily concerned with the cultural standing of children's literature, I consider the two centuries of thinking about age and the novel with which James attempted to break. In examining this subject, I draw on critics such as Michael McKeon and Nancy Armstrong who have demonstrated that the novel as a whole participates in a broad historical shift from understanding persons in terms of their social status to understanding them in terms of their internal states. I argue that this shift in emphasis from social to psychological categories also required new ways of thinking about age. These varying ideas of age affect in turn both the novel's readership and its ways of constructing character. Chapters 2 and 3 examine how some eighteenth-century novels explore different ideas of age to try to escape the disreputable, mixed-age world of popular print addressed to the semi-literate of all ages: the audience of women, children, and servants who were thought to consume too eagerly stories of criminal and sexual adventure. Chapters 4 and 5 place the novel within the more genteel nineteenth-century world of "family reading." Alan Richardson has shown that new standards of sexual and political propriety advocated by printers such as John Newbery triumphed in "official" children's literature towards the end of the eighteenth century.[48] But similar standards shaped the mainstream novel as well, by defining what was proper for middle-class people of all ages to read. Newly respectable as the standard-bearer for domesticity rather than raffish adventure, the nineteenth-century novel continued to address a mixed-age audience. Finally, the concluding chapter argues that as Modernism elevated the novel from popular entertainment to elite art form, it often described this shift in the social status of its readers as a shift in their age, helping to produce a new ideal of the novel as adults-only reading. "Adult" gained new weight as a term of aesthetic value from the increasing importance of numerical age-leveling in the twentieth century more broadly, not only in bookstores, libraries, and classrooms, but also in psychiatry, medicine, and a new framework of state-sponsored institutions ranging from kindergarten to old-age pensions.

As age-leveling and adulthood became ever more important in the social world, in the history of the novel, adults became ever more unlikely to get stranded alone on desert islands or to think they ought to enjoy reading about people who are. Daniel Defoe's solitary shipwreck scenario became instead the property of childhood. Chapter 2, "Rewriting *Robinson Crusoe*: age and the island," asks why this is so. Although Defoe's didactic work *The Family Instructor* (1715–18) is concerned to differentiate between the child and the adult according to the complexity of their understanding of God, *Robinson Crusoe* is remarkably unconcerned with age. As we see in the rapidly multiplying chapbook adaptations of Defoe's 1719 novel, its early audience was primarily differentiated by social status and by the varying degrees of literacy that were considered appropriate to people in these different social positions, whatever their numerical age. For these early readers, Crusoe's avid economic awareness was not a marker of adulthood, nor was his relative lack of sexual awareness a marker of childishness. Rather, the isolation of Crusoe's island offered a compelling fantasy of escape from an anxious web of personal and economic obligation that did not distinguish between public and private, business and family. As increasing differentiation between these personal and economic realms helped to separate the world of the adult from that of the child, age gradually became central to *Robinson Crusoe*'s reception. The novel's powerful fantasy of shipwrecked isolation was re-imagined in terms of newer ways of understanding age difference. Influenced by Rousseau's assertion in *Emile* that "this marvelous book" was the only one that any child should read, children's writers such as Joachim Heinrich Campe transformed Crusoe's island into the perfect image of childhood. Their Robinson is positioned very far away from an adult world that they saw as distinguished by the complexity of its awareness, not of God, but of sexual and economic relationships. In contrast, for neo-classical economic theorists of the mid-nineteenth century and the introductory economics textbooks that followed them, this same island became the perfect image of adulthood, which they imagined as rational, utility-maximizing individualism. Covering the longest expanse of time of all the book's chapters, this study traces *Robinson Crusoe*'s complex position in the history of the novel, the history of children's literature, and the popularization of economic theory.

While *Robinson Crusoe*'s relative lack of interest in sex took on a new importance as reading became age-leveled, so too did the avid interest in this subject displayed by Samuel Richardson's *Pamela; or, Virtue Rewarded*. Chapter 3 of this study, "Dating *Pamela*: Mr. B., *Goody Two-Shoes*, and the age of consent," compares Richardson's sense of his readers with the first commercially significant age-differentiated reader: not the adult, but rather the child – the reader envisioned in the middle of the eighteenth century in the new children's book market staked out by John Newbery. It compares Richardson's novel with another story about a girl who is as literate, as devoted to Lockean reason, and as upwardly mobile as is Pamela herself: Newbery's *History of Little Goody Two-Shoes* (1765). First published "for the YOUTH of both sexes" but later re-classified as adults-only reading, *Pamela* is a flashpoint for the representation of sexuality in relation to age. Following Michel Foucault, cultural historians have argued convincingly that sexuality is now more important to a psychological idea of the self than it was to earlier ways of understanding identity. And as psychological theories of sexual development gained more influence, so too did the idea of adulthood. The ability to offer a certain kind of consent to sexual relations is central to our contemporary idea of being an adult. A psychological sense of sexual development shapes this idea of legal consent. *Pamela* and its reception history reflect a conflict between traditional ideas of age based on social status and the challenge to these ideas represented by developmental theories of age most influentially formulated by John Locke, and popularized in part through the emergence of a market for children's literature largely framed along Lockean lines. But Locke's adult is a reasonable rather than a sexual being. Locke's ideas affect theories of sexual consent and marriage law through stressing the importance of rational consent to all contracts, not by anticipating psychological theories of sexual maturity. In *Pamela*, Locke's sense of adulthood as the mastery of immediate desires by reason becomes more separate from and more able to compete with other kinds of mastery, other ways of deciding who gets to tell whom what to do, who gets to form legally binding contracts, or who gets to hit whom without running into trouble with the law. Nevertheless, the struggle to be reasonable, like the struggle to be virtuous, is a life-long pursuit, and read in this light *Pamela* is still appropriate to a mixed-age audience. Adulthood became important enough to need books of its own when a psychological idea of the self became dominant, one that foregrounds neither reason nor virtue but rather sexuality. As we have seen, by these standards, *Robinson Crusoe* became a boy's book. The converse is true for Richardson's relentlessly erotic but also proudly Lockean *Pamela*. Always seen as a "warm" book, this novel moved only slowly out of the hands of the young reader and into those of the adult.

Letitia Barbauld, Maria Edgeworth, and Walter Scott at last give us stories whose central characters and audiences are imagined from their beginning according to a full-fledged developmental model. Barbauld's and Edgeworth's success in publishing age-leveled series whose vocabulary, syntax, and developmental content consistently foreground numerical age over social status remains a template for publishing today. Chapter 4, "Rational moralists, highland barbarians, and the taste for adventures," argues, however, that in many respects the developmental model that frames their age-leveled work still may not be the one we expect. While the continental bildungsroman explores the growth of sexual experience and introspective self-knowledge in its hero, the central characters in the works of Barbauld, Edgeworth, and Scott learn how to shop, how to avoid debt, and how to refrain from attacking their personal enemies with battle-axes or dueling pistols. That is, they reach maturity as this stage is understood by the eighteenth-century conjectural historians, becoming, not psychologically complex adults, but polite and commercial people. Barbauld, Edgeworth, and Scott share a fascination with conjectural history's theory that the life of the individual and the life of the nation recapitulate each other, reaching their highest point of development in a state of peaceful, rational commercial prosperity. This idea of maturity shapes the way their work imagines both violence and gender. Just as Barbauld and Edgeworth urge middle-class boys to acquire professional skills instead of succumbing to the real and tempting possibility of enlisting at twelve years old to fight Napoleon, so Scott shows grown men putting down their claymores and taking up a life of judicious consumption. While few writers can offer more nostalgic pleasure by describing weapons and warriors than Scott, he generally presents violence itself as a distressing phase that must be outgrown by both nations and individuals. To reach maturity, men, women, and Britain all must become rational and polite. Changing ideas of age shape not only Scott's critical reputation, but also the rise and meteoric fall in critical esteem of historical fiction as a whole. Critics such as Ina Ferris have demonstrated the role that gendered ideas of literature played in Scott's reception, arguing that *Waverley* made novels critically respectable by associating them with the masculine and professional genre of history rather than with the feminine pleasure of romance.[49] What Scott gained in terms of gender, however, he eventually lost in terms of age. When other theories of development replaced his national one, the *Waverley* novels and their scenes of violence were re-interpreted to fit a new genre, the Victorian boys' adventure story. By the twentieth century, historical fiction as a whole was widely seen as "juvenile," a sub-literary genre particularly suited to immature readers.

"When I say I like Dickens, do I simply mean that I like thinking about my childhood?" asks George Orwell, who, born in 1903, still encountered Dickens first within a mixed-age world of family reading.[50] Chapter 5, "Educating Dickens: Old Boys, Little Mothers, and school time," begins with the fact that Dickens writes for families rather than for adults. That is, in *Household Words*, *Bleak House*, and *Our Mutual Friend*, through the relationship he creates with his audience as well as through his characters, Dickens focuses on unifying his readers in terms of middle-class ideals of gender and domesticity rather than dividing them up according to age. Nevertheless, age is more important for Dickens than it was for Scott, or for Richardson or Defoe, more important within his novels themselves and in their changing critical reception. Dickens's long career saw the emergence of a critical model that tried to move reading from the mixed-age space of the home to the age-leveled space of the school. The mixed-age world of family reading that Orwell still invoked in the twentieth century was first called into question by the ideal of the adult, professional critic powerfully articulated by George Eliot and George Henry Lewes. At the start of Dickens's career, reviewers claimed he was not a gentleman. By the end of his career, his mixed-age domestic audience had not changed, but its critical status had: detractors now claimed that Dickens was not an adult. Age fascinates Dickens as well as his critics. He sometimes tries to chart the steady process of psychological development towards stable adulthood that is advocated by the continental bildungsroman and by English critics such as Eliot and Lewes. However, he is more often drawn to the scrambling of age categories: his novels swarm with Little Mothers and Old Boys. While the bildungsroman focuses on the adolescent growing into adulthood, Dickens specializes in the direct collision of childhood and old age, as critics such as Claudia Nelson have noted.[51] In this scrambling of age categories, Dickens engages with nineteenth-century debates over labor, education, and age. In particular, he considers the issue of whether labor is a key attribute of adulthood. New ways of organizing homes, workplaces, and schools made it seem that, in principle, work should also become something new: a separate, public, adult sphere of life. By the turn of the twentieth century, such debates were resolved with a new consensus that adults should go to work and children should go to school. It is at this point that the figure of the factory child is near-universally adopted as representing all of the injustice of the Industrial Revolution. But Dickens does not write about factory children, and he does not reliably divide people up by age as either students or workers.

Like its audience, the Anglo-American domestic novel of the nineteenth century did not find adulthood to be a subject of riveting interest. Towards the end of the century, however, a number of novelists began to show just such an interest, Henry James perhaps foremost among them. My final chapter, "'The time of real amusement': Henry James and the cult of adulthood," argues that James defines his idea of the adult and his idea of the novel through each other. Urging "serious" writers to turn to exclusively adult readers and subjects in his essay "The Future of the Novel: An Analysis and a Forecast," for example, he insists that nothing less than the survival of the novel itself depends on transforming its audience. If novelists do not stop writing for young people as well as old, he claims, the novel will die: "By what it shall do in respect to the 'young' the great prose fable will, from any serious point of view, practically see itself stand or fall." Complaining that the "larger part of the great multitude that sustains the teller and the publisher of tales is constituted by boys and girls," James struggles to move the novel out of the mixed-age world of family reading into the adults-only space of Modernism – a space that will eventually be given legal protection through the celebrated obscenity trials of works such as *Ulysses* and *Lady Chatterley's Lover*.[52] James writes within an older, more amorphous understanding of age in attacking as childish the middle-class and feminine tradition of domestic fiction from which he wishes to differentiate his version of the novel. And the class bias and misogyny of his new "art-novel" have been insightfully described. I focus on a different aspect of James's "elevation" of the novel: the significance of the adults-only novel within the social history of age. James shows a newly specialized interest in and enthusiasm for the idea of the adult, and for the possibilities for reading, writing, and other aspects of living that this idea enables. As he weeds out boys and girls from his audience, however, James turns to them as the focal characters of the novels of his middle period. While more popular novels by contemporary authors such as Frances Hodgson Burnett also use child focal characters, James's children are distinguished by the fact that they are not interested in childish things. Maisie, Miles, and Flora stare with absolute fascination at the future, at the modern, age-exclusive pleasures and powers of adults. One of the greatest of these adults-only pleasures is the novel as James strives to imagine it, infusing numerical age difference with an intense sense of elite aesthetic pleasure.

Another and somewhat ironic effect of the age-leveling of the novel is a twenty-first century preoccupation with adults who read children's books. Adults now cross the relatively new divide between books marketed as adult fiction and books marketed for the young with extreme self-consciousness. Such cross-reading is not new. Since its appearance in the late nineteenth-century, "adult fiction" has not been a description of what most adults actually read, but rather an aesthetic and psychological ideal riding the coattails of a demographic category. But cross-reading still draws comment. Maria Tatar, for example, ponders "why so many adults can be found browsing books in the children's section and why books for children and young adults dominate best-seller lists."[53] It triggers strong reactions that range from praise for regaining an inner Romantic child to condemnation for infantilizing culture, such as William Safire's protest that when adults read Harry Potter, it "is not just dumbing down; it is growing down."[54] In 2000, after the Harry Potter books had reliably topped its best-sellers list for years, *The New York Times* finally created separate best-sellers lists for adults and for children. As might be expected, a decade later, the mixed-age popularity of another series marketed for young adults set off a similar reaction: "The only thing more embarrassing than catching a guy on the plane looking at pornography on his computer is seeing a guy on the plane reading 'The Hunger Games'" rails *The New York Times* columnist Joe Stein in a piece plaintively titled "Adults Should Read Adult Books." The purpose of *Books for Children, Books for Adults* is not to instruct people on what they ought to read, but rather to uncover the history that makes such debates possible – the history that must be forgotten for a popular columnist such as Stein to write "I'll read 'The Hunger Games' when I finish the previous 3,000 years of fiction written for adults."[55] While this study does not attempt to cover 3,000 years, it hopes to raise questions about the assumption that a great deal of "fiction written for adults" can be found in England and the United States before the late nineteenth century. It hopes to interest others in the history that makes the conflation of age as a demographic measure and age as a measure of aesthetic excellence both so irresistible and so problematic.

CHAPTER 2

Rewriting Robinson Crusoe

Age and the island

In the centuries that followed *Robinson Crusoe*'s publication, Defoe's shipwreck plot dropped out of the mainstream of the novel to become instead a staple of children's literature. Why was this the case? To answer this question, we must consider how ideas about age shape *Robinson Crusoe* and its reception in three overlapping contexts: the history of the novel, the history of children's literature, and the popularization of economic theory. Crusoe's solitary island took on new meaning in each of these contexts as numerical age took on new weight relative to social status. In each context, an idea of adulthood gained new importance, transforming Crusoe's story. *Robinson Crusoe*'s first audience was mixed-age, and for these early readers the isolation of Crusoe's island offered a compelling fantasy of escape from an anxious web of personal obligation that shaped economic relationships. Degrees of economic or sexual awareness did not work primarily as age-markers. In contrast, later transformations of Crusoe and of his island suggest that thinking of economic decisions as different from personal ones, and thinking of a public sphere as different from a private one, required thinking of adults as ever more different from children.

Ideas about both childhood and adulthood gradually became central to *Robinson Crusoe*'s reception. Rousseau's claim that children should read nothing but "this marvelous book" prompted writers such as Joachim Heinrich Campe to give *Crusoe* a prominent place in the new world of children's literature.[1] Adapted for "the use of Young Persons," their desert island was free of sexuality and preoccupied with economics. The sexlessness that made the island so attractive to these writers was, however, one reason why Defoe's novel eventually became not quite worthy of the attention of a new figure on the literary scene, the self-consciously adult reader – the reader Leslie Stephen called "a grown-up man with a taste for high art."[2] In contrast, for economic theorists of the eighteenth and nineteenth centuries, and for the introductory economics textbooks that followed them, this same island illustrated two different versions of adult economic life. For classical economics, Crusoe's island was a microcosm of civil society progressing through historical stages to reach maturity: it was a place where nations grew up. For neo-classical economics, it housed instead the utility-maximizing individual, isolated from irrational impulses, from other people, and from history.

Shipwreck; or, desperate debts

Daniel Defoe wrote one book with readers of a certain age specifically in mind. This book is not *Robinson Crusoe* but rather *The Family Instructor*, his best-selling religious manual of 1715.[3] Unlike novels, such Protestant devotional writing was committed to differentiating readers by age. Before the middle of the eighteenth century, this genre is where we should look to find many of our familiar assumptions about numerical age and reading. This kind of writing shows how childhood and adulthood work together as age-leveled categories of development, in contrast to a sense of identity that relies more heavily on status. More specifically, developmental thinking needs a goal. For Protestant devotional writing the goal was salvation: a kind of salvation that can be reached only by learning to think in increasingly complex ways. Although such books often describe very young prodigies of religious devotion, they were not written for an audience of such exceptional children. Rather, they set out an age-leveled program of reading and reflection that leads to a certain version of maturity.

I want to stress how distinctive this focus on age-leveled reading was. It was strongly identified with theological understanding and marginal to more secular popular print. Below the classical literacy of the gentleman, different stations in life required different levels of vernacular literacy – but what called for literacy most urgently and in the most egalitarian way was Protestantism. Little Protestants, like big ones, had a newly intense responsibility to read, choose, and introspect their individual way to salvation, with less help than Catholics found in communal sacramental structures such as infant baptism. This Protestant ideal of reading the Bible and of understanding key theological points for oneself carried such burning importance that it produced the first substantial body of widely available publications that targeted young readers through vocabulary, sentence structure, and concepts deliberately chosen according to a theory of age-leveled cognitive development. In each generation from the ancient world onwards, classical literary works had been adapted for the pedagogical use of a tiny group of young gentlemen, but Puritan devotional works went after every child born with an immortal soul.[4] Convinced that in a time of high child mortality, little children "are not too little to go to hell," Puritan writers published a wide body of work specifically targeting the young, and routing them instead towards heaven.[5] With books such as James Janeway's *A Token for Children* (1672) and John Bunyan's *A Book for Boys and Girls* (1686), the Puritans and their Dissenting heirs were the first to age-level readers on a large scale.[6]

The Family Instructor is a fine example of this Protestant commitment to differentiating readers by age. As a Dissenter, a popular writer, and a polemicist, Defoe was particularly well positioned to reflect on and to shape the relationship between age and print. Although its reformed characters celebrate their spiritual reawakening by burning their own collections of disreputable "Songs, Plays, Novels, Romances, and such like Stuff" (122), *The Family Instructor* is itself a novelistic work, written in the form of dialogues embedded in narrative. It anticipates the psychological interest common to many later novels and to children's literature in its focus on individual development. The precision with which its central character's numerical age and cognitive abilities are described is part of Defoe's attempt to make the book seem convincingly mimetic. Like the readers of *Robinson Crusoe*, the readers of *The Family Instructor* are explicitly "assured that the Substance of each Narrative is Real" (*Family Instructor*, "To the Publisher"). In its treatment of age, however, *The Family Instructor* demonstrates possibilities that Defoe does not pursue in *Robinson Crusoe*, possibilities that he briefly turns to, for example, in his short but nuanced accounts of Moll Flanders's and Colonel Jack's thoughts in early childhood. *The Family Instructor*'s sights are set squarely on salvation: it is not a secular guide to child development like Rousseau's *Emile*. Nevertheless, this book's keen attention to age-leveled cognitive development makes it read like an early entry in that field.

Defoe describes his principal although nameless character, the youngest child of the eponymous Family, as a "Child . . . supposed to be come up to such Years as to be thinking and inquiring, suppose about five or six Years old" (5). *The Family Instructor*'s concepts and language are deliberately chosen to reach such an audience. For example, Defoe insists that his main speaker "asks but very little of his Father but what a Child *at that age* may be very capable of asking" (5, italics in original). The father's replies obey a similar decorum: "as this Part is spoken to a Child, and is for Children to read for their Instruction, it requires to be plain and concise . . . the more it is adapted to the meanest Understandings, the better it answers the

Design of this Undertaking" (41). Even with all this care to adapt ideas to "the meanest Understandings," one of the dialogue's main points is that some ideas are simply beyond any child's comprehension – and that this limitation is perfectly fine. Although this five- or six-year-old child speaker is precocious by our educational standards (he reads fluently, for example, and has an insatiable appetite for theology), the text pays a good deal of attention to the proper limits of his cognitive abilities, the limits that mark him as a child. "These are all hard Words, *Father*, how shall I understand them; what do you mean by that word INFINITE . . . " (18), he typically remarks. At such moments the father is careful to explain hard words using easy ones, or to reassure his son and his readers that in fact no child should understand such things without a long, careful process of education. When the child declares that he "does not understand a Word of all that" in response to a brief explication of eternity, God's omniscience, man's redemption through Christ, and the co-existence of God the Father and God the Son, his father's reply is gentle and unsurprised: "You must understand it gradually, *my Dear*, a little at a time" (23).

The Family Instructor's youngest son has rightly been compared to *Robinson Crusoe*'s Friday because of their shared hunger for catechism in simple vocabulary. As Charles Gildon points out in his contemporary attack, however, in comparison with his consistent depiction of the youngest son, Defoe was sloppy and contradictory in describing Friday's cognitive development and relation to language. Gildon imagines Friday and Crusoe explaining to their "Father D . . . n" at gunpoint the inconsistencies for which they are about to shoot him: "No shoot yet Master, me have something to say, he much Injure me too . . . Have injure me, to make me such a Blockhead, so much contradiction, as to be able to speak *English tolerably well* in a month or two, and not to speak it better in twelve Years after."[7] While the youngest son's learning process is consistently worked out, Friday's is both unnaturally quick and unnaturally retarded, frozen with "so much contradiction" at the most entertaining point of colorful, incorrect dialect. Friday sounds like the comic Welshman in a chapbook, not like a young person gradually but steadily mastering hard words.

Despite his unfamiliar theological preoccupations, *The Family Instructor*'s youngest son is recognizable as both the familiar protagonist and the familiar imagined reader of the children's literature of our own time. This developmentally nuanced child also lives in a familiar setting, the enclosed world of the household, as dependent on his parents as he is on God the Father. Finally, this work's understanding of reading as an aid to inner growth is equally familiar to us. It suggests our own sense of age as a series of steps towards psychological maturity, towards a full cognitive, emotional, and sexual development that unfolds "a little at a time" according to predictable stages. However, the youngest son is in fact the only member of the family who embodies these familiar ideas about age. Less familiar ideas about age, ideas that are central to *Robinson Crusoe* and to its early reception, play an important role even within *The Family Instructor*. This domestic hothouse of Protestant introspection and age-leveled individual development is also a set of fixed-status relationships. Even the youngest son is moved by the biblical command to "Remember thy Creator in the Days of thy Youth" to reflect on the ambiguity of age categories, wondering whether or not he is a youth: "*may be I a'n't a Youth yet*; I long to be a youth, Father, then you'll tell me who God is, that I may remember him, wont you, Father?" (17). Social historians agree that up to the early eighteenth century, most popular sources are not very interested in the sexual development that for us marks the end of childhood and the beginning of adolescence, a key psychological category that we tend to loosely equate with this earlier usage of "youth."[8] This developmental sense of "youth" coexists uneasily with *The Family Instructor*'s commitment to defining "child" and "father" through property. According to Defoe, the father of the family owes servants of all numerical ages exactly the same paternal authority and paternal care that he owes his children (with the important exception of fixing an inheritance on them): "you put the Master entirely upon the Father's Place, and the Servants in the Posture of Children" (303). No matter their age, servants remain forever "in the Posture of Children."[9] "If you who call your selves Christians and Protestants, will not instruct your Children and Servants," the narrator warns, proper order will be inverted: "you will find your Children and Servants instructing you" (4). Moreover, here the subordination of biological children themselves is an effect of economic dependency rather than of numerical age. Although the oldest children of this family protest that they are "past Tutelage, and *out of our Minority*" (169) (one daughter is said to be "about eighteen Years old" [85]), their father insists that "it is my unquestioned Duty, to make all that are under my Command, *do their duty*" (149). The introductory letter to the work agrees with him, stressing that it will "convince the Govenour of a Family of his duty" to instruct both "Children that are very *young*" as well as "those that are *grown up*" ("To the Publisher," n.p., italics in original). Unless they acquire enough property to establish independent households, all economic dependents remain forever "in the Posture of children" in the father's house – and by the end of the story, all have been saved by submission to their "governor."

While Defoe insists that the propertyless remain in the posture of children, however, he attacks the equally old-fashioned corollary idea that property quite naturally brings independence without much attention to a developmental scale keyed to numerical age. The one child in *The Family Instructor* who dies in an unregenerate state of sin is damned by his independent property. He is killed by the clash between the devotional work's focus on age-differentiated cognitive development and an older understanding of adulthood as economic independence. A well-meaning uncle dooms him by giving him an independent estate: "he has about 200 pounds a Year his Uncle . . . left him, so he thinks himself his own Master" (304). Effectively undermining his father's claim to mastery, this 200 pounds a year hopelessly scrambles the son's place in the hierarchy of age categories: a "foolish Boy *for tho he is a Man in Growth, he showed the Boy and the Fool in his Behaviour*" (304, italics in original). He squanders his fortune on an army commission and general dissipation, then dies miserably. As we shall see, independent property is an unmixed good in the world of the chapbooks, but that is not the case here. Although the moral of this story seems clear, Defoe spells it out at length anyway:

> It shows something of the mischievous Consequence of leaving Estates to Children intirely independent of their Parents . . . *and tells us*, That tho' in former Cases it might be necessary to do thus, yet it ought to be avoided as much as possible, it being in general a fatal Obstruction to Paternal Authority, a Foundation of Childrens refusing Instruction, and especially of their not bearing Reproof, beside that, often times the Consequences are Such, That the Children had better be without such Estates. (294)

While an idea of adulthood as economic independence was acceptable "in former Cases," it now conflicts with a sense of adulthood as spiritual maturity.

Here *The Family Instructor* demonstrates a common double-bind of Protestant devotional writing. As we have seen, such writing strongly supports the duty of the master of the household to control all those economic dependents who are "in the Posture of children" relative to him. At the same time, it sets out a universal scale of cognitive and moral development, one that culminates in an idea of adulthood that in principle disregards status and gender. This scale redefines the word "Gentleman" from propertied head of a household to mature, godly person. "Can you pretend you cannot serve God, and be *Gentleman*? That you cannot live a Vertuous Life, and obey the Commands of God, and yet be a *Gentleman*? This is a Reproach upon the very Name of Quality, and such a Slander on a

Gentleman, as no one will allow" (157), insists the father when his oldest son claims spiritual reformation will bring him social embarrassment. This developmental tradition links an idea of adulthood in age-leveled Puritan devotional works, children's literature, the bildungsroman, and psychological realism.

Robinson Crusoe is a more capacious book than *The Family Instructor*, one that can easily be imagined to appeal to a greater variety of readers. It draws together Protestant devotional traditions with colonial fantasies, capitalist ideals, Lockean epistemology, and picaresque adventure, winning both immediate commercial success and eventual critical respect. In *Robinson Crusoe*, however, adulthood exists only in a weak sense that is inseparable from status. That is, in this novel the authority of the economically independent master of a household remains more important than any age-leveled scale of cognitive and spiritual development. Crusoe pursues the property that brings the status of master rather than the internal development that brings adulthood. Critics remain largely unconvinced by Crusoe's repeated attempts to impose a providential framework on his story because he changes so little. Rather than outgrowing his filial disobedience and "rambling Thoughts," for example, once he is no longer physically immobilized on the island, Crusoe rambles on.[10] His oscillation between repentance and rambling in the book's opening scene remains the template for his character: "I was sincerely affected with [my father's] Discourse, and, indeed, who could be otherwise? and I resolv'd not to think of going abroad any more, but to settle at home according to my Father's Desire. But alas! a few Days wore it all off" (7).

Crusoe's oldest brother's death in the Low Country wars might fit the developmental world of *The Family Instructor*: he followed the bad course to be expected of a defiant eldest son to its properly bitter end. His middle brother's wonderfully inconclusive story, however, is a better portent of Crusoe's own picaresque life: "What became of my second brother I never knew, any more than my father or mother knew what became of me" (1). Although in terms of spiritual growth, nothing becomes of Crusoe, he does achieve the status of master on the island, where he becomes "King and Lord of all this Country indefeasibly" (85). His "Right of Possession" of the land makes him master of everything on it: crops, goats, dog, cats, parrot, Friday, mutineers. There is only one drawback: Crusoe thinks of the island as real property, which means thinking of it in terms of a certain version of family and status. What he misses is not a helpmate to have a spiritual and sexual relationship with, but rather a good conveyancer to draw up a strict settlement on his nonexistent heir: "if I could convey it, I might have it in

Inheritance, as completely as any Lord of a Mannor back in *England*" (85), he wistfully explains.

In 1829, Charles Lamb still sees *Robinson Crusoe*'s readers in similar terms, according to an old-fashioned standard that weighs status more heavily than age-leveled development. He remarks that "all ages and descriptions of people hang delighted over the *Adventures of Robinson Crusoe*."[11] Lamb is not merely saying that readers of all ages love the book Defoe published in 1719, or that age-differentiated readers love the wealth of age-specific adaptations of *Crusoe* that appeared by 1829. As he explains, *Crusoe* "is an especial favourite with sea-faring men, poor boys, servant-maids, &c. [Defoe's] novels are capital kitchen-reading, while they are worthy, from their interest, to find a shelf in the libraries of the wealthiest and the most learned."[12] Lamb's *Crusoe* is not good for the library and the nursery, or good for the library and the schoolroom, but rather good for the library and the kitchen – good for both the master and the servant. Lamb's main interest is not numerical age but social status – or, rather, he still assumes a way of describing people and how they read that combines both of these terms, one that views age through the more important frame of social status.

Like spiritual development, economic awareness is not strongly age-leveled in *Crusoe*. Defoe's novel has fascinated economic theorists, popularizers, and teachers, not to mention economically minded literary critics, through much of its long history; but it does not present economic relationships as an adult sphere of life separate from that of children. That is, it does not imagine a public world of economic decisions that is distinct from a private world of family and personal bonds. Economic relationships are still personal relationships – except when the story does away with personal relationships altogether by shipwrecking Crusoe on the island. In this the novel reminds us of an important difference between its time and our own. In the nineteenth century, rationally calculated utility won wide acceptance as the governing principle of economic relations, helping to define this sphere of life as the opposite of a private sphere of complex emotional and moral bonds.[13] This division stressed age-leveling: children and child-like people belonged in the home, and adults belonged in the economic world outside. In particular, as Margaret Hunt has shown, the crucial set of legal concepts and practices we know as limited liability slowly emerged as part of the larger separation between public and private life. Until that occurred, extended families, not individuals or institutions, risked everything and often lost everything in the ordinary course of business, unprotected by the "quite remarkable separation between personal or family property and business assets and liabilities" that we can take for granted today.[14]

In Defoe's time, the economic world was not an adults-only place. Economic relations crossed our familiar divisions between public and private, adult and child. And, because business relationships were still personal relationships, they were articulated through the same Christian ideals that defined other personal relationships. As Craig Muldrew reminds us, daily life at all levels of society in the early eighteenth century depended on credit, and debtors and creditors talked about their "trust" in each other, not about their rational self-interest. The language of trust kept its emotional and theological resonance even as it strained to explain increasingly complex economic transactions.[15] This trust economy was a worrying place to live. Eighteenth-century tradesmen routinely characterized a substantial number of the debts owed to them as "desperate," meaning they believed their creditors either would not or could not pay them. And pursuing such debts to the full extent of the law could be awkward for people who in the Lord's Prayer still asked God to "forgive us our debts, as we forgive our debtors" as routinely as they asked for their daily bread.[16]

Family was not a haven from such pressures, but rather their most intense focus. A hot topic for the early eighteenth-century Protestant homilists, for example, was the question of exactly when it might be morally permissible to refuse to bail one's parents out of debtor's prison. When, if ever, could rational, prudential considerations, including the specifics of the individual's economic behavior, weigh more heavily than the duty of any child to redeem any parent from captivity? As is suggested by the title of a popular manual, the Reverend William Fleetwood's *The Relative Duties of Parents and Children, Husbands and Wives, Masters and Servants* (1705), this sense of family is informed by status: like masters and servants, parents and children have fixed and unequal obligations that are hard to disregard. The superior party's bad behavior does not easily dissolve the inferior's obligations, as we shall see in the next chapter's examination of Samuel Richardson's *Pamela* and Mr. B. Fleetwood nevertheless questions the routine condemnation of "Children who suffer their Parents to lie in Prison or Captivity." What if such children "are just able to live themselves, and have Families of their own to maintain," and what if the parents in question "are so extravagant that there would be no end of paying for them"?[17] Similarly, people worried endlessly about when it might be morally permissible to refuse to invest capital in a relative's enterprise, or to refuse to be bound as surety that a relative would repay a loan from a third party.

Age was not as important in this household-based trust economy as it later became. Whatever their numerical age, children, servants, and wives were grouped together as dependent members of a household who all shared a certain relation to credit, one that, in principle, limited both their agency and their risk. Drawing on the credit of the head of the household, women, children, and servants could borrow only what was needed for household "necessities." They could not be imprisoned for unpaid debts; rather, the head of the household, in whose name these debts were contracted, would go to debtors' prison until either the debts were paid or the creditors relented. Women, children, and servants could, however, lose the roof over their heads. This shared relation to credit suggests that a simple opposition between childhood and adulthood numerically understood misses much of significance in the social history of age.

As an alternatively successful and bankrupt businessman who had been imprisoned for debt, Defoe understood the dangers of trust. His popular manual *The Complete English Tradesman* focuses on conducting business on credit.[18] Defoe writes, "Credit is the tradesman's life; it is, as the wise man says, *marrow to his bones*... if this be hurt, wounded, or weakened, the tradesman is sick, hangs his head, is dejected and discouraged" (156). Because a tradesman needed to extend trust to others every day in order to stay in business, this tradesman himself might have no choice but to disappoint the creditors who trusted him. Defoe describes the agonies of a tradesman who must declare bankruptcy, or "break":

> I might instance here the miserable, anxious, perplexed life which the poor tradesman lives under before he breaks: the distresses and extremities of his declining state; how harassed and tormented for money; what shifts he is driven to for supporting himself; how many little, mean, not to say wicked things, will even a conscientious tradesman stoop to in his distress to deliver himself, even such things as his soul would abhor at another time, and for which he goes perhaps with a wounded conscience all his life after. (55)

Defoe's biographers tend to hear personal experience in this passage, pointing to the little, mean, and even wicked financial shifts that Defoe himself resorted to in a vain attempt to stave off bankruptcy, betraying the trust of family and friends who continued to accept his assurances of solvency after these assurances had ceased to be true. Whether or not Defoe is drawing on his own experience, in *The Complete English Tradesman* he repeatedly begs the unfortunate tradesman to "break in time" rather than sink those who trust him deeper and deeper into debt.

This uneasiness over trust appears in displaced form in *Robinson Crusoe*. Defoe thought of debt in terms of storms and shipwrecks, and *Robinson*

Crusoe translates this metaphor into the novel's central premise. As Thomas Keymer points out, Defoe's "favourite metaphor for debt was one of drowning."[19] Speaking in a voice that is an unstable mix of Crusoe and himself, Defoe seems to refer to his own history of mixed prosperity and bankruptcy when he writes in the *Preface to the Serious Reflections* that he has been "taken up at Sea in Distress, rais'd again and depress'd again, and that oftner perhaps than in one Man's Life than ever was known before; Shipwreck'd often, tho' more by Land than by Sea."[20] The metaphor of debt as shipwreck permeates *The Complete English Tradesman* as well. A tradesman trying to ignore the necessity of declaring bankruptcy babbles nervously to himself about swimming and drowning: "I have such an adventure abroad; if it succeeds I may recover again; I'll try my utmost, I'll never drown when I can swim, I'll never fall while I can stand" (50). While a debauched tradesman may be hurt by his obvious extravagancies, the well-meaning, home-loving tradesman is in even greater danger from "sunk rocks":

> there are so many sober extravagancies, and so many grave, sedate ways for a tradesman's ruin, and they are so much more dangerous than those hare-brained desperate ways of gaming and whoring, that I think it is the best service I can do the tradesman to lay before him those sunk rocks, as the seamen call them, those secret dangers. (74)

Credit and shipwreck are rarely far apart: "He that takes credit may give credit, but he must be exceeding watchful; for it is the most dangerous state of life that a tradesman can live in; he is in as much jeopardy as a seaman upon a lee-shore" (40). Defoe likens selling at a loss during a panic to preserve one's credit to pitching cargo overboard in a storm:

> The throwing away of one half to save the other, was much better than sinking under the burden; like a sailor in a storm, who, to lighten the ship wallowing in the trough of the sea, will throw the choicest goods overboard, even to half the cargo, in order to keep the ship above water and save the rest. (41)

In his preface, Defoe even describes *The Complete English Tradesman* as a whole as a kind of sailor's manual or sea-map: "Here he [the young tradesman] will be effectually encouraged to set out well, and to avoid all those rocks which the gay race of tradesmen so frequently suffer shipwreck upon" (x).

The Complete English Tradesman tries very hard to will into plausible being some version of an isolated, economically rational individual. Its celibate young hero, the tradesman, fights single-mindedly to establish his credit. Without protest, he defers marriage and all other personal relationships, absorbs endless abuse from the bad-mannered customers who amuse themselves by riffling through his goods without buying, and finds his joy in his beautifully kept account books. Such accurate and complete books are like a sailor's helm: "If they are not duly posted, and if everything is not carefully entered in them, the debtor's accounts kept even, the cash constantly balanced, and the credits all stated, the tradesman is like a ship at sea steered without a helm; he is all in confusion" (9). These account books are important because in them Defoe imagines the possibility of effortlessly differentiating between personal and business matters. They represent an economic realm free from worrying ambiguity concerning family and friends. Marx describes Crusoe himself as just such a Complete English Tradesman, famously remarking that Crusoe keeps good account books: "our friend Robinson . . . having rescued a watch, ledger, and pen and ink from the wreck, commences, like a true born Briton, to keep a set of books."[21] Ian Watt too sees Crusoe as a fanatically methodical bookkeeper, and sees such bookkeeping as a genetic imperative of eighteenth-century English men and women:

> All Defoe's heroes pursue money . . . and they pursue it very methodically according to the profit and loss book-keeping which Max Weber considered to be the distinctive technical feature of modern capitalism. Defoe's heroes and heroines, whatever their birth or education, do not need to learn this technique. They have it in their blood.[22]

Through the early eighteenth century, however, account books were in fact generally neither so well kept nor so well able to distinguish between public and private realms. As Defoe's own life suggests, the norm was slovenly or non-existent written records, long-running verbal commitments that were mis-remembered through self-interest or error, and a habit of giving up on desperate debts out of charity, despair, or some unknowable combination of both.[23] Other critics have noted how Crusoe's own account blends tangible and intangible things, listing personal emotions in the form of public transactions: his celebrated account of Protestant interiority "stated it very impartially, like Debtor and Creditor, the Comforts I enjoy'd, against the Miseries I suffer'd" (57). In its combination of credit, debt, miseries, and comfort, Crusoe's account is perhaps more typical of its time than we might first expect, more like other account books that deal in charity, forgiveness, and despair as well as profit and loss.

In the end, Defoe himself admits that despite his heroic commitment to rational self-interest, his young tradesman may very well go bankrupt because he is still caught in the web of trust. His business affairs are in fact neither impersonal nor predictable. Although debt is the most dangerous rock on which tradesmen "so frequently suffer shipwreck," it is also the rock on which the trust economy is built: "He that gives no trust, and takes no trust, either by wholesale or by retail, and keeps his cash all himself... so no body is in debt to him, and all his estate is in his shop... I suppose the Tradesman that trades wholly thus, is not yet born, or if there ever were any such, they are all dead" (268–69). Young Robinson Crusoe's career presents a remarkable variation on this kind of trust. He seems to benefit both from an unusually high degree of individual autonomy and from an equally high degree of household solidarity. That is, Crusoe can begin his economic adventures only because he is securely positioned within eighteenth-century England's family-based web of credit and debt, despite the fact that he is a runaway son under a heavy cloud of filial disobedience. His first successful voyage is backed by 40 pounds of investment capital from his family. Crusoe explains that raising this money required a complicated process of personal negotiation, involving written correspondence and the goodwill of go-betweens:

> I carried about 40 *l.* in such Toys and Trifles as the Captain directed me to buy. This 40 *l.* I had mustered together by the Assistance of some of my Relations whom I corresponded with, and who, I believe, got my Father, or at least my Mother, to contribute so much as that to my first Adventure. (17)

Despite all the details offered, this start-up loan to an "under Age" runaway strikes Charles Gildon as improbable. He objects to the miraculous invulnerability of Crusoe's credit to his own youth and indiscretion, just as he objects to the miraculous invulnerability of Crusoe's life to shipwreck:

> it is not very probable, at least it is not very common, for People that have Money, to trust it to a young Fellow who had run from his Father, and was likewise under Age. This I say is not common; nay, I believe, never did happen to any Body in his Circumstances, but to *Robinson Crusoe*, and may well be put into the Number of the Miracles of his Life.[24]

What bothers Gildon the most is the degree of autonomy that Crusoe enjoys here in "his first Adventure." The senior Crusoes (or at least the mother) simply hand over the money and let their feckless son carry on as he pleases: "certainly his Father would have been very cautious of letting him be entrusted with Money entirely to manage it himself, since he had given him no Reason to imagine that his Prudence would dispose of it to the best Advantage" (92). That is, at the very start of his adventures, Crusoe already seems to be curiously immune to the pressures of a credit network based on personal trust. When he reaches the island, things grow still more miraculous.

Critics have noted what seems like the willful perversity of Defoe's decision to grapple with economic questions that are inherently social in nature through the figure of a solitary desert island castaway. Diana Spearman sums up this point with both insight and exasperation: "no one in his senses would choose the story of a man cast alone on an uninhabited island to illustrate a theory which only applies to the exchange of goods and services."[25] However, Defoe's desert-island scenario makes more sense when seen in terms of the informal web of personal credit and debt that defined his economic life. With Crusoe's shipwreck, the novel seems to break completely free of such bonds and escape into a delightful fantasy, one that takes two different forms.

First, on the island, Crusoe amasses a nearly limitless stock of things without trusting anyone at all. The book seems to offer a glimpse of something that looks a bit like impersonal economic activity on this isolated island, a place where Crusoe miraculously functions as an economic being but is subject to no constraining personal relationships with family or friends, debtors or creditors. As Defoe writes in *The Complete English Tradesman*, the tradesman who neither gives nor takes trust, with nobody in debt to him and all his estate in his shop – this tradesman is either not yet born, or he is dead. Or, possibly, he is called Robinson Crusoe. That is, for Defoe, imagining anything like a world of rational economic individualism means imagining a world with only one person in it.[26] In the long run, limited liability and the growth of more secure investment opportunities "offered a way out of the psychic morass" of an economic life that was supposed to follow the same rules as family life and Christian morality. In the short run, you could at least read *Robinson Crusoe*.[27]

In *Of the Laws of Ecclesiastical Polity* (1593), Richard Hooker explains that no matter how many debts remain unpaid, we must continue to trust each other to survive. Hooker's key point is that no one can do what Crusoe does on his island: "we are not by ourselves sufficient to furnish ourselves with competent store of things needful for such life as our nature doth desire."[28] In the second of his *Two Treatises on Government*, John Locke seizes on this claim by "the judicious Hooker" to explain why men move from the state of nature into society. While the isolated individual can assert his natural right to all the acorns he can pick, getting beyond acorns requires "communion and fellowship": "to supply those defects and imperfections which are in us, as living single and solely by ourselves, we are naturally induced to seek communion and fellowship with others: this was the cause of men's uniting themselves at first in politic societies," he quotes.[29] But while on the island, Crusoe, of course, is by himself sufficient. Not only is he able to make all the goatskin hats and clay pots needful for such life as his nature desires, but he also arrives there with a delightfully complete "store of things." Defoe shipwrecks not only Crusoe, but also an entire shop's worth of valuable and lovingly inventoried goods, not only the tradesman but also his stock as well.

If Crusoe's isolation represents the state of nature, his well-stocked shelves represent a state of advanced commercial society. Crusoe is a passionately efficient looter of the wreck: "I had been now thirteen days on shore, and had been eleven times on board the ship, in which time I had brought away all that one pair of hands could well be supposed capable to bring; though I believe verily, had the calm weather held, I should have brought away the whole ship, piece by piece" (60). The claim that he would have disassembled and stockpiled the entire ship if given a bit more time is no exaggeration. Crusoe never tires of gloating over the stock in his loaded "Warehouse" (79). "All of his estate is in his shop," not circulating in the doubtful form of other men's promises: "had my Cave been to be seen, it look'd like a general Magazine of all Necessary things, and I had every thing so ready at my Hand, that it was a great Pleasure to me to see all my Goods in such Order, and especially to find my Stock of all Necessaries so great" (60). Defoe's peculiar desert-island scenario allows him to create a world of multiplying goods and no other people, a satisfying imaginary solution to the real historical problem of the unstable and inescapable web of credit. "I had got home to my little tent, where I lay, with all my wealth about me, very secure," Crusoe announces, safe at last from shipwreck by land as well as sea. In this isolation, *Robinson Crusoe* may seem to anticipate a division between public and private worlds, between the abstraction of economic rationality and everything else. But Defoe, of course, writes long before neo-classical economists will re-imagine his castaway as a model for how the individual calculates utility. Busy filling his storeroom up to the ceiling with marvelous goods in complete solitude, Crusoe is more like Rumpelstiltskin spinning straw into gold than a rational economic actor, more a fantasy figure of raw desire than a proleptic illustration of principle.

Crusoe's island represents in miniature form the economic relations of a tradesman of Defoe's day – except for trust, the most important relation of them all. Although there is no need of trust on Crusoe's island, trust in fact surrounds this island as absolutely as the sea. Wolfran Smidgen points to the intensely personal nature of Crusoe's international transactions, to the notable "proliferation in *Robinson Crusoe* of friends who manage Crusoe's international dealings in money and goods."[30] Crusoe's business affairs depend on "particular friendships with virtuous individuals" rather than on generalized bureaucratic rationality or reliable impersonal institutions.[31] Although Crusoe's labor on his island will become very important to both progressive educators and economic theorists, that labor is not what makes him rich. His wealth comes from a Brazilian sugar plantation worked by slaves and entrusted to his friends. Critics have described Crusoe's island as a microcosm of this larger project: Crusoe's exploitation of Friday and of the natural resources of "his" island stands in for this larger exploitation, presenting the colonial project in miniature form. When Crusoe puts his foot on Friday's head and Friday is "swearing to be my slave forever" (172), his partner and trustees are busy buying slaves for the plantation in Brazil. When Crusoe accepts the delayed gratification of building fortifications and planting his seed corn rather than eating it, his partner and trustees accept the delayed gratification of re-investing most of the plantations' profits for years in sugar refining machinery as well as in slaves (237). What the island can offer no parallel for, however, is the existence of partners and trustees themselves.

Economic fantasy reaches its apotheosis when, after spending twenty-eight years in blissful isolation from all creditors and all debtors, Crusoe emerges a miraculously rich man. Weeping with joy so intense that it nearly kills him, Crusoe discovers that all of his business associates have been better book-keepers as well as better friends than he had any right to expect. Crusoe is rich because of the bizarre precision and fidelity with which they manage the financial affairs of a man who was lost at sea for nearly three decades. The account books kept by his friends show a fidelity to detail as well as to Crusoe that is nearly as miraculous as Crusoe's survival itself. While Crusoe was busy furnishing himself with goatskin hats and clay pots, an international network of personal trust piled up much more significant rewards: "in less than seven Months, I receiv'd a large Packet from the Survivors of my Trustees the Merchants, for whose Account I went to Sea, in which there were the following particular Letters and Papers enclosed" (238). Many more "particular Letters and Papers" follow. Indeed, the scene in which Crusoe settles accounts with the old captain he named as his heir is a celebrated mixture of joyful tears, altruism, and nearly unbearable pleasure in records of credit and debt, accurately maintained and witnessed and honestly acknowledged. "I shall give you a true Account of what I have received in all, and how I have disposed of it" (237), the old captain promises, then proceeds to make good on the promise in extensively described detail, producing appropriate documents "sign'd by my Partner and the Merchants Trustees" as well as other securities:

> I was too much mov'd with the Honesty and Kindness of the poor Man, to be able to bear this . . . I could hardly refrain Weeping . . . Every thing the good Man said was full of Affection, and I could hardly refrain from Tears while he spoke: In short, I took 100 of the Moidores, and call'd for a Pen and Ink to give him a Receipt for them. (237–38)

The shock of all this miraculous accounting nearly kills Crusoe:

> It is impossible to express here the Flutterings of my very Heart, when I look'd over these Letters, and especially when I found all my Wealth about me . . . In a Word, I turned pale, and grew sick; and had not the old Man run and fetch'd me Cordial, I believe the sudden Surprize of Joy had overset Nature, and I had dy'd upon the Spot. (239)

Although here Defoe returns Crusoe to the eighteenth-century trust economy, he presents it in a gloriously idealized form.

Robinson Crusoe's chapbook adaptations suggest that many early readers may have seen this economic fantasy as central to the story. In addition to full-length piracies, legitimate editions, and newspaper serializations, *Robinson Crusoe* circulated widely in chapbook form – or rather, as much of the story as could fit on twelve to twenty-four pages, about three by two inches in size, circulated widely in chapbook form. In fact, chapbook *Crusoes* seem to have outnumbered editions of the complete book.[32] As we shall see in the next chapter, chapbooks eventually became strongly identified with childhood, in part because John Newbery borrowed their format for his new children's books. In Defoe's time, however, chapbooks stood for a much older idea of reading, for a popular audience that did not differentiate according to numerical age. That is, they are a bridge between a very old mixed-age reading audience that seems foreign to us today and the age-differentiated audience that we inherit from the later eighteenth century.

Because chapbooks are so important to the changing role of age in the history of print, we should clarify what we mean by this much-used term. Historians disagree on the boundaries of the term "chapbook," but generally use it to describe flimsy, relatively cheap (selling for as little as a penny), tiny pamphlets.[33] They were sold by a network of traveling packmen radiating from London, where most were produced.[34] In both form and content, chapbooks showed extraordinary continuity from the sixteenth century to the middle of the eighteenth; for example, two of their best-known stories,

Guy of Warwick and *Bevis of Hampton*, were read for at least five hundred years.[35] They were crudely printed and illustrated, using old black-letter fonts long after these fonts had fallen out of favor in mainstream print, and were illustrated with cuts made from old woodblocks. Rather than containing original material, they adapted old chivalric romances, legends, bawdy tales and riddles – and, eventually, a few novels, including *Robinson Crusoe*.[36] What these adaptations kept and what they cut reflects some combination of what their prosperous London printers wanted to print and what their more popular, largely rural audience was willing to buy.

A version of readership that can be traced back to the middle ages lived on with chapbooks – and this readership did not privilege the adult. As Bennett Brockman observes, "the medieval audience seems more likely to have been divided along class lines than along age lines . . . Medieval and early modern children . . . both read and listened to the same romances as did their elders." Moreover, "when a market for printed books developed, English publishers aimed similarly at a broad spectrum of readers, including youthful ones" (3). Early modern critics and writers still describe the audience of such romances in this way, as "hopelessly plebeian and uncultivated, 'old women, servants, country squires, the sons and daughters of citizens, and children.'"[37] M. O. Grenby carefully distinguishes between level of literacy and numerical age: "Certainly, there seems little reason to believe that chapbook use was determined by age, except in so far as age would have been a factor in determining reading prowess." As he points out, "in early modern England (and Scotland, differently) other factors were just as important in determining literacy: class, gender, religion, location, parental occupation, and so on."[38] Grenby believes that chapbooks retained such a mixed-age audience through the eighteenth century.

In keeping with this mixed-age audience, chapbooks do not foreground a developmental idea of adulthood in their content. Chapbooks contain no complex adult world of theological paradoxes, economic institutions, or sexual relationships that the young hero must grow to understand, a little at a time. Instead, the chapbook hero is often young in the same way that he is often poor: both factors establish him as a sympathetic underdog, but neither limits what he can know or can do in any meaningful way. Numerical age does not shape what is possible or impossible for Bevis of Hampton, Jack the Giant-Killer, or Dick Whittington, as it does for *The Family Instructor*'s youngest son. A chapbook hero may be unusually little or unusually big, a Tom Thumb or a Tom Hickathrift, but he does not grow up. No matter how many pious speeches they include, these stories chart the gain or loss of worldly goods through strength or trickery, not the getting of wisdom. *Robinson Crusoe* contains chapbook elements and was edited into chapbook form. In his hostile parody, Charles Gildon makes Defoe's hero protest his kinship with traditional chapbook heroes. Even before he is cut down to fit within a few three-by-two-inch pages, this Crusoe already looks very like Guy of Warwick and Bevis of Hampton, two of the oldest chapbook heroes: "Cru: Your Hero! Your Mob Hero! On a foot with *Guy of Warwick, Bevis of Southhampton*, and the *London Prentice!* Your *Pyecorner* Hero! For M..w..r has put me in that Rank."[39] According to this reading, chapbook adaptations of Crusoe merely return him to his "Mob Hero" chapbook roots.

The drastic editing of chapbook adaptations of *Robinson Crusoe* targets readers by social status rather than by their numerical age. At a higher cost, other early abridgements also did so, but chapbooks offer the most dramatic example of this process. As Andrew O'Malley notes, chapbook *Crusoes* "make definite choices about what constitutes the essential elements of Defoe's text, not just deleting major events from the original narrative, but devoting often incongruously lengthy portions of their restricted space to minor episodes."[40] He suggests that chapbooks rework Defoe "to fit a new, or rather, an old, framework," a popular interest in exotic adventure and the miraculous social ascent of lowborn figures.[41] I would stress that the chapbooks' draconian editing often heightens the elements of wishful economic fantasy that we have seen in Defoe's original. These tiny books say a good deal about property. They often focus on the wonderful resolution of Crusoe's affairs by his "friends" on his departure from the island, describing in satisfying detail all the wealth that has accumulated in their hands for Crusoe during his island years.

For example, *Voyages and Travels: Being the Life and Adventures of Robinson Crusoe of York, Mariner* (*c*.1750) is only eight pages long.[42] It cuts even the episode of the footprint in the sand (Friday himself and his conversion to Christianity merit only one sentence), but spends nearly a page and a half carefully detailing all of the foodstuffs, coins, tools, clothing, and other moveable goods that Crusoe loots from the wrecked ship when he arrives on the island. Out of the total of eight pages, this catalogue of Crusoe's salvaged goods dominates the description of his island adventures. It also specifies the exact value of Crusoe's property when he finally regains it: "enquiring after my Effects in *Brasile*, [I] found I was worth 5000 Pounds Sterling in Money, besides having an Estate there worth above 1000 Pounds a Year, so making the best of my way home to *England*, by way of France,

1 Woodcut from *The Surprizing Life, and Most Strange Adventures of Robinson Crusoe*, 1770

on the fourteenth of January, and sold my Estate and Effects, beyond Sea, for the Sum of 328000 Pieces of Eight. FINIS." A longer twenty-four-page duodecimo chapbook includes as the last of its ten woodcuts one picturing Crusoe in an elegant room, decked out in clothes that indicate in careful detail his final prosperous position: a full-bottomed wig, tricorn hat, brocade jacket, and large cane. Crusoe has become a master (see Figure 1).

"Now let us hurry to establish him on this island"

It is Rousseau who begins Crusoe's life as a hero of specifically childhood reading. Rousseau is also the first to describe *Robinson Crusoe* as nothing more and nothing less than the story of the isolated individual. He insists that *Robinson Crusoe* is really all about the island: he will give Emile the "novel, disencumbered of all its rigmarole, beginning with Robinson's shipwreck near his island, and ending with the coming of the ship which comes to take him from it."[43] As we have seen, Defoe and the chapbooks triumphantly return Crusoe to an idealized version of the eighteenth-century web of credit and debt. Rousseau and the writers for children who follow his example jettison this grand finale, permanently deleting Crusoe's miraculous web of personal trust, leaving only goats, hand-tools, and storehouses. For Rousseau, however, this isolated islander is not a figure of economic rationality, but rather a child. While Defoe's Crusoe is in his mid-thirties when he lands on the island, Rousseau imagines isolation as an aspect of childhood. While the chapbook *Crusoe*s are not very concerned about either the presence or the absence of sexual content, Rousseau values the story in significant part because it allows him to describe childhood itself as an island refuge from sexual knowledge, as the opening tableau in a developmental fable. Once it has nurtured the earliest stages of the individual's complex psychological development, isolation must be abandoned for the individual to live as an adult – someone who for Rousseau is by definition a sexual and a sociable being. As Wordsworth will explain at greater length in *The Prelude*, "Love of Nature Leading to Love of Man" (Book 8), no Romantic Robinson ought to stay forever on his island.

In 1761, Rousseau advocated *Robinson Crusoe* as the one and only book that should be allowed into the carefully choreographed developmental hothouse occupied by his model child-pupil, Emile:

> there is one [book] which, to my taste, provides the most felicitous treatise on natural education. This book will be the first that my Emile will read. For a long time it will alone compose his whole library, and it will always hold a distinguished place there . . . What, then, is this marvelous book? Is it Aristotle? Is it Pliny? Is it Buffon? No. It is *Robinson Crusoe*. (184)

For Rousseau, the value of *Robinson Crusoe* lies not only in its flatly mimetic style but also in the complete isolation of its hero: Emile should learn to identify with "Robinson Crusoe on his island, alone, deprived of the assistance of his kind and the instruments of all the arts, providing nevertheless for his own subsistence, for his own preservation, and even procuring for himself a kind of well-being" (184). Emile identifies with this fictional character in order to imagine himself as the only person in a world of things:

> I want it to make him dizzy; I want him constantly to be busy with his mansion, his goats, his plantations; I want him to learn in detail, not from books but from things, all that must be known in such a situation: I want him to think he is Robinson himself, to see himself dressed in skins, wearing a large cap, carrying a large saber and all the rest of the character's grotesque equipment, with the exception of the parasol, which he will not need. (184–85)

For Rousseau, the point of Emile imagining himself as Crusoe is that he imagine himself as an isolated man, able to live in the "true castle in Spain of this happy age, when the child knows no other happiness than the necessities and freedom" (184–85). The paradoxical celebration of childhood as a happy state of both necessity and liberty claims that the child is subject to the laws of the material world, but free from the constraints and compromises of relationships with other human beings. Up to the age of fifteen, Emile himself is remarkably island-like: "He demands nothing from anyone and believes that he owes nothing to anyone. He is alone in human society; he counts on himself alone" (208).

The chapbook *Crusoes* are as devoid of sexual content as Defoe's original, but in them neither its presence nor its absence registers on an age-leveled scale of reading. Today it is hard to image a world in which sexual knowledge is not so strongly linked with adulthood. For example, William Warner draws on the idea of such "adult" reading as early as 1695 to describe the breakdown of state control of the press. Explaining the contribution that stories of "amatory intrigue" made to the rise of the novel, Warner praises "an assumption crucial to the early-modern emancipation of reading: that every mature literate adult has the right to choose his or her own reading."[44] In this account, the victory of unlicensed printing reflects a decisive recognition of the fact that adults, unlike children, have a right to sexually titillating books such as Eliza Heywood's *Love in Excess*, published in 1719. Before 1695, it is implied, state censorship frustrated this right of mature literate adults to combine reading and sexual excitement. Histories of erotic writing, pornography, and censorship, however, question this assumption. For example, Ian Moulton argues that early modern censorship was not designed to frustrate the private sexual pleasure of mature adults, because sexuality had not yet become private enough to be thought the proper business of mature adults. He claims that erotic writing instead freely "circulated throughout literate culture" of the sixteenth and seventeenth centuries. In his account, what separates this earlier time from ours is our own habit of connecting erotic writing and privacy. For Moulton, modern pornography is all about privacy, as are modern ideas of sexuality. In contrast, the separation between public and private "is not a division that existed in anything like the same form in the sixteenth and seventeenth centuries."[45] Moulton does not concentrate on age. Reflecting the early modern sensibility that it seeks to describe, for example, his book's index differs from the index of any contemporary treatment of pornography in not mentioning age as a key category organizing the propriety of sexually explicit material. This index does feature "boy," but as an object of sexual desire, not the object of protective legislation. Moulton's argument about privacy nevertheless raises the issue of age. Like the changing significance of sexual content to *Crusoe*'s reception, this argument suggests that sexual content cannot always serve as a reliable marker of adult reading.

M. O. Grenby notes that from their titles onwards many chapbooks that circulated among a mixed-age audience now look unsuitable for children: for example, *Cupid's annual festival* or *The blackamoor in the wood; or a lamentable ballad on the tragical end of a gallant lord and virtuous lady; together with the untimely death of their two children.*[46] Even as we insist that adults may, or even possibly should, read about sex and violence, we now try to keep descriptions of Cupid's festivals and the tragic deaths of virtuous and gallant families out of the hands of children. However, earlier English attempts to control print were less concerned to ensure age-appropriate lessons for the young – or age-appropriate pleasures for the adult – than to censor wanton, effeminizing, heretical, or, above all, personally defamatory language among Christians of any age.[47] Chapbooks predate this shift in the purpose of censoring the printed word from protecting important people from public defamation to protecting children from developmental disturbance. Rousseau's *Emile* is all about such age-leveled protection.

Of course, Emile's isolation is as fictional as *Robinson Crusoe* itself. As Maria Edgeworth notes, "Rousseau advises, that children should be governed solely by the necessity of circumstances; but there are *one and twenty* excellent objections to this system, the first being that it is impossible."[48] Few eighteenth- and nineteenth-century parents or teachers tried to follow Rousseau's educational prescriptions to the letter, and when they did, the effort often ended in disaster.[49] Nevertheless, Rousseau's influential comments began the tradition of seeing the act of reading *Robinson Crusoe* as being about some version of developmental psychology.

Rousseau also links Crusoe to contemporary theories of the stadial development of human society.[50] Emile is in fact living out, step by step, the development of human civilization as Rousseau imagined it. As a solitary child, Emile is like a savage. He lives in the same state of nature as John Locke's acorn-picking individual. Like Locke's individual, he must enter into a social contract in order to develop fully. This is why Rousseau deprives his Crusoe of the wealth of tools and goods with which Defoe so generously supplies him. As a savage Crusoe, Emile must rediscover every invention of human civilization, becoming a living illustration of eighteenth-century theories of political economy. Alone, he can experience only the "natural arts," but such experience will trigger curiosity about the "industrial arts," which require "the cooperation of many hands": "The former can be exercised by solitaries, by savages; but the others can be born only in society and make it necessary." We will look in greater depth in Chapter 4 at the eighteenth and early nineteenth century's fascination with the theory that the development of the individual person and the development of human civilization mirror each other, unfolding according to the same predictable template of stages outlined by the early social scientists known as the conjectural historians.[51] Here I want to note only that this theory is central to *Robinson Crusoe*'s meaning in the later eighteenth and nineteenth centuries. Johann Haken's five-volume *Bibliothek der Robinsone insweckmaszigen Auszugen* ("Library of Robinsons in Suitable Extracts"), published between 1805 and 1808, identifies this developmental scheme as the most important meaning of the popular term "Robinsonade." Haken asserts that "Robinson's story is the history of mankind and the development of its civilization in microcosm."[52] These Robinsonades' particular sense of immaturity and maturity owes much to eighteenth-century ideas about the grand sweep of human history. It is this particular developmental scheme that in the *Grundrisse* (1857) and the *Contributions to the Critique of Political Economy* (1859) Karl Marx dismisses as the "great and small Robinsonades" of Adam Smith and David Ricardo.[53] It is, perhaps, partly due to this overlap between ideas of individual development and historical development that, in contrast to its silence about sex, children's literature through this period is positively garrulous about political economy. As we shall see, the Robinsonade becomes the perfect genre with which to talk about age in this way.

Nevertheless, for Rousseau, it is not the need for industrial technology and surplus wealth that drives Emile from the island when he is fifteen years old, but rather the need for sexual relations. That is, Rousseau grants sexuality a larger role in individual development than it plays in many of the Robinsonades that follow him, or in Defoe's novel itself. As we have noted, Rousseau truncates *Crusoe* at the coming of the ship that will bear the hero away; he sees puberty rather than property as what links Crusoe to society. Although the island offers all Emile needs for both "entertainment and instruction throughout the period which is dealt with here" (185), sexual desire will all too soon transform Emile from a solitary being into a social one:

> Now let us hurry to establish him on this island while he still limits his felicity to it; for the day is nearing when, if he still wants to live there, he will not want any longer to live alone, when Friday, who now hardly concerns him, will not for long be enough for him. (185)

Here Crusoe's island is childhood itself, defined as the absence of both sexual awareness and heterosexual need. Rousseau's particular model of development creates an enormous sense of distance between adulthood and childhood, a great wave of grown-up things that must not be spoken of but that will, very soon, crash down on the young islander's head.

In making the entrance into adulthood an escape from sexless solitude, and in making this development recapitulate the development of human civilization as it was seen by conjectural history, Rousseau begins the re-writing of Defoe's novel to fit a new set of ideas for what children's literature ought to look like. In contrast to the undifferentiated reading material of earlier times, it has often been noted that a hallmark of "official" children's literature by the middle of the eighteenth century is its new concern not to mention sexual humor, sexual sins, or sexual pleasures.[54] This finding is consistent with the tendency of histories of sexuality more generally to identify the eighteenth century as a time when sex became more hidden from daily life, when it came to seem more complicated and more interesting – a fascinating secret whose discovery must be carefully staged in adolescence as the entry to adulthood. As we have seen, Ian Moulton has described the novelty of this idea of sexuality as essentially private. Without this sense of privacy, exposure to sexual content in conversation and entertainment cannot be imagined as a crucial dividing line between child and adult, as Rousseau imagines in his version of *Crusoe*.

Strongly influenced by Rousseau and widely translated, Joachim Heinrich Campe's *Robinson der Jüngere* (1779) became even more popular than Defoe's original.[55] The first English version of Campe's book was published by John Stockdale in London in 1788 as *The New Robinson Crusoe: An Instructive and Entertaining History, for the Use of Children of Both Sexes.*[56] Mary Jane Godwin translated and adapted it from a popular French adaptation as part of the Godwin family project of producing politically progressive children's literature. Like the Defoe of *The Family Instructor* rather than the Defoe of *Robinson Crusoe*, Campe focuses primarily on age-leveled cognitive development rather than on social status in constructing his implied reader. Again like the Defoe of *The Family Instructor*, Campe proudly invokes a militantly middle-class domestic space as the natural stage for model interactions between adults and children. While Emile's tutor lurks discreetly in the background as Emile plays at being a castaway, here the island itself is built out of words exchanged between teacher and pupil.

Devoted to personally educating his children at home, Mr. Billingsley, a gentleman who possesses "but a moderate fortune," tells Crusoe's story by the parlor fire over thirty-one evenings to his children and wife. Friends of the Billingsleys occasionally drop in on this family story-telling and discussion group. They are all as fascinated by the pedagogical project as is Mr. Billingsley himself, who delights in the idea that he will "one day be considered . . . the instrument and cause of his children's eternal welfare" and in watching "with silent but attentive eyes, the gradual advance of his children towards the perfection of reason and virtue" (5). The leisurely frame narrative gives the children plenty of time to ask their father to explain hard words and unfamiliar concepts, to venture their own moral judgments, and to reply to their father's leading questions, as does the youngest son in *The Family Instructor*.[57] As twenty-first-century school children are often instructed to, these children even write letters to the character Crusoe, asking him questions and offering their opinions on his conduct.

The frame narrative opens by foregrounding the responsible adult's role in age-leveling reading for children. The young Billingsleys themselves explain that they do not want to hear anything inappropriate, reminding their father of his obligation to filter out emotionally disturbing content:

MR. BILLINGSLEY. Well, my dear children, I have a book for your entertainment this evening that contains a very extraordinary story. Some parts of it will make your hair stand on end, and others will perfectly delight you.

GEORGE. Ah! But do not let it be too melancholy, papa.

HARRIET. No, my dear papa, not too melancholy; for then it will make us all cry, you know.

RICHARD. Hold your tongues; papa knows what to read, I warrant you.

MR. BILLINGSLEY. Do not be uneasy, my dears. I will take care that there shall not be any thing too tragical in it. (6)

This papa does indeed know what to read. Nothing could be further than his version of Crusoe from the old mixed-age chapbook fare still shared by most children and servants, those living in the households of less progressive parents in 1788. The sheer familiarity of this scene of age-leveled reading may make it hard for us to see just how odd it still was. There was, however, still novelty in its premise that carefully guided discussion and creative writing assignments can harness hair-raising excitement, making the acquisition of literacy, reason, and moral sense fun for everyone involved. Mr. Billingsley even dangles before his children the prospect of an educational fieldtrip to Margate, where they "will have as wide a prospect of sea as Robinson Crusoe had when he was sailing out of Plymouth harbour," if they will only "be very attentive while . . . learning geography" (10). Their response to this offer of integrated experiential learning surpasses any liberal educator's fondest hope: "*All the Children:* Oh! oh!" (10). Three decades later, Mary Jane Godwin's stepdaughter Mary Shelley will strike the same note in little Victor Frankenstein's salute to his own "peculiarly" progressive and pedagogically obsessed parents (1818): "We felt that they were not the tyrants to rule our lot according to their caprice, but the agents and creators of all the many delights which we enjoyed. When I mingled with other families, I distinctly discerned how peculiarly fortunate my lot was."[58]

Although a clear descendent of the Dissenting father in *The Family Instructor*, Mr. Billingsley contents himself with a vague deism. While the Billingsleys mention the Bible, a different book is actually in their hands. For sale by John Stockdale, it ought to be in the hands of their readers as well:

> CHARLOTTE. Where is the Coast of Guinea, papa? . . .
> HENRY. Hold, here is Sealy's Geographical Dictionary, which describes all the known world, and contains maps of every country, to which we can refer from time to time for fuller information, it being the most correct and complete work of the kind ever published. This dictionary is also enriched with a great number of beautiful views of the most celebrated cities and towns, &c. in Europe. – Look at this map . . . (15)

What is being sold here is not the Puritans' theology, but rather the age-leveled form they hammered out to teach it, and their intense sense of the family as an educational tool. But this developmental focus was still a minority way of shaping print. We shall look in the next two chapters in more depth at how this focus grew more popular through the work of John Newbery, Letitia Barbauld, and Maria Edgeworth. Here we will concentrate on what the adaptation and reception of Crusoe suggests about changing ideas of economics and age.

Like Rousseau, Campe believes that everything beyond the island itself is "unnecessary rubbish" (13). As we have noted, Defoe's Crusoe is eighteen years old on the novel's first page but thirty-four by the time he reaches the island. In contrast, Rousseau imagines the whole island phase of development ending at fifteen with the coming of sexual need. *The New Robinson Crusoe* popularized Rousseau's general sense of Crusoe as a sexless child confined to the island rather than a thirty-four year-old picaresque adventurer. However, for Campe both the numbers and the role of sexuality are quite different. While Emile's sexlessness ends at the age of fifteen, Campe's Robinson is already eighteen when he reaches the island. In contrast to Rousseau's child, Campe's eighteen-year-old is an undutiful young man who has still a great deal of growing up to do, and who on a desert island has somehow found the perfect place to do it. He does indeed grow up; the book even concludes with an admiring look at his peaceful old age. But in Campe's Robinsonade, growing up is not the story of sexual and social development that will become familiar in the bildungsroman and later psychological theory, the story Rousseau imagines beginning for Emile at fifteen. Although his story is framed by the mass domesticity of the Billingsleys' family fireside, Campe's Crusoe never marries or fathers a child. Unlike Emile, he does not grow into a sexual being. When he leaves the island at the age of thirty, now devout, self-controlled, and industrious, he instead continues a life of asexual companionship with Friday, one that allows him to indulge in the "pleasure" he learned to enjoy on the island: manual labor. He chooses the hands-on work of that little world over the more abstract financial world of his father: "Robinson's father was by profession a broker, and he wished to see his son apply to his own business, in order to take it up after his death; but Robinson, long accustomed to the pleasure of manual labour, begged his permission to learn the trade of a carpenter" (183). This Crusoe and Friday "opened the business in partnership, and during their whole lives remained faithful friends and inseparable companions... Being always actively employed about something useful, they reached a very advanced age in health and peace" (183). Exhorting the children of Hull, Crusoe sums up the moral of his story: "My dear children, obey your parents and your teachers; learn diligently whatever you have a capacity to learn; fear God; and be careful – oh, be careful! – to avoid idleness!" (183). Far from ending with a grand finale of riches hoarded up through his trustworthy friends' management of his investments, Campe's Robinson returns home "exactly as rich as when he formerly set sail" (181). And as a celibate carpenter devoted to keeping busy rather than a financial broker devoted to getting rich, he in a sense remains on the island forever. He is as permanently removed from abstract economic relationships as he is from sexual relationships.

The interest of Campe's story lies in a different idea of growth, in demonstrating the stages of human civilization. For Rousseau, only the first stage of human development can happen on a desert island, but Campe locates the whole process there. Before Campe shows his Crusoe re-inventing civilization with his bare hands, he attacks the awkward warehouse of tools and other goods that Rousseau simply wishes away. Campe advertises his re-writing of Defoe as the correction of a serious error:

> The Old Robinson Crusoe... is erroneous in one particular sufficient to destroy every advantage that this History might produce, which is, that Robinson Crusoe is provided with all sorts of European tools and

> instruments necessary to procure him many of those conveniencies that belong to society. Thus the opportunity is lost of affording the young reader a lively sense both of the wants of man in a state of solitude, and the multiplied happiness of a social life. (12–18)

Moreover, Campe divides his book into three distinct sections, the better to illustrate the development of civilization. In the first, alone and "destitute of any European tool or instrument whatsoever," Crusoe barely survives; in the second, by gaining a companion, he shows "how much man's situation may be bettered by taking even this single step towards society"; in the third, another shipwreck finally provides him with the necessities of civilized life, including bread. "This may shew you how extremely difficult it is for one man singly to provide for all his own necessities. A thousand hands are not sufficient to prepare what each of us wants every day" (40). Illustrating the rise of civilization remains important to many children's *Crusoes*. For example, the "Advertisement" to a "Juvenile and School Library" edition by Tabart & Co. (*c.*1805, London) explains that the book is worth revising for children because of "the lively picture it conveys of man residing in a state of nature, and of the means necessary to obtain a state of enjoyment and easy subsistence" (iiv).[59]

Although Campe's Crusoe was enormously popular, neither Defoe's original nor Robinsonades in general were universally accepted as good for impressionable readers. In particular, however carefully the story was re-framed, there remained something uncongenial about the idea of shipwreck to writers who wanted to stress as a hallmark of maturity the habit of forming rational economic expectations about the future. While Defoe found shipwreck an irresistible metaphor for the unpredictable disasters inherent to an economic life built on "trust," the image worked less well for a group of didactic writers who were committed to promoting the idea of probability: the rational moralists, a later eighteenth- and nineteenth-century group of pedagogical writers that we shall consider in greater depth in Chapter 4. For now I will note that they helped to popularize economic theory through such work as Letitia Barbauld's *Lessons for Children* (1778–79), Maria Edgeworth's *Practical Education* (1789) and *Forester* (1801), Jane Marcet's *Conversations in Political Economy, in which the Elements of that Science are familiarly Explained* (1816), and Harriet Martineau's *Illustrations of Political Economy* (1832). In doing so, they gave the distinction between child and adult great importance in terms of economic decision-making. For them, what distinguishes adults above all else is the ability to defer pleasure for the sake of long-term well-being.

Although the rational moralists admired *Robinson Crusoe*'s potential for depicting the rise of tool-wielding civilization, they felt it was a dangerous text because it encouraged a childish love of adventure. It participated in what critics such as Gary Kelly and Andrew O'Malley have called the "lottery mentality" of the "plebian moral economy."[60] For example, Edgeworth rejected *Robinson Crusoe* as a children's book because she believed it encouraged impulsive rambling around the world rather than the central ideal she found in Adam Smith: the dogged perseverance, based on the rational calculation of long-term benefits, that defines adulthood in a modern commercial society. She remarks that young readers' characteristic love of adventure stories is exactly why they should not read them: "voyages and travels . . . interest young people universally. Robinson Crusoe, Gulliver, and the Three Russian Sailors, who were cast away on the coast of Norway, are general favourites. No child ever read an account of a shipwreck, or even a storm, without pleasure. A desert island is a delightful place, to be equalled only by the skating-land of the reindeer, or by the valley of diamonds in the Arabian tales . . . "[61] Delightful desert island adventure is incompatible with commercial life as Edgeworth understands it, which is all about working very hard for very little: "the patient drudgery of a trade, the laborious mental exertions requisite to prepare him for a profession, must appear to [a boy] in a formidable light, compared with the alluring prospects presented by an adventuring imagination."[62]

As new, relatively impersonal institutions supplanted a household-based system of credit that was meant to follow Christian ideals, these writers show some of the ways that living consciously with economic abstractions becomes a measure of adulthood, an alternative way to be a good person. They worry about differences between classical economic theory and Christian morality, trying to distinguish enlightened self-interest or economic rationality from plain selfishness. Of course, some version of economic competence has always marked some version of adulthood. For example, being able to recognize a bad penny was one very old method of ascertaining "the age of discretion."[63] But telling a good penny from a bad one when you hold it in your hand, or a good neighbor from a bad one when he asks you for credit (like refusing to exchange a cow for a sackful of magic beans), was a more immediate business than what far-sighted adults were now imagined as doing when they went out into the world. Re-envisioned in these terms, *Robinson Crusoe* could instruct as well as delight.[64] The rational moralists' commitment to combining Christian moral teaching and economic theory explains the one moment from Defoe that tends to appear most often in their Robinsonades, Crusoe's famous discussion of the inutility of gold on a desert island:

> I smiled to myself at the Sight of this Money. 'Oh Drug!' said I aloud, 'what art thou good for? Thou art not worth to me, no, not the taking off of the Ground; one of those Knives is worth all this Heap; I have no Manner of use for thee . . . ' However, upon Second Thoughts, I took it away. (50)

In their adaptations, as in Defoe, this moment still looks backward to medieval Christian condemnations of gold as the corruptor of man, as well as forward to theoretical distinctions between use value and exchange value. While Coleridge picks up on the psychological interest of Crusoe's final decision to pocket the useless gold anyway, these writers stress Crusoe's condemnation of gold as "nasty sorry useless Stuff. . . of no manner of Value to me, because of no Use" (110). As we shall see in the following section, later nineteenth-century popularizers of economic theory discarded such ethical constraints and defined maturity more narrowly as the ability to calculate future utility. In their hands, the children's Crusoe who started with Rousseau and Campe became the face of an increasingly important version of adulthood, an illustration, and at times even a defense, of neo-classical economics. At the same time, Defoe's Crusoe himself was rejected by nineteenth-century literary critics as childish in light of their own highly specialized idea of the adult.

The servant-maid, the sailor, and the school-boy

As they become adults, young people learn today about a public world of economic institutions and abstractions that is distinct from their world of personal relationships, a world that is supposed to run on rational utility rather than on trust. They learn about it "a little at a time," as gradually as the youngest son in Defoe's *Family Instructor* learns about the Trinity. And from the late nineteenth century onwards, Robinson Crusoe has appeared in the introductory chapters of economic textbooks designed to help with this task. Now stuck forever on his solitary island rather than sobbing with joy over his friends' account books, Crusoe plays a new role as the personification of an economic theory, "marginalism" or neo-classical economics. This theory stresses the forward-looking calculations of the individual actor. In this context, the isolation of Crusoe's island takes on new significance as a metaphor for the permanent social and emotional isolation of the rational economic individual. This is the Crusoe that Max Weber famously refers to as "the *isolated economic man*."[65] Forever shipwrecked on the island, this Crusoe does nothing but choose the most marginally effective way to optimize his wealth as mechanically as a compass-needle points north. Some version of this Crusoe is still with us. "It turns out that the primitive environment of Robinson Crusoe contains the essence of choice problems that arise in complicated market economies," remarks a popular college-level textbook on macroeconomics in a chapter entitled "Work effort, production, and consumption – the economics of Robinson Crusoe": "We assume that Crusoe's choices are guided by enlightened self-interest; that is, we exploit the central economic postulate of optimizing behavior . . . when we consider the economy's responses to changes in production opportunities . . . we usually get the right answer by thinking of the parallel situation of Robinson Crusoe."[66] Insofar as he is a model for proper decision-making, this Robinson Crusoe appears to be an adult.

At the same time as economists began to use this version of Crusoe, however, literary critics began to dismiss *Robinson Crusoe* itself. Michael White sees this as an ironic coincidence: "It might seem ironic that, just as the RCE [Robinson Crusoe Economics] came to be widely deployed in economic texts in the last twenty years of the nineteenth century, Defoe's writings were receiving a somewhat disparaging treatment from the literati."[67] I would suggest that Crusoe's simultaneous rise and fall in the late nineteenth century is more than ironic. Rather, it reflects the rise in cultural importance of two different versions of adulthood: on the one hand, economic rationality, and on the other, psychological complexity, the professional literary critic's age-leveled ideal. We shall look at this standard in greater depth in Chapter 5. Here I want to point to a basic shift in the kind of criticism *Robinson Crusoe* drew. While earlier readers had complained that Defoe's novel was low-class, a crudely written, improbable story designed to thrill the semi-literate, a new kind of reader, the self-consciously adult literary critic, now brought a new charge: Defoe's novel was immature. These critics complain that Crusoe merely play-acts at adulthood, revealing Defoe's own immature understanding of the self and its relationship to others, a naiveté that is at best charming but more often deeply annoying. In these different ways, both the Crusoe of nineteenth-century economic textbooks and the Crusoe of nineteenth-century literary critics reflect the increased importance of the idea of age.

The classical economics associated with Adam Smith and David Ricardo is the study of how people try to get what they want – but also of how what they want is shaped by when and where they live, by their place on a historical timeline. Rather than imagining an isolated individual, this version of economics sees human wants in the context of the stages of social development imagined by conjectural history. Smith and Ricardo not only arrange all human wants in a hierarchy from necessities to luxuries, but also consider how wants shift from one category to another depending on the "state of society": the luxuries of primitive societies become the necessities of sophisticated ones. As we have seen, such interest in the development of society is present in Rousseau's account of Crusoe and dominates most of the Robinsonades that follow until the late nineteenth century. In contrast, neo-classical economics relies on a sense of the individual's wants as defined by nothing beyond that individual's preference. This theory produces its own Crusoe: "Suppose that an isolated economizing individual inhabits a rocky island in the sea," suggests Carl Menger's *Principles of Economics* (1871), a founding text of the Austrian school of economics.[68] This islander's sense of want is highly abstract.[69] When historicist economist Gustav von Schmoller criticizes Menger's economic theory for its reliance on "the Robinsonade," he objects to this version of *Crusoe* as a parable of economic individualism: "Clarity in abstract theory is his goal; very detailed, indeed tiresomely copious discussions of examples, mostly linked to the Robinsonade rather than to current economic conditions, is the means by which he operates."[70] Rather than living within the frayed but sticky web of personal trust that Defoe describes, the wholly rational individual of neo-classical economics exists in a kind of "logical time" that allows for only the memory and anticipation that are required to perform actions in a sequence intended to maximize the satisfaction of any given want in the future. In such texts "Crusoe" becomes the proper name of the isolated economic individual, the figure who demonstrates value, or marginal utility.

As Michael White points out, this version of Crusoe builds on the empty-handed, capital-less children's hero popularized by Rousseau and Campe rather than on Defoe's own fanatical looter.[71] That is, a figure shaped by Rousseau to represent childish isolation from sexual awareness, who then took on a new life as an illustration of a primitive state of society for young readers, is now transformed into an image of adult economic rationality. Hermann Gossen's *Entwicklung* (1854) offers not only one of the earliest elaborations of the theory of marginal utility, but also one of the earliest references to Crusoe as such a utility-maximizing individual – and he refers to Campe rather than to Defoe. Arguing that the prospect of future gain offsets the present pain of work, Gossen suggests that "in order to convince oneself completely of this, one need only read Campe's children's story, 'Robinson Crusoe'."[72] Not very influential when it was published in

1854, Gossen's text was revived by William Jevons and Robert Adamson in the late 1870s. Jevons played a central role in formulating and popularizing neo-classical economic theory in England, and he uses Crusoe to think about the nature of value: "Even Robinson Crusoe must have looked upon each of his possessions with varying esteem and desire for more, although he was incapable of exchanging with any other person."[73] Crusoe's name helped to ward off the English historical school of economics, which was concerned by the fact the rational isolated individual of neo-classical economics does not resemble any real person living at any place or time.[74] Crusoe provided a friendly face for this abstraction through the late nineteenth century.

It may seem that the isolated individual is a mere heuristic device, a way to study one aspect of human personality in general rather than a full description of what any person is actually like. However, conjectural history's theory of stadial development returns in an assertion that this figure does in fact represent a certain kind of person: the civilized adult. Jevons notes that because neo-classical economics focuses on the calculation of future utility to satisfy abstract wants, it depends on the existence of an agent who is able to perform such calculations. The "power of anticipation must have a large influence in Economics," Jevons writes in his influential *The Theory of Political Economy* (1871), "for upon it is based all accumulation of stocks of commodity to be consumed at a future time." Although the power of anticipation is central to Jevons's version of economic law, he believes that this power is not a universal human characteristic. Rather, Jevons locates it on a timeline of both individual and national development, returning to a version of the double timeline popularized by conjectural history. The laws of marginal utility apply to civilized adults but not to other people, because civilized adults are the only persons who possess the power of anticipation. Children and savages are defined by its lack: "The untutored savage, like the child, is wholly occupied with the pleasures and the troubles of the moment; the morrow is dimly felt; the limit of his horizon is but a few days off. The wants of a future year, or of a lifetime, are wholly unforeseen."[75]

Here age is seen through status: no matter what their numerical age may be, "savages" are not adults. They stand for childhood to Jevons, as they stand for childhood to Rousseau. What is new here is the stress on foresight in and of itself as the quality that defines the civilized adult. While Emile is moved by a vague but powerful desire for Sophie, Jevons's adult is moved by a vague but powerful desire for the future: "in a state of civilisation, a vague though powerful feeling of the future is the main incentive to industry and saving. The cares of the moment are but ripples on the tide of achievement and hope."[76] As a utility-maximizer, the civilized adult has an acute sense of time as limited, as valuable as it is fleeting. Haunted by this "vague but powerful feeling of the future," he constantly trades present pain for future good, calculating the value of his precious time exactly. White points out the impossibility of actually finding this utility-maximizing, rational Crusoe in Defoe. Although Defoe's castaway often does work very hard to achieve distant goals, he is also given to saying awkward things such as "my time or labour was little worth, so it was as well employed one way as another" (85). Perhaps time is of "little worth" on Defoe's island because it seems to be nearly limitless. Both classical and neo-classical economists stress that people tend to place a low value on even an essential good when we have a lot of it, which is why water costs less than diamonds. And time is as abundant as water for Defoe's Crusoe. As we have seen, *Robinson Crusoe*, unlike *The Family Instructor*, is not a developmental work. Crusoe does not get any older – or at least he shows no physical, emotional, or mental sign of aging as the years tick away into decades. The fact that he does not change as he nominally moves from thirty-five to sixty-one means that he is free to spend his nearly infinite, nearly valueless time casually, in various non-utility-producing ways. Only the later children's Crusoe consistently optimizes his resources, just as he constantly learns and grows.

If to be an adult is to be rational, as popularizers of neo-classical economic theory imply, emotion becomes the property of childhood. That is, one corollary of economic rationality is a certain Romantic version of developmental psychology, one in which Jevons's focus on the future tips over into an equally powerful nostalgia for the past, the lost homeland of emotional intensity. John Stuart Mill describes both sides of this age-leveled division of rationality and emotion in his famous account of his mental breakdown. He is driven to near-suicide by a failure to want anything. Although Rousseau makes adulthood attractive by making it the home of sexual awareness and pleasures, Mill's version of adulthood has little to recommend it other than grim duty. The product of a fabulously intensive middle-class education (his father surpassed Mr. Billingsley in his zeal, hand-lettering Greek–English flashcards for the three-year-old John Stuart), young Mill was precociously adult – which meant that he was entirely rational and entirely forward-looking. "I was accustomed to felicitate myself on the certainty of a happy life which I enjoyed, through placing my happiness in something durable and distant," he recalls, "in which some progress might be always making, while it could never be exhausted by complete attainment." As in Campe and Edgeworth, here the ideal seems to be goal-oriented drudgery rather than the actual achievement of any goal. When it is almost too late, however, Mill realizes that the same habits of mind that create his work ethic also erode it: "Analytic habits . . . are favourable to prudence and clearsightedness, but a perpetual worm at the root both of the passions and of the virtues; and, above all, fearfully undermine all desires, and all pleasures, which are the effects of association." Instead of an overly adventurous Crusoe courting shipwreck, Mill's education left him a ship without a sail, "stranded" before he even started his voyage:

> I was thus, as I said to myself, left stranded at the commencement of my voyage, with a well-equipped ship and a rudder, but no sail; without any real desire for the ends which I had been so carefully fitted out to work for: no delight in virtue, or the general good, but also just as little in anything else.

Unable to bear the prospect of living more than a year in this state, Mill saved himself by redefining his idea of happiness to stress altruism, and by taking the "Immortality Ode" as a guide to enduring the inevitable loss of one's "youthful enjoyment of life."[77]

Other nineteenth-century commentators found both ends of this age-leveled opposition of adult rationality and childhood emotion in Crusoe himself: by the end of the century, Crusoe's island was not only an icon of utility-maximizing rationality, but also a spot of time. *Robinson Crusoe* was read as an escape from the abstraction of the forward-looking mental habits of adulthood. The island was described as a small, manageable world, filled with therapeutic, hands-on experiences with arts and crafts, like Thoreau's cabin at Walden Pond. Less charitably, literary critics used Crusoe's isolation on his desert island to promote, by contrast, an idea of psychological complexity. That is, imaginatively stranding the young person on Crusoe's island could help the older reader think of himself as inhabiting a great mainland of adult knowledge, where he explored increasingly private and increasingly complicated ideas about sex and interpersonal relationships, while still firing off the occasional bulletin explaining the difference between use value and exchange value.

As we have seen, for Charles Lamb in 1829 *Robinson Crusoe* stands out from the rest of Defoe's works and from novels in general because it retains a strangely old-fashioned, mixed audience by the force of sheer habit, by "tough prescription." Lamb still sees age through the more important frame of social status. People of all social classes read *Robinson Crusoe* because people of all social classes have always read *Robinson Crusoe*, even as they diverge as readers in all other cases: "De Foe can never again hope to be popular with a much higher class of readers, than that of the servant-maid or the sailor; *Crusoe* keeps its rank only by tough prescription."[78] For Lamb, all of Defoe's novels *ought* to be read both by gentlemen and by the young, female, and servile reader because of their "interest," but only *Robinson Crusoe* still manages to reach this undifferentiated audience: *Crusoe* "is an especial favourite with sea-faring men, poor boys, servant-maids, &c. [Defoe's] novels are capital kitchen-reading, while they are worthy, from their interest, to find a shelf in the libraries of the wealthiest and the most learned" (Letter from Lamb to Walter Wilson, December, 1822).[79]

Half a century after Lamb, however, Leslie Stephen is so eager to differentiate and to elevate the novel as proper reading for grown-up gentlemen that he misremembers and simplifies Lamb's claims about *Crusoe*'s mixed audience. For Stephen, the point is that kitchen reading cannot cross over to any other room in the literary house: "'Robinson Crusoe' is a book for boys rather than men, and, as Lamb says, for the kitchen rather than the higher circles. It falls short of any high intellectual interest."[80] Stephen still thinks about reading in terms of both age and status, but for him age matters more. *Robinson Crusoe* now belongs to servants and to sailors rather than to gentlemen – but it belongs most of all to boys. While Lamb thought the book would "interest" both gentlemen and their servants, Stephen is looking for something more exclusive, for books with "high intellectual interest." Although Stephen still talks about status as well as about age, for him age has become the key term. Crusoe's island marks Defoe's novel as low in terms of both types of person: the "horrors of abandonment on a desert island can be appreciated by the simplest sailor or schoolboy." The schoolboy, however, is now an even lower sort of reader than the sailor. Stephen damns *Robinson Crusoe* with a back-handed compliment, retrospectively age-leveling its century and a half of largely mixed-age readers: "it scarcely satisfies a grown-up man with a taste for high art . . . [but] to have pleased all the boys in England for near a hundred and fifty years is, after all, a remarkable feat."[81]

For Stephen, an adult novel is a "psychological study." By this criterion *Crusoe* is a failure:

> It would indeed be easy to show . . . the story singularly wanting as a psychological study . . . Crusoe himself is all but impossible . . . For this reason, the want of power in describing emotion as compared with the amazing power of describing facts, *Robinson Crusoe* is a book for boys rather than men, and, as Lamb says, for the kitchen rather than for higher circles.[82]

Crusoe is now "all but impossible" as a character, a mere boy's sketchy attempt at describing a human being. Earlier readers knew that isolation like Crusoe's would lead in practice to mental and emotional ruin, as it did in the real-life castaway narratives that Defoe himself read. But Stephens cares about this fact: "a man living fifteen years by himself, like Crusoe, would either go mad or sink into the semi-savage state," he protests.[83] Crusoe's miraculous exploits on the island are no longer an inspiring sign of God's providence, or of the English national gift for keeping account books and building empires. They are now a sign of an immature writer. Similarly, Dickens complains that Crusoe's island experience left "no visible effect . . . on his character." Dickens also objects to another deficit in psychological complexity in the novel, the dearth of sexual feeling that helped to win its status as a children's book from Rousseau onwards, commenting that "Defoe must have been a precious dry and disagreeable article himself."[84]

Other nineteenth-century critics also agree that *Robinson Crusoe* is all about the island, but no longer assume that the island is the property of semi-literate readers of all ages. Like Stephen, they see Defoe's readers as childish, but move gradually from defining childishness through social status to defining it as an effect of numerical age. Overall, letters and reviews show an uneven but growing sense of distance between adulthood and childhood as stages of readerly development, one that can take the form of either Romantic nostalgia for an idealized child or Stephen's contempt for the young Philistine. Writers debate whether the book should be read by adults or by children, or by both, or by adults who become their childhood selves again whenever they read Defoe. Mary Poovey and Stephen Arata have described the campaign of later nineteenth-century literary commentators to elevate certain aspects of literature and reading, to "discriminate among kinds of imaginative writing and ways of consuming printed material in order to construct hierarchies within both writing and reading."[85] Kinds of writing and reading that value the appearance of simplicity and transparency were developed to describe the public economic world, while literary reading and writing came to be seen as their opposite. Ideas of age played an important role in this elevation, which we will examine in greater depth in Chapter 5.

Here I would like to note a tension in the nineteenth-century discussion that is particularly relevant to the reception of Crusoe. On the one hand, the critics' elevation of literary reading and of themselves to the status of professionals depends on a strong claim that they are adults: their rationality, expertise, and experience of life make what they do with imaginative books different in kind and more valuable to others than what young readers do with such books. In this sense, one of the most important moments in John Murray's 1886 overview of the contemporary professionalization of literature, "On Books and Reading" (*Quarterly Review* 1886), is a seemingly casual line near the end of this long essay: "Last, but by no means least, do we plead for a guide to 'Children's Books.'" Whatever else he still needs to argue for, by 1886 Murray can rely on the authority of age-leveling. As critics, "we" are adults, speaking to an audience of similarly adult readers. Some of these adults may want to turn their attention briefly from the imaginative literature appropriate to themselves to consider, like Mr. Billingsley, which books are right for children – but being a good critical reader means being grown up. At the same time, however, the psychology that these adult novels and critics explore is in significant part a Romantic one. As does John Stuart Mill, it identifies emotions themselves with an idealized vision of childhood. So, in this sense, being a good critical reader means being a child. Both sides of this age-leveled sense of reading are important to the nineteenth-century reception of Crusoe.

For an anonymous reviewer in the *National Review* in 1856, for example, Defoe's various audiences coexist uneasily: *Crusoe* "is a work of genius – a most remarkable one – but of a low order of genius." What matters for this reviewer, as it matters for Stephen, is a sense of distance between the child and the adult. *Robinson Crusoe*'s power comes from nostalgia for lost childhood, although childhood is here understood as lasting up to the age of twenty-five, insofar as the window for enjoying *Robinson Crusoe* for the first time now closes at that age:

> The universal admiration it has obtained may be the admiration of men: but it is founded on the liking of boys. Few educated men or women would care to read it for the first time after the age of five-and-twenty. Even Lamb could say it only "holds its place by tough prescription." The boy revels in it.[86]

For this reviewer, nostalgia is an unreliable prop for an adult reader's admiration, perhaps because he also thinks the reveling boy reader is stupidly selfish, as emotionally isolated as is Crusoe himself on his island. The boy reader is engaged in the very absorptive reading praised by Rousseau, picturing himself in Crusoe's place. But he fails to learn imaginative sympathy from the immature pleasure he takes in the book:

> the boy becomes his own Robinson Crusoe – it is little Tom Smith himself, curled up in a remote corner of the playground, who makes those troublesome voyages on the raft, and rejoices over the goods he saves from the

> wreck . . . He does not care a farthing for Crusoe as a separate person for [*sic*] himself.[87]

This island is a scene of immature play because the boy reader cannot recognize the difference between himself and Crusoe, or the difference between himself and anyone else.

The *Dublin University Magazine* (1856) in the same year does not imagine an audience with a "double character" of both children and adults, but rather readers doubling back to the island, returning in old age to the book they read in their childhood and through this book returning to their childhood selves. This review is both more confident about the power of nostalgia and more upbeat about the child. Here Crusoe's island becomes a Wordsworthian spot of time, a vivid childhood experience that restores emotional intensity to the aged reader: "How many in the decline of life have over the leaves of that wonder book grown young again! . . . "*That* island" . . . remains to the last the greenest spot in memory." "Children are charmed with the *story* of *Robinson Crusoe*; men of thought are not less delighted," the reviewer remarks, but his point is that this "wonder book" turns thoughtful men back into charming children, that it manages to cross a deeply significant division between ages.[88] Running away to sea and shrinking the world down to an island, to what can be seen with one pair of eyes and held by one pair of hands, is a fantasy of escape from the large, complex economic institutions within which adults now knowingly live – as well as their large and complex psychological relationships. In 1886, Harrison strikes this same Romantic note, self-consciously protesting against what seems to him the new and excessive age-leveling of literature. A "healthy . . . taste for imaginative work" refuses to dismiss not only *Robinson Crusoe* but also *The Vicar of Wakefield* as being exclusively "for the young"; it also requires one to be consistently thrilled by Shelley and Keats:

> If he thinks "Crusoe" and the "Vicar" books for the young; if he thrill not with the "Ode to the West Wind" and the "Ode to a Grecian Urn"; if he have no stomach for "Christabelle," or the lines written on "The Wye above Tintern," he should fall on his knees and pray for a cleanlier and quieter spirit.[89]

Gender plays a more consistently prominent role in the nineteenth-century reception of Crusoe than it did in eighteenth-century adaptations. When *Crusoe* is about learning rational self-control and foresight, the book is good for both boys and girls. When it is an exciting adventure tale, it belongs to a genre the Victorians gave to boys – and as we shall see in Chapter 5, most often to "boys of all ages," granting gender priority over age. For John Dennis in the *Cornhill Magazine* (1871), Defoe's one great work is *Robinson Crusoe*, *Robinson Crusoe* is all about the island, and the island is all about boys: "'Crusoe's lonely isle' has a more familiar hold upon our boys than any historic site with which they are acquainted. Few spots distinguished in geography have a greater interest than this. It is something to discover an island, but it is better to create one." Dennis's critical evaluation of Defoe's works becomes an act of cartography: "*Robinson Crusoe* stands out from its companions like a noble mountain amidst a range of stunted hillocks."[90] William Minto (1879) does not merely see boy readers imagining themselves on the island, but also sees Defoe himself setting up camp there: "Daniel Defoe was the only man of letters in his time who might have been thrown on a desert island without finding himself at a loss what to do."[91] Here Minto sees Defoe as Crusoe, but a Crusoe who looks a lot like Robert Baden-Powell. In other words, *Robinson Crusoe* was a valuable book in 1879 because it offered the same practical mastery of the world modeled by the empire-building heroes of the nineteenth-century boys' adventure story, a genre we will examine in Chapter 5.

In contrast, for twentieth-century academic critics, saving *Robinson Crusoe* as a novel for adults required distinguishing it from desert-island tales written for children. Leslie Stephen's ideal reader was a "grown-up man with a taste for high art," but the contemporary professional academic critic is the most grown-up reader of all, the reader who is most carefully distanced from the context of primary and secondary education as well as childhood itself.[92] Like Stephen, such critics equate adulthood and full literacy, as they equate childhood and lesser degrees of literacy. But they do not invoke Lamb's Crusoe-loving servants and sailors, because semi-literate adult readers no longer represent central worries about the status of the novel. Now age rather than social class is the threat to the novel's claim to possess aesthetic value. Crusoe's island looks too much like Treasure Island, Coral Island, Never-Never Land, and all the other islands on which fictional English boys stage their self-flattering adventures.[93] Crusoe's delayed gratification in building and farming his little world looks too much like a middle-class child sweating away at a lemonade stand, cheerfully ignorant of the larger institutions (Mom, Dad, inherited wealth, salaries, compound interest, bank accounts, mortgages, tax breaks, insurance plans, credit card payment schedules) that underwrite his enterprise. No matter how hard Crusoe works, it seems he is only play-acting, performing gestures in isolation from the larger structures that would give them reality.

Serious critics were often uncomfortable finding themselves in this neighborhood. In *English Literary History* in 1943, John Robert Moore tried to show that *Robinson Crusoe* is not a "little story" but rather a work of major philosophical and literary significance. He set about this task by showing that Robert Louis Stevenson misunderstood the novel, attacking the "element of unsoundness in Stevenson's estimate of Defoe." For Moore, the fact that Stevenson mistakenly saw *Robinson Crusoe* as a children's book proved that Stevenson rather than Defoe was psychologically retarded: "Stevenson, for all his idolatry, could never quite forget the childhood idea that *Robinson Crusoe* is a nursery book for 'the pleasant Land of Counterpane' ... Stevenson became a man; but he never quite put away childish things."[94] To this line of thinking, the self-sufficiency of Crusoe's island is not adulthood but rather a child's immature fantasy of adulthood. And these critics' idea of adulthood offers a sharp contrast to the neo-classical economists' utility-maxizimer. Harry Robins remarked in *PMLA* in 1952 that desert island locations suggest fantasies of omniscience and omnipotence, and fantasies of omniscience and omnipotence are childish. Robins cherished every mechanical blunder that Crusoe makes as evidence that Defoe's castaway adventure is different in kind from *The Swiss Family Robinson*. It does not "appeal to children." *Robinson Crusoe* is now a book for adults because its hero wastes so many years building boats that are too huge to move to the sea and hacking whole trees into useless twelve-hundred-pound planks. Robins noted that Crusoe's time is weirdly "unlimited," but stresses that the more of this nearly limitless time Crusoe wastes, the better:

> Were Crusoe depicted as succeeding with ease in each venture, as triumphing over every difficulty through mechanical genius or even "ingrained skill or knowledge," he would, like the castaways in *The Swiss Family Robinson*, appeal to children. But... by granting Crusoe an almost unlimited time in which these problems may be solved, and by seeing that he makes errors in judgment and performs a considerable amount of ill-planned work, Defoe made him intensely real to the adult mind, which is not fascinated by omniscience and omnipotence.[95]

For Robins, what makes the novel valuable "to the adult mind" is exactly the psychological complexity that makes it uninteresting to the child mind. That is, Robins accepts Stephen's definition of adult novels as psychologically complex, but he understands psychological complexity not as the study of sexual feeling or the impact of environmental influences on the mind, but as the study of futility. In contrast to these earlier twentieth-century critical accounts of *Robinson Crusoe*, post-colonial criticism embraces both Crusoe's island and the thematic connections it suggests between the novel and children's literature as evidence of the larger cultural project of colonialism. Rather than seeing Crusoe himself as living out the stages of history from savagery to commercial civilization, they focus on the exploitation and violence of his encounters with indigenous people.

The bonds of debt and credit that figure in Defoe's *Crusoe* are also the bonds of blood kinship and love, the principles of family duty and neighborhood charity. In contrast, the psychologically complex private world of adult novels assumes a public world of economic abstractions and institutions that are legally distinct from personal relationships. Crusoe's island is an escape from the web of trust, but not an entrance into either of these modern worlds of adults. That is one reason why the decades-long solitude of a desert island castaway seems such an unlikely premise for an adult novel today. For us, awareness of the different rules that govern the public and the private is one important difference between adults and children. We will look at some other differences in the following chapters.

CHAPTER 3

Dating Pamela

Mr. B., Goody Two-Shoes, *and the age of consent*

When the twenty-five year-old Mr. B. flirts with her, abducts her, and threatens her with rape, Pamela Andrews is fifteen years old; she turns sixteen shortly before Mr. B. marries her. What did these ages mean for Samuel Richardson and for his audience in 1740 when *Pamela* was published with runaway success? What do they reveal about the idea of adulthood and its relation to the novel? The previous chapter argues that the eighteenth century saw the beginning of a long shift in thinking about identity: age became increasingly important in comparison with social status and gender as the basis for individual agency. Novels such as *Pamela* and *Robinson Crusoe* – both in their central themes and in the retroactive age-leveling of their audiences – participated in this shift. As we have seen, *Robinson Crusoe* became a children's book, the sexlessness of Crusoe's island ultimately helping to ban it from adult literature. The converse is true for *Pamela.* Written to "*Improve the Minds of the YOUTH of both Sexes,*" Richardson's novel was seen from its publication onwards as a "warm" book.[1] As sexual awareness became a more important hallmark of adulthood, *Pamela* traveled in the opposite direction from *Robinson Crusoe*, moving from the young reader to the adult.[2]

In the last section of this chapter, I trace the evolution of *Pamela* into adults-only reading. I begin, however, with an older kind of reading audience, one that, at least at first glance, Pamela Andrews neatly embodies as a young female servant: the eighteenth-century novel's popular mixed-age audience of women, children, and servants. The "lowness" shared by all these readers subsumed their wildly varying numerical ages. More particularly, I focus on Pamela's relationship to the first commercially significant age-differentiated reader: the child reader envisioned at mid-century in the new children's book market staked out by John Newbery. A successful novel such as *Pamela* and a successful children's book such as John Newbery's *Little Goody Two-Shoes* (1765) have much in common: both are formally complex and proudly didactic. Moreover, while both kinds of book share a commitment to Lockean reason as a version of maturity, this reason does not map clearly onto modern ideas of age, nor does it outweigh social categories of identity. Rather, a combination of numerical age, Lockean ideas of development, and social status provides the context for the eighteenth-century market in both children's literature and novels. This same set of ideas also sets the terms for Pamela's marriage at sixteen to the twenty-five-year-old Mr. B. *Pamela* is about a triumphantly successful young person, and is sometimes read today as a story about "growing up." But for this novel, as for *Goody Two-Shoes*, "growing up" still means moving up in the world more than it means reaching a new psychological stage. The new authority that Pamela wins is finally defined by social position rather than by inner growth.[3] Nevertheless, in *Pamela* a specific idea of adulthood founded on the ability to reason becomes more separate from and more able to compete with other kinds of mastery. With peculiar clarity, *Pamela* shows us how a world of masters and their servants became a world of adults and their children.

hierarchy + social categories important to (mixed-age) fiction

Books: "for the youth of both sexes"

In 1896, novelist and children's writer Helen Shipton discerned something odd about the way age works in *Pamela*. She thought that Richardson lacks a strong psychological sense of age, and that this lack is typical of his time. Shipton's sense of this historical difference was powerful enough to help convince her that *Jane Eyre* was influenced by *Pamela*: she thought that Brontë had absorbed Richardson's archaic sense of age together with his plot. Shipton imagines a scene of the young and therefore "impressionable" Charlotte Brontë encountering Richardson, a scene that is all about age-leveled differences in reading and the lasting effect of early experiences on the gradual growth of a personality. The formative book lies in wait for the eager child:

> on the bookshelves in the poorly furnished parlour, or slinking out of sight among Parson Brontë's ponderous theological tomes in his dull study, was a substantial volume bound in brown calf bearing, in faded gilt letters, the title 'Pamela; or Virtue Rewarded.' Or was it in some neighbouring farmhouse that Brontë found the book – borrowed it perhaps, and carried it home with all the eagerness of a precocious child with whom books were scarce.[4]

However Brontë got hold of *Pamela*, Shipton is convinced that *Pamela* got permanent hold of Brontë, in a way that books can influence children alone:

> Whatever we read at an impressionable age fixes a kind of standard in our minds . . . The old books are there, along with the old scenes and the old faces, a part of ourselves, known as we can never know anything in later life . . . The books that they [children] read while yet too young to choose or to criticise, the books that thus become part of their inner lives and tinted the glasses through which they viewed the world.

In contrast to this sense of a sharp difference between impressionable youth and adulthood, the time of critical thinking and of personal choice, Shipton finds an anachronistic idea of age in *Jane Eyre*. An "old-fashioned standard" borrowed from *Pamela* prevents Brontë from representing youth and adulthood as Shipton expects to see these states represented in a novel. Shipton stresses numerical age. She believes that young people are impressionable, and that this impressionability explains not merely how they read, but also how they live. Rather than relying on their own capacity to reason and reflect, as do mature adults, they act under the influence of other persons:

> Another and invariable sign of an old-fashioned standard is the early maturity of those concerned in the story. Jane Eyre is *eighteen* when she passes through the crisis of her life, and not only is she invariably right and wise and judicious, but there is never a hint that she might be expected to be otherwise . . . This newly emancipated schoolgirl, after her short life of absolute subordination, reasons and reflects like a woman of forty, and never hesitates or doubts or is turned from her course by the influence of any other person.

For Shipton, an eighteen-year-old who reasons like a forty-year-old can only be the product of early exposure to a certain sixteen-year-old:

> Pamela is just *sixteen* when she acts with such unparalleled firmness and discretion, and before she is twenty she is the all-admired mistress of a great household, mother of a large family, qualified to criticise and correct the learned Locke, and to give good advice to all the ladies of her acquaintance.

Shipton is right about Pamela's numerical age. Pamela's fourth letter describes her as "fifteen last February"; her parents' second letter worries about the odds of a "poor maiden, of little more than fifteen years of age" fending off a "designing young gentleman . . . [who] has a kind of *authority* to command as your master" (italics in original).[5] While imprisoned with Mrs. Jewkes, Pamela writes that she has "lived above sixteen years in virtue and reputation," refusing to renounce "the whole sixteen years innocence" (239).

Writing at the end of the nineteenth century, Shipton expects these numbers to have a certain meaning. She expects to find in novels a psychological idea of development: the gradual growth of maturity, and with it personal independence, according to a complex but entirely predictable timetable. In *Jane Eyre*, she finds instead the idea that reason alone brings independence from the influence of others. This "old-fashioned standard" seems to her anachronistic in Brontë's 1847 novel, although to be expected in Richardson's 1740 one. While Shipton's reading itself leaves out psychological elements of *Jane Eyre* that readers today often find most compelling, such as its focus on early childhood trauma, this reading usefully highlights other elements in the novel: "absolute subordination," independence, and a Lockean sense of reason as the quality that determines to which of these two states a person belongs. Her reading is even more suggestive with regard to *Pamela* and eighteenth-century ideas of reading and age.

To understand how age works in *Pamela*, we must remember how age worked in the book market in which this novel appeared. In general, the difference that still mattered in writing and selling books was the difference between elite and popular, not the difference between the sophistication of the adult and the naiveté of the child. As soon as they could read anything at all, most eighteenth-century readers tried their luck with the same kind of books and pamphlets that they had probably already heard read out loud, the same books and pamphlets that they would read all their lives. These typically included the Bible, *Pilgrim's Progress*, other devotional works, Aesop's fables, a wealth of almanacs and chapbooks full of old chivalric or sexually frank stories and riddles – and, increasingly, novels. Charlotte Brontë still assumes familiarity with the older, traditional audience of women, children, and servants in describing the nursemaid Bessie Lee holding young Jane Eyre and the little Reeds spellbound as she recounts over her ironing "passages of love and adventure taken from old fairy tales and older ballads; or (as at a later period I discovered) from the pages of *Pamela*, and *Henry, Earl of Moreland*."[6]

Although Jane's education allows her as narrator to retroactively sort out elements of popular print and oral tradition, in this scene passages of love and adventure from folktales, ballads, and novels merge to form one familiar kind of entertainment, as women, children, and servants combine to form its natural, mixed-age, low audience. This conflation of children and semi-literate people in general minimizes the significance of numerical and developmental ideas of adulthood. Conduct-books take a similar stance, stressing the shared subordination of women, children, and servants even when addressing them as separate groups. In doing so, such writing echoes patriarchal political theory, which defines the child as a person of any numerical age whatsoever in a dependent social status.[7] This shows that ideas of age mirrored ideas of social subordination, rather than presenting an alternative to them. This sense of age is quite different from a universal scale of development keyed to the number of years lived.

In the middle of the eighteenth century, however, within the small, specialized children's book market, John Newbery made a bid to differentiate young readers more distinctly from the semi-literate lower classes of people in general by popularizing age-leveled developmental claims. Historians of children's literature generally see this as the crucial moment when children's literature emerged as a viable enterprise. Newbery published largely secular stories in commercially significant numbers specifically to delight and to instruct infants and the young in age-appropriate ways. In the process, he helped to popularize the ideas set out in John Locke's *Thoughts Concerning Education* (1692) about the importance of reason and its development in childhood. The most commonly cited date for the start of children's literature as a successful commercial enterprise is the 1744 publication of Newbery's *A Little Pretty Pocket-Book*. With this book, Newbery opened a new market: socially ambitious middle-class parents eager to buy "appropriate" books for their children – not the same two-penny trash the servants read (and we've been buying ever since, especially Newbery Award-winning books).

Such parents were eager to buy books for their children that were also produced in distinctive ways. *A Little Pretty Pocket-Book* had a small-page layout, lots of woodcuts, a bright cover, and came complete with a ball for "little Master Tommy" or a pincushion for "pretty miss Polly." It promised to enable young readers to play themselves into learning.[8] Newbery's little books still looked a lot like the little chapbooks with which they competed – in fact, they looked exactly like brighter, better-printed, and better-bound chapbooks. "The eighteenth-century publishers of children's books were under the delusion that miniature books were appropriate to miniature human beings," Julian Roberts dryly remarks.[9] But it would perhaps be better to say that in the kind of books that they produced, as well as in their tireless foregrounding of words such as "little" and "Lilliputian" in their titles, eighteenth-century publishers of children's books actively campaigned to make this "delusion" seem natural. They deliberately redefined the audience of certain little books from the lower classes of people in general to the small offspring of the middle class in particular.[10]

While chapbooks, lewd and otherwise, had long belonged to the semi-literate of all ages, in the middle of the eighteenth century chapbooks or "little books" became instead linked to children. Later eighteenth-century booksellers and buyers used the terms "chapbook" and "children's book" interchangeably, or favored the even more general term "little book."[11] There is, of course, no natural or necessary connection between little books and little readers. Today, perhaps the majority of books intended for young readers appear in picture-book formats that are larger than those of adult books. The relative cheapness of the chapbook format (even spruced up and priced up for middle-class buyers with better print, gilt edges, and colored paper binding) was a draw. But I would suggest that in this new market the chapbook format also reflects the historical confusion of the semi-literate and the young. This competition between Newbery's new "specialized fictional form" and the older, less specialized chapbooks appears in Jan Fergus's meticulous study of the book-buying habits of eighteenth-century Rugby schoolboys.[12]

In their form as well as their content, Newbery's books showcase the development of the young reader's mind. They celebrate the idea of development itself, the idea most powerfully outlined by "the great Mr. *Locke*," as *A Little Pretty Pocket-Book* respectfully invokes him.[13] John Yolton sums up the importance of this idea in Locke's thought: "Locke's man is not born a person . . . [but rather] can become a person, develop into one . . . through education, acquiring the necessary attributes of virtue and rationality."[14] Both virtue and rationality are important here: Locke, Newbery, and Richardson all assume that "reason" is not the tendency to maximize individual utility that later economics textbooks foreground in the solitary figure of Crusoe on his island, but rather the recognition of moral laws that govern how people ought to relate to each other. This version of reason underwrites their didactic impulse, their pride in leading the reader towards "the Dignity and Excellency of a rational Creature."[15]

In good Lockean fashion, *A Little Pretty Pocket-Book* argues that subduing your child's passions and making its temper "subservient to the Rules of Reason . . . is not to be done by chiding, whipping, or severe treatment, but by Reasoning and mild Discipline" (9). Both literacy itself and the habit of thoughtful discussion are crucial: "Would you have a *Wise* Son, teach him to reason early. Let him read, and make him understand what he reads. No Sentence should be passed over without a strict Examination of the Truth of it . . . A Method of Reasoning will be acquir'd, which will be of Use to him all his Life after" (8). Reading and discussing what one reads give this child not merely pleasure and good moral precepts, but also the ability to think critically, a "Method of Reasoning." While moments such as this invocation of a "wise son" foreground boys in particular, overall, the book is careful to include girls as well as boys within its idea of the child reader. The title page, for example, proclaims that it is "Intended for the Instruction and Amusement of Little Master Tommy and Pretty Miss Polly." Although it opens with two separate letters from Jack the Giant-Killer, one addressed to Master Tommy and one to Miss Polly, these letters are in fact identical, except for the pronouns and the use of "good Boy" or "good Girl." These relatively gender-neutral ideas shaped the new children's literature's age-specific audience, formal conventions, and marketing practices. Following Newbery and Locke, progressive eighteenth- and early nineteenth-century educators and printers differentiated some young readers from the old mixed-age world of low, popular print. They cultivated an upscale, specialized audience by excluding adults, even though children remained part of the novel's low audience of mixed-age readers.[16] In this sense, the child reader was "invented" before the adult reader was invented – as was the child more generally. That is, age took priority over other important frames for imagining an audience, such as social status or gender, in the practice of writing and marketing literature for young readers in particular before it was used in this way to write or market literature for adults. The new children's books promoted a positive image of these young readers as respectably middle-class and irresistibly educable. These qualities also became the core of the ideal later eighteenth- and nineteenth-century novel reader. In this sense, the young reader may be not so much a specialized niche market as the prototype of didactic fiction's audience as a whole. Helen Shipton's sense in 1896 of a great divide between impressionable young readers and critical adult readers suggests the eventual break-up of this way of thinking.

In their depiction of the nuts and bolts of the process of growing into reason, children's books promoted principles central not only to Locke's *Thoughts Concerning Education*, but also to his *Two Treatises of Government* (1689). Lockean texts represent adulthood as the effect of reason rather than social status, opposing patriarchal political theory with theories of cognitive development.[17] "Thus we are *born Free*, as we are born Rational; not that we have actually the Exercise of either; Age that brings one, brings with it the other too," Locke writes.[18] The fascinating story of the alliance of political Locke with educational Locke, an alliance made over his dead body, is well known. Locke himself explains in *Thoughts Concerning Education* that he intends to describe only the education proper to a gentleman's son (and to a large extent, to a gentleman's daughter) rather than the education proper to the great majority of children, who should instead settle into their lifelong subordinate status as quickly as possible. When he directly addresses children affected by the Poor Laws, for example, it is not to cultivate their reason but rather to regret that "their labour . . . is generally lost to the public till they are 12 or 14 years old," and to recommend that they be put to some sort of work "from infancy," or around three years old.[19] In this case, social status still dominates Locke's other ideas: no matter what their numerical age, the poor remain under patriarchal authority. Newbery's books, however, helped in the long process of popularizing the idea of the child defined in terms of stages of cognitive development corresponding to specific numerical ages rather than in terms of a permanent state of social subordination.

Lockean arguments link education and upward mobility to an expansive idea of citizenship. By the middle of the eighteenth century, debates over education and political agency began to assume the cultural prominence that they have today. When agency depends on status, education is not a central issue. However, when agency depends on reason, understood as the foundation of both political and legal consent, education becomes crucial. From the founding of the Society for the Propagation of Christian Knowledge onwards, some conservative advocates of literacy argued that it was possible to educate the poor into greater acceptance of child-like subordination. More generally, however, those who wanted to widen the franchise in England or to start a revolution in America argued that education turns children into adults by developing their reason, and that these reasonable adults turn tyrannies into republics. For example, Tom Paine's *Rights of Man* (1791–92) celebrates "mental manhood" when describing reason and its centrality to republican government.[20] In 1816, contemplating what appears to him to be patriarchy's collapse under the force of mass literacy, Coleridge notes with mixed feelings this link between books and adulthood: "Books are in every hovel . . . the Cottager's child sheds his first bitter tears over pages, which render it impossible for the man to be treated or governed as a child."[21] Letitia Barbauld's *Lessons for Children* (1823) cheerfully equates literacy with the right to human life itself: "I never saw a little dog or cat learn to read. But little boys can learn. If you do not learn, Charles, you are not good for half so much as Puss. You had better be drowned."[22]

Yet we should not exaggerate the cleanness of this break. M. O. Grenby charts the fascinating rise of the specialized eighteenth-century child reader – but he also cautions against taking age-leveled reading as the norm. He remarks instead that throughout the long eighteenth century, the "campaign to drive a wedge between books for childen and for adults was largely unsuccessful," insisting that the "weight of evidence demonstrates that, regardless of warnings against it, children (and indeed sometimes adults) continued to cross-read, using both children's and adult's texts, often in tandem."[23] In addition, social status remains important even in Newbery's deliberate targeting of the new "little Masters and Misses" whose parents could afford to go shopping for educational playthings. Social status also remains important to the fairy-tale plot of upward mobility that structures many of Newbery's books and *Pamela*, the same plot that structured older chapbooks. Indeed, one of the most popular children's books ever written, Newbery's *The History of Little Goody Two-Shoes*, still vacillates on whether "child" should be understood as a developmental or a status category. *Little Goody Two-Shoes* (price sixpenny) is a consumer object that clearly targets the specialized young reader: chapbook-sized at four inches by two and three-quarter inches, but with Newbery's distinctive cover of bright Dutch flowered and gilt paper. The book's preface directly addresses not only this "little Reader," however, but also an older "kind, humane, and courteous Reader."[24] *Goody Two-Shoes*'s introduction attacks gentlemen of property, such as Sir Timothy Gripe and Mr. Graspall, who oppress "children of six feet high," readers who are full-grown, but who will never grow out of their social subordination.[25] After criticizing the engrossing rich at some length, the introduction launches into a dialogue about whether such political satire belongs in children's books:[26]

> But what, says the Reader, can occasion all this? Do you intend this for Children, Mr. Editor? Why, do you suppose this is written by Mr. Editor, Sir? This may come from another Hand. This is not the Book, Sir, mentioned in the Title, but the Introduction to that Book; and is intended not for those sort of Children, but for Children of Six Feet, of which, as my Friend has justly observed, there are many Millions in the Kingdom . . . [27]

Alan Richardson has described how, as respectable or "official" children's literature such as Newbery's differentiates itself from cheap chapbooks, the six-foot-high dependent gives way to the innocent young reader, one defined in developmental terms as an inappropriate audience for political satire as well as sexual content.[28] This editor's claim that the Introduction addresses politically powerless "Children of Six Feet High" while the book itself addresses numerically young readers or "those sort of Children" supports this distinction. The book as a whole, however, does not. Certainly, it often directly addresses a child reader understood in developmental terms. It includes chapters in which its young heroine creates her own set of alphabet blocks on Locke's model, for example, and chapters in which she teaches children to identify letters and to combine them into words are generously illustrated with alphabets printed in both upper- and lower-case letters, directly inviting the "little Reader" to learn along with Margery Meanwell and her students: "Now, pray, little Reader, take this Bodkin, and see if you can point out the letters from these mixed Alphabets, and tell how they should be placed, as well as little Boy *Billy*" (31). These age-leveled segments, however, are framed by continued satiric commentary on how the rich manipulate parish poor laws, tithes, and justice itself: "Complaints indeed were made, but to what purpose are complaints brought to a man who can hunt, drink, and smoke with the lord of the manor, and who is also the justice of the peace?" (7). Overall, *Goody Two-Shoes* is still fascinated by the relationship between social subordination and age. It is still busy disentangling the knowing adult reader, the proper audience for political satire, from the innocent young reader, the proper audience for the new, official children's literature.

Like Newbery, Samuel Richardson sometimes invokes an older audience that is not differentiated by numerical age, and at other times plays with ways of differentiating this audience as the occasion prompts. We can see both gestures in his varying descriptions of the intended readers for his 1740 revision of Sir Roger L'Estrange's Aesop's Fables.[29] His title makes the widest possible claim: *Aesop's Fables with Instructive Morals and Reflections Abstracted from all Party Considerations and Adapted to All Capacities and design'd to promote Religion, Morality, and Universal Benevolence.* His letters, however, break down these readers of "All Capacities" into what are for us today two very different kinds of readers: children, and "the lower classes of people." To Johannes Stinstra, Richardson first remarks that this Aesop is a book "I would commend for Children," echoing the language of the book's Preface. In recommending the book for children, as in his promise of "Instructive Morals and Reflections Abstracted from all Party Considerations," Richardson seems to be angling for Alan Richardson's apolitical young innocent. However, to explain why Aesop is not as good as the novels that earned Stinstra's approbation, Richardson invokes a different readership, one defined by social status rather than numerical age. Now his Aesop is not an early example of children's literature but rather a typical example of "low" literature, something like a manual of sample letters intended for the semi-literate: "I am not at all surprized, Sir, at what you say of the Familiar Letters, and of Aesop. They were both intended for the lower Classes of People. I omitted several Letters in the former, as too high for the design."[30]

Pamela shows a similar ambiguity in terms of the age of its intended readers. Its title page and preface make two claims about age – and neither of these claims privileges adult readers. The first claim is that the novel is particularly directed to "youth." The second claim is that the novel's value is shown by its wide appeal, its power to move all kinds of people in addition to its primary "youth" audience. *Pamela*'s title page declares it was published "in order to cultivate the Principles of Virtue and Religion in the Minds of the YOUTH of BOTH SEXES." Begun as a handbook of sample letters for the use of the semi-literate, supposedly written by a daughter who has left home to go into service, the book's title page firmly links it to youth understood both as a developmental and as a status category. Richardson assumes that youth will often face the trials that come with a servile position in other people's households. Pamela herself, we are told matter-of-factly, was only eleven when she was packed off to become a servant to Mr. B.'s mother, an unexceptional age for leaving home to go into service. The preface follows up by promising "to Divert and Entertain, and at the same time to Instruct, and Improve the Minds of the YOUTH of both Sexes," by rendering "Religion and Morality . . . equally delightful and profitable to the younger Class of Readers, as well as worthy of the Attention of Persons of maturer Years and Understandings."

Here Richardson's term "youth" more closely coincides with the modern "child" than with the modern "adolescent," the developmental term with which it is sometimes conflated. As we have seen, "adolescence" strongly foregrounds the sexual development associated with puberty, while "child" holds in play the double sense of being both a status and a developmental category.[31] Moreover, particularly relevant to Pamela is Ala Alryyes's observation that "adolescence" suggests a period of psychosocial development dominated by identification with a peer group, an identification that we now cultivate and structure by secondary education and its attendant universe of age-leveled activities. While certain groups of early modern and eighteenth-century young people, such as urban apprentices, seem to have had an experience that was somewhat comparable to this, such experience does not seem typical of the central characters of early novels or their time: "the nascent novel treats solitary dependent 'children,' not boisterous groups of youth with a common 'subculture.'"[32] Pamela herself seems to invoke this association of youth with dependence rather than with a developmental timetable or the relative independence of a peer group when she protests that Mr. B.'s "unlawful restraint . . . would not have been attempted, but only that I am a poor destitute young creature, and have no friend that is able to right me" (240).

When Richardson re-packages highlights from his novels as a conduct book, he makes even more explicit his assumptions about how he sees his audience. The title page of *A Collection of the Moral and Instructive Sentiments, Maxims, Cautions, and Reflexions, Contained in the Histories of Pamela, Clarissa, and Sir Charles Grandison*... (1755) offers a traditional catalogue of hierarchical pairings rather than a single developmental trajectory.[33] Age is only one category among others, and adulthood is nowhere in sight. Richardson recommends his novels by claiming that they "amiably illustrate, and strongly enforce, the proper Virtues of *Man and Woman, Parent and Child, Old-Age and Youth, Master and Servant*!" (vi). Here "Old-Age" appears as one superior term in a series of paired hierarchical identities: "Old Age" is like "Man," "Parent," and, above all, "Master."[34] Richardson stresses status, a set of social relationships between permanently unequal individuals, rather than psychology, a universal, age-leveled process of development.

While it may surprise that the young were the central audience of *Pamela*, we know that at least two very young readers won Richardson's particular attention. Among the unpublished pro-*Pamela* poems that he recorded is "an Ode written by a Miss not 12 years of age."[35] And seven-year-old Harry Campbell won himself a future as a successful printer by crying over Pamela's suicidal thoughts by the pond. Richardson was so moved by Harry's "tears of sensibility for Pamela," which formed "two sincere little Fountains," that he took the boy, a poor widow's son, as an apprentice in his printing shop without the usual fee. Harry did not encounter the story in the way we may imagine first encountering novels, as a solitary, silent experience, but in the form of family reading. Featuring representations of attempted sexual assault and attempted suicide, family reading here seems to be a livelier business than it becomes a century later. Richardson's friend Aaron Hill describes the scene: "One Evening, when I was reading [Pamela's] reflections [on suicide] at the Pond to some Company... [Harry] was sitting before me, on the Carpet, with his Head almost touching the Book... " When Harry wept at Pamela's distress, "all the Ladies in Company were ready to devour him with Kisses: he has, since, become doubly a Favourite – and is perhaps the young's [*sic*] of *Pamela's Converts*."[36] The eleven-year-old ode writer and little Harry are both exceptional, she for her poetic skill and he for his sensibility as well as his extreme youth, being in Hill's words "perhaps the young's [*sic*] of *Pamela's Converts*." But there is no sense that either one, as a child, is a developmentally inappropriate member of Richardson's audience.

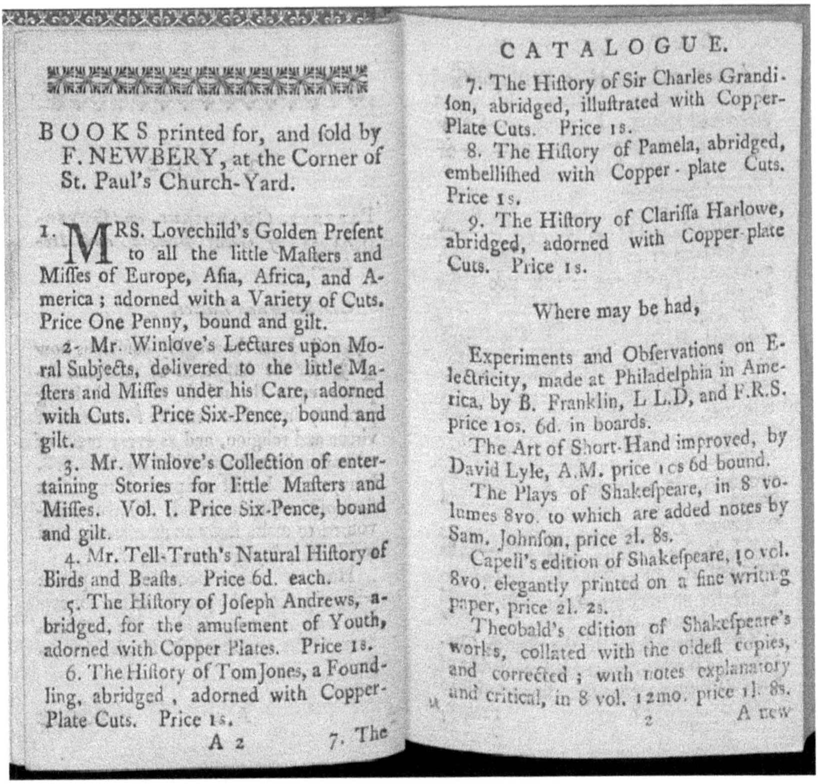

BOOKS printed for, and ſold by F. NEWBERY, at the Corner of St. Paul's Church-Yard.

1. MRS. Lovechild's Golden Preſent to all the little Maſters and Miſſes of Europe, Aſia, Africa, and America; adorned with a Variety of Cuts. Price One Penny, bound and gilt.
2. Mr. Winlove's Lectures upon Moral Subjects, delivered to the little Maſters and Miſſes under his Care, adorned with Cuts. Price Six-Pence, bound and gilt.
3. Mr. Winlove's Collection of entertaining Stories for little Maſters and Miſſes. Vol. I. Price Six-Pence, bound and gilt.
4. Mr. Tell-Truth's Natural Hiſtory of Birds and Beaſts. Price 6d. each.
5. The Hiſtory of Joſeph Andrews, abridged, for the amuſement of Youth, adorned with Copper Plates. Price 1s.
6. The Hiſtory of Tom Jones, a Foundling, abridged, adorned with Copper-Plate Cuts. Price 1s.

A 2 7. The

CATALOGUE.

7. The Hiſtory of Sir Charles Grandiſon, abridged, illuſtrated with Copper-Plate Cuts. Price 1s.
8. The Hiſtory of Pamela, abridged, embelliſhed with Copper-plate Cuts. Price 1s.
9. The Hiſtory of Clariſſa Harlowe, abridged, adorned with Copper-plate Cuts. Price 1s.

Where may be had,

Experiments and Obſervations on Electricity, made at Philadelphia in America, by B. Franklin, L L.D, and F.R.S. price 10s. 6d. in boards.

The Art of Short-Hand improved, by David Lyle, A.M. price 10s 6d bound.

The Plays of Shakeſpeare, in 8 volumes 8vo. to which are added notes by Sam. Johnſon, price 2l. 8s.

Capell's edition of Shakeſpeare, 10 vol. 8vo. elegantly printed on a fine writing paper, price 2l. 2s.

Theobald's edition of Shakeſpeare's works, collated with the oldeſt copies, and corrected; with notes explanatory and critical, in 8 vol. 12mo. price 1l. 8s.

2 A new

2 Catalogue from *The History of Pamela*, 1769

Harry Campbell was not the only eighteenth-century little boy who liked heroines in violent distress. As Jan Fergus documents, in 1784, the single novel most often bought by schoolboys at Rugby with their own pocket money was Frances Burney's *Cecilia*, which was purchased by boys ranging from the ages of ten to eighteen.[37] Fergus's research into the book-buying habits of public schoolboys also suggests the remarkable popularity of abridged versions of eighteenth-century novels among young readers. Similarly, the catalogue included in Francis Newbery's abridged *Pamela*, which is addressed to the "Parents, Guardians, and Governesses of Great-Britain and Ireland," lists not only a six-penny abridgement of *Gulliver*, but also a six-penny *History of Joseph Andrews*, and one-shilling histories of *Tom Jones*, *Clarissa*, and *Charles Grandison* (see Figure 2).[38]

The young were expected not only to read *Pamela* but to learn from it. For Richardson, the young reader generally was the ideal reader, and educating this reader was the novel's central purpose. In other words, Richardson's novel was for the young in a sense that now seems unusual to us: as educable readers of didactic fiction, the young were a model for what all readers should be rather than a marginal group somewhere to the side of literature's primarily adult audience. Richardson assumed that in order for fiction to be worthwhile, it must teach young people how to be moral – but he claimed the same thing about reading for all ages and for all stations in life. To be sure, John Newbery emblazoned *Delectando monemus*, a version of the old Horatian motto of combining instruction with delight, on his children's books, and histories of children's literature often take this motto as handy shorthand for what distinguishes later eighteenth- and nineteenth-century children's literature from the more straightforward and more theologically focused didacticism that preceded it. But this motto, of course, had a broader currency. The power to instruct in an entertaining way defines respectable eighteenth-century literature as a whole for readers of all ages. Rather than designating the sub-literary as it often does now, "didactic" was a guarantor of literary value. There was nothing very new about this neo-classical standard of literary value; what was new was the growing sense that the novel could qualify as literature under it.

Much of the "*Pamela* controversy" centers on the novel's effect on "the youth," a group sometimes understood to consist, as I have argued, of all of the dependents in a household regardless of their numerical age, and sometimes understood to consist of a more upscale set of readers progressing through a developmental process of acquiring reason that is keyed to numerical age. Complete with consumer tie-ins such as fans and teacups, *Pamela*'s enormous commercial success mirrored the social rise of its heroine, enabling it to become a synecdoche for the "market-led multiplication of lowbrow print, unregulated by traditional considerations of learning, decorum, or taste."[39] Everyone read *Pamela* – or, rather, everyone read a version of *Pamela* appropriate to his or her segment of the book market. Fashionable London readers bought increasingly expensive editions, in octavo format, with beautiful paper and engravings, while servants, children, and other chapbook-readers followed the story as it was serialized in farthing newspapers such as *Robinson Crusoe's London Daily Evening Post*, which reprinted *Pamela* over eighteen months in 1741–42.[40]

Today, *Pamela*'s focus on seduction and attempted rape would be likely to classify it as an adult or young-adult book, as would the fact that its heroine has left the sheltered circle of immediate family, friends, and teachers to deal with the power structures of the working world. In the 1740s, readers disagreed vigorously about what kind of book it was and about who should read it. Parents were told both to put the book into the hands of their children and their servants to improve their morals and to snatch it away before it destroys those morals. Attacks on the novel, such as *Shamela* and *Pamela Censured*, countered the didactic claims of Richardson's title page with vivid images of boys and girls, both servile and affluent, losing sleep over *Pamela*'s most well-thumbed erotic passages.[41] Nevertheless, *Pamela* remained widely recommended as family reading. Charles Povey went so far as to complain that the book's supporters "recommend it to Families equal to the *Whole Duty of Man* [a popular devotional manual] to instill Religion into the minds of both Sexes." A French observer criticized an English preacher for exhorting his congregation to put *Pamela* "entre les mains de leurs enfants."[42]

Pamela's unwavering focus on sex may make it a more surprising choice to us than travel narratives such as *Robinson Crusoe* or *Gulliver* for adaptation for young readers, but the controversy over its "warm" scenes did not hinder its popularity as a book suited for children in particular any more than it hindered its popularity as family reading. Because *Pamela* was widely seen as a sexually exciting book, its reception provides a measure of the eighteenth century's growing but still quite limited interest in organizing erotic material according to age. By 1804, in her introduction to Richardson's correspondence, progressive children's writer Letitia Barbauld marvels, and expects others to marvel with her, at how readily the parents of Richardson's day gave *Pamela* to their children: "Mr Lobb talks of bringing-up his son to be virtuous, by giving him *Pamela* as soon as he could read, a choice of books for a youth which we, at present, should be very much surprised at."[43] Nevertheless, several abridgements of *Pamela* were within a few decades of its appearance published exclusively for a young audience. Francis Newbery published more than one edition, and a French translation was published "*for the use of* SCHOOLS" in 1741. Since "young readers already had the novel by heart," asks Peter Sabor, "what better means of teaching them French?"[44]

One can see in such editions the partial emergence of a distinctive *Pamela* meant specifically for children, particularly with respect to sexual content. Nevertheless, flirtation and sexual assault remain essential elements of the plot even when *Pamela* is adapted to exploit the emerging children's market. Such scenes are toned down, to be sure. But in many later versions this toning down reflects the rising standard of propriety for literature in general, still understood to address a mixed-age audience, rather than a separate standard for children's reading. Reviewing Leslie Stephen's new edition of Richardson's works in 1883, for example, *John Bull* sums up the nineteenth-century literary world's sense of the impropriety of the previous century as a whole for readers of *all* ages. While Richardson does not delight in "thrusting" sin before his readers for the sheer pleasure of it, as do Fielding, Smollet, and Sterne, even Richardson's didactic ends require more licentiousness than *John Bull* thinks good for anyone. "The fact that the picture is a faithful copy of the manners of the last century necessarily makes it not edifying," explains this reviewer:

> The age was terribly coarse and licentious . . . As we read his [Richardson's] pages we are compelled to own that virtue cannot be depicted in the toils of vice, even though virtue be in the end triumphant, without our getting some ugly glimpses of the vice over which it is to triumph, and which is usually better veiled than laid bare. There are cases in which ignorance is bliss, and this is one of them. Blissful, indeed, should we be if we could be wholly ignorant of the impurities and sins of the last century.[45]

Ignorance of Richardson is bliss not merely for schoolboys, but rather for all of *John Bull*'s readers.

In any case, in later adaptations Pamela's body starts to disappear. Explicit descriptions of her bosom (with or without Mr. B.'s hand in it), neck, and "shape" tend to fade over time from the pages of most adaptations, whether they are specifically directed to children or not. Not all adaptations of *Pamela* are age-leveled. The anonymous 508-page *Life of Pamela* (1741) makes no mention at all of the age of its intended readers, for example, while *The Paths of Virtue Delineated* (1756) stridently restricts the book to "the youth of both sexes, for whose use it is solely intended."[46] Rather than improving the minds of the *youth* of both sexes as Richardson originally promised, an 1830 abridgement's title page proclaims that it is "Adapted to Inculcate in the Minds of Both Sexes the Principles of Virtue and Religion," with no reference to age.[47] Both of these two later adaptations cut most of the scene in which the cross-dressed Mr. B. attempts to rape Pamela. The Mr. B. of the earlier, 1741 *Life of Pamela*, like Richardson's Mr. B., still "thrust his Hand into her Bosom"; the scene includes most of Richardson's extended description of Mrs. Jewkes helping to hold down the screaming Pamela while Mr. B. fondles her breasts.[48] In contrast, the two later adaptations merely tell us that Mr. B. "was proceeding to indecent liberties."[49] When Pamela revives from her fit, the 1756 *Paths of Virtue*'s Mr. B. vows "that beyond her bosom he was unacquainted with her sex" (36), while the 1830 Mr. B. even more politely vows that "except in outward appearance he knew not her sex."[50] Both are more chaste statements than that of Richardson's Mr. B. who exclaims that "I know not, I declare, beyond this lovely bosom, that you are a woman" (244) or the anonymous 1741 adaptation's still lasciviously regretful Mr. B., who announces that "further than that white Bosom, I know not what Sex you are of."[51] At least one reader (using what Heather Wolfe calls an "unpracticed" and "stilted" hand, one likely to be written by a young person and closer to 1800 than 1900) nevertheless disapproved of this 1830 abridgement, labeling it "not a nice Bock."[52] This inscription's position over a frontispiece of Pamela recoiling in shame from Mr. B. suggests this reader's disapproval may be linked to the novel's characteristic sexual scenarios, although the illustration also occasioned painstaking coloring by hand (see Figure 3).

All of these abridgements of *Pamela* also flatten the formal complexity of Richardson's epistolary format into a third-person omniscient narrative, reducing the potential for conflicting perspectives, moral ambiguities, and critical thought. Pamela's distinctive, class-marked narrating voice is minimized so that her story becomes a less threatening tale, one told by an omniscient narrator in proper English. Bonnie Latimer sees such flattening in age-leveled terms, as the imposition of a restrictive didacticism thought appropriate for children onto a more free and more socially subversive text originally designed for the adult.[53] However, up to the early nineteenth century, all adaptations, including those not directed solely to young readers, make this same change in narrative structure. They all replace Richardson's epistolary structure with a third-person omniscient narrative. Leah Price detects in this consistent change of structure "the abridger's unspoken assumption that poor or young or lazy readers want nothing but plot," suggesting that adaptations were generally written for the "lower class of readers."[54] Other socially subversive aspects of *Pamela* were also toned down for the good of readers of all ages. For example, the 1741 anonymous *Life of Pamela* is also a third-person narrative told by an omniscient narrator; and in addition to eliminating Pamela's voice, this version eliminates her servant-class origins. While Richardson's original version had merely noted that things had once been better with Pamela's literate but ditch-digging family, the *Life* reveals her to be the long-lost relative of the splendidly wealthy Sir Simon Andrews: "She was now out of Danger of ever being insulted on Account of her Birth, since, being of *Sir Simon Andrews*'s family, she had as good Blood in her veins as any Commoner in England could pretend to."[55]

Thus, when we look at *Pamela*'s early reception, we can see some differentiation of audience by age, but this reading audience was still not as clearly age-differentiated as we may now assume. With hindsight, tentative, contradictory, or otherwise partial marketing strategies and authorial

3 Hand-colored frontispiece from *The History of Pamela*, 1830

intentions can take on a coherence that they did not possess at the time. Numerical age did not matter as much then as it matters now in how books are written, marketed, and consumed, because numerical age did not matter then as much as it matters now in other spheres of life.

Laws: "no will of their own"

Pamela's tendency to see status and numerical age in terms of each other reflects Richardson's world. In setting out a catalogue of hierarchical pairings rather than a single developmental trajectory, the title page of Richardson's *Collection of the Moral and Instructive Sentiments, Maxims, Cautions, and Reflexions* reflects the same conceptual framework as Sir William Blackstone's *Commentaries on the Laws of England* (1765–69), the standard reference work for common law well into the nineteenth century, and a foundational work for Anglo-American juridical culture.[56] Like the book market, Blackstone's common law had a history of weighing status more heavily than numerical or developmental ideas of age. As Carolyn Steedman points out, Blackstone states that the contract between servant and employer represents the first of the "three great relations of private life" that concern the law: "According to Blackstone, the others – between husband and wife, and parent and child (or guardian and ward) – were founded on this first and primary one."[57] That is, status difference provides the model for age difference, rather than age providing the model for status, as we might expect today. Robert Steinfeld reminds us that by "servants" we should not imagine merely domestics such as chambermaids and footmen, but the much wider category of economically dependent persons. For a century or so after Locke, the concept of free labor spread only slowly: "all those who worked for others for compensation on whatever terms were in some sense 'serving' their masters."[58] It was not until the late nineteenth century that whipping and imprisonment were finally abolished as legal remedies for a servant's breach of contract. As Douglas Hay explains, with the repeal of nearly all such penalties in 1875, "a type of contract originally based on the need to subordinate labor was restated as if it were a contract between fully equal parties."[59] Chief Baron Pollock's influential ruling against the repeated imprisonment of a potter for leaving his employer in 1857 suggests the shifting relation of numerical age and status in this context. Unlike the legitimate imprisonment of apprentices, Pollock argued, such imprisonment "would not be suitable and proper in the case of a man grown up and of full age, possibly surrounded by a wife and children."[60]

In this sense, our familiar checklist of adult personal qualities – puberty, reason, labor, and worldly knowledge – did not confer agency in the sixteenth, seventeenth and early eighteenth centuries. Property did, by removing one from dependency on others. Those who remained economically dependent had to remain perpetual children: subject to physical correction from their master, and unable to cast a vote in public elections or to hold political office. In 1769 Blackstone still assumed that all propertyless members of a community necessarily exist "under the immediate dominion of others."[61] A propertyless man cannot have a vote, because a vote is the full expression of an independent will and a propertyless man cannot have such a thing: "only such are excluded" from the franchise, Blackstone writes, "as can have no will of their own."[62] While elite boys could attain real power as members of parliament, many people lived out their lives in a child-like dependent status. Domestic service gave the master of the household paternal power over all its members, no matter what their actual numerical age.[63] In 1771, an Anglican minister could still blandly write that most subjects "must ever in a great degree be . . . mere children; and pay of course a due submission to the authority of their political elders."[64] Rigorously dividing up the social world according to numerical ages was still a relatively novel idea in the eighteenth century. At the middle of the eighteenth century, it was still useful to think instead about adulthood in terms of mastery, the status of an independent gentleman, the one who has the power to choose and the power to hurt. Reflecting on the long process through which reasoned consent supplanted status as the basis for common law from the vantage point of the late nineteenth century, Sir Henry Maine sums up the influential medieval precedents: "What a man had largely determined what he was."[65]

Seventeenth- and eighteenth- century legal, religious, and political writing often justifies the power of superiors through patriarchal theories. These theories might seem at first to emphasize age difference by explaining social inequality through a series of analogies between kings and fathers, subjects and children. However, since lordship trumps fatherhood every time, strict patriarchal theory is not in fact very good at distinguishing between the rights and duties of children and those of adults. The subordination of the child as a metaphor for the subordination of the subject outweighed its literal meaning. As Robert Filmer points out with relish, "many a child, by succeeding a king, hath the right of a father over many a grey-headed multitude."[66] Filmer's child-father is not an isolated paradox of political theory. Estates as well as kingdoms passed from father to son, bringing with them rights based on status, not on age. In his discussion of the rise of the novel in the context of the intellectual shift from Robert Filmer's patriarchalism to John Locke's model of reasoned consent, Ala Alryyes reflects on this moment in the history of age. He notes that children are everywhere in patriarchal political theory, while the idea of adulthood is relatively unimportant:

> Aries argues that "the child" in its modern sense – as a distinct social and biological category – did not exist till the eighteenth century. Yet, in a curious twist, it seems it is not the child who was missing before then, but rather the adult. For the dependent subject, a child, is ubiquitous.[67]

Alryyes notes a blank space in eighteenth-century political thought, a blank space for which Locke's rational contract-maker may be a kind of placeholder, and that will only gradually become filled with ideas of adulthood such as psychological maturity.

Following Michel Foucault, cultural historians have argued convincingly that sexuality is more important to a psychological idea of the self than it was to earlier ways of understanding identity.[68] And as psychological theories of sexual development gained more influence, so too did the idea of adulthood. In particular, adulthood became more widely associated with the ability to give a certain kind of consent to sexual relations. For example, Pamela's youth and the ten-year age difference between her and Mr. B. disturb us because they raise the possibility that this novel is the story of a sexual predator and his young victim. The 1980 Penguin edition suggests this anxiety. The blurb on the back cover erases the age gap between Pamela and Mr. B., as it downplays all the other power inequalities between them. It describes the novel instead as an inoffensive piece of young adult fiction, a funny coming-of-age story with a perfectly matched and perfectly equal heroine and hero: it is "an absorbing, often comic, highly charged love story of two countrified, bumptious, ignorant, egotistical and superbly human young people." This description of Pamela and Mr. B. as a pair of equally comic "young people" seems to reflect a submerged concern that a sixteen-year-old may not legitimately consent to sexual relations with a man who is a decade older than she is. It implies a psychological basis for sexual consent, a sense that people become appropriate sexual partners according to a certain well-established developmental timetable.

This concern with psychological readiness for sexual consent did not carry the same weight in the eighteenth century. In 1740, as we shall see, the common law still recognized as valid the marriages of twelve-year-old girls. Far from reflecting any widely accepted idea of adulthood, eighteenth-century marriage law was more of a free-for-all among popular custom, the church, the state, and propertied families. As Lawrence Stone remarks, "marriage law as it operated in practice in England from the fourteenth to the nineteenth century was a mess."[69] Particularly relevant for *Pamela* is the flashpoint created by crossing a fluid sense of age with an unswerving commitment to property. In terms of sexual assault rather than marriage, the age of ten years was an important legal dividing line. The Westminster rape statute of 1576 defined rape as "the unlawfull and carnal knowledge and abuse of any woman above the age of ten years against her will, or of a woman-child under the age of ten years with her will, or against her will."[70] This law was far from a dead letter. At London's Old Bailey in 1747, for example, John Hunter was acquitted of the rape of ten-year-old Grace Pitts because she willingly went into a room with him and sat on his lap in exchange for an orange. "You must prove Force and Violence in this Case in a Person above ten Years of Age," Hunter's Counsel stressed.[71] Sex with twelve-year-old girls was legal up to 1875, when the age of consent was raised to thirteen. It was not until 1885 that the Criminal Law Amendment raised the age of consent from thirteen to sixteen, making "carnal knowledge" of a girl between thirteen and sixteen a misdemeanor, and of a girl under thirteen a felony.

Within the novel, Pamela's ability to consent is not in question. When finally offered the advantageous marriage to Mr. B., no one doubts that she can accept it. In the context of sexual assault as well as marriage, it is not Pamela's youth in and of itself but rather her "innocence" that matters. When Mrs. Jervis describes Pamela as a wonderfully "innocent young creature" (61), Mr. B. counters that innocence, artlessness, and virtue are not necessary attributes of youth. Mrs. Jervis accepts this distinction, offering to die to protect Pamela from rape not because she is a sixteen-year-old, but because she is a virtuous sixteen-year-old: "You shan't hurt this innocent; for I will lose my life in her defence. Are there not . . . enough wicked ones in the world for your base purpose, but you must attempt such a lamb as this!" (96). The meaning of Pamela's age depends on her degree of sexual experience. It also depends on her relation to property.

"So young a girl!" Pamela exclaims when confronted with the prospect of marriage to Mr. Williams at the age of sixteen: "I think I should be very forward were I to shew any inclination to be so soon a wife" (188). Here Pamela invokes a certain idea of when it is proper for people to marry, and when it is "forward" in them even to consider doing so. This kind of forwardness implies not just sexual immodesty, but also, and perhaps even more strongly, social ambition. As a servant who marries a wealthy gentleman, Pamela Andrews catapults from one set of age norms to another set that is quite different. Although popular custom, the church, the state, and propertied families could still disagree on this point, by the middle of the eighteenth century, "marriages between children under twelve for girls and fourteen for boys came usually to be seen as illegal under the common law."[72] This age of consent for marriage is still remarkably low in comparison to today's standards, and like the Westminster rape statute, it still had force in everyday life. Despite this low legal age, however, for most women and men the actual age of marriage was relatively late, somewhere in the mid-twenties. A cultural consensus that marriage ought to be part of one's assertion of economic independence determined this late age: marriage was properly part of setting up one's own household.[73] As a sixteen-year-old servant who listens to her superiors' "good advice to keep myself to myself . . . [and] take care to keep all the fellows at a distance" (47), Pamela is entirely typical of her class and time. Such advice was standard, and was widely heeded. The power of the widespread "no followers" rule depended on the idea that whatever his or her numerical age, a good servant was not to be a sexually mature adult but rather a childlike dependent within the master's household. At sixteen years old, an eighteenth-century servant who says that she or he has no thoughts of marrying is not being coy or hypocritical, but rather realistic about the probable decade or so that must pass before marriage as an aspect of economic independence might be achieved.[74]

When the problem was the opposite one, a question of settling the inheritance of a considerable estate rather than of acquiring property, the marriage age plummeted. In this context, Pamela is no longer "so young a girl!" That is, although her numerical age remains the same, its meaning is reversed. In an aristocratic context, the sixteen-year-old Pamela is an entirely proper candidate for marriage. As Judith Lewis explains, the proportion of maternal death from childbirth or related problems was as high for aristocratic women as it was for the rest of the population because aristocratic women were far more likely than poorer ones to become mothers in their teens. The aristocratic propensity to marry adolescent girls as young as fourteen outweighed the many medical benefits of wealth through much of the eighteenth century: "the practice of arranging the marriages of young adolescent girls increased the possibility that they would die in childbirth . . . Early arranged marriages and wet-nursing most certainly offset expected social and economic advantages."[75]

Pamela and its reception history reflect a conflict between traditional ideas of age based on social status and the challenge to these ideas represented by developmental theories of age most influentially formulated by

Locke, and popularized in part through the emergence of a market for children's literature largely framed along Lockean lines. But Locke is interested in adult reason, not adult sexuality. Locke's ideas eventually affect theories of sexual consent and marriage law through stressing the importance of age as a factor in the ability to rationally consent to all contracts, not by anticipating psychological theories of sexual maturity. The eighteenth-century rise in the age of consent to marriage to twelve or fourteen from even lower common-law precedents reflects a shift from agency based on status to agency based on reason, a shift also seen in contract and criminal law more generally. Brewer claims that the capacity to form a legally binding contract becomes the exclusive property of adults as reason becomes the dividing line between childhood and adulthood – but an idea of reason that assumes twelve-year-olds can form legally binding marriage contracts must still give us pause.[76] The eighteenth-century legal age of consent to marriage was often associated with puberty as well as with reason, but it is still distant from a psychological idea of sexual maturity, or of sexual awareness as the central attribute of adulthood. Eighteenth-century literary texts often seem similarly off-center if we read for this idea of maturity.

Happy endings: "coming into power"

John Newbery's stories tend to imply that as one's reason grows, one acquires more property rather than more psychological complexity. This focus on property and status may help to explain what seems odd about both Newbery's and Richardson's stories to a more thoroughly age-leveled audience today. The conclusions of both *Goody Two-Shoes* and *Pamela* reflect the concerns of "youth" understood as dependence rather than as psychological immaturity. Both stories feature the kind of "love and adventure" central to the popular traditions savored by Bessie Lee and her young listeners in *Jane Eyre*. As in the chapbooks they draw on, in these stories economic independence takes the place that emotional independence holds in the twentieth century's psychological developmental schemes. Although both books feature young heroines, neither one is a psychological coming-of-age story. The inner quality that matters most is virtue, and Pamela Andrews and Margery Meanwell are equally virtuous at the beginning, middle, and end of their tales. Both stories describe how a girl becomes, not a woman, but a lady – how she achieves a measure of power through acquiring property. In this shared plot, both stories are true to their chapbook origins. As Andrew O'Malley has shown, the goal of a chapbook hero or heroine is not to become a more empathetic, more sexually fulfilled, or more self-aware person, but rather to triumph over one's enemies by galloping through them in a coach-and-six, throwing coins to the poor and leaving one's baffled oppressors gnashing their teeth in the dust.[77] In this sense, Pamela and Margery marrying are like Robinson Crusoe coming into his riches. This chapbook-like triumph is what will worry Barbauld about *Pamela*'s ending, which threatens her belief in the heroine's "delicacy" by raising the suspicion "that she married him for '*The gilt coach, and dappled Flanders' mares*.'"[78]

Like a chapbook heroine, the heroine of *Little Goody Two-Shoes* does not grow and develop, but rather survives and triumphs. *Goody Two-Shoes* delivers exactly what its title page promises: the story of how, through her Lockean education, Margery Meanwell gets an estate:

> The Means by which she acquired her Learning and Wisedom, and in Consequence thereof, her Estate; set forth at large for the benefit of those,
>
> *Who from a State of Rags and Care,*
> *And having Shoes but half a Pair,*
> *Their Fortune and their Fame would fix,*
> *And Gallop in a Coach and Six.*

Goody Two-Shoes' clearest announcement of a developmental progression blurs biological growth and social mobility. The movement is not "child to adolescent to adult," or "girl to woman," but rather "Girl to Woman to Lady": "the Neighbours came in Crouds to see the Wedding; for they were all glad, that one who had been such a good little Girl, and was become such a virtuous and good Woman, was just going to be made a Lady" (131).

Margery tells her students at A,B,C College a story that implies that the true reward of female virtue is not a fulfilling marriage, but rather the sole possession of an estate. Captured by pirates, young Miss Lovewell proves she values her chastity above her life. Converted by her virtuous example, the reformed pirates defeat their unreformed brother-pirates and bring Miss Lovewell safely to the Manilla Islands, where her story, like Pamela's, takes on a life of its own, making friends of all who hear it: "when her Story was known, she was treated with great Respect, and courted by a young Gentleman, who was taken ill of a Fever, and died before their Marriage was agreed on, but left her his whole Fortune"(94). Becoming an heir rather than a wife, Miss Lovewell gets the estate without even the temporary encumbrance of a husband.[79] She uses it to rescue her parents, who have been living on cabbage and water in the countryside ever since the failure of her father's business.

We might expect Margery's wedding to Sir Charles Jones to be the climax of her development, the moment when she becomes "a Lady." However, Margery appears to assume her new title only after her husband's death, as if she too were merely his heir rather than his wife. We are briefly told that Margery and Sir Charles enjoy six years of "inexpressible happiness," but the seventh year brings Margery something more concrete: "being seized of a violent fever [Sir Charles] died, and left her full of Grief, tho' possessed of a large Fortune" (134). Margery is called "Lady Jones" only after Sir Charles has died. That is, first we are told that Sir Charles has died, and then Margery is re-named: "We forgot to remark, that after her Marriage, Lady Jones (for so we now must call her) ordered the Chapel to be fitted up, and allowed the Chaplain a considerable Sum out of her own private Purse, to visit the Sick" (134).

Similarly, the true emotional climax of Margery's story is not her courtship, or her wedding itself, but rather her settlement, the legal arrangements that ensure she will own property and have power after her husband's death. Property law plays a spectacular role at her wedding:

> Just as the clergyman had opened his book, a gentleman richly dressed ran into the Church, and cry'd Stop! Stop! . . . The people were greatly surprised to see Sir Charles stand Motionless, and his Bride cry and faint away in the Stranger's Arms. This seeming Grief, however, was only a Prelude to a Flood of Joy, which immediately succeeded, for you must know, Gentle reader, that this gentleman . . . was little Tom Two-Shoes, Mrs. Margery's brother, who was just come from beyond Sea, where he had made a large Fortune, and hearing, as soon as he landed, of his sister's intended wedding, had ridden Post, to see that a proper Settlement was made on her; which he thought she was now intitled to, as he himself was now able and willing to give her an ample Fortune. (132)

Margery's wedding is bathed in joyful tears: "They soon returned to the Communion table and were married in Tears, but they were Tears of Joy" (133). Everyone in this church appears to be sobbing not merely over the appearance of the bride's long-lost brother, or over the marital union itself, but also over the eleventh-hour establishment of the bride's contractual property rights. Margery's legal rights to property both within and after her marriage establish for her a new kind of agency, one that is celebrated in the next chapter, "The True Use of Riches." Here the narrator explains exactly what property means. Because of Margery's settlement, at her husband's death she gets "Power": "At her first coming into Power, she took care to gratify her old Friends" (138). After briskly disposing of both Sir Charles and married bliss, the chapter settles down to describing in loving detail exactly what Lady Margery does with her power. She exercises it in two overlapping spheres: charity to the poor and delicious revenge on the gentlemen of property who destroyed her family of origin.[80]

Richardson does not go quite as far as does *Goody Two-Shoes* in stressing status and property. His Cinderella has a compelling inner life, and she marries Prince Charming rather than simply inheriting his estate. We must confess, however, that Mr. B.'s estate remains the most charming thing about him: as Sir Henry Maine would say, he is what he owns. Union with Mr. B. offers Pamela fulfillment or maturity not through sexual or emotional growth, but rather through property. Critics have often noted that Mr. B. is an unimpressive figure: not very bright, transparently vain, much given to waffling, bullying, and bluster. "It is not easy to conceive of Pamela's being rewarded by marrying him," Barbauld notes, after listing some of the obvious unattractive aspects of Mr. B.'s character, "unless her regard for external circumstances was greater than the author would wish to have supposed."[81] "We think little of Mr B —, his character, or his motives, and are only delighted with the preferment of our favourite, because it seems to give so much satisfaction to herself," echoes Walter Scott.[82] For Richardson, however, Mr. B.'s unappealing qualities do not matter because he is Pamela's master. That is what she insists on calling him, both before and after marriage. Scott himself points to this explanation for Richardson's otherwise puzzling or unsatisfying characterization of his hero and heroine: "But in Richardson's time, the bonds of subordination in society were drawn very strictly, and he himself seems to have had high and exaggerated ideas of the importance of wealth and rank." Despite this historical awareness, Pamela's forgiveness of Mrs. Jewkes on the grounds that the housekeeper merely obeyed "the command, forsooth, of a generous master" still leaves Scott fuming that "there is want of taste in this humiliation." He cannot shake his sense that "the character of Pamela is somewhat sunk by the eager gratitude with which she accepts the hand of a tyrannical and cruel master . . . There is a parade of generosity on his side, and of creeping submission on hers, which the case by no means calls for."[83]

What Mr. B. owns is who he is, awkward as that point may be if we approach the novel looking for the glamour of an appealing, emotionally complex hero/villain, not the glamour of property. The 1980 Penguin edition back-cover blurb suggests the embarrassment involved in fitting this couple into more modern, psychologized roles by opting to call Mr. B. merely Pamela's "dead mistress's son," not "my wicked, wicked master," or "my dear master," as Pamela relentlessly names him.[84] Indeed, Mr. B.

is one of the last heroes who can rely so completely on status doing the work of personality for him. Lord Byron will have to be brilliant as well as titled to make all of England and the continent desire him. To win Elizabeth Bennet, Mr. Darcy must display not only Pemberley, but also an array of attractive personal qualities and a process of personal growth documented by letter in convincing detail. And to marry Jane Eyre, Mr. Rochester must manage to get himself humbled and blasted by fire, transformed both inwardly and outwardly: Thornfield alone is not enough. But to make Pamela (and Richardson) love him, Mr. B., doltish as he is, needs only to be the legitimate owner of estates in Bedfordshire and Lincolnshire. He is the hero of Richardson's novel for the same reason that he is – at twenty-four, the same age at which William Pitt the Younger became Prime Minister of England – a Justice of the Peace: by the right of his status, not his personal qualities.

And yet: both *Pamela* and *Goody Two-Shoes* also reflect the specifically Lockean developmental ideals promoted by the new official children's literature. Although they do not focus on psychological growth, they do stand for the kind of triumph of reason that struck Helen Shipton. Pamela Andrews and Margery Meanwell are printer's heroines, advertisements for the power of literacy.[85] As readers have noted, in its linking of reading to reason and agency, *Pamela* is a thoroughly Lockean production.[86] The conservative Henry Fielding saw this threat in the novel. In lampooning its uppity heroine's "vartue," *Shamela* attacks not only Pamela's morality, but also her claim to be educated. Similarly, *Joseph Andrews* contains inset cautionary tales about the doomed nature of the Lockean enterprise: in two separate instances, Fielding shows us how literacy brings to the children of laborers inappropriate social ambition, then anger, wickedness, and early death. It is no accident that his Fanny is illiterate.[87]

In contrast, both Margery and Pamela are conspicuously rational and conspicuously literate. Richardson takes the time to assure us proudly that Pamela is "not afraid of spirits" (57). Like Margery, who does not turn a hair at spending a night in a building the whole village believes to be haunted, Pamela is shown to be uncontaminated by the popular superstitions of uneducated, child-like servants. As we have seen, *Goody Two-Shoes* describes Margery's education and her own career as a teacher. Pamela is also a testament to the importance of education, although her own education occurs before she writes her first letter. Hence Pamela does grow and develop – but not through the experience of being flirted with and assaulted by Mr. B. at the age of fifteen. Rather, she develops through the experience of being educated by Mr. B.'s mother from age eleven to age fifteen.[88] Pamela's mistress gave her an education that leaves her "qualified above my degree" (43), and critics have often noted that literacy is Pamela's weapon in her "downright rebellion" (163) against her status. Mr. B. calls her letters home her "treasonable papers" (265): even more than her beauty, her letters win her a measure of power over him.

Pamela reasons clearly. Challenging Mr. B.'s power over her, she thinks in terms of property rights and their origin, sounding like the Locke of the *Second Treatise on Government* (1690): "Though the earth and all inferior creatures be common to all men, yet every man has a 'property' in his own 'person.' This nobody has any right to but himself," Locke writes, imagining the beginnings of private property.[89] Pamela revisits this issue: "And pray, said I (as we walked on) how came I to be his property?" (163). She is also clearly interested in her own process of reasoning, reflecting on, re-stating, and questioning her chains of deductions:

> I told her all that had passed; for, ruminating on every thing, I thought . . . to keep a secret of such a nature, would be, as I apprehended, to deprive myself of the good advice which I never wanted more; and might encourage him to think I did not resent it as I ought, and would keep *worse secrets*, and so make him do *worse by me*. Was I right, my dear mother? (57)

In this letter to her own mother, Pamela strikes the perfect balance between respect for authority and independent thought that Locke holds can be achieved only through close, daily personal interaction. Like the ideal tutor in Locke, and later in Rousseau and Edgeworth, Pamela's mistress gave her years of such teaching. This teaching's lasting effect was not the gentlemanly familiarity with the Latin or Greek classics that progressive educators scorned, but rather the achievement that they most praised: the careful exercise of personal judgment. Pamela passes on this prized quality in Richardson's sequel, *Pamela in Her Exaulted Condition*, where her career as a Lockean educator takes pride of place. Like any other well-informed, well-intentioned, and wealthy English mother, in this later volume Pamela systematically works through *Some Thoughts Concerning Education*. Her generally positive although not uncritical reflections on "this noble writer" (409) fill nearly fifty pages. For Ian Watt, in this sequel, Pamela manages to become not merely a lady, but a gentleman. Suggesting the strong eighteenth-century links between adulthood and status, Watt describes Pamela's development into a "grown-up" as a gender-bending process. He sums up eighteenth-century ideas of literary value as "the norms of the mature, rational and educated male world."[90] These are the norms that are opposed to the popular reading of women, children, and servants. When

Pamela leaves this mixed-age group of subordinates behind, there is only one thing that she can develop into:

> If we venture so far as the second part of *Pamela* . . . the novel's Augustan quality becomes much more obtrusive: it is an important part of Richardson's general ideological commitment that his servant girl should eventually develop into someone who speaks with the voice of a man, and a very grown-up one at that – an Addison or even a Locke.[91]

While Richardson is mindful of the importance of reason to the achievement of such a gentlemanly voice, he does not neglect property, as we shall see.

Marrying down: "entirely the act of my own will"

The anxiety Richardson diffuses is not the danger of Mr. B. being a sexual predator, but rather the danger of Mr. B. being a feckless heir. While his story needs to establish Pamela's ability to consent, its still more urgent challenge is to protect Mr. B.'s family estate. This concern was voiced in the public debate over the Act for the Better Preventing of Clandestine Marriages (1753), also known as Hardwicke's Marriage Act. Hardwicke's Act gave parents new power to void the marriage of their daughters or sons if they were under twenty-one when they promised to marry, and invalidated all clandestine marriages.[92] As we have seen, earlier laws often granted the ability to make contracts for marriage and for other purposes at a much earlier age. The Act's intention was to protect a family's property by making it more difficult to profit by either the seduction or the abduction of unwary young heirs and heiresses. To accomplish this goal, the Act also divided people according to age much more clearly than did many earlier laws concerning contracts. The Act implies two different categories of legal persons. On the one hand are infants or young people who lack the ability to reason required for consent to a contract, in Locke's sense of these terms. On the other are adults, who are capable of reason, and so are free to contract.

The debate over the Clandestine Marriage Act suggests how questions of property, as well as ideas of reason, continued to inform schemes of age differentiation. While the advocates of the Act were motivated by a desire to prevent the seduction of heirs and heiresses, opponents to the Act, who argued for setting the legal age of marriage close to puberty rather than twenty-one, wanted to keep the marriage market as liquid as possible. For example, in his pamphlet criticizing the Act, *An Inquiry into the Force and*

Operation of the Annulling Clauses... (1754), Henry Stebbing argues that even a father who is arranging a marriage for his daughter thinks of only two things: puberty and property. Such a father implicitly admits that the ability to consent to a contract "follows close at the heels" of the ability to procreate: "This capacity [to contract] follows close at the heels of the capacity of Procreation, and the natural appetite to marriage. Every man confesses this who marries his daughter at fifteen, sixteen, or seventeen years of age (which there is scarcely a Parent in the Kingdom who would not do so for the sake of an advantageous match)."[93] Stebbing claims that parents will go as low as fifteen years of age to secure an advantageous match, but not to twelve, ten, or eight, because they are waiting for the "capacity of Procreation" to appear. This new standard relies on a category of physical development rather than the older precedent of the common law, which, as we have seen, could go as low as eight years old for consent to marriage. But here the "natural appetite to marriage" is more closely linked to the physical capacity to produce an heir rather than a psychological idea of sexual maturity. The need to protect and to transmit property still drives these newer versions of legal personhood.[94] In the case of the *Earl of Buckinghamshire* v. *Drury* (1762), Lord Hardwicke himself stressed property and class in commenting on the power that he helped to give propertied families over their children's marriages: "There are many considerations, which may induce them, besides strict equality in settlements – inclination of the parties – rank and quality of the person – convenience and propriety in families – bringing together and uniting different parts of the same estate; all of these are proper reasons."[95]

Even as a very young storyteller, Richardson seems to have taken aim at this alliance of marriage law and propertied interests. With breath-taking ingenuousness, he describes one of the earliest tales he made up to amuse his school-fellows: "a history... on the model of Tommy Pots... it was of a servant-man preferred by a fine young lady (for his goodness) to a lord, who was a libertine. All my stories carried with them, I am bold to say, a useful moral."[96] The traditional ballad of Tom Pots is careful to specify that the fine young lady this servant marries is not merely the Earl of Arundel's daughter, but his sole heir. (One can barely imagine the reception Tom Pots would get in Lord Hardwicke's court.) Similarly, although the Clandestine Marriage Act itself is several years away, Richardson seems to side with the advocates of a more liquid marriage market in setting Pamela's age at sixteen. His heroine has the "capacity of Procreation": the early pages of the novel carefully document others' comments on how she has just blossomed into womanhood: "Every body talks of how you are come on . . . you are very pretty" (45). Like nearly every other "Parent in the Kingdom," Richardson is delighted to marry his girl off at sixteen for the sake of an advantageous match. However, Pamela's advantageous match is by necessity Mr. B.'s spectacularly disadvantageous one. In setting Mr. B.'s age at twenty-five, Richardson also respects the concern to protect property that permeated the debate over clandestine marriage. Richardson needs to establish Mr. B.'s ability to consent to a marriage contract more urgently than he needs to establish Pamela's ability to consent. Not the teenaged maid, but the master – or, rather, the master's estate – is what is in danger.

The 1730–31 court cases of *Rudd* v. *Rudd* suggest what happens when the heir rather than the servant-girl is sixteen. In 1720, Sir John Rudd, a sixteen-year-old baronet, fell in love with and married a servant, Lettice Vaughan, in a clandestine ceremony. His appalled family had no direct legal recourse. Instead of questioning the validity of the marriage, they immediately sent Sir John to Holland and persuaded Lady Rudd that he had died, tricking her into a second marriage. In two separate court cases, the first in the Consistory Court in 1730 and the second in the Court of Arches in 1732, Sir John's family used this marriage to argue that Lady Rudd had committed adultery and bigamy. The favorable judgment they ultimately won enabled them to gain for Sir John a full divorce through a private Act of Parliament in 1734. In this case the family's private means (their money, "low cunning, duplicity, and blatant manipulation of the law"), proved stronger than the couple's legal ability to form a marriage contract.[97]

Although such marriages between eligible young bachelors and servants were rare, the threat to property and status represented by a marriage such as Sir John Rudd's was too real to ignore.[98] In fact, several of the failed bills leading up to Hardwicke's Act aimed specifically to prevent master–servant misalliances.[99] A pamphlet defending the Clandestine Marriage Act warned of exactly this danger, insisting that the legal age of consent needed to be set high enough to protect "a boy of sixteen, heir apparent to an Estate, whose Fancy is captivated with his Mother's Maid."[100] Mr. B.'s marriage to his mother's maid is clearly a clandestine one, although both his parents are dead: he carefully conceals it from his only living relative, his mannish sister Lady Danvers, whose rage on discovering what he has done is intense enough to oblige Pamela to jump out of a window and run for it. "This affair is entirely the act of my own will" (367), Mr. B. assures Pamela on the night before their wedding, between kisses. Insisting that he is not a lovesick boy but rather a reasonable man with the right to dispose of himself and his family's estate, Mr. B. sounds as if he has his hand on the Bible in court. Noting that her own lack of property means no marriage settlements are being read, signed, or sealed, Pamela too reflects on the relations among poverty and power, property and will: "'Good, dear sir, what can I say! How poor is it to have nothing but words to return for such generous deeds! And to say, I *wish* – What is a wish, but the acknowledged want of power, and a demonstration of one's poverty in everything but *will*" (368). Unlike William Blackstone, here Pamela claims that a will can exist even without property. But this kind of will seems to be a paradoxical thing, little more than "the acknowledged want of power." Later, she explains that a will that cannot be exercised is a mysterious thing, one that can be known only dimly: "'People, Mrs Jewkes,' replied I, 'don't know how they shall act, when their wills are in the power of their superiors'" (458). Here a will that is "in the power of [one's] superiors" seems to be locked up and hidden away as completely as any other precious object in the master's house. Benjamin Rush, the American physician, strikes a similar note in praising "youth who have never known or felt their own wills till they were one and twenty years of age."[101]

Mr. B. once did come very close to feeling and exercising his will improperly, to being a feckless heir – not with Pamela Andrews, but with Sally Godfrey. As he tells the story, he would have been the victim of the gap between the age of majority, which is the age of reason and so the proper age of legal culpability, and the lower age of binding marriage contracts before Hardwicke's Act. When he was at Oxford, Mr. B. was nearly entrapped in an unsuitable marriage. Lured into intimacy with Sally Godfrey, he is then threatened at sword-point "with instant death, if he did not engage to marry the young lady on the spot" (499). Two different aspects of "youth" are highlighted in this account: Sally's sexual weakness, and his own minority: "I was not then of age; and the young lady, who was not half so artful as her mother, yielded to my importunities" (452). Conducting this particular affair before the Clandestine Marriage Act, Mr. B. is not yet "of age," but he is already legally capable of forming a marriage contract. His marriage to Pamela is constructed to answer every one of these worries.

Yet despite Richardson's caution, some of his readers persisted in seeing Mr. B. as a foolish boy, and in sharing Lady Danvers's outrage. Most famously, Henry Fielding in his parody *Shamela* insists that *Pamela* is a danger to the sons of landed families everywhere. He wants to keep Richardson's book away from its intended readership, "youth" defined as the economically dependent as well as the numerically young. Fielding refuses to put it "either into the hands of my Daughter, or my Servant-Maid." But he does not see either kind of girl as the book's most important potential victim: once servant-maids start behaving like Pamela, "if the Master is not a Fool, they will be debauched by him; and if he is a Fool, they will marry him. Neither of which, I apprehend, my good Friend, we desire should be the Case of our Sons." The important question here is what "we desire should be the Case of our Sons."[102]

A new age?

The women, children, and servants of the mixed-age audience of eighteenth-century novels did not find in these books psychological studies of the developmental transition from childhood to maturity. They found instead stories about the struggle to achieve some measure of agency within a dependent position, as Pamela and Margery do through education.[103] The next chapters will focus on how the nineteenth century redefined the novel's ideal readership, first as the genteel, mixed-age, middle-class family circle, and then as the psychologically complex adult, preferably a professional critic. Perhaps in part because of its "old-fashioned standard" of age, Richardson's first novel barely made it into the canon of standard-edition novels first published in the nineteenth century as part of this elevation of the form.

Unlike *Clarissa* and *Sir Charles Grandison*, *Pamela* does not appear in Letitia Barbauld's pioneering effort in canon-formation, the fifty-volume series *The British Novelists* (1810). *Pamela* won only qualified praise even in Barbauld's Introduction to Richardson's correspondence: "The fame of this once favourite work is now somewhat tarnished by time, as well as eclipsed by the author's subsequent publications . . . we must acknowledge that the faults are great, but the beauties are genuine."[104] Barbauld's standard of literary value is didactic, but reflects her path-breaking commitment to age-leveling reading according to a developmental scheme. As we noted above (see p. 76), she has particularly strong reservations about using sexually warm material to teach virtue to young people. The fact that *Pamela* has more titillating scenes than *Clarissa* while being just as didactic as *Sir Charles Grandison* made it increasingly awkward to place as sexual awareness was more rigorously assigned to adults and didacticism to children.

Sir Walter Scott did include *Pamela* in his influential *Ballantyne's Novelist's Library* (1821–24) as part of his policy of representing the complete works of individual authors, although he also echoed "the judicious criticism of Mrs Barbauld." Like Barbauld, Scott claims a didactic purpose for the novel, but his ideal reader remains more prominently shaped by status than does hers. While Richardson declares that he writes for "the youth of both sexes," Scott imagines *Pamela*'s readers as young women in low circumstances. Scott resembles Fielding rather than Barbauld in his concern about the novel's impact on it readers: he still fears triggering social ambition in servants more than he fears triggering sexual awareness in children. In fact, while Fielding wants to keep *Pamela* out of the hands of both his daughter and his servant-maid, Scott assumes that the novel will matter, for good or for ill, to the servant-maid alone. He remarks that *Pamela*'s "good effects must of course have operation among young women in circumstances somewhat similar to those of the heroine." Rather than imagining young people discovering the secret of sex in *Pamela*, Scott imagines the book leading servants to miscalculate their odds of social mobility. He goes so far as to assert that such a reader is "not hypothetical":

> in that rank [similar to Pamela's], it may be questioned, whether the example is not as well calculated to encourage a spirit of rash enterprise, as of virtuous resistance . . . it may occur to a humble maiden, (and the case we believe is not hypothetical,) that to merit Pamela's reward, she must go through Pamela's trials; and that there can be no great harm in affording some encouragement to the assailant. We need not add how dangerous this experiment must be for both parties.[105]

Scott addressed the sexual impropriety of Richardson's warm scenes, the objection that in the course of depicting virtue triumphant, Richardson risks "scenes which excite evil passions . . . familiariz[ing] the mind of the readers with impure ideas." He does not address this danger in age-leveled terms, however, and concludes that it is in any case overstated, insisting that "the whole recollection is soothing, tranquillizing, and doubtless edifying." In fact, overall, Scott questions the didactic merit that *Pamela*'s admirers claim for the work, "the merit of doing more good than twenty sermons," not because the novel is too warm, but rather because it is too cold. The reasoning and reflection that Helen Shipton will see as admirable although precocious are for Scott simply "cold-blooded": "there is a strain of cold-blooded prudence which runs through all the latter part of the novel, to which we are obliged almost to deny the name of virtue."[106]

Leslie Stephen offers a final example of the shifting weight of age compared to factors such as status and gender in assigning literary value to novels. Stephen admires much of *Clarissa*, respects much of *Sir Charles Grandson*, but loathes that "gigantic tract called 'Pamela' – beyond all comparison the worst of [Richardson's] works."[107] Although Stephen included most (although not all) of *Pamela* in his edition of Richardson's collected Works, his introduction clearly warns readers off the book as a trashy tract, at once preachy and salacious. Sneering at the novel's "twopenny-tract morality," Stephen claims that it "succeeds neither in being moral nor amusing."[108] He blames *Pamela*'s failings on Richardson's own lowness. Stephen is an open snob about Richardson's social status, describing him as "always the obsequious and respectful shopkeeper" who never reached anything higher than "fourth-rate London society."[109] Stephen is even more withering about the women who constituted such a large part of the novel's first, low audience. Echoing with approval "Fielding's masculine contempt for the whinings of 'Pamela,'" Stephen attacks the "court of silly women whose incessant flatteries must generate in [Richardson] an unnatural propensity to twaddle."[110] "Twaddle" is didactic writing, which Stephen associates not only with women, but also with children. Richardson's "moral prosings . . . [or] capacity for spinning out indefinite twaddle of a superior kind" remind Stephen of his own childhood reading:[111]

> In our youth we used to read a poem about a cruel little boy who went out to fish and was punished by somehow becoming suspended by his chin from a hook in the larder. It never produced much effect upon us, because we felt that the accident was, to say the least, rather exceptional; at most, we fished on, and were careful about the larder. The same principle applies to the poetic justice distributed by most novelists.[112]

The only good thing that Stephen has to say about *Pamela* relates to its status as a warm book. Commenting on the difficulties that Jonathan Edwards had with his congregation over "equivocal books," Stephen acknowledges that *Pamela* may be "amusing" after all – not to the critical intellect of the adult but to the sexual curiosity of youth. He imagines young people reading it as part of a course of "loose conversation and equivocal books":

> Edwards got into trouble by endeavouring to force his own notions of discipline amongst certain young people, belonging to "considerable families" who were said to indulge in loose conversation and equivocal books. They possibly preferred Pamela, which had just then revealed a new source of amusement to the world, to awakening sermons.[113]

In fact, these "young people" were young men from twenty-one to twenty-five, and they were reading, not *Pamela*, but rather the venerable and proto-pornographic *Aristotle's Masterpiece* and then harassing the local girls with their new gynecological knowledge. Jonathan Edwards, on the other hand, was a Richardson fan. He enjoyed *Sir Charles Grandison*, referred to *Clarissa* as "tending much to promote virtue and piety," and quotes with evident approval a 1752 review of *Pamela* that claims it is a book that deserves "to be spoken of in terms of high Respect which has afforded entertainment to Readers of all Ranks."[114] His mention of "Readers of all Ranks" rather than a specific age-leveled group of readers, or even "Readers of all Ages" is significant: as Richardson himself so often does, here Edwards thinks of people in terms of their social status rather than their age, and hopes to amuse and to instruct as many of them as possible in non-age-leveled ways. Edwards's enthusiasm for Richardson suggests the complexity and breadth of eighteenth-century ideas about novels and novel-readers. Stephen's sense of the role that *Pamela* was likely to play in this small episode in American colonial history is skewed by the nineteenth-century process of canonizing the novel in part through retrospectively age-leveling individual works. We have seen how this process shaped Robinson Crusoe's shifting critical status, and will examine it in greater depth in the following chapters.

By the late twentieth century, Pamela's lowness had become a critical asset rather than a liability. Literary critics who sought a less elite object of study valued the heroine's status as a female servant, and her connection to "the youth of both sexes" no longer drew attention. For example, *Pamela* is central to Nancy Armstrong's *Desire and Domestic Fiction* (1987) and to the powerful feminist understanding of the novel's history that Armstrong helped to shape. In this reading, Richardson's "servant girl" stands for a modern idea of the woman that emphasizes the cultural power of the middle-class woman's domestic authority. Focusing on the triumph of such "female forms of power" in the nineteenth and twentieth centuries, Armstrong does not pause over the still-blurry boundaries among eighteenth-century women, children, and servants. The idea of the woman that emerges from this work stands in sharp contrast to the child.[115] The domestic woman's authority over private life gives her a compelling new status: as the influential supervisor of this vital realm she escapes the dependence and subordination of childhood. However, the cover art of *Desire and Domestic Fiction* blurs these boundaries once more, recalling the question of age. The book jacket does not feature an image of such a powerful domestic woman but rather James Peale's haunting 1804 portrait of a little girl with a doll.[116] Armstrong's decision to position this image so prominently on a key work about the social power of gender suggests the lingering power of the older associations, the need to explore more fully the relation between such issues and a wider social history of age.

CHAPTER 4

Rational moralists, highland barbarians, and the taste for adventures

With Letitia Barbauld, Maria Edgeworth, and Walter Scott, we move away from Samuel Richardson's status-haunted world. Popular and critically influential, these three writers all imagine their central characters and their audiences according to a full-fledged developmental model. Barbauld and Edgeworth may seem odd intellectual companions for Scott in thinking about age. He popularized the historical novel, a genre now marketed to both young and adult readers, while they produced successful age-leveled series that showed publishers how to finely calibrate vocabulary, syntax, and content according to numerical age. Nonetheless, all three of these writers share the same developmental model – and it is a model that remains strange to ideas of growing up today. While the continental bildungsroman more familiarly explores the growth of sexual experience and introspection in its hero, the central characters of Barbauld, Edgeworth, and Scott achieve maturity as this stage is understood by the eighteenth-century conjectural historians. Rather than becoming psychologically complex adults, they become polite and commercial people. Rather than exploring the passions of youth as a mirror of revolutionary change, these authors teach a version of maturity defined as the prudential morality suitable for a commercial and secular world. Proudly didactic, Barbauld, Edgeworth, and Scott have a double goal: to explain the historic rise of civility, rationality, and commerce, and to teach their readers to model their own development on this history.

Changing ideas of age affect the critical standing of the genre that Scott founded, historical fiction. His developmental model links violence and childishness: despite the nostalgic pleasure of his descriptions of claymores, battle-axes, and lances, Scott argues that violence is a phase that must be outgrown by both martial nations and young men. As Barbauld and Edgeworth urge middle-class boys to resist the real and tempting possibility of enlisting at twelve years old to fight Napoleon in favor of the long education required for a profitable profession, so Scott's heroes put down their swords and take up a life of judicious consumption. Representing individual development in these terms won his novels critical respect. When other theories supplanted conjectural history's account of individual development, the *Waverley* novels and their scenes of violence were re-interpreted to fit a new genre, the Victorian boys' adventure story. By the early twentieth century, historical fiction was widely seen as "juvenile," as a sub-literary genre suited to young readers – and often, with rich confusion, to psychologically immature readers of all ages. At this time, the wider didactic purpose that unified Barbauld, Edgeworth, and Scott's writing for all ages itself became identified with childhood reading.

"These two infancies"

At the center of the continental bildungsroman is not the young person, the protagonist and ideal imagined reader of eighteenth- and nineteenth-century English didactic novels, but rather his modern relative: the adolescent. That is, the bildungsroman's framework is psychological rather than moral. Both the bildungsroman and the didactic novel focus on growth, but differ in that the continental bildungsroman has a greater investment in the emotional and sexual energies of youth that it sets out to shape. While any developmental narrative creates the potential for nostalgia, the bildungsroman's focus on stormy passions takes exceptionally good advantage of this opportunity. English novels about young people tend to focus on their movement from a family of origin to a new family through marriage. The continental bildungsroman, in contrast, positions the adolescent in a much wider canvas. As Franco Moretti has shown, the genre helped to popularize adolescence by characterizing that stage of life as a glamorous fusion of sexual awakening and longing for revolutionary political change. The bildungsroman focuses on youth, although it gestures towards an idea of adulthood that it identifies with the renunciation of sexual and political turmoil. Once its hero decides to embrace the stability of professional success and domestic happiness, the story is over.

It is important for twentieth-century critics to distinguish these stories of youth from children's literature. For example, Moretti criticizes English authors of this genre by claiming that they have inadvertently written children's books. He points to what appears to him to be the incontestable superiority of the continental bildungsroman over its English analogue by demanding "Can you picture a child reading *Wilhelm Meister*, *The Red and the Black*, *Lost Illusions*? Impossible. But *Waverley* and *Jane Eyre*, *David Copperfield* and *Great Expectations*: here we have the 'great tradition' of children's literature."[1] In 1960, Leslie Fiedler strikes the same note on a broader scale, suspecting that the entire Anglo-American novel is in fact children's literature: the "great works of American fiction," he notes gloomily, "are notoriously at home in the children's section of the library."[2] What is striking in these comments is the difficulty of trying to age-level English and American fiction retroactively. Viewed historically, *Waverley* is not a children's book – but Moretti is right that neither was it written for the adult. The tradition that Scott represents is not children's literature as we know it today, not fiction targeting a narrow subset of child or adolescent readers defined by a psychological scheme of developmental stages tightly keyed to numerical age. Neither is it appropriate for the new adult audience that took shape from the later nineteenth century onwards. For that literary world, "adult" became an indispensable critical standard, demarcating a child-free cultural space that included everything from high art to pornography – or, as in the case of James Joyce's *Ulysses*, texts that could look like both. The psychological complexity of a novel's characters became a key criterion of literary value, a value that was associated with the maturity of its author and its readers. In the next two chapters we will explore the rise of this standard from critics of Dickens through the early work of Henry James. In this chapter we will focus, rather, on developmental writing that does not draw so heavily on this psychological sense of adulthood either to structure its narratives or to evaluate their literary success.

To understand how age works in Barbauld, Edgeworth, and Scott, we must think about how different ideas about the ways individuals change over time relate to different theories of historical change. Mikhail Bakhtin connects the bildungsroman and historical novel through a general sense of their shared interest in development. He sees a "great awakening of a *sense of time*" as distinguishing the "everyday working consciousness of the vanguard" of writers who publicized the Enlightenment.[3] Central to this sense of time is its interest in causality playing across the past, the present, and the future both of individuals and of historical epochs. Time becomes newly visible in landscapes and cityscapes, on the one hand, and in "man in the process of becoming," on the other.[4] Bakhtin's appreciation of this sense of time in Walter Scott is well known: "His eye could see time in space," he writes of Scott.[5] I want to suggest that Barbauld and Edgeworth share Scott's habit of seeing time in the faces of both nations and individuals.

More particularly, Moretti reads the bildungsroman by linking developmental psychology to revolution. He argues that the continental bildungsroman expresses the dramatic social transformations of the Europe of its time through the transformative sexual passion and emotional turbulence of adolescence. In contrast, in his account, the English bildungsroman suffers from arrested development. The novels of Scott, Brontë, and Dickens are today the "great tradition of children's literature" rather than adult literature because Scott, Brontë, and Dickens reflect the childishness of the English middle class. In comparison to the continental bildungsroman, the English bildungsroman is "far more elementary and limited." According to Moretti, the English bildungsroman excludes the moral ambiguity that is central to an adult understanding of the world, especially the moral ambiguities raised by non-marital sexual encounters, because it is the product of a "middle-class endowed with little daring and dim self-consciousness."[6] Other critics tell a different story about literature and history in this period. Social historians such as Leonore Davidoff and Catherine Hall argue that in the decades from the 1790s to 1850, the English middle class was remarkably daring and self-conscious: the "articulate middle-class men and women, involved . . . in building up the material, social and religious base of their identity, [were] battling as a proselytizing minority for their place in the world and the rightness of their view of that world."[7] Persuaded by this account of the self-definition of the English middle class, I read their developmental narratives in its light. Rather than a timorously failed adulthood, I see other ideas of age being worked out in these stories. Like Davidoff and Hall, I see a militant middle class asserting the rightness of its view of the world through linked attempts to win critical respectability for the novel and for the children's book in the early nineteenth-century.

To do this, Barbauld, Edgeworth, and Scott draw on the stadial theory of historical change propounded by the "conjectural historians," key figures in the emerging social sciences of the eighteenth century. Dugald Stewart came up with the phrase "conjectural history" to describe a mode of thought that runs through Adam Smith's work.[8] Important to much of the work of other Scottish Enlightenment figures such as Adam Ferguson, John Millar, and David Hume, conjectural history was enormously influential, becoming the "common sense of educated men" through much of the nineteenth century. As Ronald Meek has explained, conjectural history drew together Enlightenment beliefs about scientific method, causality, and a sensationalist theory of knowledge, producing a secular and historical understanding of human interaction with the environment: "Man . . . not only made himself and his institutions: he and his institutions in an important sense *were themselves made* by the circumstances in which from time to time and from place to place he happened to find himself."[9] Claiming that these changing circumstances followed a regular pattern, conjectural history described societies and the individual living through the same set of stages.[10] For example, Robertson remarks that North America offers European observers the opportunity to watch man's "progress through the different stages of society, as he gradually advances from the infant state of civil life towards its maturity and decline."[11] The conjectural historians' stadial theory goes from infancy (hunting), to rude although vigorous youth (pasturage and agriculture), to polished sophistication (commerce), to luxury and corruption (decline and death). Because each nation of the world may be at a different point on the timeline at any given moment, the historian can move backwards in time by moving around in space. For example, the eighteenth century's Native American tribes, Scottish highlanders, and rural Irish all represent the same primitive stage of development as does the infancy of Greece or Rome, or of England itself.[12]

In Barbauld, Edgeworth, and Scott, we see not merely how an idea of human development influences a theory of history, but also how a theory of history influences an idea of human development.[13] These authors share with the conjectural historians a commitment to identifying commercial rationality with maturity, seeing it as the climax of individual growth as well as of national growth. Likewise, as the "common sense of educated men," the analogy between the infancy of civilization and the infancy of the individual is so pervasive that Edgeworth objects to its excessive influence on plans for early education. This analogy misleads no less an authority than the Abbé Condillac into subjecting the six-year-old Prince of Parma to an overly abstract course of study, one that is beyond the boy's comprehension:

> After having made him reflect upon his own infancy, the abbé judged that the infancy of the world would appear to his pupil "the most curious and the most easy to study." The analogy between these two infancies seems to consist chiefly in words; it is not easy to gratify a child's curiosity about the infancy of the world.[14]

Although she here remarks that the analogy between "these two infancies seems to consist chiefly in words," elsewhere she grants it a good deal of substance. Edgeworth consistently describes Ireland as childish, for example, and urges the country to grow up by becoming a rational commercial society such as England.[15] More broadly, her work asserts that although a six- or seven-year-old cannot yet comprehend the history of the progress of the human mind, he is ready to start enacting it. He is ready to learn to become a prudent, far-seeing member of commercial society. Barbauld, Edgeworth, and Scott will teach him how.

These authors consider irrationality, impulsiveness, and violence to be the qualities that distinguish both literal children and the nations that they imagine as children. For example, Adam Smith points to a puzzling act of "childishness" as essential to a founding moment of commerce: the breakup of feudal authority. The market itself grew out of the ridiculous "folly" of landed aristocrats oblivious to their true interests as well as out of the praiseworthy "industry" of merchants. Armed to the teeth and backed by hordes of ferocious retainers, the great feudal lords were vanquished by toys: "To gratify the most childish vanity was the sole motive of the great proprietors" in abandoning their feudal obligations, Smith fumes: "For a pair of diamond buckles perhaps, or for something as frivolous and useless, they exchanged . . . the price of the maintenance of a thousand men for a year, and with it the weight and authority which it could give them." Smith stresses the "childishness" of feudal lords, the fact that they "sold their birth-right . . . for trinkets and baubles, fitter to be the playthings of children than the serious pursuits of men."[16] Such irrationality is what Barbauld, Edgeworth, and Scott are eager to educate out of both children and nations, ensuring they choose instead their own long-term self-interest.

Histories of children's literature and education now often credit Barbauld, Edgeworth, and writers whom their age-leveled series influenced, such as Sarah Trimmer, with re-imagining and re-configuring the book market in terms of developmental psychology, making their project sound nearly identical to that of the bildungsroman. However, although their work includes ideas that are continuous with the tenets of developmental psychology, their general sense of maturity as rational life in a commercial world belongs to conjectural history. Their commitment to this way of thinking may be one source of the horror they inspired in canonical Romantic writers. Canonical Romantics often saw writers such as Barbauld and Edgeworth as witches – in Charles Lamb's memorable phrase, "the Cursed Barbauld Crew, those Blights and Blasts on all that is human in man and child."[17] Unlike the canonical Romantics, Barbauld and Edgeworth do not see a painful but fascinating gulf between the creative imagination of childhood and the general dreariness of adult life. Their narrative assumes progress rather than the Fall, a steady increase in reason rather than a traumatic loss of wonder.

Two of Barbauld's and Edgeworth's best-known pieces illustrate this similarity of purpose. One of Barbauld's most anthologized essays translates Stoic philosophy into commercial terms. She heads the essay with a passage from Elizabeth Carter's 1758 translation of Epictetus: "What is more reasonable, than that they who have taken pains for any thing, should get most in that particular, for which they have taken pains? They have taken pains for power; you for right principles: they for riches; you for the proper use of the appearances of things" (20). Barbauld makes something new of the Stoic principle that one should tranquilly accept the consequences of one's own choices by rewriting it in terms of children and shopping. In both Carter's translation and Barbauld's essay, "riches" are clearly an inferior object of desire, a choice that ranks a distant second to "proper use." For Barbauld, however, the wealth of commercial society has also become the controlling metaphor that frames all choices:

> We should consider this world as a great mart of commerce, where Fortune exposes to our view various commodities, riches, ease, tranquility, fame, integrity, knowledge. Everything is marked at a settled price. Our time, our labour, our ingenuity, is so much ready money which we are to lay out to the best advantage.[18]

To enforce her moral, Carter goes on to describe how archers and blacksmiths gain skill in the particular crafts with which they have taken pains. Barbauld keeps talking about shopping, and starts talking about children as well: "Examine, compare, chuse, reject; and do not, like children, when you have purchased one thing, repine that you do not possess another which you did not purchase."[19] In this passage, children stand for the inability to rationally choose and abide by the consequences of our choices. To be childlike is to fail to do the ethical cost–benefit analysis that reveals integrity and tranquility to be the most valuable goods on the shelf. Here the old ethical principle is important, but important too is a new interest in a commercial world and in what age means in such a place. Barbauld's child fails as a consumer as well as a Stoic, recalling Adam Smith's "childish" feudal aristocrats, dazzled by diamond buckles into forfeiting their political power.

Barbauld creates a developmental model for teaching rational choice through age-leveled reading. As Mitzi Myers has shown, Barbauld is a key founder of the rational moralist school of writing for children, the popularizer of its distinctive form, the "moral tale," and of its distinctive idea of the child, the "child of reason."[20] This version of the child is often overlooked in favor of a more simple opposition between the Puritan child, full of original sin and dear to early nineteenth-century Evangelicals, and the Romantic child, full of natural innocence and dear to Victorian gentlemen. In contrast to both, Barbauld's "child of reason" was a creation of the Enlightenment.[21] She insists that children do not learn from memorizing the aphorisms traditionally included in children's books, but rather from reflecting under painstaking supervision on what they read and experience, gradually learning habits of critical thinking.

Edgeworth particularly admired "Against Inconstancy in our Expectations." Her own well-known story "The Purple Jar" reads like a miniature novelization of that essay, one that borrows Barbauld's pedagogy as well as her subject matter: "Rosamond, a little girl of about seven years old, was walking with her mother in the streets of London. As she passed along, she looked in the windows of several shops, and she saw a great variety of different sorts of things, of which she did not know the use, or even the names." Rosamond wants everything: "Dear, if I had money, I would buy roses, and boxes, and buckles, and purple flower-pots, and everything." When her mother asks "What, all! Do you wish for them all?" Rosamond offers this deadpan reply: "Yes, Mama, all." But "The Purple Jar" is not a story about greed. It is a story about inconstancy in our expectations, a story about surmounting an important obstacle to rational choice. When Rosamond asks her mother to confirm her (wrong) choice of a purple pot over new shoes, she is told "my dear, I want you to think for yourself":

> "Well, my dear, have you decided?"
> "Mama!–yes–I believe. If you please–I should like the flower-pot; that is, if you won't think me very silly, Mama."
> "Why, as to that, I cannot promise you, Rosamond. But when you are to judge for yourself, you should choose what will make you the happiest; then it would not signify who thought you silly."[22]

Rosamond must choose the greatest rational prospect of happiness; she is not supposed to be swayed even by an otherwise laudable emotion, concern over what a parent thinks of her choice. The fact that her first choice turns out to be wrong is not the main point: as critics have observed, nearly all the other choices Rosamond makes in this story series are right. When Rosamond faces yet another consumer choice in the next story (this time between a useful red leather case for sewing needles and a gimmicky stone painted to look like a plum), the importance of rational and independent choice is what she remembers: "What do you think, Mama? but I need not ask you, because I know you will say, as you did about the purple jar, '*think for yourself, my dear.*'"[23] Rosamond chooses utility over novelty, keeps track of her sewing needles, and is rewarded by being invited to join her father and brother in several "entertaining" experiments involving one of these needles and a magnet. Barbauld would agree with this moral: learn to choose carefully whatever offers the greatest long-term happiness, then abide by your choice. And you will be rewarded with a delightful family experience popularizing Enlightenment scientific exploration.

Such stories take seriously as a sign of modernity the judicious consumption of the goods offered by commercial society. For Edgeworth, learning what to buy and what to leave on the shelf is more than useful training in self-discipline. Such consumption is in itself central to a modern, moral life. For example, the climax of her novel *The Absentee* (1812) is the decision of a nearly bankrupt aristocratic family to pay their debts and then flee the high cost of life in London. They return to a cheaper life in their Irish castle – but they also tastefully redecorate the ancestral home. "I should like to set the fashion of something better in that country," declares Lady Clonbrony.[24] Although she is a comic character, the novel seems to agree with Lady Clonbrony's belief that brand new furniture (as long as it is within budget) will help set the fashion for "something better" in archaic Ireland. Old-fashioned sofas are joyfully thrown on a bonfire, making room for elegant white velvet ones, hand-painted with natural flowers. The renovation of the old castle is an image for the enlightened paternalism with which the family will now manage its estate, but the significance of redecorating is not merely metaphorical. The novel asks us to accept the presence of modern furniture in the ancient castle as itself a step in the right direction.

This scheme of development assumes a generally secular idea of human nature. Barbauld and Edgeworth believe that people are usually more devoted to protecting their reputations and their profits than their souls. An unsigned review in the *Quarterly Review* attacks Edgeworth for her worldly, "reasonable kind" of morality, for promoting "a system of manners regulated by prudence and a sense of propriety" rather than by Christian doctrine.[25] The review is quite right that Edgeworth's novels, like Adam Smith's economics, focus on the rational calculation of long-term self-interest. Edgeworth made her intellectual reputation claiming that the really important difference between children and adults is such a prudential morality. Both the educational handbooks and the fiction that she published throughout her long lifetime offer detailed guidelines on how to move English children and Ireland as a whole from a state of impulsive irrationality into rational and self-controlled economic agency, into a state of adulthood defined as commercial life. The review is also quite right in its sense that there is something about this focus that is faintly but unmistakably antithetical to the Tory *Quarterly*'s Church-and-King-mob way of thinking.

Barbauld defended Edgeworth in a letter to the *Quarterly* that links her prudential morality to the idea of human nature promoted by the conjectural historians. She argues that people are more likely to be influenced "by ridicule, by sound logick, by conjuring up all the forms of worldly ruin and distress that wait upon improvidence and vice" than by appeals to the supernatural:

> there is a large, a very large class in this kingdom called Christian, upon whom religious motives do not operate, because they are not religious; but they are accessible to motives drawn from worldly prudence, from the common feelings of humanity, from a sense of honour . . . however Theologians may dispose of the individual in another world, in this, society is much obliged to anyone who will teach them to pay their debts, and be kind to their neighbours.[26]

Rather than being ideal Christians, members of a commercial society ought to behave decently – or, at a minimum, pay their debts.

The conjectural historians' stadial theory and the work of Barbauld and Edgeworth reflect not only an enthusiasm for commercial society but also a broader Enlightenment interest in establishing an unbroken chain of cause and effect that gives significance to the particulars of experience. It was because the conjectural historians were so strongly committed to the principle that the development of society is both continuous and knowable that they filled in the blanks in the sequence of causal relationships between primitive hunters and their commercial selves with conjecture. As Meek explains, "the task of conjectural history . . . was to exhibit the mechanisms, the chains of causes and effects, whereby men might come, or better, typically do come from rudeness to polish. What was aimed at was an account free from 'jumps.'"[27] Barbauld and Edgeworth see age within this larger eighteenth-century intellectual framework, strands of which were in the process of becoming economics, anthropology, social history, and political science. Many critics have perceptively discussed the significance for their innovative writing for children of landmark texts in educational theory. Barbauld and Edgeworth indeed engaged deeply with John Locke's *Some Thoughts Concerning Education*, Hartley's theory of the association of ideas, and (in a more contestatory mode) Jean-Jacques Rousseau's *Emile: Or, On Education*. Nevertheless, their fundamental ideas of both maturity and development itself are also shaped by conjectural history. We can see this way of thinking even in Barbauld's canon-forming fifty-volume series, *The British Novelists* (1810), with its introductory essay "On the Origin and Progress of Novel-Writing." Not merely the introduction but the series as a whole is a conjectural history, like David Hume's essay "On the Rise and Progress of the Arts and Science."[28] Barbauld's series established an unbroken chain of development from old, rude continental romances up to polished British novels of "the present time," and helped to redefine novels as a specifically British and a specifically modern production.[29]

Similarly, Barbauld's and Edgeworth's model of the age-leveled series of books – perhaps their most lasting achievement – also reflects this interest in unbroken development.[30] Rather than borrowing the chapbook's fairy-tale plots of stunning upward mobility, their books illustrate a different trajectory: small, predictable stages in continuous cognitive, moral, and emotional progress.[31] Barbauld published *Lessons for Children of Two to Three Years Old* (1778), followed by *Lessons for Children of Three Years Old* (1778), *Lessons for Children of Three to Four Years Old* (1779), *Hymns in Prose, for Children* (1781), and (together with her brother, John Aiken) the six-volume *Evenings at Home*, designed for "the Instruction and Amusement of Young Persons" (1792–96). Both *Lessons* and *Hymns* were reprinted consistently in both England and the United States; the last British reprints that McCarthy identifies are 1878 for *Lessons* and 1905 for *Hymns*.[32] Edgeworth also published carefully demarcated series addressed to different segments of the book-buying public, identified by age: for example, *The Parent's Assistant; or Stories for Children* (1796), *Practical Education* (1798), *Early Lessons* (1801) for very young children, *Moral Tales for Young People* (1805), and a continuation of *Early Lessons* (1822).

Barbauld and Edgeworth combined the desire to establish age norms with a keen attention to individual variation. Edgeworth recommended not merely age-leveled series, but also age-leveling all books read by individual young people through a careful process of selection and editing.[33] Parents or teachers should recommend specific passages and censor others based on the reader's development: "As young people grow up they will judge of the selections that have been made for them; they will perceive why such a passage was fit for their understanding at one period, which they could not have understood at another." Considering the difficulty of fitting an individual reader's needs within a larger scheme, Edgeworth's answer is an Enlightenment call for still more empirical observation and recording of data: "We are sensible that order is necessary in reading, but we cannot think that the same order will suit all minds . . . If parents would keep an accurate list of the books which their children read, of the ages at which they are read, it would be of essential service in improving the art of education."[34]

Their developmental model requires a long, resource-intensive process of education, one that was incompatible with the early participation in the workforce expected of the great majority of young people of their time, an expectation we will consider in more depth in the next chapter. It was also incompatible, as we shall see, with the early enlistment in the military experienced by many middle-class boys, an incompatibility that is noteworthy because the writings of both Barbauld and Edgeworth were strongly linked to the middle-class home.[35] Edgeworth wrote a separate series of *Popular Tales*[36] addressing those lower in the social scale but, like Barbauld, her true sphere of influence was the ambitious middle-class household. Barbauld and Edgeworth went farther than did Newbery in distinguishing between reading for the middle-class young and cheap print for the semi-literate of all ages. Renée Balibar sums up this similarity between Barbauld's *Early Lessons* and one of Barbauld's and Edgeworth's favorite French writers for children, Arnaud Berquin: they "marked the end of the chapbooks of the former regime," popularizing instead "a sort of book that relegated hornbooks and ancient alphabet primers to the archaic past, and one which no longer belonged to Utopian literature as did those written by the theoreticians of education."[37] As Barbauld puts it, *Lessons for Children* sought to challenge not only the content, but also the material form of children's publishing: she deplored "the want of *good paper*, a *clear and large type*, and *large spaces*."[38] With fine paper, wide margins, large, clear print, and a minimum of words per page, Barbauld created the look that still makes high-end children's books recognizable at a glance today. This look carries a price tag and marks a social class: Barbauld's books were easy for beginning readers to decipher, and difficult for anyone below the middle classes to buy.[39]

Like Newbery promoting children's books, Barbauld argues for the value of novels in the name of both instruction and delight – but she gives special praise to domesticity, the fighting word of the emerging middle class. She insists that "entertainment is their [novels'] legitimate end and object," but stresses that reading is not only "the cheapest of pleasures; it is a domestic pleasure."[40] Similarly, the idea of education as domestic entertainment is an important context for *Waverley*. Scott even breaks the frame of young Waverley's own mid-eighteenth-century childhood to note the continuing boom in educational playthings in 1814. He has mixed feelings about the faith middle-class parents put in teaching through the "insinuating method of instructive games," about their eagerness to buy whatever promises their children "instruction through the medium of amusement":

> The history of England is now reduced to a game at cards, the problems of mathematics to puzzles and riddles, and the doctrines of arithmetic may, we are assured, be sufficiently acquired by spending a few hours a-week at a new and complicated edition of the *Royal Game of the Goose.* (13)

The British Critic (August 1814) agrees that *Waverley* as a whole acts as a testament to the importance of proper domestic education: "it is to this first source that we are constantly referred for a just and sufficient cause of all the wandering passions as they arise in his [Waverley's] mind."[41]

Both Edgeworth and Barbauld themselves belonged to writing, liberal-minded, intellectual families who were committed to advancing reason, social reform, and science through progressive education. Unlike Mary Wollstonecraft, they both wrote as ladies, with the sanction of their economically secure and socially respected families. Both were versatile women of letters: Barbauld was a celebrated poet as well as literary critic, essayist, and children's writer, while Edgeworth was known for educational writing before she turned to the novel. They both advocated alternatives to the elite public schools and their Latin- and Greek-based curriculum. The daughter of a Warrington Academy teacher, Barbauld and her husband founded Palgrave Academy, known as something of a "nursery of radical principles."[42] Together with her father, Edgeworth home-schooled her many younger siblings and published the bible of progressive middle-class childrearing and education, *Practical Education.* Despite real differences, Edgeworth found an essential role model in Barbauld, and Barbauld included Edgeworth in her shortlist of distinguished contemporary novelists.

Although they were pioneers in age-leveling books for young people, Barbauld and Edgeworth believed that didactic purpose unifies writing for all ages. Worthwhile fiction should teach readers how to be modern, moral, and British, making "didactic" the greatest honor that Barbauld could think of to award novels: "it is not necessary to rest the credit of these works on amusement alone . . . When allied with some great moral end . . . they [fictitious adventures] may be termed didactic," she concludes.[43] The goal of all reading is education, and the goal of education, as we have seen, is to teach one to "examine, compare, chuse, reject" among a range of practicable options. The emotionally responsive, critically thinking middle-class reader that Barbauld cultivates in *Lessons for Children* is the same kind of reader that she tries to call into existence for the novel in *The British Novelists.* In her Foreword to *Belinda* (1801), Edgeworth asks her readers to consider the book a "moral tale" rather than a novel, since novels have unleashed on the world so much "folly, errour, and vice."[44] In *The British Novelists*, Barbauld uses the term "novel" but makes the same case for the novel's moral teaching.[45] Scott shares this didactic purpose. He stresses "the moral lessons which I would willingly consider as the most important part of my plan, although I am sensible how short these will fall of their aim, if I shall be found unable to mix them with amusement."[46] As for Richardson, the child or young person whose grasp of good principles is strengthened by enjoying and reflecting on a well-written book is a model for the ideal older reader.

All this praise of didacticism may sound odd to us at least in part because of a specific turn in literary history. As we shall see in the next chapters, the late nineteenth and earlier twentieth centuries created a particular theory of how reading works, one that places didacticism at the lowest point of a hierarchy of age-leveled fiction. These critics associated didacticism exclusively with childhood, arguing that the young passively absorb lessons from easy books while adults actively engage with the challenges of complex ones. Under this model, "didactic" is the near opposite of critical thought. To be an adult is to think critically, while to be a child is to be inscribed with reductive morals. Edgeworth, Barbauld, and Scott all work with a different model of didactic fiction. They do not assume a contrast between passive young readers and active adult ones. Rather than our age-leveled hierarchy of reading, their starting point is Samuel Johnson's *Rambler* No. 4, a reflection on Horace's famous motto translated as "And join both profit and delight in one." As we saw in the previous chapter, Newbery emblazoned *Delectando monemus*, the Horatian exhortation to combine instruction with delight, on the frontispiece of his *Little Pretty Pocket-Book*, and histories of children's literature often take this motto as a handy shorthand description of what distinguishes late eighteenth- and nineteenth-century children's literature as a whole from the more straightforward and more religious didacticism that preceded it. Barbauld, Edgeworth, and Scott's engagement with Johnson reminds us that this motto had a much broader currency.[47]

Samuel Johnson does not idealize either adulthood or adult novel-readers. The most he hopes for is that good novels will fill the empty heads of novel-readers of all ages before something worse does. Young people share with ignorant and idle people of all ages the need for instruction: "These books are written chiefly to the young, the ignorant, and the idle, to whom they serve as lectures of conduct, and introductions into life."[48] Although Johnson foregrounds the young, he does not age-level reading as a whole by offering a superior, adult reader to contrast with a passive young reader. Once readers are no longer young, ignorant, or idle, it seems that even the best novels will have nothing left to offer them. Barbauld, Edgeworth, and Scott rework Johnson to define novel-reading as active and critical, but they too do not create a contrast between passive children and active adults. Like Johnson, they tend to foreground young readers but also to think of the novel's teaching as helpful for all ages. In the 1830 "Introduction" to *Ivanhoe*, for example, Scott assumes not only that "young persons" form an important part of his reading audience but that they are in fact "the most common readers of romance."[49] He explicitly discusses his novels in terms of their mixed-age audience, their ability to amuse and to teach readers of different ages. "To elder persons it [*Waverley*] will recall scenes and characters familiar from their youth; and to the rising generation the tale may present some idea of the manners of their forefathers," he remarks, breaking both his audience and British history down by generational style. Scott also notes that he has been blamed for "misleading the young, the indolent, and the giddy" by mixing historical information with fiction. He asserts, however, that "by introducing the busy and the youthful to 'truths severe in fairy fictions dressed,' I am doing a real service."[50] Novels can trigger intellectual curiosity in both the busy older reader and the young reader with fewer responsibilities.

Eighteenth-century critics argued over whether the convention of poetic justice promoted or defeated the didactic goal of novels. By rewarding Pamela's virtue with riches, for example, does Richardson reduce chastity to mercenary self-interest? Alternatively, by rewarding Clarissa's virtue with death, does he deny God's justice? They also worried over the related question of whether the readerly sympathy created by mixed characters was compatible with this didactic purpose. Scott's earliest reviewers stress the problems of poetic justice and mixed characters. They assume that these are central critical issues for readers of all ages. "The rule of poetical justice has obtained such currency, that whatever the author rewards he is supposed to approve," Nassau Senior observes in the *Quarterly Review* in 1821, with no reference to age.[51] In 1823, the *New Monthly Magazine* explicitly discusses poetic justice and mixed characters with regard to their effect on Scott's mixed-age audience. It fears Scott will mislead not only young readers, such as the lively child who learned to admire Louis XI from *Quentin Durwood*, but "riper" older readers as well:

> [We protest against] the misfortune of the greatest genius of the age conveying false impressions to the public of the great political concerns of man – of his blunting the sympathies of youth with the cause of human civilization,

> and begetting a precocious indifference to public interests . . . Nor is it enough to say that these works are not intended for youth; for youth will read them; and not only so, but even those of riper years will find it difficult to resist their influence.[52]

Scott himself does not say his works are "not intended for youth." He thinks carefully about how the convention of poetic justice may affect reflective young minds and disagrees with most reviewers about the probable result, refusing on principle, for example, to reward Rebecca's virtue with Ivanhoe's hand in marriage:

> it is a dangerous and fatal doctrine to teach young persons, the most common readers of romance, that rectitude of conduct and of principle are either naturally allied with or adequately rewarded by the gratification of our passions, or the attainment of our wishes . . . a glance on the great picture of life will show that the duties of self-denial, and the sacrifice of passion to principle, are seldom thus remunerated.[53]

Although he disagrees about the best way to go about it, Scott does not doubt that young persons are his "most common readers" and that the novel's central purpose is a didactic one.

On *Waverley*'s appearance in 1814 Edgeworth complimented the author by observing that the novel's appeal was in no way limited by its audience's age. Her account foregrounds alert, careful reading: "We have this moment finished *Waverley*. It was read aloud to this large family, and I wish the author could have witnessed the impression it made – the strong hold it seized of the feelings both of young and old."[54] Here Edgeworth describes a scene of middle-class family reading. Instead of reading the Bible out loud to his household, including his servants, Richard Lovell Edgeworth reads a novel out loud to his wife and children only. *Practical Education* and other well-received works made the Edgeworthstown domestic circle an icon of middle-class progressive educational ideals. Shedding the disreputability of the novel's older semi-literate mixed-age audience of women, children, and servants, Edgeworth's portrait of reading *Waverley* to this particular family elevates the genre to the status of delightful instruction. The Edgeworths analyze Scott's narrative voice, pacing, word choice, characters, and settings just as carefully as they analyze the qualities of a fossil or the veins of a flower: "my brother wishes that *bridal garment* were *shroud*; because when the heart is touched, we seldom use metaphor," she reports. They also object to the "occasional addresses from the author to the reader. They are like Fielding, but for that reason we cannot bear them, we cannot bear that an author of such high powers, of such original genius, should for a moment stoop to imitation."[55]

In Edgeworth's account, *Waverley* stimulates critical thought as well as emotion in a mixed-age audience. Her letter models rational understanding even as it praises emotional response. She singles out the novel's "pathos" for special praise, for example, and gives readerly enthusiasm plenty of space: "Believe me, I have not, nor can I convey to you the full idea of the pleasure, the delight we have had in reading *Waverley*." But she values the novel most for offering readers (and listeners) of all ages a strong sense of the "probable." *Waverley's* plot reinforces the audience's habit of rationally calculating likely outcomes, the central goal of Edgeworth's own pedagogy: "The mind is prepared by unseen degrees for all the changes of feeling and fortune, so that nothing, however extraordinary, shocks us as improbable." Similarly, the novel's new information about the Scottish Highlands is valuable because, however extraordinary it may be, it too is somehow probable: "We never are harassed by doubts of the probability of any of these modes of life; though we did not know them, we are quite certain they did exist exactly as they are represented."[56]

The power of the mixed-age audience did not disappear overnight. Anne Lundin points to a continuing "lack of rigid demarcation between adult and children's literature" as late as 1900 in both England and the United States, noting that many books that seem today to belong exclusively to the children's market continued to be reviewed, and bought, as having general interest. The top ten best-sellers in the United States between 1875 and 1895 included *Heidi*, *Treasure Island*, *A Child's Garden of Verses*, *Huckleberry Finn*, *Little Lord Fauntleroy*, and *King Solomon's Mines*.[57] The presence or absence of illustrations, today a good indicator of the dividing line between children's books and others, also does not work in this way in the nineteenth century, which took to new heights the interplay between the writer, illustrator, and consumer of novels, gift books, and anthologies for all ages.[58] A booming range of product tie-ins also ignored our age divisions, as in the notable case of the late nineteenth-century best-seller *Trilby*, whose heroine's famously desirable naked feet were reproduced in ice cream. They "could actually be bought by schoolchildren as an ice-cream confection. This commodity allowed Trilby's fans to possess, suck, and devour those one-in-a-million, highly reproducible feet."[59] Although reviewers today still periodically describe a good book as being suitable for readers "from six to sixty," the idea that good books (and good fetishistic ice creams) are good for everyone, regardless of age, did not survive the nineteenth century as a serious assumption of increasingly professional literary critics, as we shall see in the next chapter. For early nineteenth-century novelists and reviewers, "adult" was not yet an important term for organizing the literary world – but they were increasingly interested in age.

A virgin knight

To understand further what age means in Barbauld, Edgeworth, and Scott, we must consider more closely two things often taken today as markers of adulthood when age-leveling textual, television, film, or internet content: sex and violence. For these authors, both sex and violence occupy a distinctive place in the life of the individual and of the nation. We have seen how the gradual age-leveling of sexual content helped to move *Pamela* and *Robinson Crusoe* from a mixed-age audience to audiences marked as adult or child, respectively. But Barbauld, Edgeworth, and Scott frame sexual content in terms of the politeness that distinguishes a mature commercial nation rather than the freedom that characterizes a psychological idea of adulthood. Even more remarkably, while we are likely today to take going to war as a marker of adulthood, the field of battle did not work in quite this way for these authors, or in the Napoleonic and Revolutionary period more generally. Although war is one of Walter Scott's great subjects, it is conspicuous by its absence from the children's literature championed by Barbauld and Edgeworth. Both Scott's garrulity about violent times and Barbauld and Edgeworth's silence, however, reflect ideas of maturity drawn from conjectural history. If commercial rationality means adulthood, war marks the childishness of both the nation and the individual. In the final chapters of Scott's novels, his heroes hang up their weapons and turn to their account books.

Edgeworth and Scott were congratulated for raising the novel to cultural respectability through demonstrating its power to combine instruction with an unambiguously unsalacious delight. They had finally managed to make novels stop being sexy. Edward Waverley not only has the unmarked name of a "virgin knight" but, unlike Wilhelm Meister, he is also a virgin. While we may assume that this de-eroticized respectability made early nineteenth-century novels safe for young readers, it more importantly made novels safe for England. That is, it made the novel consonant with literate England's understanding of its place in history. Edgeworth's and Scott's work seemed modern because it was polite. As cultural historians have frequently noted, the standard of propriety went up for civil Englishmen and women in the late eighteenth and early nineteenth centuries. The "young person" mattered a great deal to this way of thinking about novels, but in a different way from how this figure matters to our contemporary understanding that certain novels are good for adults exactly because they would be very bad for children. For most of the nineteenth century, English novels as a whole contained no more non-marital sex than did England's children's books. For Barbauld, Edgeworth, and Scott, the young person in the library was a kind of canary in the coalmine, a warning system for writing that would soon corrupt everyone. Rather than sheltering young people in particular from age-inappropriate content, the code of politeness demonstrated the progress of English civilization as a whole. Scott strikes this note in criticizing the coarseness of the correspondence of James I and the Duke of Buckingham, claiming it abounds in "the grossest as well as the most childish language."[60] For all ages, membership of modern society implied decency in reading, speaking, and writing.

Similarly, Barbauld links literary and national history, seeing the presence or absence of sexual content as a marker not of age but of nationality and historical progress. She distinguishes the best contemporary British writing from the coarseness of the English past and the voluptuousness of the French. The "morals of young people" are important – but more broadly, politeness makes novels modern and British, representative of the contemporary "national character." Barbauld does not imagine an adult reader with distinct rights that should influence what certain novels ought to be. French novels

> are not merely exceptionable, they are totally unfit to enter a house where the morals of young people are esteemed an object . . . The awful frown with which the better part of the English public seem disposed to receive any approaches, either in verse or prose, to the French voluptuousness, does honour to the national character.[61]

William Warner foregrounds age in describing the critical consensus that Barbauld helped to create. In his account, two points were central to early nineteenth-century canon-forming anthologizers, essayists, reviewers, and novelists: "first . . . that novels should be written in such a way that teenagers of both sexes can read them without harm; and second, they view novel-reading as part of a reader's moral education."[62] However, these two points are really one. That is, the schoolboy or young lady represents most dramatically the potential dangers and potential benefits of novels, but the purpose of any good novel is to combine pleasure with moral education. Through roughly the first half of the nineteenth century, the novelist's and reviewer's main goal is not to separate adult fiction from that appropriate to children or to young people, but rather to separate respectable fiction as a whole from scandalous trash.

It is true that Scott's own commercial venture into canon-formation, the ten-volume series *Ballantyne's Novelist's Library* (1821–24), takes a less austere stance on the gratification of our passions. Later literary critics sometimes credited Scott with rescuing the English novel from sexually repressed and repressive women by including in the *Novelist's Library* all of Smollett, all of Fielding, all of Mackenzie, and both of Sterne's novels. In 1951, for example, Michael Sadleir praised Scott's inclusion of such "marvellously full-blooded, ribald English novels, supposedly passed over by Barbauld because she was a 'stickler for feminine decorum.'"[63] Nonetheless, in his own novels Scott worked within the rules of critical respectability that Barbauld and Edgeworth had hammered out. Scott's favorite eighteenth-century authors assumed that a generous measure of sexual content was acceptable for all readers, regardless of age – but Scott's novels assume that sexual content is not acceptable for any reader whatsoever, regardless of age. No one has ever praised the Waverley Novels as marvelously ribald. From the start, their heroes and heroines were recognized as models of propriety rather than of sexual passion. Coleridge insists that "moral" is "too high and inwardly a word" for Scott's work but, although he cannot for a moment grant Romantic interiority to the Waverley Novels, he does acknowledge a politeness that makes them appropriate to their contemporary audience. This is Scott's one advantage over "Fielding, Richardson, and Sterne – in moral, or if that be too high and inwardly a word, in *mannerly* manliness of taste . . . I sincerely trust that Walter Scott's readers would be as little disposed to relish the stupid lechery of the courtship of Widow Wadham, as Scott himself would be capable of presenting it."[64] For his contemporary readership, what Scott excluded from his own novels was as important as what he put in them: "Scott's realism was not eighteenth-century realism with its descriptions of sexual peccadilloes and its scatological references. There was none of the odor of 'the bad century' in Scott's world, nothing that could not be read to the whole family."[65]

To his detriment, young Edward Waverley himself does not appear to read a single polite English novel. Instead, he browses through a catalogue of "chivalrous and romantic lore": Shakespeare, Milton, Spenser, Drayton, Froissart, "the usual" classical authors, Italian poetry, and French memoirs and romances. "Young Waverley drove through the sea of books, like a vessel without a pilot or rudder," Scott explains, and these years of wild and solitary reading produce "evil consequences, which long continued to influence his character, happiness, and utility." That is, Waverley's archaic tendencies blossom in Scotland in large part because he was formed by a "large and sombre library, with no other light than was afforded by the decaying brands on its ponderous and ample hearth" rather than a scene of polite and enlightened domestic reading.[66]

Waverley's "sea of books" looks old-fashioned and aristocratic. It is apparently worlds away from the militant middle-class respectability that shaped the mixed-age reading of 1814. Nevertheless, in a testament to the power of these standards, Waverley's library has in fact been quietly edited to fit them. Although we are told that his ancestors spent two centuries filling their library shelves "without much scrutiny or nicety of discrimination," Scott himself is actually as nice and discriminating as Barbauld or Edgeworth.[67] There are no bawdy English chapbooks on the shelves of this library, and although Waverley does read continental romances, their pages of amorous intrigue seem to have been snipped out. The library at Waverley Honor is as relentlessly high-minded as are the Waverley Novels themselves. Scott explains in his General Preface that Waverley's library reflects collections that he used in his own youth. Among these are Allan Ramsay's celebrated Edinburgh circulating library, which, as Scott tells us, "exhibited specimens of every kind, from the romances of chivalry and the ponderous folios of Cyrus and Cassandra, down to the most approved works of later times."[68] Ramsay's circulating library contained works that had become objectionable according to the standards of literary respectability that Scott follows in *Waverley*. For example, Grenby points out that "Robert Woodrow, in his famous lament about the corrupting effect of Allan Ramsay's Edinburgh library, regrets that 'young boyes' were among those reading the library's 'villainous profane and obscene books and playes.'"[69] Scott writes that "I was plunged into this great ocean of books without compass or pilot," like Waverley sailing without a pilot through his sea of books.[70] But the hazards of the literary ocean in which Scott himself learned to navigate have been removed from Waverley's middle-class shelves – not only for the good of the young, but for the good of readers of all ages.

Scott consigns to the past not only sexual content, but also the glory of violence. Through the historical novel, he promotes instead commercial modernity. His debt to Edgeworth in inventing this genre has long been acknowledged, perhaps most gracefully by his own 1829 Preface to *Waverley*: "Without being so presumptuous as to hope to emulate the rich humour, pathetic tenderness, and admirable tact, which pervade the works of my accomplished friend, I felt that something might be attempted for my own country, of the same kind with that which Miss Edgeworth had so fortunately achieved for Ireland."[71] Like Edgeworth, Scott uses a model of individual development created in the image of conjectural history.

In his novels, the personal development of the elite male hero mirrors the historical development of the nation. In particular, both nations and young men must be persuaded to lay down their weapons – and to pick up, instead, consumer goods. Scott's stories are built around the opposition between the lawless laird Redgauntlet and the young lawyer Alan Fairford, or any other juxtaposition of old military aristocracy and new commercial power. Exciting as it is, military violence is something to be outgrown. *Redgauntlet*'s hero, for example, is praised for possessing the modern virtue of moral restraint rather than the dangerously archaic virtue of military valor: "This is civil courage, Darsie; and it is of little consequence to most men in this age and country, whether they ever possess military courage or no."[72]

As critics have noted, young Edward Waverley is a paradigmatic Scott hero in living out the disorderly but exciting early stages of conjectural history in the Jacobite Highlands, then embracing instead the peace of modern commercial life. Flora MacIvor's dismissal of the courage that Waverley shows in battle is withering. Although no coward can be called a man, mere physical courage does not raise men above the status of "other male animals": "'For mere fighting,' answered Flora, 'I believe all men (that is, who deserve the name) are pretty much alike; there is generally more courage required to run away. They have besides, when confronted with each other, a certain instinct for strife, as we see in other male animals, such as dogs, bulls, and so forth.'"[73] *Waverley* as a whole seems to agree with Flora. Showing bravery while killing, getting injured, or generally participating in the violence of battle is likely to be central to one's development in the later genre of the Victorian boys' adventure story, which more enthusiastically promotes this way of proving that one "deserves the name" of man. But violence does not work this way for Edward Waverley. Both Waverley's Jacobite battles and his reading stand for a certain kind of old-fashioned childishness. They are brilliant but "useless": "like a child among his toys, [the sixteen-year-old Waverley] culled and arranged, from the splendid yet useless imagery and emblems with which his imagination stored, visions as brilliant and as fading as those of an evening sky."[74] The only other figure who is as childish, as brilliant, and as useless as Edward Waverley among his old romances is Richard the Lion-Hearted among the paynim: "In the lion-hearted king, the brilliant, but useless, character of a knight of romance was in a great measure realised . . . his reign was like the course of a brilliant and rapid meteor."[75] Scott compares Waverley to a sunset and Richard to a meteor, but both are archaic, both representing historical dead-ends.

Although Waverley appears on more than one battlefield in the course of the novel (usually, although not always, in a conscious state), fighting does not prove that he has achieved manhood, the strongly gendered maturity of the boys' adventure story. Instead, Scott coolly describes how the battle of Preston triggers Waverley's "instinct for strife." Surrounded by primitive clansmen and the sound of their primitive bagpipes, Waverley feels fever and madness overcome his mind:

> It was not fear, it was not ardour: it was a compound of both, a new and deeply energetic impulse that with its first emotion chilled and astounded, then fevered and maddened his mind. The sounds around him combined to exalt his enthusiasm; the pipes played, and the clans rushed forward . . . the muttering sounds of the men to each other began to swell into a wild cry.[76]

Fever, madness, and "enthusiasm" are not generally positive terms for Scott. For example, unregulated energetic impulses famously kill off *Ivanhoe*'s villain (1819), who "unscathed by the lance of his enemy . . . died a victim to the violence of his own contending passions."[77] Scott's goal is not to prove Waverley's physical courage, but instead to move him and his world away from the wildness of war. Key turning points tend to mark progress in this direction. For example, more valuable than moments such as Waverley's madness at Preston are those in which he recognizes that he has strayed into the wrong moment of history:

> It was at that instant that, looking around him, he saw the wild dress and appearance of his Highland associates, heard their whispers in an uncouth and unknown language, looked upon his own dress, so unlike that which he had worn from his infancy, and wished to awake from what seemed at the moment a dream, strange, horrible, and unnatural.[78]

The Highland clans and their military valor are a horrible dream, one from which Waverley's true, rational, modern self must awake.[79] And awake he does.

Like *The Absentee*, *Waverley* ends with a joyful vision of a beautifully redecorated castle. The novel carefully works up to this climax. Edward Waverley and his bride capture the attention of the Scottish countryside, so lately up in arms, with their tasteful new carriage: "The nuptial party travelled in great style. There was a coach and six after the newest pattern, which Sir Everard had presented to his nephew, that dazzled with its splendour the eyes of one half of Scotland." Where outbuildings were destroyed by war, Waverley's money has been busy improving: "the heavy stables, which had been burnt down, were replaced by buildings of a lighter and more picturesque appearance." Next comes a "new greenhouse stocked with the finest plants." The crowning touch reminds us of why all of these high-priced consumer goods deserve such admiration. Like Lady Clonbrony's white velvet sofas, they are part of "something better," part of the peaceful commercial prosperity that Scott sees as the successor to military violence. A painting of Waverley and Fergus MacIvor (whose actual head is still rotting on a pike for treason) transmutes such violence into a curio, making Highland lawlessness into the stuff of tourism:

> It was a large and spirited painting, representing Fergus Mac-Ivor and Waverley in their Highland dress . . . painted on a full-length scale by an eminent London artist. Beside this painting hung the arms which Waverley had borne in the unfortunate civil war. The whole piece was beheld with admiration and deeper feelings.[80]

This remarkable painting "drew tears" from the eye of the beholder. Like the best-selling *Waverley* itself, it is a brilliant consumer good, one that manages not merely to replace but to sell the archaic violence that came before it.

This nuptial journey represents the progress from violence to commercial prosperity outlined by the conjectural historians. In their writing, war often appears as a ruinously expensive folly. With the notable exception of Adam Ferguson (himself both a Highlander and a soldier, as well as a social philosopher), the conjectural historians often see war not as un-Christian, but rather as childish, as a wasteful preference for immediate emotional satisfaction that mature persons will avoid whenever possible.[81] "The powder that is spent in a modern review is lost irrevocably, and occasions a very considerable expense," frets Adam Smith;[82] although he does not doubt that sovereign nations must defend themselves, soldiers on parade leave him cold. "The art of war is essentially that of destruction," Barbauld states in a piece typically titled "The Cost of a War."[83] While Scott describes youths growing out of war, Barbauld and Edgeworth prefer to refuse to represent anyone engaging in it. Even the heroes of Edgeworth's novels do not tend to join any branch of military service. One of the very few who does, Captain Godfrey Percy of *Patronage* (1814), is repeatedly praised not for courage under fire but rather for keeping "his resolution to live within his pay." And although *Patronage*'s ideal family has the usual *Life* of Lord Nelson on a drawing-room table, the only person who pays any attention to it is a cowardly and hypocritical Frenchman, who tries to ingratiate himself by praising "our naval hero."[84]

It is remarkable that Scott, the conjectural historians, and the writers of respectable children's literature all dismiss military courage as being "of little consequence to most men in this age and country" at the very time when England was engaged in the most sustained military venture that modern Europe had yet seen. Yet as respectable children's writers, Barbauld and Edgeworth were in fact quite typical in this regard. As Grenby demonstrates, during the Revolutionary and Napoleonic wars there was a striking lack of war stories for children – during the very decades when England was usually at war with France, often under direct threat of invasion, and awash with wartime propaganda in other forms: "An imaginative war literature for children developed only after Waterloo."[85] N. A. M. Rodger remarks that describing eighteenth-century Britain "without mentioning the Royal Navy is . . . as difficult as writing a history of Switzerland without mentioning mountains, or writing a novel without using the letter 'e.'"[86] But writers of respectable children's literature make a determined effort to avoid both branches of the military.

Grenby offers two reasons for this remarkable lack. First, respectable children's authors avoided war stories because children were fighting in wars. By land and sea through the long wars of the Revolutionary and Napoleonic period, fighting was commonly the business of the young person and even of the child. These authors responded to the real possibility of their middle-class boy readers going to war either by openly criticizing or, more often, by simply excluding military adventure as a subject. When they do mention military service at all, they directly urge boys not to enlist: "probably the most recurrent motif of the children's literature about war during the French Revolutionary and Napoleonic eras . . . [is] the frequent warnings to boys not to be seduced by the glamour of military life and not to run off to join the armed services." Although a few texts expressed pacifist principles, most simply feared middle-class boys signing up to fight: "they were anti-enlistment rather than anti-war."[87] Second, Grenby describes a broader incompatibility between celebrating war and the values of respectable children's literature, which were the values of polite commercial sociability that we have seen the conjectural historians and Scott advocate. Committed to teaching "commercial values and skills such as diligence and industry, trustworthiness and thrift, enterprise and ambition, prudent expenditure and judicious benevolence," respectable children's writers feared that the unpredictable adventures of military heroes inculcated the opposite.[88]

Edgeworth directly addresses the fact that for Georgian middle-class boys, no adventure stories could be safely fictional. "The taste for adventures is not repressed in boys by the impossibility of its indulgence," she explains, which is why she insists that most middle-class boys should not read *Robinson Crusoe.* Girls, however, are welcome to enjoy the book. Unlike their brothers, these Georgian girls are like later middle-class child readers as a whole. For them, adventure stories are fiction: "To girls this species of reading cannot be as dangerous as it is to boys," Edgeworth writes, because, unlike boys, "girls must soon perceive the impossibility of their rambling about the world in quest of adventures."[89] Since Edgeworth's idea of education for boys is education for a profession, however, there is in fact one group of boys for whom such reading is appropriate – boys heading for war:

> The taste for adventure is absolutely incompatible with the sober perseverance necessary for success in any other liberal professions . . . this species of reading should not early be chosen for boys of an enterprising temper, unless they are intended for a seafaring life, or for the army.[90]

Robinson Crusoe will draw boys to the military, and the military, although necessary, often involves gambling with one's life as well as with cards or dice. Rather than prudently calculating the "rational probability of success" in professional life, young military men see success as the "gift of fortune": "the profits of commerce and of agriculture, the profits of every art and profession, can be estimated with tolerable accuracy; the value of activity, application, and abilities, can respectively be measured by some certain standard . . . but every man will allow that, in point of good fortune, at any game of chance, he thinks himself upon a fair level with every other competitor."[91]

Through both childhood enlistment and uncommercial adventureousness, military life ran counter to the developmental ideas of age advocated by respectable children's literature. While such literature imagined a long, carefully graduated, carefully standardized education unfolding in a domestic space sheltered from major danger or responsibility, military service featured both life-or-death violence and the "entire absence of any official training scheme or curriculum for the boys."[92] Childhood enlistment itself contradicted the ideal of rational choice as the crowning achievement of a long education. Historians such as Holly Brewer claim that societies whose legal systems tend to place a high value on rational, informed consent also tend to place a high value on the idea of adulthood.[93] Through the early nineteenth century, military enlistment did not require either. This was the age of "Casabianca": the popular poet Felicia Hemans sees a great deal of pathos but nothing inappropriate or illegal in the "gallant child" dying on the burning deck at the age of twelve at the Battle of the Nile. And there was no reason she should have: children routinely enlisted in the military.[94] The army and navy had long accepted boys as young as five years old, although twelve or fourteen appears to be a more typical age. George III was told on contemplating the navy that "'fourteen is as late as so hardy a profession can be embraced with the smallest chance of success.'"[95]

We may smile at Samuel Taylor Coleridge's brief enlistment in the army at the age of twenty-one as an act of youthful folly, but his brother Frank became a midshipman at the age of eleven.[96] Jane Austen's brothers Francis and Charles each joined the navy at twelve, and William Wordsworth's brother John went to sea at the age of sixteen. Walter Scott's brother Robert was probably twelve or fourteen when he joined the navy.[97] "The sea officer's career began in childhood," as Rodger states. Ordinary sailors as well as officers often joined as children, making up a significant proportion of any ship's company: "On the high seas, each line of battleship in the Royal Navy generally carried upward of fifty boys aged between six and eighteen."[98] The navy's examination for lieutenant did invoke a numerical age requirement, stipulating that applicants be at least twenty years old as well as have at least six years of service at sea. However, examining boards could disregard the minimum age for capable youths. George Eliot, for example, became a lieutenant in 1800 when he was barely sixteen: "he had been at sea since he was ten, he had already distinguished himself in two battles, and he had been taking charge of a watch for more than a year."[99]

A sense of age that had become archaic in middle-class commercial society still governed a navy in which Horatio Nelson and most of his successful fellow-officers commanded grown men at the age of twelve.[100] Status weighed more heavily than numerical age. Midshipmen were "young gentlemen," not children, defined more by their status than by their numerical age. Very young officers were not sheltered by their age from either danger or responsibility.[101] As Robert Southey matter-of-factly explains in his 1813 *Life of Nelson*, guard duty on the Thames was "considered as too inactive a station for a boy," so the twelve-year-old Horatio Nelson set sail for the West Indies.[102] On land, too, boys joined the militia and the army and might well command their elders before they reached an advanced age.[103] Although he purchased his first army commission at seventeen, Sir Arthur Wellesley, the future Duke of Wellington, was not a precociously talented officer but merely a typical son of a wealthy family.[104] When the Royal Navy tidied up its system of ranks in 1794, it seemed to try to articulate the slippery relationship between numerical age and social status. It discarded the older category of "captain's servant" in favor of "three classes of 'boy,' of which 'Boy First Class or Volunteer' was explicitly reserved for young gentlemen intended to become officers."[105]

The late nineteenth century eventually restructured the British military on the same age-leveled lines as the British book market. Although its new naval rating of "Boy, first class" may still sound like an odd military rank to us, unlike the twelve-year-old young gentlemen of the previous era, these boys entered the service no younger than fourteen and were educated separately at a training college before starting active duty. In addition, ordinary sailors claimed the new status of adult – or at least they asked to be treated "more like men." They claimed an increasingly professional status based on their higher level of specialized training, as well as their general intelligence and self-discipline. In 1901, the editor of the lower-deck newspaper the *Bluejacket* protested "this addressing of present day fleetmen in words more fitted for infant school children than grown up men." He summarized seamen's letters objecting to what they felt was infantilization by the philanthropic efforts of Agnes Wilson, popularly known as the "Mother of the Navy": "The days of tracts . . . whose words are those of a mother addressing very young children, are gone . . . [Ratings] want to be talked to and treated to a higher quality of appeal to their intelligence; to be treated more like men."[106]

"Juvenile (for all ages)"

Age carried a new weight in discussions of literary value by the turn of the twentieth century: for the first time, "adult" became widely used as a synonym for "good." A vocabulary of age supplemented that of status and morality. Rather than merely being instructive, entertaining, witty, rakish, vulgar, or elegantly refined, works of fiction now could be mature or immature. The historical novel's critical standing reflects the growing importance of this new criterion. Like didactic fiction, the historical novel fell to sub-literary status as it became identified with young readers.[107] As the most distinguished writer of historical fiction, Scott took his place on one of the lower rungs of a new age-leveled literary hierarchy. The rise of the Victorian boys' adventure story hastened Scott's critical decline, making it easier to retroactively age-level his historical novels by associating them with this new genre. While Scott's original reviewers are eager to argue that he is proper reading for a gentleman, by the later nineteenth century, critics are equally eager to claim that he is not proper reading for an adult.

Age-leveling became a vexed issue for historical novels a few decades after Scott's death: "Historical novels of this period like Doyle's own *Rodney Stone* (1896) or *The White Company* (1890), or R. D. Blackmore's *Lorna Doone* (1869), or Stanley Weyman's *The House of the Ws* (1890) are notoriously hard to classify by age group."[108] Critical discussion of such novels often triggers the confusion implicit in using "adult" as at once a term of value and a description of numerical age. For example, Avrom Fleischman's major discussion of the historical novel includes the remarkable category of "juvenile (for all ages)": "Most Victorian historical novels may be readily identified by reference to three sets of qualities: antiquarian, juvenile (for all ages), or tendentious." Fleishman struggles with an unclear generic boundary between the later nineteenth-century historical novel and "juvenile fiction": "Kingsley leads us to the brink of another world, if he does not actually keep us there throughout: it is the playful, legendary world of juvenile fiction."[109]

Fleishman's "juvenile (for all ages)" is the opposite of the Romantic "children of all ages" in that he is playing with the relationship between age-leveling and a negative transcendent value rather than a positive one. For Fleishman, juvenile fiction means not only fiction that is in practice written for and marketed to young people, but also commercially successful fiction that seems to him aesthetically inadequate, even though it was written for or marketed to adults, or to a general reader of any age. Distinguishing "the juvenile from the adult fiction" is especially difficult, for example, when discussing "the inundation of late Victorian historical novels": "It is these latter that fill the lists of Baker and Nield; their perennial progeny still make the best-seller lists. There was Charlotte M. Yonge, who filled a half-century with an oeuvre in which it is difficult to distinguish the juvenile from the adult fiction."[110] When comments such as these blur status and age, we seem to come full circle: the young is the popular and the popular is the young. We could be in the eighteenth century scorning chapbook readers. What has changed, however, is the naturalness of the conflation of these two categories. Fleishman lives within a self-consciously age-leveled literary world. Rather than comfortably disdaining a semi-literate audience by combining youth and non-elite status, he feels that he *ought* to be able to distinguish the juvenile from the adult. Establishing the historical novel as a critically important genre depends on this distinction, on moving these particular novels out of the category of juvenile literature and into adult literature.

More specific ideas about age, as well as the growing importance of numerical age itself, influenced historical fiction's rise and meteoric fall in critical esteem.[111] As we have seen, Scott's novels present growing up not merely in Romantic terms that are consonant with developmental psychology or the continental bildungsroman, but more powerfully in terms of conjectural history's ideas about age. That is, adulthood means not merely puberty or emotional sophistication, but, more importantly, the achievement of commercial rationality. Reflecting this interest, early reviewers often describe Scott as a valuable crash course in conjectural history's stadial theory. Thomas Love Peacock, for example, admires Scott for "depicting, with the truth of life, the features of human nature in a peculiar state of society before comparatively little known."[112] *The British Critic* appreciates Scott's examination of "the state of society that prevailed in the northern part of this island," which reveals "that in our own country, and almost in our own age, manners and characters existed, and were conspicuous, which we had been accustomed to consider as belonging to remote antiquity, or extravagant romance."[113] In an unsigned review, Scott himself praises his own insight into the "aboriginal": "the Highlanders . . . this keen-spirited and aboriginal race."[114] More critically, Hazlitt questions the nostalgia implicit in such touring through the early stages of civilization: "Would [Scott] really carry us back to the early stages of barbarism, of clanship, of the feudal system as 'a consummation devoutly to be wished'?"[115] As Hazlitt suggests, when it comes to the pleasures of densely plotted historical fiction, and especially the pleasures of violence, Scott and his first audiences manage to have it both ways. For them battles are a good subject for serious novels because the hero and his nation grow out of them by the end of the book.

When other ideas of age made the maturity envisioned by conjectural history look shallow, however, Scott's novels lost depth as well. An 1828 review is one of the very first to criticize Scott in print by the standard of psychological depth, invoking a specifically Romantic idea of interiority. This reviewer still, however, presents lovers of Scott as bad readers, plain and simple, rather than as young readers. Quoting "Julian and Maddalo"'s question, "Where is the love, beauty, and truth we seek / But in our minds?," Frederick Denison Maurice condemns Scott's novels as superficial. Scott looks "at humanity and nature in their outward manifestations, instead of seizing them in their inward being."[116] On reading *Guy Mannering* in 1815, Wordsworth similarly complains that in both it and *Waverley* the characters "excite little interest"; he objects to the "laborious manner in which everything is placed before your eyes for the production of picturesque effect."[117] Scott may have labored, but his reader is required to do too little work. Stephen Arata has discussed the nineteenth-century rise of the ideal of reading as work, especially in relation to Stevenson and Henry James.[118] These Romantic discussions of interiority invoke a similar ideal. According to Coleridge, the problem with Scott is that he is too easy. Reading him is not strenuous intellectual work: "My criticism was *confined* to the one point of the higher degree of intellectual activity implied in the admiration of Fielding, Richardson, and Sterne . . . [Scott's popularity is due to his ability] to amuse without requiring any effort of thought, and without exciting any deep emotions."[119] Characters with deep feelings require readers who are deep thinkers – but here Coleridge still characterizes shallow reading as popular trash rather than as children's literature. That is, social status still outweighs age in his thinking about literary value. The opposition of psychological depth (which great art offers) to shallow pageantry (which makes Scott popular) became standard in the critical deflation of Scott: the *Athenaeum*, for example, takes as acknowledged fact in 1871 that the "psychological element of the novels is their weakest point."[120]

Eventually, the age of Walter Scott's imagined readers shifted downwards, in part because numerical age came to matter more in reading and marketing books, as well as in fighting battles as military service was restructured after Waterloo. The boys' adventure story, often with a patriotic battle setting, was one of the most popular genres of children's literature from the middle of the nineteenth century into the early twentieth, a genre perhaps best summed up by the long career of G. A. Henty. Claudia Nelson describes the impact of Henty on historical fiction: "it took the arrival of G. A. Henty on the literary scene – as the most influential boys' writer of the late nineteenth century – to enthrone macho manliness as the genre's dominant ethic."[121] Henty's young heroes do their bit on battlefields ranging from the Punic Wars to Waterloo to the Crimea, in books that appeared from the 1860s into the 1900s. Much changed between children's literature's ban on military adventure in the time of Nelson and the publication of Henty's *By Conduct and Courage; a Story of Nelson's Days* (1904). While Georgian children's writers tried to restrain middle-class boys from enlisting to fight Napoleon, Victorian children's writers assumed that such boys would spend a long childhood dreaming over adventure stories before fighting for the British Empire.

By Conduct and Courage reflects these changes. Rather than being eleven or twelve years old, Henty's hero, Will, is fully fifteen by the time he joins the Navy. And when he gains command of a cutter soon after, Henty expects the reader to marvel along with the secondary characters at this spectacle of a sixteen-year-old commanding grown men:

> "It must surely seem very ridiculous to you," she said, "to be giving orders to men old enough to be your father."
>
> "I can quite understand that it seems so to you," he said, "for it does to me sometimes; but custom is everything, and I don't suppose the men give the matter a thought. At any rate they are as ready to follow me as they are the oldest veteran in the service."

Unlike the Georgian writers, Henty also approves of the fact that "adventure is always tempting to boys": "Will had thought the matter over in every light, and concluded that he could not do better than join the navy for a few years. Putting all other things aside, it was a life of adventure, and adventure is always tempting to boys."[122] Military violence is central to this praiseworthy life of adventure. Will's life at sea consists of little more than a long series of fights, escalating from boxing with a bully to battling pirates to fighting the French. Henty describes the rising body count with approval.

The bonds of heterosexual domesticity have little standing in this world. As we have seen, the Georgian writers' worst fear was a boy running away from home and towards war. In contrast, when Will's best friend runs away from home with him, nearly everyone they meet applauds them both for it:

> "You will do," was the verdict of an old soldier. "I can see that you have both got the right stuff in you. When one fellow saves another's life, and that fellow runs away and ships in order to be near his friend, you may be sure that there is plenty of good stuff in them, and that they will turn out a credit to His Majesty's service."

Bonds between one adventurous fellow and another seem to take priority over all others. Those who are not charmed by the two boys' unity are physically subdued by it: "'As I told you,' Will answered [a big bully] quietly, 'my friend and I are one. I don't suppose that single-handed I could fight a great hulking fellow like you, but my friend and I are quite willing to do so together.'" The two boys' bond rivals or even surpasses marriage: "'I think,' the sailor said to Will seriously, 'you are a fortunate fellow to have made a friend like that. A good chum is the next best thing to a good wife. In fact, I don't know if it is not a bit better.'"[123]

As this passage implies, gender works in complicated ways in the boys' adventure story. In the next chapter, we will argue that powerful Victorian ideas about gender could outweigh age difference, much as powerful ideas about status had earlier outweighed age difference. As Claudia Nelson has demonstrated, "the Victorian stereotype of childhood had much in common with the feminine ideal." That is, a good girl and a good woman were fundamentally the same kind of person. What made a good boy or a good man, and how similar or different they were, was, however, a trickier question. Nelson suggests that "women became archetypes [such as the Angel in the Home], while men could only hope to be adults."[124] In the next chapter, I shall argue that mid-Victorian men, at least, could not yet hope to be adults – that "adult" is too gender-neutral a concept to carry much weight in a world so thoroughly awash in ideas of womanliness and manliness. In any case, gender rivaled age as a strategy for organizing this aspect of the book market – whether explicitly stated or not, the adventure story was the boys' adventure story. The adventure story and its near-relative, historical fiction, belonged to "boys of all ages" but most particularly to fathers and sons. In contrast, girls and their mothers got the domestic story (although anecdotes about sisters reading their brothers' adventure stories abound in Victorian memoirs), and, eventually, the domestic novel.[125] "It was to be a story for boys; no need of psychology or fine writing . . . Women were excluded," writes Robert Louis Stevenson of *Treasure Island* (1881–82). This audience of boys included not only Stevenson's stepson, but also his father: "I had counted on one boy, I found I had two in my audience. My father caught fire at once."[126]

When the Waverley novels were read in the context of the boys' adventure story, they stopped describing the evolution of adult, commercial society from the childishness of warfare, and became instead boyish celebrations of what Walter Bagehot calls "the fighting times." In the process of making the novel into the property of adults only, Modernist writers also furthered this redefinition of Walter Scott as an author of adventure stories for boys. Henry James, for example, sees Scott as a kind of literary Baden-Powell, a story-telling big brother enthralling the little ones over the campfire: "we can liken him to nothing better than to a strong and kindly elder brother, who gathers his juvenile public about him at eventide, and pours out a stream of wondrous improvisation. Who cannot remember an experience like this? . . . And thoroughly to enjoy him, we must again become as credulous as children at twilight."[127]

In 1858, Walter Bagehot regrets that Scott addressed the young reader by "invariably attempt[ing] an account of youthful, sometimes of decidedly juvenile, feelings and actions." In some ways, Bagehot's young reader is still the passionate but critically reflective thinker imagined by Barbauld and Edgeworth: "Superficial the reading of grown men in some sort must ever be: it is only once in a lifetime that we can know the passionate reading of youth; men soon lose its eager learning power." Bagehot's young reader is judicious as well as passionate, as eager to "adjudicate" the qualities of a new novel as he is to love them: "The generation which is really most influenced by a work of genius is commonly that which is still young when the first controversy respecting its merits arises; with the eagerness of youth they read and re-read; their vanity is not unwilling to adjudicate. This is the kind of reading that Edgeworth describes in recounting her family's engagement with *Waverley*, hot off the press. Bagehot's opinion of the young reader goes downhill, however, as his essay progresses. There is an unmistakable put-down in his remark that "there is much in very many of them [the Waverley novels] which is admirably fitted for the delight of boyhood."[128] Bagehot's young readers are briefly female as well as male in their addiction to heterosexual romance plots. By the end of the essay, however, the young reader has become the boy-reader of adventure stories, who delights in the flashy violence of endless tournaments rather than in eager learning. Bagehot sees this appeal not as lower class, but as childish. He describes *Ivanhoe* as the ultimate boy's adventure story, foregrounding simple, pageant-like violence:

> The charm of *Ivanhoe* is addressed to a simpler sort of imagination – to that kind of boyish fancy which idolizes the mediaeval as "the fighting time." Every boy has heard of tournaments, and has a firm persuasion that in an age of tournaments life was thoroughly well understood. A martial society, where men fought hand to hand on good horses with large lances.[129]

Similarly, Leslie Stephen firmly reclassifies Scott as children's literature, as he reclassified *Robinson Crusoe*. He claims that boys rather than men like fictional accounts of battles – even though he also worries that what boys may in fact like best of all is the even newer genre of the school story:

> *Ivanhoe*, let it be granted, is no longer a work for men, but it still is, or ought to be, delightful reading for boys. The ordinary boy, indeed, when he reads anything, seems to choose descriptions of the cricket-matches and boat-races in which his soul most delights. But there must still be some unsophisticated youths who can relish *Robinson Crusoe* and the *Arabian Nights* and other favourites of our own childhood, and such at least should pore over the "Gentle and free passage of arms at Ashby".

Having "descended from the library to the schoolroom," Scott becomes a kind of holiday uncle for boys needing a virtual experience of manly outdoor life:

> But if *Ivanhoe* has rightly descended from the library to the schoolroom, we should not be ungrateful to Scott for wasting his splendid talents on what we can hardly call by a loftier name than most amusing nonsense . . . The

> pleasure of that healthy open-air life, with that manly companion, is not likely to diminish.[130]

Virginia Woolf extends her father's project of placing Scott critically. *To the Lighthouse* (1927) offers these defensive reflections from Mr. Ramsay, who feels his own work going the way of old Sir Walter's novels. In Mr. Ramsay's self-serving musings, "that healthy open-air life, with that manly companion" is revealed as the sexual prudishness of the English novel, the criticism voiced by Moretti. Mr. Ramsay bases his attempt to defend Scott on the premise of French voluptuousness. Mr. Ramsay frames

> one or two reflections about morality and French novels and English novels and Scott's hands being tied but his view perhaps being as true as the other view . . . The whole of life did not consist in going to bed with a woman, he thought, returning to Scott and Balzac, to the English novel and the French novel.[131]

There is some poignancy in Mr. Ramsay's attempt to hold on to the idea that the novel's treatment of sexual content is a marker of national identity. In Woolf's own Modernist world, it has already become a marker of age.

By the middle of the twentieth century, a new genre closely related to historical fiction drew particularly loud and particularly interesting age-leveled criticism: fantasy. In a 1954 *New Statesman* review of *The Lord of the Rings*, for example, Maurice Richardson issued a call to arms against fantasy's rising popularity. He first links fantasy to the boys' adventure story, remarking that *The Two Towers* will "do quite nicely as an allegorical adventure story for very leisured boys." When encountering critics who praise the book in any other terms, however, Richardson feels that he can barely "restrain myself from . . . slouching through the streets with a sandwichman's board inscribed in jagged paranoid scrawl in violet ink: 'Adults of all ages! Unite against the infantilist invasion.'"[132] Richardson's inscription of "adults of all ages" on his imaginary sandwich board suggests some of the ambiguities inherent in describing literary value in terms of age. On the one hand, age-leveling may imply a sliding standard: rather than positing one universal measure of what makes fiction good or bad, critics and readers see different books as good or bad for people of different ages. Age-leveled school reading, publishers' lists, best-seller lists, public library collections, literary awards, and literary criticism seem to reflect this way of thinking. On the other hand, the enormous weight of "adult" as the end-point of developmental psychology, and the end-point of these same developmentally oriented educational institutions, suggests that adulthood is an absolute good. As in the bildungsroman, "adult" is the intellectual, ethical, and sexual ideal that we strive to achieve, the ultimate standard of excellence.

Like the Romantic call for "children of all ages" to find spiritual food in fairy tales that we will examine in the next chapter, Richardson's appeal to "adults of all ages" follows a distinctive rhetorical strategy. It links a particular numerical age that is enjoying new cultural cachet to a fashionable personal quality – eighteenth-century childhood with wonder; twentieth-century adulthood with critical intelligence – qualities that never coincide perfectly with this numerical age itself. Such calls claim both that these qualities define a particular numerical age and that they transcend this age as a universal human good. Just as some adults may lower themselves to infantile self-indulgence, Richardson implies, so some children may rise to adult intelligence. This rhetorical slippage is built into any cultural norm, any category that moves between empirical observation and moral exhortation. Given fantasy's continuing liminality in terms of age-leveled reading, we may or may not be surprised to see Richardson denounce J. R. R. Tolkien as infantile. But Richardson also reviles one of the twentieth-century's icons of its proudly adult literature, Tolkien's admirer W. H. Auden. According to Richardson, Auden is immature, a failed adult who "has always been captivated by the pubescent world of the saga and the classroom."[133] "The pubescent world of the saga and the classroom" recalls the didacticism of Barbauld, Edgeworth, and Scott, as well as Scott's scenes of battle, but it places these things on a different scale of development from that of the conjectural historians. Here the landmark is puberty, and the embarrassment of physical, mental, and emotional changes associated with the end of childhood. "Pubescent" suggests a psychological framework, but even more strongly than the bildungsroman's glamorization of adolescence, "pubescent" makes adulthood look good.

In his 1890 review essay, "Should Children Have a Special Literature?" Edward Salmon ventriloquizes the response of old-fashioned parents to the shifting book market, summing up nearly a century of change with one question about the young readers of 1890: "Their fathers read Scott as children; why should not they?"[134] Merely naming Scott captures a great deal about this new book market. Why should they spend time and money pursuing a specialized kind of reading for their children, such parents wonder, when all forty-eight volumes of the Waverley Novels sit ready on the shelf, and when they themselves cannot remember a time when they did not know Scott's books? Salmon's essay as a whole, however, advocates differentiating the book market by age. His mention of Scott in this context is, in fact, a bit disingenuous because of the critical transformation that the Waverley Novels had undergone from the middle of the nineteenth century onwards: by 1890, Scott had already become a children's author. The Waverley Novels were already praised, or damned, as belonging to the new "special literature" for children that Salmon supports. Accordingly, a new answer to Salmon's question was clear, an answer that still works today: separate young people from novels written specifically for adults, leaving the adult audience to enjoy them in private while children find their own age-appropriate works in a clearly signed section of the library or bookstore.

As late as 1871, the year that Leslie Stephen dismissed Scott as delightful reading for boys, however, the *Athenaeum* could still rely on the young reader as a practical measure of literary value for all readers. In contrast to the kind of literary standards that Scott and Dickens share even (or especially) in their treatment of drunkenness and non-marital sex, this reviewer senses something new in George Eliot. A "taint of animalism" in *Adam Bede* "makes it inferior":

> Would any lady put *The Heart of Midlothian* out of her daughter's reach? Or would any gentleman dread the effect of the Baron of Bradwardine on his son? In this respect there is another curious resemblance between Scott and Dickens . . . no one has ever charged the *Pickwick Papers* with any tendency to promote excess. The story of *Little Em'ly* is equally free from all taint, not only of prurience, but even coarseness. In the character of Hetty Sorel, Miss Evans has shown how closely she could tread in these footsteps; but there is a nameless something even there – a taint of animalism – which makes it inferior.[135]

This "curious resemblance" between Scott and Dickens, like their shared distance from George Eliot, was capable of being evaluated in quite opposite terms, as we shall see in the next chapter.

CHAPTER 5

Educating Dickens
Old Boys, Little Mothers, and school time

As long as the critically respected novel was defined as middle-class family reading, it was dominated by Charles Dickens. As we have seen, this model of reading puts the family novel in the place of the family Bible and imagines old and young savoring the same humor, pathos, and drama, and learning together, over and over again, the same moral lessons.[1] Dickens's long career, however, saw the emergence of a new critical model that moved reading from the mixed-age space of the home to the age-leveled space of the school. At the start of Dickens's career, hostile reviewers claimed he was not a gentleman; by the end of his career, they claimed he was not an adult. Dickens's mixed-age domestic audience had not changed, but its critical status had. During his lifetime, age-leveled critical standards spread from children's literature to the novel in general. In addition to the familiar claims of the young, we see the emerging claims of a new figure: the adult reader. The ideal version of this reader is the professional intellectual, an ideal powerfully articulated by critics such as George Eliot and George Henry Lewes. Critics who understood themselves as being and as advocating for this new kind of reader struggled, with increasing frustration, to make sense of Dickens. Even Dickens himself eventually mocks the standards of family reading through the account in *Our Mutual Friend* (1864–65) of Podsnappery, the adult's self-serving suppression of unwelcome realities on the pretext of shielding "the Young Person."

Although Dickens resembles Barbauld, Edgeworth, and Scott in thinking of good novels as family reading, his idea of family differs from theirs. As we have seen, these writers imagine the middle-class family home as the place where adults educate children according to a carefully age-leveled scale charting the growth of reason in a commercial world. Their parents teach their children how to think, how to read, and how to shop. In contrast, families in Dickens tend to be bundles of bizarre developmental trajectories held together by a commitment to gender difference: his novels swarm with Little Mothers and Old Boys. He does sometimes try to chart the kind of steady psychological development towards stable adulthood that is advocated by the continental bildungsroman and by English critics such as George Eliot and George Henry Lewes. However, he is more often drawn to the scrambling of age categories. In individual characters, Dickens presents strikingly random combinations of responsibilities, freedoms, internal qualities, and numerical age, combinations that may be pathetic, grotesque, attractive, or comic, or all of these things at once.

Dickens sometimes uses such figures to call for social reform – but he does not, as we might expect, use them to protest against child labor. By the early twentieth century a new age-leveled map of public space had become visible: adults, or at least adult men, belonged in the workplace, and children, especially boys, belonged in schools. It is at this point that "child labor" at last became a disturbing oxymoron, and the figure of the factory child came to represent all of the injustice of the Industrial Revolution. But Dickens does not write about factory children. Although age is important for Dickens, he still does not consistently divide people up by age as either students or workers.

"The same keen and wonderful faculty"

Because children's literature was a thriving business in Dickens's time, some critics wonder why he had very little to do with it. For example, Michael Patrick Hearn feels "it is surprising that Dickens did not write more, and better, books for boys and girls."[2] One reason may well be Dickens's greater commitment to the model of family reading than to an age-leveled literary world. As we have seen, children's literature imagines two specialized readers: the child and the adult. As Perry Nodelman reminds us, although addressed to a child reader, the genre seeks the approval of a "hidden adult," one who believes in a deeply meaningful distinction between what children and adults ought to read.[3] The contrast between these two perspectives energizes this writing. Dickens himself occasionally wrote for this specialized market. The most significant example is *Holiday Romance* (1868), a novella written on commission for the children's monthly *Our Young Folks*, which offered this preview in December 1867: "Charles Dickens has written a story *for you alone*. Although he has written so beautifully about children and in their service, he has very seldom written for them."[4] *Holiday Romance* consists of four stories supposedly written by four children ranging in age from "half-past six" to nine. Unlike Dickens's novels, it is structured by interest in the gap between the perceptions of children and of adults.

Although commissioned by and advertised for the children's market, *A Holiday Romance*'s best readers are in fact adults. It deliberately privileges a self-consciously adult perspective, relying for its humor on the adult reader understanding what the children do not. Dickens himself notes this fact, writing "I hope it is droll, and very childlike; though the joke is a grown-up one." The opening lines give a fair sense of how such "grown-up" humor works:

> THIS beginning-part is not made out of anybody's head, you know. It's real. You must believe this beginning-part more than what comes after, else you won't understand how what comes after came to be written. You must believe it all; but you must believe this most, please. I am the editor of it. Bob Redforth (he's my cousin, and shaking the table on purpose) wanted to be the editor of it; but I said he shouldn't because he couldn't. HE has no idea of being an editor.[5]

The amusing naiveté of *A Holiday Romance* is not aimed at the child reader, imagined as equally naive, but rather at an adult reader, the only reader sophisticated enough to get the joke. Here Nodelman's hidden adult is barely hiding at all. Dickens laughed and cried while writing the piece, and passed it around to friends who reacted in the same way. Such readers find this kind of humor both funny and moving because they are interested in a gap between the child's and the adult's perception.

Unlike most of Dickens's other shorter works and novels, however, *A Holiday Romance* was not a success with its contemporary public.[6] It was reprinted in full only in the twentieth century, perhaps because by then works such as E. Nesbit's *The Treasure-Seekers* (1899) and Richmal Crompton's *Just William* (1922) had popularized the device of the entertainingly naive child narrator. In contrast, Dickens's wildly popular novels and stories do not privilege an adult perspective but rather concentrate on the unified audience of family reading. In fact, while adults were the best readers of the novella that Dickens wrote for a children's magazine, children were some of the best readers of his novels in general. As Hearn notes, "Of course all of [Dickens's] massive novels were devoured in their day as eagerly by children as by their parents, for at that time the great divorce between juvenile and adult literature had not yet been finalized."[7] For example, William Makepeace Thackeray's two daughters were avid Dickens fans. Thackeray describes how, at ten years old, one not only reads but re-reads Dickens independently:

> All children ought to love him . . . I know one who when she is happy reads *Nicholas Nickleby*; when she is unhappy reads *Nicholas Nickleby*; when she is tired reads *Nicholas Nickleby*; when she is in bed reads *Nicholas Nickleby*;

> when she has nothing to do reads *Nicholas Nickleby*; and when she has finished the book reads *Nicholas Nickleby* over again. This candid young critic, at ten years of age, said: "I like Mr Dickens's books much better than your books, Papa."

"Lucky is he who has such a charming gift of nature as this," concludes Thackeray, "which brings all the children in the world trooping to him, and being fond of him."[8] Neither the content nor the style of Dickens's novels aims to exclude these troops of children and redefine their implied reader as an adult.

Dickens describes his own childhood self as reading not the new age-leveled children's literature that was already popular with politically progressive or socially ambitious parents, nor the kind of genteel family reading that he himself would popularize so successfully. Instead, sometime between the ages of five and nine, he read his father's collection of mainly eighteenth-century novels; Dickens gives these books to the young David Copperfield as well. This collection was not adapted for children. Dickens remembers this reading as an intensely private experience, not part of an educational family circle: "the picture" that "always rises in my mind" is a small boy "sitting on my bed, reading as if for life." Like generations before him, Dickens had a father who assumed his son would read his books. Like Walter Scott, Dickens includes eighteenth-century novels with sexual content in his own much-cherished memories of childhood reading:

> From that blessed little room, *Roderick Random*, *Peregrine Pickle*, *Humphrey Clinker*, *Tom Jones*, the *Vicar of Wakefield*, *Don Quixote*, *Gil Blas*, and *Robinson Crusoe* came out, a glorious host, to keep me company. They kept alive my fancy, and my hope of something beyond that place and time, – they, and the *Arabian Nights*, and the *Tales of the Genii*.[9]

In this recollection, a nineteenth-century sensibility that values genteel family reading wrestles with the awareness that an earlier, much-loved reading experience was distinctly less genteel. Surprisingly, Dickens's response is a kind of age-leveling that reverses our own habits: he suggests that sexually explicit novels are fine for children, but not for adults. As it so often does, the issue of propriety crystallizes around *Tom Jones*. These novels "did me no harm; for whatever harm was in some of them, *I* knew nothing of it . . . I have been Tom Jones (a child's Tom Jones, a harmless creature) for a week together."[10] A "child's Tom Jones" is harmless because he is able to identify with a character who has sexual experiences without recognizing these experiences as sexual. As he works out his own model of genteel family reading, however, Dickens is even happier expatiating on being a sexless Robinson Crusoe for ever than on being a harmless Tom Jones for a time.

In its very title, Dickens's lyrical essay "Where We Stopped Growing" both acknowledges and rejects the expectation that people grow as readers across time, the expectation that shapes both children's literature and the adult novel. Dickens argues that the adult is a good reader insofar as he defies this expectation and retains a child's emotional response to texts. In particular, Dickens insists that as an adult he keeps his childhood habit of identification with central characters. Like Rousseau's Emile, Dickens's childhood self did not so much read *Robinson Crusoe* as become Robinson Crusoe. But Dickens feels more nostalgia than Rousseau at the prospect of leaving Crusoe's sexless island. Dickens claims that he stopped growing at the point when Crusoe and all of his goods "fit" him perfectly:

> We have never grown the thousandth part of an inch out of Robinson Crusoe. He fits us just as well, and in exactly the same way, as when we were among the smallest of the small . . . Never sail we, idle, in a little boat, and hear the rippling water at the prow, and look upon the land, but we know our boat-growth stopped for ever, when Robinson Crusoe sailed round the Island.[11]

As Robert Louis Stevenson's *Child's Garden of Verses* will proclaim, there is no bark like a book. This is the same little boat that will drift through *The Wind in the Willows* (1908), carried by the same irresistible current of Romantic nostalgia that flows from the mighty ocean of the "Immortality Ode" through the children's literature of Victorian and Edwardian England. "On these magic shores children at play are for ever beaching their coracles. We too have been there; we can still hear the sound of the surf, though we shall land no more," writes J. M. Barrie of Never Never Land. In this investment in an idealized child reader, "When We Stopped Growing" suggests the possible distance between an interest in childhood and a commitment to a set of age-leveled norms crowned by adulthood.

In contrast to Dickens's nostalgic focus on childhood, the bildungsroman tends to value adolescence, as we saw in the previous chapter. Both adolescence and adulthood are psychological categories of development in that they both focus, not on movement through a social world, but on mapping an inner self. We shall explore later how, in Dickens's lifetime, advanced literary critics such as George Henry Lewes and advanced novelists such as George Eliot began to insist that the study of such psychological development should give value to novels as well as to individual lives. By this standard Dickens often came up lacking, as later critics also point out: "There is no point in comparing Dickens's conversions . . . with the slow and often eddying movement traced in George Eliot or Henry James," notes Barbara Hardy.[12] G. K. Chesterton puts this claim more baldly: Dickens is "never successful in describing psychological change."[13] Franco Moretti argues that because Dickens transforms the dire external circumstances of his waifs rather than their inner lives, his novels are more fairy tale than bildungsroman, offering the pleasures of wish fulfillment through miraculous reversals of fortune rather than the detailed examination of psychological growth.[14]

Dickens's earliest novels most openly embrace the idea that character and perception do not change in essentials over time. These novels celebrate when we stopped growing. Little in the central characters of *Oliver Twist* or *Nicholas Nickleby* tempts critics even to look for developmental psychology. Young Oliver is richly readable as an ideal Romantic child, or an allegorical figure for innocence, or a fantasy of middle-class incorruptibility, or a melodramatic appeal for social reform, but not as a study in emotional, sexual, or cognitive growth. So remarkably compelling is the model of the bildungsroman, however, that at times critics have tried to read even the irrepressibly episodic *Pickwick Papers* in terms of it. Sometimes the middle-aged Mr. Pickwick's engagement of Sam Weller becomes his long-overdue moment of psychological development. *Pickwick*'s sales took off with the introduction of Sam, and it is true that Pickwick then becomes a more interesting character as well as one with more moral authority. But the story does not find itself when Pickwick engages Sam because in that moment Pickwick becomes an adult, but rather because in that moment he becomes a master. As Bruce Robbins notes, Mr. Pickwick and Sam Weller are the last of the English novel's great master–servant pairs, a line that stretches back through Pamela Andrews and Mr. B. all the way to Friday and Robinson Crusoe.[15]

Even more often, critics transform *Pickwick* into a bildungsroman by focusing on Pickwick's encounter with the injustice of debtor's prison. If Pickwick were moving towards adulthood, the Fleet would certainly be a likely turning-point. As Philip Rogers points out, however, the starving debtors are in fact a mere bump on Pickwick's picaresque road rather than a "formative stage in a continuous, cumulative process of moral *Bildung*."[16] Pickwick remains an "elderly child," the most sustained, positive version in Dickens's canon of the scrambling of age categories that fascinates him throughout his career.[17]

Dickens does eventually write a version of the bildungsroman, producing novels that focus on a very young central character who manages to grow up by the last page. In comparison to the continental bildungsroman, however, even *David Copperfield* and *Great Expectations* can seem psychologically crude. The bildungsroman often has a strong autobiographical element, but although it is clearly a portrait of the young novelist, *David Copperfield* does not consistently chart the kind of psychological development that is central to this genre, and important to the critical standards of later nineteenth-century realism more broadly. In his autobiographical fragment on the same personal history he uses in *David Copperfield*, Dickens himself suggests that these criteria were not altogether his. Dickens does not chart important changes in his own psyche, he implies, because nothing important ever changed. The nine-year-old Dickens was a miniature version of the established novelist: "Whatever was comical in this scene, and whatever was pathetic," Dickens writes of his father and his father's friends happily signing a useless petition in debtor's prison, "I sincerely believe I perceived in my corner, whether I demonstrated or not [*sic*], quite as well as I should perceive it now."[18] Charles Forster's biography stresses Dickens's ageless perception of London, his insight into "the character and weaknesses of the grown-up people around him":

> "I certainly understood it," he has often said to me, "quite as well then as I do now." . . . It seems almost too much to assert of a child, say at nine or ten years old, that his observation of everything was as close and good, or that he had as much intuitive understanding of the character and weaknesses of the grown-up people around him, as when the same keen and wonderful faculty had made him famous among men. But my experience of him led me to put implicit faith in the assertion he unvaryingly himself made.[19]

Like the elderly children and childish elders who populate his novels, Dickens himself can be so fixed as to seem unstable. What Forster's *Life* presents as precocity was also seen as retardation by a reviewer. Robert Buchanan in 1872 links academic and psychological growth, and sees Dickens as incapable of either:

> Charles Dickens, having crushed into his childish experience a whole world of sorrow and humorous insight, so loaded his soul that he never grew any older. He was a great, grown-up, dreamy, impulsive child . . . He saw all from a child's point of view – strange, odd, queer, puzzling . . . all in the childish fashion . . . even that hard circle [of English literary culture] began to love the quaint, questioning, querulous, mysterious guest, who would *not* become a pupil.[20]

Whatever Dickens's own life may represent to such critics, with its unending energy, failed marriage, and late "dark" reform-minded novels, it is not age-leveled growth structured by a school curriculum, or the continental bildungsroman's double compensation of domestic happiness and professional success for the loss of the political world.

Of all Dickens's heroes, Pip perhaps comes the closest to the kind of growth central to the bildungsroman. When Pip describes the succession of stage coaches that takes him away from his childhood home, for example, he evokes that genre's lyrical sense of irrevocable change. Here the "we" of the coach's passengers becomes the "we" of the bildungsroman, intensifying the genre's forward-looking excitement with backward glances at a forever-vanishing home: "We changed again, and yet again, and it was now too late and too far to go back, and I went on."[21] Unlike many Dickens heroes, Pip does in fact change internally as well as externally, growing from a loving child into a snob. Nevertheless, Dickens also presents him as in essence unchanging, and not merely by making him speak impeccable English from his village childhood onwards. Even worse than his infatuation with Estella, the great error of Pip's life is his failure to value properly Joe Gargery, an error that he rights on recovering from his near-fatal illness and brush with (yet again) debtor's prison. Dickens does not, however, say that Pip achieves through time and suffering a new, adult understanding, but rather that time and suffering return Pip to the original and correct perceptions of his very earliest childhood. And one measure of Joe's goodness is that he himself does not grow in any way throughout all the eventful years that separate his time with young Pip and their final reunion: "There was no change whatever in Joe. Exactly what he had been in my eyes then, he was in my eyes still; just as simply faithful, and as simply right."[22] In this assertion that both Joe himself and Pip's view of Joe are "exactly" what they were decades ago, Dickens argues for the continuity of perception across a lifetime against more age-leveled expectations.

While Scott foregrounds the individual's growth as a miniature version of national development, Dickens is interested in age in and of itself, independent of a national referent. But he is not fascinated by adulthood, the endpoint of the bildungsroman's developmental story. Dickens's novels usually describe growing backwards more energetically than they describe growing up. As critics such as Claudia Nelson have noted, for Dickens, age categories are "by no means stable," and they are most interesting, in both positive and negative ways, when they take on each other's attributes.[23] Examining the careless wish that a pretty child might never grow up, Dickens remarks that in making such wishes, "the imagination" does not "enter into such details as the picturing of childhood come to old age, or of old age carried back to childhood."[24] His own imagination, however, enters very eagerly into just such details. Even the ancient woodwork of the Six Jolly Fellowship Porters "seemed in its old age fraught with confused memories of its youth . . . Not without reason was it often asserted by the regular frequenters of the Porters, that when the light shone full upon . . . an old corner cupboard of walnut-wood in the bar, you might trace little forests there, and tiny trees like the parent tree, in full umbrageous leaf."[25]

In contrast to the bildungsroman's focus on the adolescent, Dickens is drawn to the extremes of childhood and old age, preferably in bizarre combinations. In his work people as well as paneling enact the implosion of these stages of life, sometimes in fairy-tale language. That "horrible young changeling," David and Dora Copperfield's incompetent boy servant, grows like a human version of Jack's beanstalk in David's strangely preoccupied imagination, hurtling towards old age:

> I watched him as he grew – and he grew like scarlet beans – with painful apprehensions of the time when he would begin to shave; even of the days when he would be bald or grey. I saw no prospect of ever getting rid of him; and, projecting myself into the future, used to think what an inconvenience he would be when he was an old man.[26]

Even crossing the Channel has a way of playing tricks with age: "Unless it be a delusion born of my giddy flight, the grown-up people and the children seem to change places in France. In general, the boys and girls are little old men and women, and the men and women lively boys and girls."[27]

Childhood and old age merge perhaps most spectacularly in the horrifying reprise of the finale of the traditional Ages of Man that *Bleak House* stages at the Smallweed's tea table. The four Smallweeds are neither children nor adults, but rather a vividly imagined pack of "old faces . . . hover[ing] over the teacups, like a company of ghastly cherubim." As their family name suggests, the growth of a Smallweed is at once too fast and too slow, populating their family tree exclusively with "little old men and women."[28] The prime of life is missing from the Smallweed family, leaving only grandparents and grandchildren.[29] Obsessed with trivets and shrieking about pound notes, senile Grandmother Smallweed has the strongest claim to carry old age back to childhood: "There has been only one child in the Smallweed family for several generations. Little old men and women there have been, but no child, until Mr Smallweed's grandmother, now living, became weak in her intellect, and fell (for the first time) into a childish state." Conversely, at the age of ten, Judy Smallweed is already too old to be a child: "She once or twice fell into children's company when she was about ten years old, but the children couldn't get on with Judy, and Judy couldn't get on with them. She seemed like an animal of another species, and there was instinctive repugnance on both sides." The Smallweeds are not even properly human, but rather a regressive throwback through the evolutionary family tree: "the house of Smallweed, always early to go out and late to marry . . . has had no child born to it and . . . the complete little men and women whom it has produced have been observed to bear a likeness to old monkeys with something depressing on their minds."[30] In resembling old monkeys, the Smallweeds suggest post-Darwinian ideas of human development; in particular, they suggest the fears of racial degeneration that were increasingly popularized in the later nineteenth century by such writers as Max Nordau, Cesare Lombroso, Havelock Ellis, and Henry Maudsley.[31] In such writing, the habit of imagining the history of mankind and the history of the individual in terms of each other takes a more ominous form than it held for writers influenced by conjectural history.

In contrast to such age-scrambled nightmares, Dickens also presents the crossing of childhood and old age in an idealized tableau, as in the wanderings of the precocious Little Nell and her child-like grandfather. "It is true that in many respects I am the child, and she the grown person – that you have seen already," this grandfather candidly remarks in the first chapter of *The Old Curiosity Shop*.[32] For Dickens, the reversal of childhood and old age can be as beautiful as it can be grotesque; Little Nell's grandfather is only one of the many Dickens men cared for by little girls with the author's evident approval. Whether they are ugly or charming, such age reversals are always interesting to Dickens. But although age fascinates Dickens, adulthood does not.

"The child's (I don't mean Skimpole's) rhyme"

For Dickens, not developmental psychology but rather nineteenth-century domestic ideology finally defines both his readers and his characters. His novels affirm that the true womanliness and manliness of the middle class trump the decaying prestige of aristocrats like Lord Verisopht and Lady Tippens. In terms of their readership as well as in how they represent age, these novels subordinate the difference between the world of adults and the world of children to the domestic space and the gender roles that middle-class adults and middle-class children share. Dickens delights in the unchanging girl-woman, and worries over the equally static but often much more troubling boy-man. Dickens's focus on a static sense of gender reflects his historical distance from a twenty-first century ideal of adulthood that is less strongly marked by gender. Winthrop Jordan observes that both Dickens's England and Antebellum America were "not concerned with any bimodality between childhood and maturity, but rather with proper roles within the home." The difference that mattered most was the difference between manhood and womanhood, not the difference between adulthood and childhood. Nineteenth-century ideas of the distinct and complementary natures of manhood and of womanhood "perceptually overrode adulthood."[33] In Dickens and in the family reading that followed in his wake, maturity was a quite different thing for Little Mothers and for Old Boys. He is interested in how social expectations, and labor in particular, relate to age. But manliness and womanliness easily trump any non-gendered notion of the adult.

I will examine first some of the positive versions of Dickens's trajectory-twisting sense of age, characters whose static nature is seen as a good thing. Many, although not all, of these positive figures are feminine. As critics since G. K. Chesterton have pointed out, Dickens frequently embodies nineteenth-century domestic ideals in what he sees as the deeply satisfying figure of the Little Mother, a figure whose nurturing identity does not change in any important way across her lifetime.[34] I want to focus here, not so much on the domestic ideology to which these unchanging figures conform, as on the basic fact that they do not change. Little Motherhood transcends social class as well as time, blurring the difference between paid and unpaid domestic labor. Any girl working in any household is likely to be an appealing character with womanly, homelike qualities in Dickens. He has a keen eye for the possible misery of children performing domestic work – but such work never does his girls any permanent harm whatsoever. In this sense the Little Mother's premature responsibility is not really premature at all. Those who work outside the home, however, are a much more unsavory lot.

A "follower's" orphaned daughter, thirteen-year-old Charley Neckett is a working-class Little Mother, laboring in the Smallweed's vile home to support herself and her two younger siblings. As Trooper George remarks, she singlehandedly manages to "give the house almost a wholesome look." Charley's "motherly, womanly" bonnet, apron, and manner do not fit her numerical age, but they do express her nature perfectly:

> a very little girl, childish in figure but shrewd and older-looking in the face – pretty-faced too – wearing a womanly sort of bonnet much too large for her, and drying her bare arms on a womanly sort of apron . . . The little girl

> took it [baby Emma], in a womanly sort of manner belonging to the apron and the bonnet . . . "Then he's as good as gold," said the little creature – O, in such a motherly, womanly way![35]

Although Charley is "shrewd and older-looking in the face," we are assured that she is "pretty-faced too." She is precocious in financially supporting and nurturing younger siblings at the carefully specified age of thirteen, but her "motherly, womanly" nature is presented as natural, positive, and ageless. She is a pathetic figure because her burdens are so great, but she is also an intensely appealing one, a Little Mother rather than a freak. This static sense of womanliness stands in strong and reassuring contrast to the politically active, intellectually ambitious, or sexually irregular middle-class women who stray from their domestic role elsewhere in Dickens's novels.[36]

David Copperfield's Agnes Wickfield is a middle-class Little Mother. Like so many of Dickens's heroines, she is from early childhood responsible for a weak father, one who could sincerely declare along with Little Nell's grandfather that "It is true that in many respects I am the child, and she the grown person." Little Dorrit and her father present the same tableau, and Lizzie Hexam and the Gaffer are a late variation on it. As a Little Mother, Agnes does not develop. She has always been "the Agnes whom we know," as David crushingly informs Dora Spenlow when she wonders whether she might learn to imitate Agnes's virtues: "Agnes has had her father to take care of for these many years, you should remember. Even when she was quite a child, she was the Agnes whom we know."[37] Because Agnes has been her father's "little housekeeper" ever since she stepped into her dead mother's place, she has never once set foot in a classroom:

> "You have never been to school," I said, "have you?"
> "Oh yes! Every day."
> "Ah, but you mean here, at your own home?"
> "Papa couldn't spare me to go anywhere else," she answered, smiling and shaking her head. "His housekeeper must be in his house, you know."

Her tranquil brightness exists outside time; as a child encouraging David with his homework and as a wife encouraging him with his novels, Agnes is always the same: "I see her, with her modest, orderly, placid manner, and I hear her beautiful calm voice, as I write these words. The influence for all good, which she came to exercise over me at a later time, begins already to descend upon my breast."[38] Dora, of course, is the reverse image of Agnes:

equally unchanging, she is forever an incompetent "child-wife" rather than a supernaturally competent Little Mother.

When viewed through a developmental paradigm, this unchanging Little Mother has an eerie, Dorian Gray-like quality. Nearly half a century before Wilde hides Dorian's portrait in the attic, Dickens hangs Agnes's portrait on the parlor wall. Living with such profoundly static characters, young David has some trouble telling the difference between people and their portraits. In the case of Agnes's father, all that is required is a second look:

> A gentleman entered, at sight of whom I turned to the first-mentioned portrait again, to make quite sure that it had not come out of its frame. But it was stationary; and as the gentleman advanced into the light, I saw that he was some years older than when he had had his picture painted.

Reassuringly, Mr. Wickfield is visibly older than his portrait. The portrait of Mrs. Wickfield, however, is also a portrait of her daughter, and this slightly gothic cross-generational likeness helps scramble any idea of change across time. David imagines that the portrait grew older while Agnes remained a child: "It seemed to my imagination as if the portrait had grown womanly, and the original remained a child." Rather than growing old and ugly as Dorian's does, Agnes's portrait grows "womanly." But both portraits externalize a sense of change that must be excluded from the person in question, but that cannot be excluded from the story as a whole. How can David describe a little girl growing up to be a woman if she has been supremely womanly all along? His answer is to say she becomes the perfect image of a portrait:

> And the little girl I saw on that first day at Mr. Wickfield's, where is she? Gone also. In her stead, the perfect likeness of the picture, a child likeness no more, moves about the house; and Agnes . . . the better angel of the lives of all who come within her calm, good, self-denying influence – is quite a woman.[39]

Agnes has become "the perfect likeness of the picture." A similarly elaborate and displaced version of growth happens with Charley Neckett. In this case it is her own sister who makes it possible to describe Charley growing up and nevertheless to "suppose Time to have stood still." Emma becomes the perfect likeness of what her sister was: "So far as my small maid is concerned, I might suppose Time to have stood for seven years as still as the mill did half an hour ago; since little Emma, Charley's sister, is exactly what Charley used to be."[40]

For Dickens, Little Mothers are charmingly pathetic figures, undamaged but rendered more interesting by their early experiences of work and responsibility for family members. Working-class Little Mothers may be "shrewd" like Charley, the Marchioness, or Jenny Wren, while middle-class little mothers are angelic like Nell or Agnes, but all of them are appealing. This is the same kind of appeal that Wendy Darling will have, absorbed in the midst of Neverland in darning the Lost Boys' socks and dosing them with imaginary medicine. As James Barrie remarks, "Wendy was every inch a woman, though there were not very many inches."[41] In contrast, to an observer who values gendered domestic ideals less and a developmental ideal of adulthood more, the Little Mother's precociousness is a kind of monstrosity. To Henry James, for example, Jenny Wren is "a little monster; she is deformed, unhealthy, unnatural; she belongs to the troop of hunchbacks, imbeciles, and precocious children who have carried on the sentimental business in all Mr. Dickens' novels; the little Nells, the Smikes, the Paul Dombeys."[42]

Dickens represents girls' non-domestic labor quite differently. That is, when he looks at working girls, what concerns him is not child labor or premature responsibility, but rather gender deviance. In *The Old Curiosity Shop* as well as in *Bleak House*, Dickens juxtaposes a good Little Mother with a bad female employer who has been unsexed as well as removed from the developmental timeline by working as a child at something other than domestic labor. Sally Brass and Judy Smallweed are both ugly, cruel employers, as unpleasant as their respective little household drudges, the Marchioness and Charley, are endearing. They both worked as children, Sally as a legal clerk for her father and Judy as an artificial flower-maker. Each also has a brother whom she closely resembles. Dickens remarks of the Marchioness that "There never was such an old-fashioned child in her looks and manner. She must have been at work from her cradle." Sally Brass is also marked by early labor: "having devoted herself from infancy to this one pursuit and study," she "could know but little of the world, otherwise than in connection with the law." Dick Swiveller links Sally Brass and the Marchioness as similarly "supernatural" figures. A woman who more-or-less passes as a "professional gentleman," Sally is as "supernatural" as the household's tiny cook and maid-of-all-work: "'This is a most remarkable and supernatural sort of house!' said Mr Swiveller, as he walked into the office with the bill in his hand. 'She-dragons in the business, conducting themselves like professional gentlemen; plain cooks of three feet high appearing mysteriously from underground.'"[43] The Marchioness, however, will become Dick's fairy-tale savior, nursing him through a dangerous illness with motherly skill. She is supernaturally good at being feminine, that is, supernaturally natural, according to domestic ideals. She ends up married in an idyllic suburban cottage, exerting a steadying influence on the no-longer swiveling Dick.

In contrast, Sally remains a dragon to the last. Rumors fly that she has become ever more masculine: "Some said with confidence that she had gone down to the docks in male attire, and had become a female sailor; others darkly whispered that she had enlisted as a private in the second regiment of Foot Guards . . . There were many such whispers as these in circulation."[44] In fact, Sally is last glimpsed in exile from all domestic spaces, out on the street where no good girl should be. Together with her brother, Sally becomes not a soldier or a sailor, but rather a kind of allegorical figure of national ruin, as do street children in *Bleak House*, *Household Words*, and *A Christmas Carol*. The once merely ugly and greedy Brass twins now become obscene specters, "the embodied spirits of Disease, and Vice, and Famine":

> These forms were never beheld but in those nights of cold and gloom, when the terrible spectres, who lie at all other times in the obscene hiding-places of London, in archways, dark vaults and cellars, venture to creep into the streets; the embodied spirits of Disease, and Vice, and Famine. It was whispered . . . that these were Sampson and his sister Sally; and to this day, it is said, they sometimes pass, on bad nights, in the same loathsome guise, close at the elbow of the shrinking passenger.[45]

Sally and Sampson Brass embody the same social fears and the rhetorical figures that cluster around street children for Dickens and for his reform-minded contemporaries. Lurking in kennels and eating offal, they degenerate from human to wolfish animal. They recall the child-figures of Ignorance and Poverty hiding in the robe of Father Christmas, foreboding the doom of mankind:

> Where graceful youth should have filled their features out, and touched them with its freshest tints, a stale and shrivelled hand, like that of age, had pinched, and twisted them . . . Where angels might have sat enthroned, devils lurked, and glared out menacing. No change, no degradation, no perversion of humanity, in any grade, through all the mysteries of wonderful creation, has monsters half so horrible and dread.[46]

These figures seem to be both religious types of eternal sin and modish examples of monstrous degeneration, suggesting thrilling vistas of geological time, like the Megalosaurus waddling through the opening pages of *Bleak House*. Similarly, in contrast to Charley, the natural Little Mother,

Judy Smallweed, the former artificial flower-maker, is freakish rather than feminine, resembling her equally horrible twin brother rather than a motherly ideal. But Judy is even more like a monkey than she is like a man: "she so happily exemplifies the before-mentioned family likeness to the monkey tribe, that, attired in a spangled robe and cap, she might walk about the table-land on the top of a barrel-organ without exciting much remark as an unusual specimen."[47] Although she has never worked in the streets of London, Judy has worked outside the home. Like Sally, she embodies the anxieties that were common about the moral and even racial degeneration of such working girls.[48] Whether or not they engaged in prostitution, the girls who worked for a living among the mostly male young peddlers, crossing-sweepers, and other street children were clearly not Little Mothers. While Charley is agelessly feminine, Judy is geologically old: "In the active superintendence of this young person, Judy Smallweed appears to attain a perfectly geological age and to date from the remotest periods."[49]

The stasis that Dickens's Little Mothers and Old Boys share has very different consequences for each in terms of labor. While his good girls work hard from cradle to grave, Dickens allows some men to remain boys at play forever – but only if they can afford it. Dickens describes men who are entitled to perpetual leisure, not as aristocrats, but rather as lucky children. The Old Boy who is independently wealthy and philanthropically inclined, such as *Bleak House*'s aptly named Boythorn, does not conform to developmental age standards for heterosexual manhood, or any other sort of manhood, but neither is he condemned as immature or freakish.[50] Boythorn is a wealthy, good-hearted and impulsive permanent bachelor who likes talking about his schooldays. Mr. Pickwick is another wealthy and benevolent Old Boy, who no more works than he grows up, and whose permanent childishness is presented as a good thing. After leaving the debt-ridden Mr. Micawber, who is forever "confused" about their relative ages, David Copperfield finds himself in yet another age-scrambled relationship at his aunt's house. His dealings with Mr. Dick are on "this odd footing: that, while Mr. Dick came professedly to look after me as my guardian, he always consulted me in any little matter of doubt that arose, and invariably guided himself by my advice."[51] Mr. Dick has an independent income: although mentally incompetent, he is a thoroughly good Old Boy. The boyishness of grown men who do not possess independent wealth, however, presents a real problem.

"The little old woman of the child's (I don't mean Skimpole's) Rhyme," Mr. Jarndyce flounders, momentarily associating Esther Summerson, one of Dickens's best Little Mothers, with Harold Skimpole, probably the very worst of his Old Boys.[52] While a static sense of character may avoid gender anxieties about un-domestic women, it has the opposite effect regarding the parallel problem of the feckless or sexually irregular middle-class man. Little Mothers may be naturally suited to morally sustain the home, but if Old Boys refuse to become professional men and support families, the whole domestic project languishes in debtors' prison. Impecunious Old Boys are a disturbing sight: "He had more the appearance, in all respects, of a damaged young man, than a well-preserved elderly one," Esther remarks of the indolent Skimpole, describing his appearance as "a romantic youth who had undergone some unique process of depreciation." Lazy Mr. Turveydrop, who fantasizes about being the bosom companion of the Prince of Wales, is even stranger and even harder to place on any scale of age: "He was not like youth, he was not like age, he was not like anything in the world but a model of Deportment."[53] Juxtaposing Skimpole and Charley, Esther describes them as opposing varieties of childhood: "he was such a mirthful child by the side of the graver childhood we had seen, that he made my Guardian smile." Although Mr. Jarndyce smiles at "that elderly young gentleman," after seeing his impoverished family, we clearly are not meant to.[54]

"The strongest and the strangest opposition"

Today we are likely to assume a certain understanding of age and labor, the clear-cut division that informs Sarah Cleghorn's devastating quatrain in 1916: "The *golf links* lie *so* near the *mill* / That almost every day / The laboring *children* can look out / And see the *men* at play."[55] Here adulthood (or at least manhood) and childhood are assumed to be distinct states, and the difference between them is properly marked by entrance into the labor force – and entrance into a factory, a space dedicated to labor alone. When social class overrides this trajectory and makes children work while men play, the effect is grotesque. Dickens, however, does not share this understanding of labor as appropriate to adults only. His view of age and labor is instead largely traditional. Most English children had always worked in homes, farms, or workshops – often under extremely dangerous conditions. Throughout the eighteenth and much of the nineteenth centuries, the labor of such children was either taken for granted or praised by wealthier observers.

Dickens combines approval of such working children with enthusiasm for a Romantic ideal of the child – a combination that was also unexceptional for his time. As Hugh Cunningham observes, an opposition between Romantic childhood and child labor was less important in the nineteenth century than it became in the twentieth century, as a long, complicated process of historical change was rephrased as a simple and compelling story about rescuing children from factories. By the end of the First World War, the spectacle of little children laboring in the mills of the Industrial Revolution became central to the story of the growth of a liberal social conscience.[56] Some readers may seem to remember this story in Dickens. For example, some sociologists now reject the very phrase "child labor" as "fogged-over with too many Dickensian images to permit clear view."[57] Yet Dickens did not actually supply these Dickensian images. He was a notable friend of childhood and of various kinds of social reform, but he did not view work as an adult realm, or see child labor as a violation of children's rights.

On an everyday basis, the working children Dickens himself saw were not in "the mill" but in more traditional roles: in domestic service, in the streets, or on the stage. These are the working children who typically figure in his novels. *Nicholas Nickleby*'s Smike and *The Old Curiosity Shop*'s Marchioness demonstrate Dickens's awareness of the hard labor of child domestic servants, and may also suggest that there is something a bit puzzling to him about their age. These characters do not know how old they are. As a hulking boy, Smike still wears an infant's neck frill, and the mystery of the Marchioness's age is the subject of Dick Swiveller's elaborate fantasies. In comic and tragic registers, *Nicholas Nickleby*'s gin-guzzling Infant Phenomenon and *Bleak House*'s semi-savage Jo may also suggest a similar sense of puzzlement. This sense is not, however, the same thing as the twentieth-century critique of child labor. Although children working in domestic service, theatres, or streets caught Dickens's attention, what he objects to is particularly unkind treatment of them. He does not suggest that working for a living is in and of itself inappropriate for any child. Charley Neckett, for example, is rescued from being the Smallweed's small drudge by becoming Esther Summerson's "little maid." Dickens's autobiographical fragment about his time in Warrens's blacking warehouse refers bitterly to "some young relation of Mealy's – I think his little sister – [who] did imps in the pantomimes" at Drury Lane. Dickens is not, however, disturbed by the employment of a working-class child in the theatre, but rather by the loss of status implied by his own association with such a person. Even when he returns later to theatrical children in *Household Words*' sympathetic piece, "Gaslight Fairies," he does not identify them as exploited because of their age. Rather, playing with the traditional description of fairies as "little people" Dickens calls pantomime performers of all ages a "class of small people" and "these little people."[58] He focuses in particular on a family that includes performers ranging in age from twenty-three to eight years old:

> I select Miss Fairy, aged three-and-twenty, lodging . . . with her mother, Mrs Fairy, disabled by chronic rheumatism in the knees; and with her father, Mr Fairy, principally employed in lurking about a public house . . . Miss Rosina Fairy, Miss Angelica Fairy, and Master Edmund Fairy, aged respectively, fourteen, ten, and eight . . . Miss Fairy has an engagement of twelve shillings a week . . . at this time of year the three young Fairies have a nightly engagement to come out of a Pumpkin as French soldiers.[59]

Although their different ages are carefully noted, none of them marks any of these gaslight fairies as not properly employable. Dickens imagines sick and drunken parents as well as siblings "clinging to the spangled skirts, and contesting for the nightly shilling or two, of one little lop-sided, weak-legged Fairy."[60] It is not clear, however, whether this particular little weak-kneed fairy is in fact a woman or a child.[61]

Dickens's lack of sustained engagement with factory children may reflect their relative lack of visibility in his everyday life. It also seems related to his traditional, weakly age-leveled sense of labor. As Olga Nieuwenhuys points out, the rise of the very idea of "child labor" as a morally offensive or even a noteworthy category of work coincides with the rise of the factory: "From its inception, the notion of child labor was associated with factory work."[62] In contrast to the spaces where the great majority of children traditionally worked, the factory provided a new, unambiguous image for entering a labor force. Here the line between adulthood and childhood can be seen as the central division of human life.

When Dickens's attention was directed to factory children, he expressed concern and a desire to do something for them. After reading the Report of the Children's Employment Commission of 1843, for example, he was distressed enough to suggest "writing and bringing out a very cheap pamphlet called An Appeal to the People of England on Behalf of the Poor Man's Child, with my name attached, of course." But he did not.[63] "I mean to strike the heaviest blow in my power for these unfortunate creatures," Dickens writes to E. M. Fitzgerald in 1837, sympathizing with the Ten Hours Movement agitation to improve the lot of factory children.[64] But when Dickens really unleashes the heaviest blow in his power, we get the knock-out sentimental wallop of Jo the dying crossing-sweeper or Smike the dying Yorkshire school cripple. Although Little Nell travels through a landscape of demonic factories in *The Old Curiosity Shop*, and *Household Words* campaigns against factory children's mutilation and murder by improperly fenced-in industrial machinery, the unfortunate young creatures of the factories remain hard to find. None of his novels offers a sustained attack on child industrial labor.[65]

An 1838 reviewer feels that Dickens ought turn his attention from other vulnerable and suffering groups and write instead about children who work in factories:

> But there is a public crime more vast than either of these [the oppression of workhouse orphans and Yorkshire schoolboys, or milliner's slaves], and capable, from its peculiar character, of being put down, in whole or in part by legislative enactment. I mean, the *working little boys and girls to death in the factories.*[66]

This italicized protest strikes a note that will dominate by the turn of the century. Once a burden on the local squire, the children of the poor became imperial Britain's future.[67] Concern that factory children grew up unfit to serve the Empire helped to spur increased legislation on the closely related issues of child labor and education.[68] What Frances Trollope's *The Life and Adventures of Michael Armstrong, the Factory Boy* (1840) had called "hideous premature old age" was contrasted with the healthy, hard-working, military-ready adulthood created by a childhood in the country.[69] As the 1909 Minority Report of the Royal Commission on the Poor Laws (1905–9) claimed, the laboring town boy was a "'weedy', narrow-chested, stunted weakling, whom even the recruiting sergeant rejects and who succumbs prematurely to disease."[70] In this view, child labor disrupted progression through a set of age-leveled norms leading to healthy adulthood.

The fact that Dickens values a Romantic ideal of the child but does not generally oppose this ideal to child labor suggests the distance between an ideal figure and such a set of age-leveled norms. Judith Plotz has shown how social class framed Romantic childhood. When the child was meant to embody an ideal of rosy innocence, emotional responsiveness, and spiritual purity, it was all too easy to disqualify grimy, hard-bitten workers from the status of "real children" no matter how chronologically young they in fact happened to be.[71] For example, Dickens describes himself as a Romantic child who has been tragically misplaced among young workers at Warren's blacking warehouse. "It is wonderful to me how I could have been so easily cast away at such an age," he writes of his debt-ridden parents' decision to set him to work at eleven or twelve, "a child of singular abilities: quick eager, delicate, and soon hurt, bodily or mentally." Dickens's calm acceptance of boys such as Bob Fagin and Poll Green spending their childhoods in the blacking warehouse stands in marked contrast to his flaming outrage that he was "thrown away at such an age."[72]

What interests me here is the way that Dickens combines anxiety over status and anxiety over age. The class identity that Dickens feels himself losing on being set to work is also an age trajectory. Like children's literature, this middle-class sense of age focuses on a carefully calibrated and resource-intensive process of personal development, one that leads to material rewards as well as personal satisfaction. It is all about education. At the core of Dickens's fury is a longing for school:

> No words can express the secret agony of my soul as I sunk into this [working-class] companionship; compared these henceforth everyday associates with those of my happier childhood – not to say with Steerforth, Traddles, and the rest of those boys [at David Copperfield's old school]; and felt my hopes of growing up to be a learned and distinguished man, crushed in my bosom.[73]

In this sense, a boy is not just any young male person, but rather one who is in the process of becoming a "learned and distinguished" man: "the misery it was to my young heart to believe that day by day what I had learned, and thought, and delighted in, and raised my fancy and my emulation up by, would pass away from me, little by little, never to be brought back any more; cannot be written." Making matters worse, unlike the selflessly supportive sisters of his novels, Dickens's own sister remained a forward-looking schoolchild rather than disappearing as he did into the immediate needs of the family economy. While he sank into the blacking warehouse, she landed a scholarship at the Royal Academy of Music:

> I could not bear to think of myself – beyond the reach of all such honourable emulation and success. The tears ran down my face. I felt as if my heart were rent. I prayed, when I went to bed that night, to be lifted out of the humiliation and neglect in which I was. I never had suffered so much before. There was no envy in this.[74]

Once he escapes the blacking warehouse, Dickens's young stand-in, David, again aspires to being a distinguished professional. This aspiration, however, first requires re-establishing him within a framework of age-leveled developmental norms – which means going to school:

> It seemed to me so long, however, since I had been among such boys, or among any companions of my own age, except Mick Walker and Mealy Potatoes, that I felt as strange as ever I have done in my life. I was so conscious of having passed through scenes of which they could have no knowledge, and of having acquired experiences foreign to my age, appearance, and

> condition as one of them, that I half believed it was an imposture to come there as an ordinary little schoolboy.[75]

Dickens is conscious that a gap in perception separates him from the other schoolboys. It is caused by experiences that are foreign, not to an age-leveled norm for all children, but rather to the condition of being a schoolboy. In this moment social class is experienced and interpreted in terms of age. Studying his schoolbooks in Mr. Wickfield's beautiful old house under the domestic influence of Agnes, David imagines becoming again, not merely a schoolboy, but rather a boy: "I sat there, sturdily conning my books, until dinner-time (we were out of school for good at three); and went down, hopeful of becoming a passable sort of boy yet." "Although Mr. Micawber was just as much confused as ever about my age and standing, he always remembered, as a genteel thing, that I was a pupil of Doctor Strong's," David notes with amusement, but Mr. Micawber is not alone either in his confusion about age or in his reliance on school as a social marker.[76]

David's story may reflect not merely Dickens's own movement back and forth between the social categories of schoolchild and laborer, but also a larger uncertainty of his time in placing young people in these categories. Legislation making education compulsory was the most effective way to limit and ultimately eliminate child labor. Social historians have long pointed to the rise of children's toys and books as signs of the emergence of a "new world of childhood" throughout the eighteenth century, but it was state-sponsored universal compulsory schooling that gave this separate world its own territory. An important effect of such schools was "to remove children from the adult world . . . to distance the world of childhood from that of adulthood." While the "much-feared idle child of the eighteenth and early nineteenth century" had to be saved from the sin of dependency on his social superiors, the National schoolchild had to be saved from short-sighted exploitation by adults.[77] For the first time, in principle although not yet in practice, compulsory schooling and a minimum school-leaving age cut across all classes.

This separation of a children's world of school and an adult world of work took shape slowly and unevenly. Like most of his middle-class contemporaries, Dickens did not argue that all children should be students rather than workers. Instead, he claimed they should be both. He was one of the many enthusiastic supporters of the Short-Time system, a scheme to combine child labor with education that was started by the early Factory Acts and widespread by 1845. In *Household Words*, Dickens is part of the decades-long chorus that claimed, not that half-time education was better than none at all, nor that it was as good as full-time education, but rather that it was better than full-time education.[78] As Edwin Chadwick argued, "compulsory detention to mental instruction in all elementary schools should be limited to three hours daily," leaving time for exercise and for "the freedom for productive occupation of children."[79] Dickens's *Household Words* essay "The Short-Timers" (1861) presents this position even more cheerfully: "since the introduction of the Short-Time system it has been proved here that eighteen hours a week of book-learning are more profitable than thirty-six, and that the pupils are far quicker and brighter than of yore." Dickens argues that poor children find industrial work a refreshing break from the mental ardors of education, citing "the common sense of mankind," which recognizes that schoolboys become inattentive after lunch. Such education will produce better workers and household servants, and, above all, better soldiers. It "would make them part of England's glory, not its shame – of England's strength, not its weakness – would raise good soldiers and sailors, and good citizens, and many great men, out of the seeds of its criminal population."[80]

By the end of the nineteenth century, what Dickens saw as an ideal resolution had come to seem an infuriating contradiction. By the 1890s, the Short-Time system was largely discredited as "one of the most preposterous fallacies ever trotted out by an interested class to hoodwink the community." Exhausted half-time children who fell asleep at their desks not only presented a pathetic spectacle, but also lowered the overall test scores of those schools that combined them with full-time students.[81] Although not fully abolished until 1919, the system became increasingly untenable in the face of a new consensus that adults, or at least adult men, belonged in the workplace, while children, especially boys, belonged in school. Class difference remained important, of course. As late as 1899, even the Fabian children's writer E. Nesbit seems to agree that state-funded schooling would be worse than no school at all for the likable young heroes of *The Story of the Treasure Seekers*: "Then we left off going to school, and Father said we should go to a good school as soon as he could manage it," explains Oswald Bastable as the family fortunes collapse. The little Bastables actually observe a group of "Board School children" with some interest, but do not think of asking these "poor and needy" to join their own imaginative games. The Bastables are finally rewarded for their pluck and their unshakable sense of their own class identity with Rugby and Balliol, as well as with an orgy of Christmas feasting and presents: "This ending is like what happens in Dickens's books," Oswald blandly observes.[82]

Nevertheless, by the early twentieth century compulsory schooling, for the first time, grouped most children together in classrooms according to age rather than dispersing them throughout the working world. This change had a range of unanticipated consequences. Perhaps most relevant for theories of age is the fact that schoolchildren were ideal research subjects. Unlike Rousseau's one and only Emile, or Letitia Barbauld's singular Little Charles, National schoolchildren came in cohorts: "attention shifted from the individual middle-class baby to the mass of children, now available for inspection with the coming of compulsory schooling."[83] The burgeoning field of child-study was important to the growth of psychology as a professional discipline. Schools were re-imagined as places where age-cohorts advanced together, rather than places where bright or dull individual students found their proper level, regardless of age, as they had in the old elite public schools.[84] The first medical norms for physical and mental development were differentiated according to social class, describing the children of the poor as likely to be smaller, weaker, and intellectually slower than the children of the middle class. These were replaced by one set of universal age-leveled norms, describing the stages leading up to the healthy adult on whom Britain's future depended.

Dickens's educational satire takes on a new resonance in this context. As George Orwell points out, not only are factory children conspicuous by their absence in Dickens's novels, but a different figure appears instead – the schoolchild: "There are plenty of pictures of suffering children in his books, but usually they are suffering in schools rather than in factories."[85] Even *Hard Times*, which opens with all the fanfare of a novel devoted to the problem of the industrial worker and mentions a little girl whose arm was torn off by mill machinery, still ends by demanding kinder treatment of schoolchildren. Dickens's most sustained treatment of both factories and education, *Hard Times* as a whole teaches us to feel sympathy for the rationally educated children of Bounderby's friend Gradgrind, not the children laboring in Bounderby's factory. Although Dickens praises school as an alternative to a prematuring aging world of work in David Copperfield's case, he more often attacks it as a place that destroys Romantic childhood.

At first glance, Dickens might seem to illustrate the painful contrast between healthy military manhood and the stunted weakness of the industrial child laborer in *Bleak House*: while Trooper George radiates martial vigor, that "little, damaged man," Phil Squod, is a human catalog of the bodily ruin inflicted by the Industrial Revolution. A tinker's assistant at the age of eight, Phil worked in a number of other hazardous occupations. He explains that "what with a dozen years in a dark forge, where the men was given to larking; and what with being scorched in a accident at a gasworks; and what with being blowed out of winder, case-filling at the firework business; I am ugly enough to be made a show on!" This history has crippled and disfigured him: "Everything seems to have happened to his hands that could possibly take place, consistently with the retention of all the fingers; for they are notched, and seamed, and crumpled all over."[86] This former child laborer, however, does not really represent the kind of hideous premature old age that came to be associated with urban working children. He is extremely strong and healthy, extremely hard-working, and extremely good-natured; although small and damaged, he is a man, not an old child or a childish elder. At moments he even suggests the wonder and goodness of a proper Romantic childhood. Not only is he devoutly loyal to George, but he also cannot count very well and dreams of the countryside. He talks about a dream of grass and swans to the "real country-boy," Trooper George, who ducks his head in his morning washbowl "like a military sort of diver . . . standing with his body well bent forward, to keep the wet from his martial legs."[87]

Looking for the unhealthy aging particularly associated with urban working children, we might return to the Smallweeds. Trooper George's military vigor is even more flamboyantly contrasted with this gruesomely wizened family. Sounding like a recruitment pitch, the narrator juxtaposes George's "developed figure" and overwhelming martial vigor to the Smallweeds' stunted, pinched selves. Trooper George is a human broadsword, while the Smallweeds are crooked little oyster-knives at best:

> A special contrast Mr George makes to the Smallweed family. Trooper was never yet billeted upon a household more unlike him. It is a broadsword to an oyster-knife. His developed figure, and their stunted forms; his large manner filling any amount of room; and their little narrow pinched ways; his sounding voice, and their sharp spare tones; are in the strongest and the strangest opposition.[88]

Trooper George and the Smallweeds present the "strongest and the strangest opposition." This tableau might seem to showcase the difference between healthy adult recruit and wizened child laborer that helped to motivate education and factory legislation. Unlike Phil Squod, however, the grotesquely stunted Smallweeds have not in fact been crippled by industrial work and poverty. They are a ruthless clan of urban misers. Although they generally begin to work at a young age, the root of whatever blights their family tree is not "child labor" itself, but rather an overly rational education and the greedy worldiness that Dickens associates with such an education.

Both *Hard Times* and *Bleak House* follow this pattern. Although they celebrate Romantic childhood, they do not oppose this ideal to child labor. With their early experience of work, Judy and Bart Smallweed might seem to have little in common with the wealthier and non-laboring sister and brother, Louisa and Tom Gradgrind. Dickens, however, claims that all Smallweeds and all Gradgrinds are stunted by confinement within the same "narrow world of fact": "The house of Smallweed, always early to go out and late to marry, has strengthened itself in its practical character, has discarded all amusements, discountenanced all story-books, fairy tales, fictions and fables, and banished all levities whatsoever." Like Louisa and Tom, neither Judy nor Bart has experienced gender-appropriate imaginative graces and delights:

> Judy never owned a doll, never played at any game, never heard of Cinderella . . . And her twin brother could not wind up a top for his life. He knows no more of Jack the Giant Killer, or of Sinbad the Sailor, than he knows of the people in the stars. He could as soon play at leapfrog, or at cricket, as he could change into a cricket or a frog himself.

Overly rational education has damaged the Smallweeds for at least three generations. Grandfather Smallweed's mind "holds, as well as it ever held, the first four rules of arithmetic and a certain small collection of the hardest facts. In respect of ideality, reverence, wonder, and other such phrenological attributes, it is no worse off than it used to be."[89] Similarly, *Hard Times* claims that the same rational worldliness characterizes schoolchildren and factory workers, marking both M'Choakumchild's students and Coketown's grown factory operatives with premature old age. Dickens acknowledges that "the English people" are "hard-worked," and notes that he "would like to give them a little more play."[90] Although the novel considers trade unionism as a potential solution to the misery of factory workers, however, its ultimate answer is quite different. The novel's final vision is of Louisa Gradgrind Bounderby, at last "grown learned in childish lore," ministering equally both to infancy and to industrial manhood. Children and working men form one audience as she spends her time "trying hard to know her humbler fellow creatures, and to beautify their lives of machinery and reality with those imaginative graces and delights, without which the heart of infancy will wither up, the sturdiest physical manhood will be morally stark death."[91]

In part through foregrounding age-leveled norms, school emphasized gender less than did most homes and workplaces. *Our Mutual Friend*'s eager National schoolgirl Mary Anne, "so imbued with the class-custom of stretching out an arm, as if to hail a cab or omnibus, whenever she found she had an observation on hand to offer to Miss Peecher, that she often did it in their domestic relations," is the great-great grandmother of Hermione Granger, her right arm forever reaching for the sky.[92] Of course, obvious inequalities remained between the treatment of girls and boys. The Factory and Education Acts themselves were intended to enforce gender as well as age norms; hopes of making "the norm of the male breadwinner . . . a reality" helped to justify the demand that all children be kept out of the workplace.[93] The Industrial Revolution eventually helped to create the ideal of the "family wage" earned by an adult male far away from home. The implications for women of this movement of labor outside the household have been insightfully examined. Its implications for girls are at times surprising. The same dead-end, unskilled sweatshop or industrial jobs that were dangerous to the future earning-power of boys were seen as perfect for girls, who were not meant to have any future earning-power at all. That is, exactly because they were never supposed to grow into adult laborers, girls could be the ideal child laborers.[94] Nevertheless, the long battle had begun to classify girls as well as their brothers as schoolchildren rather than a source of paid or unpaid support to the family. To the extent that standardized testing evaluated teachers and schools and justified state funding, the schoolchild was a relatively un-gendered figure.

Dickens's novels often lament school's disruptive effect on gender. Agnes Wakefield, we remember, never set foot in a classroom. The collision of M'Choakumchild with that embodiment of domestic virtue, Sissy Jupe, provides an extended example. Sissy's "pretty, modest head" is incapable of absorbing facts or figures, and Dickens clearly implies that it should not be required to. Like Charley Neckett, another excellent caregiver and terrible student, Sissy's proper place is the home, not the schoolroom:

> M'Choakumchild reported that she had a very dense head for figures; that, once possessed with a general idea of the globe, she took the smallest conceivable interest in its exact measurements; that she was extremely slow in the acquisition of dates, unless some pitiful incident happened to be connected therewith.

Sissy's praiseworthy inability to grasp the difference between the Golden Rule and the "elements of Political Economy" illustrates *Hard Times*'s attack on utilitarian political philosophy, but it also makes a claim about gender and school. In case we miss this point, Sissy and Louisa explain it:

> "It would be a fine thing to be you, Miss Louisa!" she said... "I should know so much, Miss Louisa. All that is difficult to me now, would be so easy then."
>
> "You might not be the better for it, Sissy... You are more useful to my mother, and more pleasant with her than I can ever be," Louisa resumed. "You are pleasanter to yourself, than I am to myself."[95]

An exemplary student, Louisa is a domestic disaster. Of course, her brother, Tom, and the pupil-teacher, Bitzer, are also good students and bad people, but the novel offers no boyish equivalent of Sissy's unschooled domestic goodness.

Dickens's well-known essay "Frauds on the Fairies" (*Household Words*, 1 October 1853) explores the same satirical impulse towards contemporary children's literature and education that characterizes *Hard Times* and *Bleak House*. In this essay, Dickens's very commitment to a Romantic child-like ideal seems to work against age-leveling labor. Put simply, to cure debilitating exhaustion, Dickens does not seem to advocate less work but rather more fairy tales. The essay opposes the liberating power of childlike "fancy" to the dreariness of social reform. As "nurseries of fancy," fairy tales counteract aging, preserving in older people and in England as a whole a Romantic childhood. Fairy tales

> greatly helped to keep us, in some sense, ever young, by preserving through our worldly ways one slender track not overgrown with weeds, where we may walk with children, sharing their delights... A nation without fancy, without some romance, never did, never can, never will, hold a great place under the sun.[96]

The Smallweeds are wizened because they lurk in dark and weedy "worldly ways" rather than appreciating fairy tales, which are a refreshing path where young and old stroll together. To illustrate the contrast between these two ways, Dickens offers a mock didactic rewrite of "Cinderella" as a vehicle to promote popular movements to reform society "on enlightened, liberal, and free principles."[97] One target of his satire is the early closing movement, the effort to secure a Saturday half-holiday and a ten-hour workday for retail employees, part of the long campaign to shorten work hours. Until the Factories and Shops Act of 1885, shops typically traded six days a week and closed at 10:00 pm or later on weekdays, often keeping their staff at work as long as customers kept coming.[98] In Dickens's parody, Cinderella looks "behind a watering-pot for six lizards, which she changed into six footmen, each with a petition in his hand ready to present to the Prince, signed by fifty thousand persons, in favour of the early closing movement" (171). In 1890, George Howell summarized the argument for early closing in *The Conflicts of Capital and Labor*, arguing that "excessive work" damaged the physical and mental health of a great nation.[99] What is interesting here is not that Dickens at roughly mid-century does not appear to share this opinion, but rather the solution to the nation's mental and physical exhaustion he seems to propose instead: people of all ages should read imaginative literature. Rather than demanding that we protect young people from labor so they are free to read fairy tales, Dickens demands that we protect fairy tales for the good of people of all ages.

Like the unreformed Louisa Gradgrind, the intellectual, pamphlet-reading Cinderella of "Frauds on the Fairies" looks like a student rather than a sister or mother. She imposes gender-bending liberal reform on the kingdom, turning all women away from love and towards the glories of "public life": "She also threw open the right of voting, and of being elected to public offices and of making the laws, to the whole of her sex; who thus came to be always gloriously occupied with public life and whom nobody dared to love" (174).These are the concerns that shape the age-scrambled figures who populate Dickens's novels. Rather than being subsumed under age-leveled categories of development, gender dominates Dickens's sense of whether age-leveling is appropriate at all: for Little Mothers it is not, while for Old Boys it may be, but often fails. Age-scrambling is ugly when it threatens national health, military readiness, or the gender roles of domestic ideology. But Dickens identifies none of these dangers with the factory child in particular or with child labor itself. As we have seen, he is more likely to view school as the enemy of childlike wonder than as an instrument to remove children from an adult world of labor.

"He never was and never would have been a student"

In *Living Liberalism*, Elaine Hadley calls attention to the "intimate but obviously nondomestic, nonfamilial, nonpersonal and decidedly grown-up private sphere of a liberal individual" in the middle of the nineteenth century. This new and "decidedly grown-up" cultural space gave authority to the professional intellectual's participation in public life.[100] According to Hadley, this particular way of thinking about age, private life, and politics became important in England in the middle of the nineteenth century. As we have seen, Dickens himself does not revere the adult. More particularly, he does not generally accept the equation of academic and psychological benchmarking that becomes increasingly important to professional intellectuals such as literary critics. In fact, Dickens is good at separating illiteracy from immaturity. He sees the gap in perception between the educated and the uneducated as a different thing from the gap in perception between the old and young, and as interesting in its own right. "No one who can read ever looks at a book, even closed and on a shelf, like one who cannot," he remarks.[101] Dickens is captivated by the strangeness of the city of unintelligible symbols inhabited by the illiterate, the place where both the very old Krook and the very young Jo live and die. Similarly, Dickens pauses to try to imagine what it means to be both fully grown and innumerate, as Phil confides to Trooper George that he knows that he is "something with a eight in it" because he remembers he was eight years old on one April Fool's Day, and has seen the holiday come around countless times since then.[102] Unlike Dickens himself, however, his reviewers eventually began to focus on adulthood. Such a combination of academic and psychological benchmarking became crucial to figures such as George Henry Lewes as they claimed that the professional literary reviewer was part of the "grown-up" liberal sphere of sincere but abstract cognition rather than the private, self-interested sphere of family life. Critics such as Lewes age-level the novel through advocating the professional intellectual as its ideal reader. They conflate adulthood with education, especially a university-level liberal education.

Today, child and adult readers are an ever-more separate and ever-more specialized business not merely because of the choices of individual consumers in the literary marketplace but because of a standardized, age-leveled educational program fostered by state-sponsored schools and libraries. Reading is not merely age-leveled, but grade-leveled. The distance we have come is suggested by Thackeray's well-known description of his editorial policy as editor of the *Cornhill Magazine*: "At our social table we shall suppose the ladies and children always present."[103] This injunction to act as if "the ladies and children" are always present contrasts with a focus on the developmental differences between adults and children. Like Thackeray, early in Dickens's career, reviewers cared more about shared gentility than developmental difference. They tried to recommend novels that delighted and instructed without offending against the politeness that was the house style of the middle class. Since good novels rewarded virtue and punished vice in genteel language, what made a novel good was exactly what made it good for readers of all ages. When they do mention age, such reviewers assert a shared middle-class identity whose power is affirmed by the fact that it includes young and old alike.

Dickens's early reviewers evaluate his novels according to these standards of middle-class family reading. They foreground social status in assessing his works, often assuring their readers that although very funny, Dickens is also genteel. This gentility needed a good deal of vouching for. The *Quarterly Review*, for example, claims that Dickens himself is "uninitiated" in the "grace, repose, and ease of good society," revealing his outsider status through the "ill-bred good-breeding" of his would-be genteel characters.[104] Other reviewers praise Dickens for what he does better than anyone else throughout his career: create humor and pathos by describing a range of social classes in language that is widely accessible and never offends against the code of middle-class politeness. That is, what may sound to us like a concern about developmental age in descriptions of Dickens as family reading is equally likely to be a claim about the class status of Dickens and his readers. George Henry Lewes strikes this note in an 1837 review of *Sketches*, *Pickwick*, and *Oliver Twist*: "Although he takes us into scenes of the lowest description . . . yet there is not a single coarse word, or one allusion that could call a blush into the cheek of the most fastidious.[105] Similarly, Mary Russell Mitford praises *Pickwick* by stressing the breadth of audience as well as of subjects that Dickens reaches without sacrificing middle-class propriety: "It is fun – London life – but without anything unpleasant: a lady might read it all *aloud* . . . All the boys and girls talk his fun – the boys in the streets; and yet those who are of the highest taste like it the most."[106] Dickens's own Preface to *Pickwick* (1838) solicits his core audience of middle-class readers, announcing his allegiance to what Ford calls "the new code that literature must be suitable reading for the family parlour."[107] "Throughout this book," Dickens promises, "no incident or expression occurs which could call a blush into the most delicate cheek." This delicate cheek may belong to a child, but it is at least equally likely to belong to a lady.

Dickens's reviewers also, however, associate age and social class to criticize him. Rather than being like ladies in their delicacy, children can be like the working classes in their irrationality, and Dickens is thought to appeal strongly to such irrational readers. The *Quarterly Review* claims that most of Dickens's readers obey emotion rather than reason because they are either "the young" or "the lower orders." Anything published in weekly shilling numbers ought to be written with this impressionable audience in mind:

> We are not afraid that the rational portion of Boz's readers may be misled . . . yet the numerical majority of the young, and of the lower orders – (for whom books in shilling Numbers have the *appearance* of being mainly designed) – judge from feelings, and are fascinated by the brilliant fallacies which reach the head through the heart.[108]

"The rational portion" of Dickens's readers are neither children nor lower class, but their reading experience is not the standard that the *Quarterly* uses to judge his work. Claiming that Dickens is loved by the semi-literate of all ages, reviewers credit him with educating their feelings and impulses rather than their thoughts: "There are even millions who are just emerging from ignorance into what may be called reading classes; all of whom Mr Dickens is educating to honesty, good feeling, and all the finer impulses of humanity." Although complimentary, the leading article in *The Times* eulogizing Dickens in 1870 still associates the reading habits of young people with those of the lower classes, on the one hand, and those of older people with "a higher class": "It has been his peculiar fortune . . . to excite the interest of the young and the uninstructed, without shocking the more refined taste of a higher class and a more mature age."[109]

The cultural aspect of education is still in the foreground in the early reviewers' common comparison of Dickens to Thackeray. The point of mentioning Dickens's relative lack of education is that this lack reveals Dickens is not a gentleman. Thackeray himself parodies the frustration of reviews such as the *Quarterly* (here called "the cauliflowered god") at readers' refusal to accept the social authority of such "cultivation":

> "Unhappy people! Deluded race!" one hears the cauliflowered god exclaim . . . "Know ye that your new idol hath little Latin and less Greek? Know ye that he has never tasted the birch of Eton . . . ? Discern ye not his faults of taste . . . ? Come back to your ancient, venerable, and natural instructors. Leave this new, low, and intoxicating draught at which ye rush, and let us lead you back to the old wells of classic lore . . . " But the children of the present generation hear not; for they reply, "Rush to the Strand! and purchase five thousand more copies of the *Christmas Carol*."[110]

In a lecture first given in 1853, Thackeray insists that neither education nor age limit Dickens's audience, praising "the charities of Mr Dickens . . . which he has conferred upon us all; upon our children; upon people educated and uneducated." Good novelists such as Dickens are "week-day preachers," and like good preachers in the pulpit on Sunday, they manage to reach an audience of all ages and all levels of education. In addition to valuing child-like qualities in all readers, Thackeray concentrates on the youngest members of Dickens's audience, praising him for making "such multitudes of children happy."[111] In this lecture Dickens himself eventually becomes a child of nature, one whose "art" is open to criticism but whose genius is undeniable. In this Romantic view, childhood is good and education is unimportant: Thackeray notes that "there is no man that teaches us to be gentlemen better than Joseph Addison" but implies that Dickens does something better still in teaching us to be children.

This line of criticism has a long life. In 1903, Alice Meynell still praises the uneducated Dickens's childlike nature. She dismisses the gentleman's early socialization as trivial: "The vulgarity that is attributable to his [Dickens's] early ignorance of social manners is a very unimportant thing." After insisting that the uneducated Dickens's grammar is in fact better than the classically educated Thackeray's, she compares Dickens to a child. Rather than the irrationality or vulgarity of the working class, this association suggests the delicacy of Ariel: "Instead of charging him with the vulgar alertness of the street (and this seems to be the accusation used by those who aver that they can no longer read him), we ought to acknowledge the Ariel-delicacy of images and allusions, and the simplicity of his caprice, resembling the simplicity of an unpreoccupied child."[112]

Deborah Epstein Nord addresses this idea of Dickens as childlike by perceptively discussing a transitional generation of critics, late nineteenth- and early twentieth-century figures such as Virginia Woolf and F. R. Leavis. Because they first encountered Dickens as children themselves, Nord argues, such writers later felt a need to assert an "adult" aesthetic appreciation by repressing both their own childhood love for him and Dickens's own "preoccupation with the persistence of childhood within adulthood."[113] The critics' negative version of an uneducated, childlike Dickens, however, reflects more than a specific generation's experience of Dickens. It is as old as critics' attempts to assert the status of the professional intellectual. Rather than positively invoking the approval of a ten-year-old "candid young critic" as did Thackeray, for example, George Stott in 1869 contrasts Dickens and his young readers with the intellectual. He claims that like women, children, and other "weak people," Dickens is overly emotional, but even that is less deplorable than is Dickens's failure to comprehend the "intellectual excellence" of academic disciplines:

> Mr Dickens is no doubt entitled to the credit of making weak people, women, and children, cry copiously; but we do not think there is a single passage in his writings which a pure and cultivated taste would pronounce beautiful. But if Mr Dickens is insensible to beauty, he is no less so to intellectual excellence, and the aims and pursuits of intellectual men . . . Theology, philosophy, science, history, seem all closed books to him.[114]

Hostile to the political satire of Dickens's later works, the *Quarterly* similarly offers an age-leveled attack on the "gaping idiocy of adult persons" who admire it. Here high intellectual cultivation is incompatible with taking any pleasure whatsoever in reading Dickens:

> Though Dickens' works are still by far the most popular of the age we have never met a single man of high cultivation who regarded Dickens in the light of an artist at all, or looked upon his books as greatly worth the attention of persons capable of appreciating better things . . . [We reject] the gaping idiocy of adult persons ready to accept the satyr [*sic*] as the very embodiment of greatness and nobility.[115]

No one emblemizes this line of criticism in more interesting ways than George Henry Lewes. As George Levine notes, Lewes represents "the resistance of Victorian intellectuals to Dickens as a truly serious novelist."[116] More particularly, Lewes was a significant late nineteenth-century contributor to the emerging discipline of psychology, committed to working out theories of literary value in terms of the individual's emotional and cognitive development.

Lewes's work often tries to age-level reading rigorously through a certain idea of the individual's intellectual development, a development keyed to academic institutions.[117] As we have seen, in 1837, Lewes himself praises Dickens for harmonizing low subjects with the polite language of middle-class family reading. In 1872, however, Lewes does not talk about social class, but rather about abstract thought. Lewes's ideal reader is now the professional intellectual, and the professional intellectual is less compatible with the family circle than is Bill Sykes. Age-leveling is now important to Lewes's claim that the professional literary reviewer is part of the "grown-up" liberal sphere of well-founded individual opinion rather than the private, self-interested sphere of family life. Lewes's statement of the root cause of Dickens's failings also sums up the importance of the age-leveled institutions of intellectual life to these ideas of novel-writing and reading: "He [Dickens] never was and never would have been a student." Never having been a student, Lewes maintains, Dickens never learned to think rather than to feel. He is incapable of the cornerstones of adult cognition: logic, the habit of reflection, the habit of generalization, and historical knowledge:

> [Dickens] presents an almost unique example of a mind of singular force in which, so to speak, sensations never passed into ideas. Dickens sees and feels, but the logic of feeling seems the only logic he can manage. Thought is strangely absent from his works. I do not suppose a single thoughtful remark on life or character could be found throughout the twenty volumes.[118]

Feeling intensely and living outside history, Dickens makes an excellent Romantic child, but Lewes faults him for lacking the professional intellectual's flair for generalization: "one sees no indication of the past life of humanity having ever occupied him . . . he never connects his observations into a general expression, never seems interested in general relations of things."[119] Surveying a century of criticism, George Ford remarks that "the attacks on Dickens since 1872 seem to be variations on a theme by Lewes" because Lewes so well "anticipated the shifts of taste which were to welcome Tolstoy, Flaubert, Meredith, and James."[120] These are the shifts in taste that also help to create the adult reader.

Lewes's changing opinions about Dickens show the terms through which higher education became synonymous with a certain idea of adulthood, one that replaced the genteel family circle as the measure of literary value. Lewes tries out a piece of rhetorical sleight-of-hand that will become increasingly common in literary criticism through the first decades of the twentieth century, blurring the difference between "adult" as a term of evaluation and "adult" as a literal description of numerical age. As Lewes himself freely acknowledges, according to his criteria, with the exception of professional intellectuals, most people read as children, whatever their numerical age. But his sense of "adult" as a term of value is nevertheless given weight by the nineteenth-century standardization of age-leveled children's literature and age-leveled education in general. Lewes is still self-conscious about using this framework of evaluation. He worries about the fact that "there probably never was a writer of so vast a popularity whose genius was so little *appreciated* by the critics. How are we to reconcile this immense popularity with this critical contempt?"[121]

He gives two different answers to this question. Sometimes he claims that liking Dickens is a sign of immaturity. Like earlier reviewers, Lewes stresses Dickens's popularity with actual children and with childlike people who are unable to think rather than to feel: "For the reader of cultivated taste there is little in [Dickens's] works beyond the stirring of their emotions – but what a large exception!"[122] Lewes believes that because most readers never progress from sensation to ideas, they remain Dickens's natural audience, however old they become: "Think how little the mass of men are given to reflect on their impressions, and how their minds are for the most part occupied with sensations rather than ideas, and you will see why Dickens held an undisputed sway" (572). Such readers know the difference between representations of life and life itself perfectly well, but the more crude the representation, the better they like it. Just as children prefer hobbyhorses to the work of Dutch masters or skillful engravers, so general readers prefer the stock emotional effects of Dickens to the realism of George Eliot. Happily galloping about on the wooden horse of Dickensian characterization, such readers are childish:

> Give a child a wooden horse, with hair for mane and tail, and wafer-spots for colouring, he will never be disturbed by the fact that this horse does not move its legs, but runs on wheels . . . this wooden horse, which he can handle and draw, is believed in more than a pictured horse by a Wouvermanns or an Ansdell . . . Just as the wooden horse is brought within the range of the child's emotions, and dramatizing tendencies . . . so Dickens's figures are brought within the range of the reader's interests. (572)

At other moments, however, Lewes admits to taking pleasure in Dickens himself: "We do not turn over the pages in search of thought, delicate psychological observation, grace of style, charm of composition; but we enjoy them like children at a play, laughing and crying at the images which pass before us" (576). Lewes cannot imagine himself straddling a hobbyhorse, but he is willing to put himself, at least momentarily, within this theatrical audience: *we* enjoy Dickens like children at a play. Here he suggests a new and openly specialized standard of literary value, one that foregrounds questions of technique that are of interest only to the professional literary critic and that create a "bias of technical estimate" (573). At moments like this one, what Dickens's general readers lack is not the adult's reflective intelligence or emotional maturity, but merely the professional critic's technical knowledge.

What truly puzzles Lewes is not the fact that Dickens is popular with children, or that Dickens is popular with uneducated people of all ages, but rather that Dickens is popular with undeniably intelligent professional men, with the "learned and thoughtful." Although he contrasts the specialized "reader of cultivated taste" to the child, Lewes is too honest to consistently limit the status of adult to such critics. Some general readers are in fact children, and all general readers are *like* children, but some of these general readers are also judges on the bench. Dickens was "the delight of grey heads on the bench" as well as "the study of youngsters in the counting-house and school-room" (570):

> [The theatrical analogy explains] how learned and thoughtful men can have been almost as much delighted with the works as ignorant and juvenile readers; how Lord Jeffrey could have been so affected by the presentation of Little Nell, which most critical readers pronounce maudlin and unreal. Persons unfamiliar with theatrical representations, consequently unable to criticise the acting, are stirred by the suggestions of the scenes presented; and hence a great philosopher, poet, or man of science, may be found

applauding an actor whom every play-going apprentice despises as stagey and inartistic. (576–77)

Here a great philosopher, poet, or man of science who enjoys Dickens proves only that he is not a literary critic, not that he is "ignorant or juvenile." Although he does so with great difficulty, Lewes acknowledges that such a naive reader may still be an adult – explanding his idea of adulthood to include the members of professions other than literary criticism.[123]

With increasing vitriol, other critics claim there is something not properly adult about Dickens through the early twentieth century. Moments of excess in Dickens's novels that were once evidence of low breeding become instead evidence of psychological immaturity. This new take on his lack of education assumes the kind of developmental framework standardized in state-sponsored schools as well as in children's books by the end of the century, a framework that separates adult and child readers and correlates levels of literacy with levels of cognitive and moral progress. Under this model, the best adult is a professional intellectual influenced by continental thought. Writing under the pen-name of George Eliot, such an adult produces in *Middlemarch* what Virginia Woolf (continuing her father's penchant for age-leveling literature) will call "one of the few English novels written for grown-up people."[124] The fact that the comparison of Dickens with Eliot has more twentieth-century resonance than the reviewers' earlier critical set-piece, the comparison of Dickens with Thackeray, reflects a general shift from a critical vocabulary of social status to one of developmental age. Both comparisons begin with the fact that Dickens is uneducated – but while the comparison with Thackeray proves that Dickens is not a gentleman, the comparison with Eliot proves that Dickens is not an adult. This is the criterion of literary value that Modernism will inherit and develop. George Ford notes that when Dostoevsky was asked to recommend books for a child in 1880 he included all of Dickens but warned that a number of his own novels were not "suitable for your daughter," adding, "For an adult in the twentieth century, such a qualification is in itself a recommendation."[125]

Dickens is still a child for V. S. Pritchard in 1954, but for Pritchard childishness no longer means wonder, irrationality, or a lack of historical awareness, but rather the dysfunctional repression of sexuality. Although Dickens was willing to forgive Fielding his representation of Tom Jones's sexual encounters, Pritchard will not forgive Dickens his omission of such experiences. For Pritchard, "childishness" means a specifically sexual dysfunction that typifies the Victorian period, a decline from the eighteenth century when novels were written from the point of view "of the grown man":

> What replaced the sane eighteenth-century attitude to sex in the comic writings of Dickens? . . . Even Sterne is a grown man. These writers are secure. In Dickens, the ground is the high visual sense and sharp ear of the experienced child who is insecure . . . Dickens' grotesque sense of physical appearance is the kind of sense the child has.[126]

This line of criticism reaches a crescendo in Aldous Huxley's description of both Dickens and his characters as grotesquely failed adults. Huxley writes in strongly psychoanalytical terms; his Dickens is a regressive example of "adult infantility," just like the "gruesome old Peter Pans" he creates:

> The creator of the later Pickwick and the Cheeryble Brothers, of Tim Linkinwater the bachelor and Mr. Garland and so many other gruesome old Peter Pans was obviously a little abnormal in his emotional reactions. There was something rather wrong with a man who could take this lachrymose and tremulous pleasure in adult infantility . . . An infantile man is one who has not developed at all, or who has regressed towards the womb, into a comfortable unawareness . . . A writer who can tearfully adore these stout or cadaverous old babies, snugly ensconced in their mental and economic womb-substitutes and sucking, between false teeth, their thumbs, must have something seriously amiss with his emotional constitution.

Now "abnormal" and "pathological," Dickens is still guilty of vulgarity, but his vulgarity has reached a "really monstrous" scale: "The pathetic parts of *The Old Curiosity Shop* . . . are vulgar . . . because their disease . . . professes to be the most radiant health."[127] After all those years, Huxley still invokes the social stigma of the blacking warehouse.

Huxley feels that Dickens is offensively oblivious of age norms. In contrast, I have argued that Dickens is nearly as interested as is Huxley himself in the grotesque aspects of mixing up age categories, although unlike Huxley, he foregrounds work over sexual development. Although Dickens's interest in age-scrambling is in part readable in terms of the nostalgia for sexless childhood that characterizes Victorian and Edwardian children's literature, as Huxley claims, it also represents a wider interest in age. It reflects the new ways that age came to matter for labor and for education in the wake of the Industrial Revolution. After Dickens's death, melodramas on the London stage began to pay a new kind of attention to age-leveling. The London theatre from the 1880s onward took a new "delight" in the contrast in "perception between adults and children."[128] Characters once united by their common victimization were now carefully differentiated according to their age-appropriate perceptions of their troubles. Ironically, more young children worked on stage in the century's last decades because of this rise in roles that stressed the child's proper distance from the adult world. Carolyn Steedman explains that unlike pantomime imps or fairies, these stage-children played a certain version of the child, one that foregrounded a sense of "dislocation between the adult's and the child's understanding of events." As we have seen, the rise of mass compulsory education helped to define an adult world of work that was separate from a child's world of school – but, in part, the increased demand for working children to play such roles was an unintended consequence of this separation: "The feature of children's parts written later, and with new repertoires of reading and understanding childhood provided by child-study, mass schooling and child psychology, was the adult's understanding that the children could not possibly understand."[129] This chapter has considered the slow and uneven emergence of some of these new repertoires of age-leveled norms – norms that shaped ideas not only of childhood but of adulthood as well. As we shall see in the next chapter, such fascination with "the adult's understanding that the children could not possibly understand" points towards Modernism's break with the model of family reading, as well as towards studies of the child's perspective by authors as diverse as Henry James, E. Nesbit, and Frances Hodgeson Burnett. We will examine what this interest in age became in the hands of the brash young reviewer who greeted the publication of *Our Mutual Friend* by attacking Jenny Wren as a little monster, a fit addition to Dickens's sentimental "troop of hunchbacks, imbeciles, and precocious children": Henry James.

CHAPTER 6

"The time of real amusement"
Henry James and the cult of adulthood

As we have seen, like its audience, the Anglo-American domestic novel of the nineteenth century was not strongly interested in adulthood. Towards the end of the century, however, a number of novelists begin to find adulthood a subject of arresting interest, Henry James perhaps foremost among them. In his "Preface" to the New York Edition of "The Pupil" (1891) James laments the end of the "classic years of the great Americano-European legend," the end of the sense of national difference that had structured his early work. "The Pupil," he writes, recalls

> the years of limited communication, of monstrous and unattenuated contrast, of prodigious and unrecorded adventure. The comparatively brief but infinitely rich "cycle" of romance embedded in the earlier, the very early American reactions and returns (mediæval in the sense of being, at most, of the mid-century), what does it resemble to-day but a gold-mine overgrown and smothered, dislocated, and no longer workable?[1]

In "The Pupil" itself, however, James discovers another gold mine. He discovers a new locus of limited communication, monstrous and unattenuated contrast, and prodigious and unrecorded adventure, one that is not at all played out but rather only just becoming workable: the modern conception of age. More specifically, James makes the mystery and glamour of adulthood loom as suggestively as the mystery and glamour of Europe itself. Such glamorous mystery is his great subject, and he creates it for the adult in the teeth of a vigorous novelistic practice that sees neither mystery nor glamour in either adult characters or adult readers.

James develops his idea of the adult and his idea of the novel in tandem. We have seen how from the eighteenth century on, both pro- and anti-novel discourse routinely conflated numerical age with other categories of identity such as social class and gender. To some extent, James still draws on this older and looser understanding of age in attacking as childish the popular and feminine tradition of domestic fiction; the class bias and misogyny of the new "art-novel" he advocates have been insightfully described.[2] Here I want to focus on a different aspect of James's "elevation" of the novel: the significance of the adults-only novel within the social history of age. James shows a newly specialized interest in and enthusiasm for the idea of the adult, and for the luminous possibilities for reading, writing, and other forms of living that this idea suggests to him. James's vision of adulthood combines aristocracy and the art of the novel, drawing on the fin-de-siècle alliance between the aesthetic movement and high society that helped Modernism reframe novel-reading as an activity of the intellectual elite.[3] It also draws on the version of the adult reader that we examined in the previous chapter: the professional intellectual developed by critics such as George Henry Lewes and George Eliot. Indirectly, James's advocacy of the adult reader helps to make possible one of the most celebrated episodes in the history of Modernism, the reclassification of the representation of some sexual desires and acts from pornography to critically respectable literature.

James uses the new age-leveled standards of his literary criticism not only to evaluate his own work and the work of his contemporaries, but also to retroactively age-level the novels of his mid-nineteenth-century childhood. He re-classifies as children's literature novels that hope to achieve social reform through sentimental or journalistic appeals to a domestic, mixed-age audience. He explores his ideas of age as the measure of literary value through describing two novels that follow this older rhetorical strategy, *Hot Corn* (1853) and *The Lamplighter* (1854), and one that does not: *The Initials* (1850). Although James's attack on "childish" novels is clear, what exactly constitutes the prodigious adventure of the adult novel remains more ambiguous, defined most powerfully by contrast to his idea of the young reader.[4]

The nearness counted so as distance

James formulates his idea of the adult and his idea of the novel through each other. Urging "serious" writers to turn to exclusively adult readers and subjects in "The Future of the Novel: An Analysis and a Forecast" (1899), for example, he insists that nothing less than the survival of the novel depends on transforming its audience. If novelists do not stop writing for young people as well as old, he claims, the novel will die: "By what it shall decide to do in respect to the 'young' the great prose fable will, from any serious point of view, practically see itself stand or fall."[5] For well over a century, novelists often said that the novel would "stand or fall" by what it did with respect to the young – but they meant the opposite of what James means here. When Richardson intended "to improve the Minds of the Youth of Both Sexes," for example, he took the young reader as his ideal reader, and this reader's moral education as the novel's central purpose. Ironically, James wrote this essay for the very mixed-age audience that it attacks. Republishing it in 1956 in the book to which it lends its title, Leon Edel claimed that the essay remained unknown to literary critics for half a century because it appeared in an anthology intended for family reading. This "long-buried essay of Henry James's . . . is reprinted now for the first time" because James "wrote it for one of those 'universal anthologies' which our fathers used to purchase from itinerant salesmen as 'educational sets,' designed to make the entire family aware of the world's literary heritage from Babylon to the Mississippi."[6] That is, James's success at separating the novel from its mixed-age audience left this piece of his own writing stranded on the wrong side of the divide.

James's interest in adulthood puts him at the forefront of an effort to reorganize the literary marketplace. As we have seen, children's literature became a specialized affair over a century earlier, with its own age-specific audience, formal conventions, and marketing practices, but the English-language novel that James inherited had not yet specialized its audience by age. Early in his career as a reviewer, even James himself relies on the principle that educating the young person is the key measure of literary value, although he also struggles ingeniously to reconcile this principle with his interest in a set of works composed according to a very different one: French realism.[7] In 1874, James still invokes the standard of educating the young person, even in defense of that "elaborate picture of vice," *Madame Bovary*. He argues that Flaubert's novel is a great work because it follows the principle of poetic justice, which means that it must be "capable really of being applied to educational purposes":

> "Madame Bovary," we confess, has always seemed to us a great work, and capable really of being applied to educational purposes. It is an elaborate picture of vice, but it represents it as so indefeasibly commingled with misery that in a really enlightened system of education it would form exactly the volume to put into the hands of young persons in whom vicious tendencies had been distinctly perceived, and who were wavering as to which way they should let the balance fall.[8]

In his later criticism, however, James makes the active rejection of the novel's ministry to young persons, wavering or otherwise, the centerpiece of the modernist novel's claim to be taken seriously as an aesthetic object.[9]

Sometimes James objects to the massive and literal presence of young people as novel-readers. He dreads the enormous economic power of the many "boys and girls" who buy books, or who have books bought for them: "Nothing is so striking in a survey of this field, and nothing to be so much borne in mind, as that the larger part of the great multitude that sustains the teller and the publisher of tales is constituted by boys and girls."[10] Even as James tries to elevate the status of the novelist as an artist, he acknowledges that novelists are largely "sustained" by this role as children's storyteller.[11] At other times, James uses terms such as "childish," "infantile," or "puerile" to describe what is wrongheaded about the critical standards and reading habits of his "babyish critics." Examples of James's use of a critically charged vocabulary of age to describe his relation with his audience could be multiplied. In criticizing the Anglo-Saxon public's appetite for dialogue on stage rather than in his novels, for instance, he describes this unthinking consumption as taking place "on the scale and with the smack of lips that mark the consumption of bread-and-jam by a children's school-feast."[12] Later, he dismisses American reviews of *The Wings of the Dove* as reflecting "a public more than usually childish . . . I confess, however, that that is my chronic sense – the more than usual childishness of publics."[13] "With the imbecility of babyish critics the serious writer need absolutely not concern himself," James pronounces categorically.[14] Finally, in a letter to William Dean Howells, James describes the prefaces to his collected works as "a sort of plea for Criticism, for Discrimination, for Appreciation on other than infantile lines – as against the so almost universal Anglo-Saxon absence of these things; which tends so, in our general trade, it seems to me, to break the heart."[15]

To grasp the novelty, and the tenuousness, of James's late-century reversal, we need to keep in mind the publishing landscape in fiction when he was writing. The mixed-age market and the more specialized children's market often overlapped. A list of turn-of-the-century American best-sellers will surprise anyone who imagines the mixed-age "crossover" appeal of *Harry Potter* to be something new. Given the continuing familiarity of many of these titles today, this surprise is an index of the power of our idea of adulthood. In fact, late nineteenth-century adults eagerly bought, read, and discussed many books that were primarily directed to children. Between 1865 and 1914, best-sellers included *Heidi*, *Alice's Adventures in Wonderland*, *Little Women*, and *Little Lord Fauntleroy*. And while critics ever since T. S. Eliot have tended to distinguish sharply in terms of age between *The Adventures of Tom Sawyer* (a "boys' book") and *Adventures of Huckleberry Finn* ("a book which boys enjoy" but which "does not fall into the category of juvenile fiction"), through the first decades of the twentieth century both best-sellers were simply praised as equally good for "boys of all ages" – which meant that they were good for a male of any age at all.[16] Gender outweighed age as a criterion for identifying appropriate readers. The permeability of the mixed-age and the specialized children's audiences in England as well as in the United States is suggested by the booming sales of James's own transatlantic friends and rivals who wrote for both audiences, including Robert Louis Stevenson, Frances Hodgson Burnett, and Rudyard Kipling.[17]

These two overlapping book markets, one for children and one for mixed-age readers, were well established by the late nineteenth century. What was not established was the one market that contemporary academic literary critics tend to take as the norm for our work, the market for critically respectable adults-only novels. As Beverly Lyon Clark has shown in her path-breaking work on the construction of American children's literature, through most of the nineteenth century even leading literary reviews such as William Dean Howells's *Atlantic Monthly* evaluated novels according to the didactic and domestic ideals of family reading. They stressed continuity between adults and children rather than adults' deeply interesting differences. Within this critical framework, what made a novel good was exactly what made it good for readers of all ages. These reviewers mention age not in order to foreground developmental difference, but rather in order to affirm a shared set of domestic ideals by demonstrating that these ideals embrace young and old alike. In doing so, they remain loyal to criteria established much earlier in the century, as when Edgeworth "read aloud" *Waverley* "to this large family."[18] In contrast, in his own fiction and criticism, James champions the emerging market and critical framework of the "art-novel" – which is the adults-only novel. He includes characterizations of novel readers in terms of gender and social class that are familiar from the previous century – rejecting semi-literate readers in favor of those with properly instructed taste, and enervated ladies in favor of professional men – but he focuses most energetically on adulthood, a category as subtle and unfixed as any distinction that transfixes the attention of his novel's characters.

Clark has written incisively about James in regard to the isolation and critical devaluation of children's literature in the early twentieth century. She argues that James, and the increasingly professionalized critics who championed his work, denigrated young readers and manipulated child characters, committing "literary child abuse, if you will," in order to raise the status of the "adult" novel.[19] For example, Clark claims that James strips Maisie in *What Maisie Knew* of the anger that any real child would surely feel at the parental neglect this character experiences. More broadly still, Clark objects to the way James and his champions scorn the world of women and children reading together imagined by nineteenth-century domestic fiction. While I agree with much of Clark's analysis, I am more interested in charting James's construction of the adult than in judging it, for two reasons. First, the social and cultural politics associated with James's revaluation of the domestic seem more mixed than Clark implies – a point made especially well in recent work on James from a queer perspective.[20] Second, and more important to me in this context, in order to invoke the real feelings of a child – the feelings that James is accused of stripping from Maisie, for example – Clark necessarily invokes a real world of adults, too. The real child is the real adult's diacritical opposite: they define one another in their difference. In this regard, this approach pays an unintended compliment to James's "adult reading" by crediting the stability of the adult–child distinction, even though it values this distinction differently from how James does. In contrast, I am interested in how James tries to imagine and to promote the category of the adult, a category that proves remarkably difficult to define.

James's campaign for an adults-only novel is one episode in the long social and intellectual history of age. In his lifetime, the concept of adulthood became more important as age became more widely understood in terms of psychological theory rather than political theory. In the eighteenth and earlier nineteenth centuries, as we have seen, theories of social subordination more strongly inflected age. Childhood and youth were often equated with any state of dependency rather than understood as a specific set of psychological attributes that everyone ought to experience and to leave behind according to the same timetable, regardless of social position.[21] The idea of age as social status and the idea of age as an internal psychological state are not mutually exclusive. But as a psychological sense of age became more important, so too did the idea of adulthood.

Demographic changes helped to raise the importance of adulthood in the late nineteenth and early twentieth centuries. People tended to have fewer children and to live longer after those children left the home, eroding the finality of marriage and parenthood, the happy ending of the domestic novel. As lifespans increased and family size fell, people were more likely to see themselves neither as children nor as parents: adulthood became "more a psychological state than a social status."[22] Medical and psychological theories put a new emphasis on age norms, in particular in terms of sexuality. While changes in social status, such as marriage or the inheritance or acquisition of property, had once moved a person out of the category of childhood, now the mere increase of years in and of itself was supposed to bring with it a precisely calculated set of internal and external changes, each age associated with a host of "distinct biological and psychological traits and behavioral norms."[23] Consciousness of numerical age also increased as new explicitly age-leveled institutions, ranging from kindergarten to old-age pensions, became more likely to structure individual lives.[24] These changes affected the relation between literature and the legal category of pornography. Writers, readers, and courts could eventually reclassify certain sexually explicit texts as critically respectable literature in part because they could draw on a new idea of literary value that assumes an audience made up of adults only.[25]

Marriage, gender roles, and domestic life of course remained important as markers of age and identity. They remain important in James's own work as well. His focus on a psychological idea of adulthood more often ironizes rather than simply excludes domesticity, and his demand "for Appreciation on other than infantile lines" has mixed results in terms of gender. He routinely lumps together "the ladies and the children" under the general category of "the reader unreflective and uncritical." Similarly, when James wants to describe modern, intelligent conversation, he claims that such talk is "as far as possible removed from that of the nursery and the schoolroom": "The wide glow was bright, was favourable to 'real' talk, to play of mind, to an explicit interest in life, a due demonstration of the interest by persons qualified to feel it: all of which meant frankness and ease, the perfection, almost, as it were, of intercourse, and a tone as far as possible removed from that of the nursery and the schoolroom."[26] Of course, the nursery and quite often the schoolroom are gendered spaces, dominated by female nurses and teachers. Interestingly, the glowing space of mental play that James praises here, Mrs. Brookenham's drawing room, is also gendered female. Here the idea of adulthood helps James to develop the figure of the society lady, a person "qualified" by age and experience to show an explicit interest in life.[27]

When discussing writers rather than readers, James claims that men fail even more spectacularly than women at what he calls the fiction's game of "playing at 'grown-up.'" While the morality of women's genteel domestic fiction is indistinguishable from stories targeting girl readers, the fiction men write, to James's disgust, is indistinguishable from the boys' adventure story. James finds this genre even more intellectually primitive than genteel domestic fiction (despite his baffled but ardent admiration for Robert Louis Stevenson):

> The female mind has in fact throughout the competition carried off the prize in the familiar game, known to us all from childhood's hour, of playing at "grown-up"; finding thus its opportunity, with no small acuteness, in the more and more marked tendency of the mind of the other gender to revert, alike in the grave and the gay, to those simplicities which there would appear to be some warrant in pronouncing puerile. It is the ladies who in a word have done most to remind us of man's relation with himself, that is with woman. His relations with the pistol, the pirate, the police, the wild and the tame beast – are those not what prevailingly the gentlemen have given us?[28]

While women's domestic fiction explores "man's relation with himself, that is with woman," the adventure story can offer only "puerile" thrills to boys of all ages.

Unlike women's domestic fiction, however, James's novels are notorious for undermining the idea of marriage as a convincing marker of adulthood. In these novels, marriages either fail to happen or fail to function as a satisfying conclusion to personal development. "Of course you couldn't have, for the present, another evaporated marriage from me!" James remarked early in his career to William Dean Howells.[29] He sympathized with the difficulties that his unconventional endings raised for Howells as the editor of *The Atlantic*. Nevertheless, James continued to specialize in "evaporating" marriage. He undermines marriage both as the literary convention that marks the right and proper ending of a novel and as the social institution that marks the right and proper end of youth. The novels of James's middle period retain elements of the domestic novel's heterosexual marriage plot, but they rework this plot in nonpurposive ways that open new possibilities.

The complexity that James imagines for psychological states conflicted with the attempt to imagine these states as norms for specific ages. As he eloquently writes, complex psychological states often do not correspond to any such timetable. Struggling to describe "so shifting a consciousness," for example, he notes that one does not cease to be young in all aspects of one's life at any one particular moment:

> Everything depends . . . on what one means by one's youth – so shifting a consciousness is this, and so related at the same time to many different matters. We are never old, that is we never cease easily to be young, for ALL life at the same time: youth is an army, the whole battalion of our faculties and our freshnesses, our passions and our illusions, on a considerably reluctant march into the enemy's country, the country of the general lost freshness; and I think it throws out at least as many stragglers behind as skirmishers ahead – stragglers who often catch up but belatedly with the main body, and even in many a case never catch up at all.[30]

Here James combines a keen sense of the unevenness of psychological development with a romantic sense of age as simple negation. Youth is a loosely organized army of stragglers and skirmishers rather than a unified state, while the state of being "old" is all too simple and all too dreary: it is "the enemy's country, the country of the general lost freshness." This familiar romantic sense of age as nostalgic loss stands in marked contrast to James's own contribution, the idea of adulthood as a complex and appealing psychological realm of age-specific pleasures, one that borrows the glamour of an aristocratic entitlement to pleasure.[31]

From the speaker of Gray's Ode savoring the doomed bliss of the little boys playing at Eton to the White Knight's melancholy farewell to Alice, we are used to stories structured by such romantic nostalgia, in which older focal characters watch young ones. But James reverses the direction of this gaze. No literary child has ever watched adults with quite the same electrified and electrifying attention as do the focal child characters of Henry James's middle period. Their gaze gives a new strangeness and new attraction to adulthood. Morgan, Maisie, Miles, and Flora are immersed in the social world of adults in order to highlight their deeper and tantalizing exclusion from it, like the yearning telegraphist awash in fashionable Mayfair telegrams in *In the Cage*. James points out this parallel between a working-class character watching aristocrats and children watching adults. They all "wonder" in the same way: "The range of wonderment attributed in our tale to the young woman employed at Cocker's differs little in essence from the speculative thread on which the pearls of Maisie's experience, in this same volume – pearls of so strange an iridescence – are mostly strung. She wonders, putting it simply, very much as Morgan Moreen wonders."[32] James's child characters do not spend their time in the typical settings of nineteenth-century literary children, opening Christmas presents, adventuring, playing, or learning with other children, but rather in the social world of adults. They are not at all interested in conventionally childish things. They are not even particularly childish themselves. Instead, they resemble James's adult characters in their passion for intense observation. But what they observe is adults. Or rather, they observe their own distance from adulthood.

A story James recalled towards the end of his life also describes the function of the children who are focal characters of the novels and stories of his middle period. James remembered going with his father to New York City, spending a great deal of time "at his side and in his personal haunts."[33] He remarks that when the two of them "took the boat to town to do things," they did something together that his father could not do alone: "My part may indeed but have been to surround his part with a thick imaginative aura; but that constituted for me an activity than which I could dream of none braver or wilder."[34] As James surrounded his father, so James's fictional children surround his adults with "a thick imaginative aura." James's works sometimes have been praised for taking a new interest in children's inner lives.[35] Their newest object of interest, however, is not the child but rather the adult. James famously describes himself as "addicted to seeing 'through' – one thing through another, accordingly, and still other things through *that*" (emphasis in original).[36] The way James sees adulthood through childhood made adulthood more visible, both in his own fiction and in the larger literary marketplace, in how books were written, understood, publicized, and sold. Max Beerbohm's brilliant parody, "The Mote in the Middle Distance" (1906), pays ironic homage to this habit of James's children. Beerbohm makes this intense, wondering observation ridiculous by directing it where we might usually expect children's attention to go, towards a typical childish object. His story's two "hypersubtle innocents, Keith and Eva Tantalus," are not a bit subtler than Maisie or Morgan.[37] What makes them funny is not their way of seeing or the fact that they think so much about how they see, but rather what they look at: not adult sexual intrigues, but their own Christmas stockings. Like the inhabitants of Mrs. Brookenham's drawing room, the little Tantaluses concentrate on vibrations rather than fixing their eyes on objects:

> He was perhaps on the verge of putting this question to her, when, waving her hand to include both stockings, she said "Of course, my dear, you *do* see. There they are, and you know I know you know we wouldn't, either of us, dip a finger into them." With a vibrancy of tone that seemed to bring her voice quite close to him, "One doesn't," she added, "violate the shrine – pick the pearl from the shell!"[38]

In contrast to Beerbohm's Tantaluses in their nursery, James's children are fascinated tourists in the strange country of adults. Seeing the place through their eyes, we become fascinated by it as well. For example, "The Pupil" is structured by a failed marriage plot: the fortune-hunting Moreens recklessly run up debt trying to catch rich European husbands for their daughters, and are ruined when these suitors drift away. But to summarize the story in this way is to misrepresent it. Its power comes from the gaze of young Morgan Moreen, who spends his days observing these financial and sexual machinations in fascinated detail. The sleazy Moreens become truly interesting only when their son concentrates his attention on them as samples of the adult world. Morgan analyzes his shiftless parents with the combination of emotional distance and intellectual fascination that James prescribes for both writing and reading novels. It is this distance that creates "fascination." Sharing this distance brings Morgan and his tutor together:

> They looked at the facts a good deal after this and one of the first consequences of their doing so was that Pemberton stuck it out, in his friend's parlance, for the purpose. Morgan made the facts so vivid and so droll, and at the same time so bald and so ugly, that there was fascination in talking them over with him, just as there would have been heartlessness in leaving him alone with them. Now that the pair had such perceptions in common it was useless for them to pretend they didn't judge such people; but the very judgement and the exchange of perceptions created another tie.[39]

Increasingly threadbare and marginal to the European capitals through which they wander, Morgan and his tutor are increasingly unified by their shared obsession with his "so vivid and so droll . . . so bald and so ugly" parents. I do not mean to diminish the eroticism of their bond, of "the subjection to *him* [Morgan] of the beguiled, bewildered, defrauded, unremunerated, yet after all richly repaid youth," but rather to point out that both Morgan and his tutor are positioned on the same side of the age divide imagined by this story, both spectators of the parody of family life enacted by the adult Moreens.[40]

Similarly, in *The Turn of the Screw*, children find childhood boring and adulthood, imagined as sexual knowledge, rivetingly attractive. In this story marriage is never a possibility, either for the governess-narrator with her forbidden desire for the Master, or for Miss Jessel and her forbidden desire for Peter Quint. Instead of a marriage plot affirming domestic ideals, James offers a pair of young orphans' fascination with the sexual passions of adults outside marriage. As Elliott M. Schrero reminds us, when *Turn* was published in 1898, the story was not about the possibility that the governess-narrator was hallucinating but rather about a central terror of middle-class families: the sexual contamination of their children by their servants.[41] Educational writers from John Locke onward begged parents, with a sense of conscious futility, to keep children out of the hands of servants. If to later readers it may seem that the governess suffers from a murderous panic on this subject, the same must be said about the era that produced James.

"It was all the romance of the nursery and the poetry of the schoolroom" the governess exclaims about the charm of Miles and Flora – but she eventually discovers that these children are charming because they are merely playing at being children. Their happy play is "a spectacle they seemed actively to prepare and that engaged me as an active admirer."[42] Miles and Flora are typical James children in that they are thoroughly uninterested in childhood, although they are unusual in at least trying to hide their lack of interest. What they watch through the whole novella with desperate attention, of course, are the sexual intrigues of the ghostly servants. The governess explains: "Oh, yes, we may sit here and look at them, and they may show off to us there to their fill; but even while they pretend to be lost in their fairytale they're steeped in their vision of the dead restored. He's not reading to her . . . they're talking of THEM – they're talking horrors!" As the governess watches the children, so the children watch Peter Quint and Miss Jessel: "Their more than earthly beauty, their absolutely unnatural goodness. It's a game . . . it's a policy and a fraud! . . . They haven't been good – they've only been absent. It has been easy to live with them, because they're simply leading a life of their own. They're not mine – they're not ours. They're his and they're hers!"[43] Children often lead a "life of their own" in nineteenth-century fiction, but as the governess clarifies here, Miles and Flora actually do not live in such a self-enclosed and innocent world. Rather, they do their best to live vicariously in Peter Quint and Miss Jessel's world: "They're his and they're hers!"

James's fullest exploration of the possibilities of seeing adulthood through childhood is Maisie. This book also reflects his complex relationship to the mixed-age literary marketplace and, more specifically, his complex relationship to a contemporary who wrote for this marketplace with marked success, Frances Hodgson Burnett. Marcia Ann Jacobson points out James's debt to his contemporaries for his focus on Maisie's point of view, and suggests the originality of what Maisie looks at:

> James's handling of the child's point of view is remarkable for its care and sensitivity, but not for its uniqueness. James had Burnett and Grahame as models; in writing from Maisie's point of view, he was simply making his child novel conform to other examples of the genre. But unlike James, neither Burnett nor Grahame forces the child protagonist to confront the adult world.[44]

Burnett was an acquaintance of James, and Jacobson claims that James "probably" knew Burnett's *The One I Knew Best of All: A Memory of the Mind of a Child*. Serialized in *Scribner's* (January to June 1893), one installment appeared in the same issue as James's own "The Middle Years."[45] James had written an extremely critical review of Burnett's successful play *Esmeralda*, and reviewers compared them as promising young transatlantic talents. In 1883, for example, a reviewer in the *Quarterly Review* preferred Burnett's early novels to the "philosophic instruction and dawdling sentimentality" of James's *Daisy Miller* and *The Portrait of a Lady*.[46]

In any case, Burnett was hard to miss. Among James's own contemporaries, she was the writer who stood most clearly for the domestic, mixed-age audience. In terms of sales and critical success, James's and Burnett's careers are inverse images of each other. Burnett was one of the highest-paid writers of their time, often compared to Dickens. She continued to write throughout her career for a relatively undifferentiated audience. *The Secret Garden* (1910), for example, was first published in serial form in a literary magazine for a mainly adult market. *Little Lord Fauntleroy* (1886), the best-seller that defined Burnett in her day, was the first book she intended for the children's market, but it was also enthusiastically read and praised by adults according to the older standards of family reading. She experienced consistent best-sellers and declining critical status as the professional critical practice of age-leveling literature diverged from the popular market for domestic reading.

Clark shows, however, that Burnett and James also share "subtle affiliations," particularly in terms of the literary ideal of gentility.[47] Both Burnett and James wrote at a "time when gentility had been claimed by the middle classes yet still had filiations with the aristocracy."[48] The genteel pleasure that perhaps figures most largely in the work of both is Anglophilia. James wrote as an American abroad and Burnett as an Englishwoman in America, both flaunting their cosmopolitan sophistication.[49] In early works such as *Daisy Miller*, James found in Americans abroad a subject that genuinely interested him as well as one that made his reputation. In 1888, however, James writes to his brother William about a worrying development: the Atlantic is shrinking on him. Instead of a sense of infinitely interesting distance, he now sees only "a big Anglo-Saxon total." And for James, a big Anglo-Saxon total is not worth writing about:

> For myself, at any rate, I am deadly weary of the whole "international" state of mind – so that I ache, at times, with fatigue at the way it is constantly forced upon one as a sort of virtue or obligation. I can't look at the English and American worlds, or feel about them, any more, save as a big Anglo-Saxon total, destined to such an amount of melting together that an insistence on their differences becomes more and more idle and pedantic.[50]

Even worse, James accuses himself of willfully mistaking individual peculiarities for national peculiarities, claiming his "ironic or critical disposition" had diversified the bland sameness of "life and human nature etc." by seeing national differences where none ever really existed.[51] Although he is dead weary of this false and/or rapidly eroding sense of transatlantic difference, James cannot do without such a structure of difference to frame his work.

What he is after is a strange and endlessly intriguing combination of intimacy and distance. While early in his career he creates this effect through transatlantic plots and characters, later he creates it through his treatment of age.[52] This sense of endless distance from what is closest to hand describes the aesthetic interest of human relationships in James's works. "The nearness counted so as distance," says the admiring young writer of the aura of the English country house he visits at the opening of "The Lesson of the Master." "There were shades of meaning in it and a vague perspective of history which receded as you advanced," he continues, sounding like Maisie observing her mother's affairs.[53]

As James and Burnett engage differently with Anglophilia, so they rework the glamour of aristocrats in quite opposite ways. James describes the emergence of an idea of adulthood that looks aristocratic not only because his characters tend to be wealthy, but also because they tend to be relatively free of the middle-class family. Judged in terms of domestic ideals, his adults are spectacular failures. Seen through the eyes of his focal child characters, however, they have the glamour, the freedom, and the enthralled audience of a cultural elite. Yet they are a cultural elite admired not by social subordinates, an admiration that would emphasize class difference, but by children, an admiration that emphasizes age difference. In contrast, for Burnett, it is the child who is the perfect aristocrat. Not the knowing society lady but Little Lord Fauntleroy is her signature figure. Moreover, in contrast to James, Burnett represents the triumphant appropriation of aristocratic glamour by genteel domesticity. Raised with selfless devotion by his perfect mother, Dearest, Fauntleroy crosses the Atlantic and wins back his ancestral estate by melting the heart of his curmudgeonly grandfather, the Earl of Dorincourt, through the flawless display of middle-class good manners and virtues. Burnett returns often to the figure of the aristocratic child who embodies domestic ideals. For example, Sara Crewe, in *A Little Princess*, is motherly, self-controlled, and charitable, while Marco Loristan, the eponymous protagonist of *The Lost Prince*, is the product of an all-male household that is perhaps even more passionately devoted to his education and good manners, and to the mending and brushing of his clothes, than is Dearest herself to bringing up Fauntleroy.

Burnett's children have a social authority that is all the more unquestionable because they are children and defined by Burnett as incapable of affectation. She presents their beautiful aversion to vulgarity as natural to them. "And lies – well, you see, they are not only wicked – they're *vulgar*," Sara Crewe remarks, starving with unshakable gentility in her garret. "'Sometimes' – reflectively – 'I've thought perhaps I might do something wicked – I might suddenly fly into a rage and kill Miss Minchin, you know, when she was ill-treating me – but I *couldn't* be vulgar.'"[54] William James describes his brother's early stories in similar terms: "They give a certain impression of the author clinging to his gentlemanliness though all else be lost, and dying happy provided it be *sans déroger*."[55] Like Sara Crewe, Henry James could not be vulgar. However, Burnett naturalizes social distinction through the unerring good taste of the temporarily impoverished young aristocrats-in-disguise who are often the central figures of her books. In contrast, James analyzes vulgarity and its social roots in often horrified or bigoted, but always fascinated, detail in works like *The American Scene*.[56]

Burnett's and James's fullest treatments of the perceptions of a child focal character show this same combination of similarity and difference, this same split over the relation of adulthood and domesticity. As its title suggests, Burnett's autobiographical *The One I Knew Best of All: A Memory of the Mind of a Child* focuses in part on the gap between what a child's mind perceives and what it can express – the same gap that interests James in *Maisie*. Burnett stresses the often overlooked sensitivity of an observant young person:

> It is difficult to realize constantly that a mite . . . is a person, and that this person is ten thousand times more sensitive to impressions than one's self, and that hearing and seeing one, this person, though he or she may not really understand, will be likely, in intervals of innocent destruction of small portable articles, to search diligently in infant mental space until he or she has found an explanation of affairs, to be pigeonholed for future reference.[57]

Particularly relevant to James is Burnett's interest in the gap between perception and language in childhood: "There must be so many thoughts for which child courage and child language have not the exact words," she writes. Burnett explores the fact that her heroine "was too young to have had in her vocabulary the words to put her thoughts and mental arguments into – and yet they were there."[58] "She had ever of course in her mind fewer names than conceptions," James similarly notes of Maisie, also insisting that this shortage of names does not stop his young person from forming accurate ideas about the relations of the adults who surround her.[59]

Revealingly, however, the group that Burnett's Small Person observes with such acute but inarticulate insight is the domestic tableau of mother, nursemaid, and new baby sister. The thought that she cannot find words for is her awareness that the nursemaid only pretends to let her hold the new baby, discreetly supporting it herself out of concern for its safety. In contrast, Maisie observes a scene that is the opposite of child-centered. She figures out, but does not say, that the appearances and disappearances of the adults in her life have nothing to do with her and everything to do with their relations with each other. She loves Sir Claude, and deduces that his becoming her stepmother's lover explains his drawing back from Maisie herself:

> It sounds, no doubt, too penetrating, but it was not at all . . . She had ever of course in her mind fewer names than conceptions, but it was only with this drawback that she now made out her companion's absences to have had for their ground that he was the lover of her stepmother and that the lover of her stepmother could scarce logically pretend to a superior right to look after her. Maisie had by this time embraced the implication of a kind of natural divergence between lovers and little girls.[60]

The question of the "divergence" between lovers and little girls is a rich one for James, one to which we will turn later. Here I want to point out that Burnett sometimes describes her heroine as a similarly fascinated and similarly powerless observer of her world: "It was the people about her, the things she saw, the events which made up her small existence, which were absorbing, exciting, and of the most vital and terrible importance sometimes."[61] For Burnett, however, this is true only "sometimes," and the absorbing events often involve other children as well as adults. Burnett's fond attention is finally concentrated on her heroine's own mind, her sheltered domestic circle and "small person" itself, rather than on the adult world that occasionally impinges on her. Burnett celebrates the child and domestic ideals, while James celebrates the adult living outside any domestic circle that functions in a conventionally recognizable way. Maisie grasps very early the important truth that "the grown-up time was the time of real amusement and above all of real intimacy." Although she finds much in it to be of "an almost terrifying strangeness," she lives in a world of adults pursuing their own lives. The closest Maisie comes to childish things is studying "to produce on Lisette [her doll] the impression of having mysteries in her life, wondering the while whether she succeeded in the air of shading off, like her mother, into the unknowable."[62] Their imaginations heated by the romantic plots of novels, Mrs. Wix and Maisie endow Maisie's absent parents and stepparents with a very thick imaginative aura indeed. Maisie and Mrs. Wix pass their time together describing in loving detail what they should not presume to imagine: "Mrs. Wix reminded her disciple . . . that the 'real life' of their companions, the brilliant society in which it was inevitable they should move and the complicated pleasures in which it was almost presumptuous of the mind to follow them, must offer features literally not to be imagined without being seen." Exactly because it is almost presumptuous to imagine the complicated pleasures that the adults are up to in their "real life" away from children, such imagining is irresistible. The moral flaws of Maisie's parents and step-parents are obvious, but they remain awe-inspiring figures nevertheless: "She was awestruck at the manner in which a lady might be affected through the passion mentioned by Mrs. Wix; she held her breath with the sense of picking her steps among the tremendous things of life." Here the tremendous things of life are adult sexual intrigue: "Maisie accepted this hint with infinite awe."[63]

James was not alone in his turn-of-the-century campaign to age-level the novel's audience. In 1895, Thomas Hardy in his preface defended *Jude the Obscure*'s sexual content on the grounds that his novel was "addressed by a man to men and women of full age."[64] As we have seen, Virginia Woolf made the standard of adulthood retroactive in praising George Eliot's *Middlemarch* as "one of the few English novels written for grown-up people."[65] But Eliot herself believed novels ought to educate young people about moral choices, while Hardy claimed that the hostility that greeted his attempt to write for men and women of full age had the effect of "completely curing me of further interest in novel-writing."[66] In contrast, James found an incitement to further novel-writing in his idea of adulthood.

The mystery of the tabooed book

A paradox is built into critics' praise of certain novels as "adult": such books are never what most adults actually read. Rather, these books are valued for their aesthetic or ethical qualities – but crucially, in a strongly age-leveled world such as our own, such literary value seems more valuable yet when we describe it in terms of developmental ideals and blur the difference between these ideals and a numerical or demographic sense of adulthood. This standard is circular: adult literature is what adults would read if they themselves were properly adult. Like his own novels and autobiographical writings, James's criticism of popular novels suggests the amorphousness as well as the importance of the category of adulthood. James offers three criteria for the adult novel, three attempts to explain his stark assertion that good novels can have nothing to do with young people. One is negative, one is extremely general, and one is positive but quite limited in scope. First, James claims that an adult novel must not be didactic. Second, an adult novel must be interesting or intelligent. Finally, an adult novel must be about sexual relationships, although it should not include explicit descriptions of sexual acts. Although these criteria convey useful information, none of them can really account for the aura of the adult novel, any more than demographic criteria can account for the aura of adulthood. To understand how James makes the literary value of the adult novel, like the shifting pearls of Maisie's experience, glow with "so strange an iridescence," we need to consider his use of the structure of difference itself.

The first of these criteria for the adult novel is relatively straightforward. The novel's role as educator of a mixed-age audience remained quite powerful through James's own lifetime and beyond. Nevertheless, both the didactic novel's defenders and those who disliked the form, such as James, increasingly tend to talk about didacticism more exclusively in terms of the young. In a vivid 1898 description of a hypothetical young reader encountering James, for example, Norman Hapgood persists in imagining the novelist as a liberal version of the young person's teacher. Young Americans learn something from James's novels, Hapgood suggests, and what they learn is that there is an alternative to the "limitations and rigidities" of their world. They may think this alternative is Europe, but it is really Henry James's personal universe:

> Imagine a young American . . . Suppose him just enough irritated at and balked by the rigid world he knows to be ready to attack it, but weaponless. *Roderick Hudson* falls into his hand. He settles back in his lounge before he has read ten lines, with the excitement of feeling that he has found the needed secret and that it is a long and full one . . . Before he has read a week he longs to see the Madonna of the Chair, because Henry James has mixed it with his universe by some flitting adjective . . . There is a world that laughs at the limitations and rigidity that annoyed him – that is gay, intellectual, unproselytizing . . . he buys photographs of Italian paintings, studies atlases, plans a trip to Europe, and reads Merimee and Trugenieff.[67]

James himself confessed to a "considerable warming of the heart" on reading Hapgood's book, and this description of the baffled and isolated young person discovering "the needed secret" in novels is likely to warm the heart of any English professor who ever hopefully constructed an introductory syllabus.[68] In queer studies' autobiographical accounts of novel-reading, we see such moments save lives. Nevertheless, James insists that this scenario is not his intention – although his review of Hapgood's book itself cannot quite shake the tone of giving advice to the young person. It describes Hapgood as muddled but promising: "he strikes me, as yet, rather as feeling for his perceptions – hunting for his intelligence. But he is doubtless on his way to find these things, and there are gleams in his predominant confusion that suggest that they may prove excellent." Even understood in the most cosmopolitan terms imaginable, didacticism is not appropriate to the adult novel.

A decade after defending *Madame Bovary* according to the didactic standard, James renounces in "The Author of Beltraffio" (1884) his hope that great literature can educate young people. The author's exquisite seven-year-old son, Dolcino Ambient, is killed by a dispute over age and reading when his mother decides he is better dead than corrupted by his father's novels. While this is clearly wrong, Mr. Ambient also acknowledges that Dolcino should not read his novels while young. Only this story's naive narrator believes that intensely good novels are good for young people as well as old:

> I asked her husband if it were his opinion in general, then, that young people shouldn't read novels.
>
> "Good ones – certainly not!" said my companion. I suppose I had had other views, for I remember saying that for myself I wasn't sure it was bad for them if the novels were "good" to the right intensity of goodness. "Bad for *them*, I don't say so much!" my companion returned. "But very bad, I'm afraid, for the poor dear old novel itself."[69]

As a writer, Mr. Ambient's first concern is the good of the novel, not of the young; moreover, these two kinds of good are now a zero-sum game. Good novels are by definition bad for young people, so writing with a sense of an audience that includes young people is bad for the future of the novel.

It is difficult to define what the novel ought to do instead of educating people in either social norms or in an ironical detachment from these norms. James himself writes of this purpose in the most general terms possible, bringing us to his second criteria for the adult novel: "The only obligation to which in advance we may hold a novel without incurring the accusation of being arbitrary, is that it be interesting. That general responsibility rests upon it, but it is the only one I can think of." For James, "interesting" and "intelligent" are fairly interchangeable terms; for example, "The Future of the Novel" attacks the novel's "great mistake of failing of intelligence."[70] Neither term, however, has much satisfying specificity. As Mark McGurl points out, the modernist novel reflects both a relatively new interest in a general human quality called intelligence (as opposed to specific talents or capacities) and a relatively new anxiety over the difficulty of defining this quality, despite the rise of new instruments such as the IQ test that professed to do so. As Charles Spearman complained in 1920, although "the teacher tried to cultivate intelligence, and the psychologist tried to measure intelligence, nobody seemed to know precisely what intelligence is."[71]

James's third criterion for the adult novel, the recognition of sexual relationships, raises different issues. Although rife with its own ambiguities, the loss of virginity was easier to specify than the presence of intelligence. This may be why James often substitutes the one for the other. For example, James begins "The Future of the Novel" by lamenting the novel's unreflective and uncritical audience, but soon shifts to criticizing this audience's lack of sexual experience. James refers to "our long and most respectable tradition of making [the novel] defer supremely in the treatment, say, of a delicate case, to the inexperience of the young":

> In the English novel (by which I mean the American as well), more than in any other, there is a traditional difference between that which people know and that which they agree to admit that they know . . . [the Anglo-American novel] strikes me as addressed in a large degree to "young people," and . . . this in itself constitutes a presumption that it will be rather shy. There are certain things which it is generally agreed not to discuss, not even to mention, before young people.[72]

That is, in talking about age and the novel James redefines a very general problem of bad writing being encouraged by unreflective and uncritical readers as a much more specific problem of genteel discretion before the sexually inexperienced. As does the society he analyzes in *The Awkward Age*, James decides where to draw the line between the adult and the young person by the presumption of virginity or its lack. When James lumps together women and children as readers, he is not moved by the same sense of their shared social subordination that moved earlier commentators to lump together these two figures, in opposition to the gentleman reader. Rather, James is building up the role of sexual knowledge. Why build up the importance of sexual knowledge in this way instead of blaming silly novels on the usual suspects, for instance, social class or gender? In this rhetorical strategy "The Future of the Novel" reflects its place in the history of sexuality, a late-nineteenth-century moment in the long process described by Michel Foucault through which sexuality takes on greater cultural importance. Sexuality becomes the open secret that can potentially explain everything from weak bodies and weak minds to weak books. This open secret also marks adulthood.

"The Future of the Novel" has often been celebrated as a plea for the explicit representation of sexual desire in English novels, a repudiation of repressive Victorian standards of literary gentility. In this critical narrative, James's essay points directly to Modernism's sex scenes, to D. H. Lawrence and to the 1921 trial of *Ulysses* for obscenity. Leon Edel, for example, grandly identifies the demand that English novelists be allowed to talk about sex as the "throbbing question raised by [James] in his Olympian search for the novel's future," although James's contemporaries George Moore and Thomas Hardy made similar demands ("I invented adultery," Moore boasted).[73] More recently, Tessa Hadley offers a more nuanced version of this narrative by celebrating James's late novels for achieving "a grown-up reconciliation with, and honoring of, the sensual side of life." She sees James's "aristocratic" style as his way "of writing himself out of that common-sensical middle-class middle-ground which the English-language novel had made its own . . . that had always been profoundly ill at ease with worldliness, with glamour, and with sex."[74]

There is some truth to this critical narrative. James does indeed link being "grown-up" to talking about sex, as well as to an aristocratic style in general. And the conclusion of "The Future of the Novel" does indeed demand that novelists be free to represent "the great relation between men and women, the constant world-renewal." This story of Henry James as the champion of the sexual liberation of the English novel is, however, incomplete and in some ways misleading. One problem is that James does not in fact describe sexual acts in his novels. As Peter Brooks reminds us, while James praised the "seriousness" of French novelists such as Zola and appreciated in principle George Sands's attempt to describe the "ardent forces of the heart," he also consistently criticized the French novel as "unclean."[75] The critical narrative of modernist sexual liberation focuses on the explicit representation of acts and desires more narrowly than James does himself. Michael Moon aptly suggests that wishing for an explicit sexual encounter in a James novel is a bit like wishing for a named sexual partner in his biography rather than valuing the "mobile, various" nature of desire James offers.[76] More centrally important to this study, this critical narrative fails to consider the fact that Henry James did not merely ripen into adulthood himself, but also helped to make this sense of adulthood possible. That is, the sexual liberation narrative takes a "grown-up" appreciation for "the sensual side of life" as a given. It does not consider the increasing consciousness of age in general and of adulthood in particular in the late nineteenth and early twentieth centuries as a historical process.

In contrast, in talking about sexual content, James himself often foregrounds the history of age. He is not troubled, for example, by the absence of sex scenes in Dickens and Scott because they are Dickens and Scott, perfect representatives of their own time. For James, encounters with novels seem to rival sexual encounters themselves in quirky indescribability, but he tries to describe the experience anyway in order to defend the difference of the nineteenth-century novel from the kind of novel that he thinks his own time requires: "One can only talk for one's self, and of the English and American novelists of whom I am fond, I am so superlatively fond that I positively prefer to take them as they are. I cannot so much as imagine Dickens and Scott without the 'lovemaking' left, as the phrase is, out. They were, to my perception, absolutely right." But what was right for Dickens and Scott is no longer right for twentieth-century novelists:

> Why not therefore assume, it will accordingly be asked, that discriminations, which have served their purpose so well in the past, will continue not less successfully to meet the case? What will you have better than Dickens and Scott? Nothing certainly *can* be . . . The difficulty lies in the fact that two of the great conditions have changed. The novel is older, and so are the young.

What does James mean by remarking that the young, as well as the novel, are now older?

He claims that in the eighteenth century, "when society was frank, was free about the incidents and accidents of the human constitution, the novel took the same robust ease as society." Instead of talking about a general loss of frankness about sexual aspects of the human condition, however, James shifts to talking about something else: age. He suggests that in the nineteenth century, something new about age caused a kind of censorship unknown to the novel of the previous century. The young became intrusively present: "The young were then so very young that they were not table-high. But they began to grow, and from the moment their little chins rested on the mahogany, Richardson and Fielding began to go under it."[77] By describing the young as having grown old enough to rest their little chins on mahogany table-tops, James suggests the intrusion of their felt presence into an adult realm of conversation, of literature and literary criticism.

As we have seen, in one important sense this statement is historically untrue. In this moment, James is in fact trying to call a new adult cultural realm into being, not to defend such a place from the suddenly intrusive gaze of the young. The sexually frank eighteenth-century novel was not an adults-only pleasure. Richardson and Fielding wrote for a mixed-age audience, claiming to educate readers of all ages. In another sense, however, James is right: new standards of genteel propriety are often imposed on readers of all ages by invoking the young. It is not that the young have somehow grown old enough to bother adults, but rather that the social categories of childhood and adulthood have grown important enough to conflict.

James does not merely theorize about such a shift; his own development as a novelist reflects it. As we have seen, the canonical work of James's middle period makes adulthood interesting by heightening this effect of distance, focusing on child characters who gaze longingly at adults and their world of complex sexual relationships across a seemingly impassable gulf. Adulthood is not yet interesting, however, in James's first novel, *Watch and Ward*, originally published as a serial in *The Atlantic Monthly* in 1871 and then as a book in 1878. James eventually disowned *Watch and Ward* by excluding it from his collected works. This early work reveals something of how his own ideas of age grew out of, as well as grew away from, those of his more popular and less age-demarcated predecessors. In James's later work, not only are the sexual lives of adults a tabooed book whose half-open pages are constantly glimpsed by children, but sexual desire between generations is also equally veiled and equally intriguing.[78] *Watch and Ward* differs from such later work in that it does not gaze longingly at adulthood. *Watch and Ward* is also an explicit inter-generational romance, but one whose young heroine is largely unmoved by older people and their sexual desires, either for each other or for herself.

Watch and Ward is undeniably amateurish in comparison to James's later novels. Twenty-nine-year-old Roger Lawrence, the kind man who adopts the novel's twelve-year-old heroine, Nora Lambert, simply raises her to be his wife. He explains his plan to his first love: "You know that, two years ago, I adopted a homeless little girl. One of these days she will be a lovely woman. I mean to do what I can to make her one. Perhaps, six years hence, she will be grateful enough not to refuse me as you did . . . I have begun at the beginning. It will be my own fault if I have not the perfect wife."[79] Although it baulked at coarse language, the genteel literary code welcomed this mixed-age heterosexual romance plot for its mixed-age audience. As Alfred Habegger notes, *Watch and Ward* is James's "first and last attempt to write a happy love story about the leading couple in American fiction of the 1850s and 1860s, the middle-aged lover and the precocious girl."[80] For this novel's first audience, a seventeen-year age gap such as that between Nora and Roger was charming rather than scandalous.

Even the fact that James was *not* simply writing this familiar story in *The Awkward Age* was not apparent to all of his contemporary readers. An anonymous 1899 review in *Literature* persists in reading the story it expects to find. This reviewer praises as "credible and, even in a suppressed sort of way, touching" the finale in which "the elderly Mr. Longdon . . . gradually overcomes the shock of the contrast between the faded romances of the past and the rather slangy prose of the present – a recovery which at last becomes so complete that he makes Nanda his wife."[81] In his review of Louisa May Alcott's novel *Moods*, James himself attacked this mixed-age heterosexual romance plot, not as sexually predatory towards minors, but rather as clichéd: "We are utterly weary of stories about precocious little girls. In the first place, they are in themselves disagreeable and unprofitable objects of study; and in the second, they are always the precursors of a not less unprofitable middle-aged lover."[82] As early as 1938, critics noted the irony of James attacking the same couple he would build so many novels around, middle-aged men and precocious and desirable girls such as Isabel Archer, Verena Tarrant, Maisie Farange, and Nanda Brookenham.[83]

Although *Watch and Ward* introduces Roger's marriage plot as benevolent, it also expresses some anxiety about this plot's possibly "egotistical" nature. The narrator assures us that "in the constant strife between his [Roger's] egotistical purpose and his generous temper, the latter kept gaining ground, and Nora innocently enjoyed the spoils of victory." Roger fails to fascinate either his ward or the reader, not merely because he is fussy and decent, but also because he inhabits a James novel that has yet to commit itself to the glamour of adulthood. A recurring source of humor is Roger's inability to flirt with his ward or to arrange Byronic scenarios to make himself glamorous in her eyes: "She has seen me scratching my head, she has seen me counting on my fingers! Before she is seventeen she will be mortally tired of me . . . I ought to snub her and scold her and bully her and tell her she's deplorably plain, – treat her as Rochester treats Jane Eyre," Roger mourns. He contemplates but cannot carry through the continental methods of the Countess and little Aggie, or Gilbert Osmond and Pansy: "If I were only a good old Catholic, that I might shut her up in a convent and keep her childish and stupid and contented!"[84] Since Nora's perceptions focus mainly on climbing trees and school rivalries rather than Roger's doings, he is right to worry about his marriage plot. To bring about the final match, James is reduced to a flurry of melodramatic coincidences that leaves Nora wandering the city streets without a penny in her pocket, with no alternative but rescue by Roger.

Roger himself is a very rough draft of *The Awkward Age*'s Mr. Langdon and *What Maisie Knew*'s Sir Claude, kind gentlemen who interest themselves in a girl or very young woman and who fail, in various fascinating ways, in their efforts to help her as they intend. Roger already has the gentility, the money, and the aura of romantic disappointment common to these men. Roger succeeds much better than any of them, however, and his story is much less interesting than any of theirs, because he is free to simply marry the girl he adopts. Although it includes a younger woman and an older man, as well as a number of letters and journal entries describing trans-Atlantic travel, in this very early novel James has not yet found his great subject, the aesthetic possibilities of "the unique phenomenon of a distance, however close it may be." This structure of difference will help James elevate adulthood and the adult novel from demographic description to a literary ideal.

To turn from *Watch and Ward* to James's 1913 memoir, *A Small Boy and Others*, is a bit of a shock. While Nora is cheerfully oblivious of Roger, in James's memoir we see avid cross-generational observation doubled. Here the observer is split into an adult narrator who watches his child self with an intensity that is topped only by the rapt attention with which this child self watches the adults around him. And in this narrative, even as a small boy, Henry James had always been in pursuit of one thing: the truly adult novel. In this memoir James stages tantalizing close encounters between his younger self and what he suggestively calls "the tabooed book, of whatever description." Versions of this encounter become a centerpiece of Modernism, invoked in obscenity trials as late as the 1962 trial over the British publication of *Lady Chatterley's Lover* with which *For Adult Audiences* began. "The tabooed book" is the adult novel: a synecdoche for the sexual knowledge, critical intelligence, freedom from middle-class morality, and general glamour of twentieth-century adulthood itself. As we saw in the Introduction, in the 1960 *Lady Chatterley* trial age-leveling triumphed over gender and social status as a principle for organizing reading when the court agreed that "Society cannot fix its standards by what is suitable for a young person of 14." In the encounters with tabooed books that James describes, we likewise see the importance of age for describing readers.

A Small Boy and Others contains three such encounters with at least potentially tabooed books, three candidates for the status of adult novel: Solon Robinson's *Hot Corn* (1853), Maria Cummins's *The Lamplighter* (1854), and Baroness Tautphoeus's *The Initials* (1850). *The Initials* itself illustrates the dynamics of such a scene. "No girl of seventeen can read a work of this description without danger," the hero declares on surprising his beloved with George Sand. "I am surprised that you did not yourself perceive that it was not suited to a person of your age or – – –," he declares.[85] The scene moves on from this blank, presumably a reference to sexual inexperience, to the read-aloud test of gentility: "'It is not exactly adapted for reading aloud,' said Hildegarde with some embarrassment. 'That is an infallible criterion by which you may know what to read for the next ten years,' said Hamilton."[86] The danger of the tabooed book tends to be directly linked to marriage when the young person is female, as in this scene. In the climax of *The Awkward Age*, for example, Nanda's famous revelation that she has read a tabooed book confirms her unmarriageability. Even in such cases as Hildegarde and Nanda's, however, the problem is specifically age and the assumption of virginity rather than gender itself. Hildegarde will be able to read all the French novels she likes, with all the silent, salacious privacy such novels require, once she is twenty-eight and married. Similarly, although "too hideous" and "so revolting" in connection with Nanda, the forbidden novel, whose title is never given, is unobjectionable reading for her mother, Mr. Vanderbrook, or the very recently married Aggie.[87]

Hot Corn is perhaps James's flashiest tabooed book. His description of his near-encounter with it demonstrates in miniature the techniques that "The Future of the Novel" and his middle works use to construct a specific idea of adulthood and to surround this idea with a thick imaginative aura. James invokes a "very old" world full of "great vague connections," then offers sexual knowledge as this world's only definite content. Young James does not read this tabooed book but rather overhears his father's *New York Tribune* friends discussing it during a visit to the newspaper office. James implies that *Hot Corn* falls under the masculine category of pornography. Playing with its suggestive title, he implies at some length that the "mystery of the tabooed book" is sexual knowledge. He presents sexual knowledge as the never-quite-discovered, always-interesting secret of adulthood.

First appearing as a series of sketches in the *Tribune* (1853), Solon Robinson's *Hot Corn* shares the adult, masculine glamour of the newspaper itself. James describes the "big" world of *Tribune* reporters, his father's friends. The measure of his admiration for these young men is the fact that he supposes them to be "very old": "It was big to me, big with the breath of great vague connections, and I supposed the gentlemen very old, though since aware that they must have been, for the connections, remarkably young."[88] *Hot Corn* promises the young James access to these great vague adult connections. What makes this a funny scene is the gap between what the child believes and what all the adults (James as memoirist, *Tribune* men, and reader) know, or seem to know – the suggestion that the allure of *Hot Corn* is pornographic:

> I also became aware that even the most alluring fiction was not always for little boys to read . . . I recall my prompt desire to make acquaintance with it no less than the remark . . . that the work, however engaging, was not one that should be left accessible to an innocent child.

James enjoys describing at some length his young self as puzzled by the "ranker actuality" of *Hot Corn* and its author, "the improper Mr. Robinson," wondering exactly "where his impropriety . . . could possibly have dwelt." The book is described as a minor "success of scandal," a tawdry pleasure rightly veiled from an innocent child. It is the child's exclusion that creates the mystery and excitement; here sex is fascinating because it is a secret, not a secret because it is fascinating. Moreover, the secret of *Hot Corn* becomes an object of permanent wonder because it is never revealed: "Neither then nor afterwards was the secret of 'Hot Corn' revealed to me, and the sense of privation was to be more prolonged, I fear, than the vogue of the tale, which even as a success of scandal couldn't have been great."[89] The book remains one of the intriguing blank spaces at the center of James's text, a mystery strongly tinged with scandal. In this description of a young person glimpsing a naughty book James subordinates gender to age. Although lethal means are not necessary in this case, young James must be saved just as the young Ambient boy must be saved from sexual knowledge. As we shall see, however, except in James's description of it, *Hot Corn* was not exactly a naughty book.

Far from merely enjoying "a vogue . . . which even as a success of scandal couldn't have been great," *Hot Corn* was a best-seller that crossed over to the stage "with a blast second only to that of *Uncle Tom's Cabin*."[90] Moreover, the book is largely a reformist tract, a set of interlocking sentimental stories written by a journalist in full crusade against the exploitation and neglect of the urban poor, the gender gap in wages, and, above all else, the legal sale of alcohol. It is "Dedicated to Horace Greeley, and to his co-laborers, the editors of the New York Tribune; the Friends of the Working Man, the Advocates of lifting up poor down-trodden humanity; the Ardent

Supporters of, and Earnest Advocates for, the Maine Law; the Wishers for Better Rewards for Women's Labor, And All Honest Industry, This Volume is Respectfully Dedicated by your Friend and Fellow Worker, The Author." *Hot Corn* opens by inviting the reader to see and then alleviate poverty in the streets of New York at night:

> Visit this city – walk with me from nine o'clock to midnight, through the streets of New York . . . read the first interview of the author with little Katy, the Hot Corn girl, and the story of her life . . . and you will then exclaim "What does it mean that I see these things in the very heart of this great commercial city, where wealth, luxury, extravagance, all abound in such profusion?" Surely the condition of the people, the ways and wants of the poor, cannot be known, or they would be improved.[91]

These life scenes are fragmentary bildungsromans, on the domestic model of *Jane Eyre* rather than the cosmopolitan *Education of Wilhelm Meister*. Through them, we follow several different child victims as they either die young from poverty and drunken abuse, are corrupted by their environment, or reform their own angry and undisciplined natures, becoming married, Protestant, productive members of society. Dramatized, *Hot Corn* was one of a number of wildly popular and thoroughly respectable mid-century temperance melodramas that drew a "new middle-class audience" to a newly genteel version of the theatre. P. T. Barnum explains the success of his own theatre (one of those that staged *Hot Corn*) in terms of the same standards that defined the domestic mixed-age novel: "I abolished all vulgarity and profanity from the stage, and prided myself upon the fact that parents and children could attend the performances . . . and not be shocked or offended by anything they might see or hear."[92] In print, *Hot Corn* contains more references to prostitution than does its dramatization, but it too at least aspires to be militantly genteel. "It is a work for the fireside of every family," declares the publisher's "Introduction": "It is a work of high tone, that must do good . . . [and] will prove one of the most acceptable to the moral portion of the community, ever published."[93]

What makes *Hot Corn* an adult book in James's account is neither its stories of growing into mature domestic virtue nor its social reformist agenda, but rather its sexual content. In his retelling, a fairly well-respected plea to uplift down-trodden humanity directed to the family audience becomes an adults-only pleasure, an open secret. To our eyes, and possibly to the incisive eyes of Henry James, *Hot Corn* is undeniably an example of "the city-as-mystery genre [which] exploited the prurient appetites of readers who sought voyeuristic titillation."[94] But prurient titillation works best when it has a plausible cover story, and *Hot Corn* does. Although it contains girls driven to prostitution by poverty, sometimes combined with trickery, none of these scenes achieve the heated intensity of *Pamela* or *Clarissa*, and they are heavily outnumbered by passages such as the deathbed pro-temperance plea of Little Katy, the child who hawks the eponymous hot corn through the streets of New York.

Moreover, although the book is written in the voice of a *Tribune* man, it does not share the all-male conviviality created by James's description of the *Tribune* office. Instead, it directly addresses a genteel domestic audience of socially ambitious mothers and fathers. "Mothers, mothers – mothers that sleep on soft couches – hear me, hear me – hear of the bitter fruits the rum trade bears – the rats had devoured the life blood of that child," Robinson implores. "Parents, don't nickname your children," he begs, warning against "low-bred" names:

> Parents, don't nickname your children, it is a step down that may carry them to the bottom of the ladder . . . Never call William, Bill; or Catherine, Kate . . . it will, perhaps, be the direct cause of their ruin as they grow up. Who would think of speaking a foul word to Miss Mary Dudley? Who would speak with respect to Moll Dud? Parents, think of it.[95]

The 1854 edition includes a closely printed page of testimonials from Christian papers: we are told, for example, that these sketches "evince a dramatic skill worthy of Dickens, and powerfully appeal in behalf of the poor, vicious, and down-trodden, on grounds which sound Christian morality and feeling cannot help but approve of." Solon Robinson himself assures us in the "Author's Preface" that for each volume sold, "a portion of the purchase money will go to ameliorate the condition of the poor."[96]

James's description of his near-encounter with *Hot Corn* mimics his middle work in its exclusions as well as in its creation of sexual knowledge as the open secret that marks adulthood. It cuts out the economic dimension of age, the problem of working children and idle elders that mesmerizes Dickens. These issues are foregrounded in Maria S. Cummins's *The Lamplighter* (1854), a book with which James's parents unsuccessfully tried to satisfy his demand for a "grown-up" novel. James secretly rejected *The Lamplighter* as a children's book disguised as an adult one. He remembers his "absorbed perusal" of *The Lamplighter*, "over which I fondly hung and which would have been my first 'grown-up' novel – it had been soothingly offered me for that – had I consented to take it as really and truly grown-up. I couldn't have said what it lacked for the character, only I had my secret reserves."[97] *The Lamplighter* was in fact neither a children's book nor a "really and truly grown-up" one but rather family reading, another example of the mixed-age genre that the author of *A Small Boy and Others* had spent his career breaking up and reclassifying. Aimed at the read-aloud audience of the family fireside, this mid-century sentimental and reformist work sold even better than *Hot Corn*.

What was it about *The Lamplighter* that disqualified it for James as a "grown-up novel"? It is illustrated and it describes characters broadly for a didactic purpose – but the same is true of *Hot Corn*. *The Lamplighter* is as sentimental, reforming, and pro-temperance as *Hot Corn*. According to many of the standards that now separate children's literature from adults', the books look similar, and look similarly adult. Both are long (*Hot Corn* is 408 pages; *The Lamplighter* 480); both include complicated sentences and high-flown vocabulary; both describe injustice and have an explicit agenda of social reform. Both also echo *Jane Eyre* in describing angry, mistreated, pagan little girls growing into self-controlled Protestant ladies. The one marked difference is sexual content. *The Lamplighter* lacks *Hot Corn*'s interest in connecting poverty and prostitution, and lacks its detailed descriptions of the crowded sleeping arrangements of the urban poor. Like *Hot Corn*, *The Lamplighter* begins with night falling on a squalid world of unredeemed urban streets. Perhaps significantly, however, its young heroine (though dirty and unloved) is perched in the doorway of a house rather than being a fully-fledged street-child:

> It was growing dark in the city . . . Upon the wooden door-step of a low-roofed, dark, and unwholesome-looking house, sat a little girl, who was gazing up the street with much earnestness . . . the narrow streets and dark lanes [were] dirtier and more cheerless than ever; for, mixed with the mud and filth which abound in those neighborhoods where the poor are crowded together, the beautiful snow had lost all its purity.[98]

The Lamplighter's Gerty is always at least liminally connected to a domestic space, dark and unwholesome though it may be, while Katy the Hot-Corn Girl consorts with street-walkers. For the purpose of making adulthood glamorous, sexual knowledge is a better secret than is poverty, child labor, or drunkenness.

What James gains from the fleeting encounter he stages between *Hot Corn* and childhood innocence is a lasting sense of wonder. Different in context as it is from the Wordsworthian child's wonder at mountains and cataracts, this moment still reads as a version of the sublime in its enduring power to disturb as well as to uplift. What transfixes James's younger self is not any random or unspecified sense of wonder, however, or finally even wonder at adult sexuality in particular. What little James encounters in this moment is the sublimity of distinction. He is haunted forever after by wonder at "discrimination" itself:

> The pang occasioned by this warning has scarcely yet died out for me, nor my sense of my first wonder at the discrimination – so great became from that moment the mystery of the tabooed book, of whatever identity; the question, in my breast, of why, if it was to be so right for others, it was only to be wrong for me. I remember the soreness of the thought that it was I rather who was wrong for the book – which was somehow humiliating: in that amount of discredit one couldn't but be involved.[99]

The qualification "of whatever identity" matters here. What James wants is the power of a secret, not its content. While a developmental story such as the bildungsroman can end with the revelation of sexual knowledge, James's open-ended dramas of divided perception and cognition need the structure of simultaneous closeness and difference, an unbridgeable but always-fascinating gap.

Although James never reads the tabooed book, he finally meets his first grown-up novel in Baroness Tautphoeus's *The Initials* (1850). Like a transatlantic innocent in one of his own novels, he encounters the baroness aboard ship, in a "fluttered little cabin," although he is going no farther than New Brighton: "When one blest afternoon on the New Brighton boat I waded into *The Initials* I saw how right I had been [to doubt *The Lamplighter* was truly "grown-up"]. *The Initials* was grown-up and the difference thereby exquisite; it came over me with the very first page, assimilated in the fluttered little cabin to which I had retired with it."[100] What constitutes this exquisite difference? What made James so certain, from the very first page, that *The Initials* "was grown-up"? In formal terms such as vocabulary, length, and sentence and plot structure, *The Initials* and *The Lamplighter* are similar and are equally unlike a nineteenth- or twentieth-century children's book. But neither is marked by the conspicuous formal complexity or opaqueness of plot that increasingly characterize James's own writing and that help to make so surprising, to a twenty-first-century critic, the very proposition that Henry James ever felt himself to be in uncomfortable proximity to young readers.

Unlike *Hot Corn* and *The Lamplighter*, *The Initials* is not a bildungsroman. It does not trace the development of a young person to adulthood. While both *Hot Corn* and *The Lamplighter* focus on the pathos of child victims and assume a reader eager to follow their gendered development, in *The Initials* children are background noise. The presence of the heroine's unpleasant little brother in a crowded coach is merely a good excuse for the heroine to escape to the hero's more elegant and comfortable coach. The marriage plot is similarly beside the point. Although the young English hero ultimately marries a young German lady, the novel focuses more on observing the German social scene, on "German characters and life," than on the hero and heroine's conscious and unconscious development into husband and wife. The opening pages tackle misunderstandings of social precedence caused by the difference between English and German inheritance customs. We are never allowed to forget that the hero is a tourist, and are constantly encouraged to learn from his cross-cultural blunders. The first barrier between himself and his future wife, for instance, is German table manners. Although Hildegarde attracts Hamilton with her perfect "German beauty" ("blue eyes, blooming cheeks, red lips, and a profusion of brown hair"), she disgusts him by eating with her fingers:

> The young ladies, to Hamilton's infinite astonishment, took the chicken-bones in their fingers and detached the meat from them with their teeth! He felt at once convinced that they were immeasurably vulgar, thereby forming an erroneous conclusion very common on the part of his travelling countrymen, who are not aware that the mode of eating is in Germany no such exact criterion of manners as it is in England.[101]

The threat of being disinherited by Hamilton's uncle allows the novel to spend hundreds of pages exploring such erroneous conclusions, before abruptly closing with the hero and heroine in serene possession of his estate. The exquisite difference from *The Lamplighter* that is visible from "the very first page" of *The Initials* is its wealthy setting, cheerfully worldly tone, and above all, its avid, nonjudgmental interest in the cultural differences between the high society of Germany and that of England. What James finds in this novel is the foregrounding of difference itself, the combination of intimacy and distance that will shape his conception both of nations and of adults.

An Englishman in Germany, an American in Paris, or a child in the midst of the sexual intrigues of an elite, non-domestic world: all are variations on this kind of difference. Viewing adulthood from a child's perspective combines such intimacy and such distance, giving the figure of the adult at once a strangeness and a reality that it might not otherwise possess. That is, it helps to infuse the flat fact of adulthood as a numerical or demographic category with the glamour of adulthood as an ideal. The very uncertainty of the nature of adulthood – an uncertainty that reveals itself in everything from the not-at-all-new phenomenon of crossover fiction to the relative historical novelty of the psychological norm itself – makes the category of the adult a fascinating one. We perhaps still feel the emotional pull of the adult's glamorous mystery, the combination of nearness and distance built into this figure which, like the country house in "The Lesson of the Master," seems to recede as you advance.

Adulthood as a category seems equally elusive, given the confusion of demography and value in writing about it. This study began by considering the cameo appearance of the fading idea of age as status in the 1960 trial over the British publication of *Lady Chatterley's Lover* (1928). It seems appropriate to end by noting D. H. Lawrence's role in popularizing the newer sense of adulthood whose history we have traced. Lawrence, a former school librarian, knew Burnett's work well and often wrote in conscious opposition to it. In her discussion of common elements in *Lady Chatterley's Lover* (1928) and *The Secret Garden* (1910), Judith Plotz describes the sense of age she finds in Lawrence's work, the sense of age that, I argue, James, Lawrence, and other Modernist writers helped to create. Plotz remarks that in breaking with what he saw as the "dreary norms" of middle-class domestic fiction, Lawrence cannot simply write "for adults" but must also write "*against* children."[102] That is, he must fight to position his novels at a certain point on a relatively new age-levelled scale. This Modernist construction of adult readers, characters, and authors remains a compelling one. In many ways, it is still consonant with important assumptions that economics, politics, law, education, medicine, and psychology make about the self, today as well as in the early twentieth century. In the past few decades, however, it has become easier to recognize this ideal as belonging to a historically specific moment in the life of the novel. The growth of scholarship on the history of children's literature, childhood, and age more generally has made more visible the rise of adulthood as a demographic category. We can see how the relatively new social importance of this category has blurred demography with particular moral and aesthetic evaluations to create an always threatened ideal: adulthood as a standard of excellence for readers, characters, and authors.

Notes

1 INTRODUCTION

1. C. H. Rolph, ed., *The Trial of Lady Chatterley: Regina V. Penguin Books Limited* (Baltimore: Penguin Books, 1961).
2. Henry James, "Future of the Novel: An Analysis and a Forecast," in *The Art of Criticism: Henry James on the Theory and the Practice of Fiction*, ed. William R. Veeder and Susan M. Griffin (University of Chicago Press, 1986), 243.
3. Philippe Ariès, *Centuries of Childhood: A Social History of Family Life* (New York: Vintage Books, 1965).
4. Mitzi Myers, "The Erotics of Pedagogy: Historical Intervention, Literary Representation, the 'Gift of Education,' and the Agency of Children," *Children's Literature* 23 (1995): 3.
5. M. O. Grenby, *The Child Reader, 1700–1840* (Cambridge University Press, 2011), 91.
6. Andrea Immel and Michael Witmore, eds., *Childhood and Children's Books in Early Modern Europe, 1550–1800* (New York: Routledge, 2006), 5.
7. Ian Watt, "Serious Reflections on *The Rise of the Novel*," *Novel: A Forum on Fiction* 1, no. 3 (1968): 205–18.
8. Edward H. Jacobs, "Eighteenth-Century British Circulating Libraries and Cultural Book History," *Book History* 6, no. 1 (2003): 1–22.
9. William Beatty Warner, *Licensing Entertainment: The Elevation of Novel Reading in Britain, 1684–1750* (Berkeley: University of California Press, 1998), 134.
10. Mitzi Myers, "Moral Majorities?: Reconceiving the Literary World We Have Lost," *The Lion and the Unicorn* 19, no. 1 (1995): 138.
11. Frances Ferguson, "The Afterlife of the Romantic Child: Rousseau and Kant Meet Deleuze and Guattari," *The South Atlantic Quarterly* 102, no. 1 (2003): 222.
12. Keith Thomas, *Age and Authority in Early Modern England* (Oxford University Press, 1976), 205.
13. Steven Mintz, "Reflections on Age as a Category of Historical Analysis," *The Journal of the History of Childhood and Youth* 1, no. 1 (2008): 93.
14. Ibid.

15. Thomas, *Age and Authority in Early Modern England*, 205.
16. Ibid.
17. Ibid., 207.
18. Ibid.
19. Mintz, "Reflections on Age as a Category of Historical Analysis," 92.
20. Adam Fox, Paul Griffiths, and Steve Hindle, eds., *The Experience of Authority in Early Modern England* (New York: St. Martin's Press, 1996), 20.
21. Ibid.
22. Ilana Krausman Ben-Amos, *Adolescence and Youth in Early Modern England* (New Haven: Yale University Press, 1994), 10–11.
23. Ibid., 10.
24. Thomas, *Age and Authority in Early Modern England*, 222.
25. OED "boy": "1918 *Army Orders* Nov. 35. The following additional column will be *inserted* in the table of corresponding ranks . . . Royal Air Force . . . Air Mechanic, 3rd Class. Private, 2nd Class. Clerk, 3rd Class. Boy. 1924 *R.A.F. King's Regulations* I. p. vii, Airman, or Airmen. These words, wherever they occur, will be held to include a warrant officer, a N.C.O., an aircraftman, and a boy."
26. Thomas Alan King, *The Gendering of Men, 1600–1750* (Madison: University of Wisconsin Press, 2004), 22.
27. Ibid.; T. E. James, "The Age of Majority," *The American Journal of Legal History* 4, no. 1 (January 1960): 30. Of course, guardians who held land in trust for medieval wards also had an interest in making such wardship last as long as possible.
28. Fox, Griffiths, and Hindle, *The Experience of Authority in Early Modern England*, 21.
29. Ibid., 38.
30. Paul-Gabriel Boucé, *Sexuality in Eighteenth-Century Britain* (Manchester University Press, 1982).
31. Thomas Cobbett, *A Fruitfull and Useful Discourse Touching the Honour Due from Children to Parents* (London, 1655). Quoted in Gordon J. Schochet, *The Authoritarian Family and Political Attitudes in 17th-Century England: Patriarchalism in Political Thought* (New Brunswick, NJ: Transaction Books, 1988), 67.
32. Ben-Amos, *Adolescence and Youth in Early Modern England*, 6.
33. Joseph Goldstein, "On Being Adult and Being an Adult in Secular Law," *Daedalus* 105, no. 4 (Fall 1976): 69–87.
34. Holly Brewer, *By Birth or Consent: Children, Law, and the Anglo-American Revolution in Authority* (Chapel Hill: Published for the Omohundro Institute of Early American History and Culture, Williamsburg, Virginia, by the University of North Carolina Press, 2005), 1.
35. G. Stanley Hall, *Adolescence: Its Psychology and Its Relations to Physiology, Anthropology, Sociology, Sex, Crime, Religion and Education* (New York: D. Appleton and Company, 1904).

36. Jeffrey Jensen Arnett, "Emerging Adulthood(s): The Cultural Psychology of a New Life Stage," in *Bridging Cultural and Developmental Approaches to Psychology: New Syntheses in Theory, Research, and Policy*, ed. Lene Arnett Jensen (Oxford University Press, 2011), 255–75.
37. Joan D. Atwood and Corinne Scholtz, "The Quarter-Life Time Period: An Age of Indulgence, Crisis or Both?," *Contemporary Family Therapy: An International Journal* 30, no. 4 (2008): 233–50.
38. Jeffrey Jensen Arnett and Susan Taber, "Adolescence Terminable and Interminable: When Does Adolescence End?," *Journal of Youth and Adolescence* 23, no. 5 (1994): 517–37.
39. James E. Côté, *Arrested Adulthood: The Changing Nature of Maturity and Identity* (New York University Press, 2000), 37.
40. Jean Piaget, "Intellectual Evolution from Adolescence to Adulthood," *Human Development* 51 (2008): 40–47, 46. Reprint of *Human Development* 15 (1972): 1–12.
41. Arnett and Taber, "Adolescence Terminable and Interminable," 520.
42. Adam Smith, *An Inquiry into the Nature and Causes of the Wealth of Nations* (Oxford: Clarendon Press, 1976), vol. 1, 2.
43. Thomas, *Age and Authority in Early Modern England*, 231.
44. Alexander Pope, *The Dunciad*, lines 147–48.
45. Fox, Griffiths, and Hindle, *The Experience of Authority in Early Modern England*, 32.
46. Leslie Paris, "Through the Looking Glass: Age, Stages, and Historical Analysis," *The Journal of the History of Childhood and Youth* 1, no. 1 (2008): 111.
47. Beverly Lyon Clark, *Kiddie Lit: The Cultural Construction of Children's Literature in America* (Baltimore: Johns Hopkins University Press, 2003). For another stimulating exception to the habit of seeing the history of the novel and children's literature as unrelated, see Felicity A. Hughes, "Children's Literature: Theory and Practice," *ELH* 45, no. 3 (Autumn 1978): 542–61.
48. Alan Richardson, *Literature, Education, and Romanticism: Reading as Social Practice, 1780–1832* (Cambridge University Press, 1994).
49. Ina Ferris, *The Achievement of Literary Authority: Gender, History, and the Waverley Novels* (Ithaca, NY: Cornell University Press, 1991).
50. George Orwell, *Inside the Whale, and Other Essays* (Harmondsworth: Penguin, in association with Secker & Warburg, 1962).
51. Claudia Nelson, *Precocious Children and Childish Adults: Age Inversion in Victorian Literature* (Baltimore: Johns Hopkins University Press, 2012).
52. James, "Future of the Novel: An Analysis and a Forecast," 243.
53. Maria Tatar, "No More Adventures in Wonderland," *The New York Times*, 10 October 2011, sec. A23.
54. William Safire, "Besotted With Potter," *The New York Times*, 27 January 2000, sec. Opinion, 27.
55. Joel Stein, "Adults Should Read Adult Books," *The New York Times – Room for Debate*, 28 March 2012, www.nytimes.com/roomfordebate/2012/03/28/the-power-of-young-adult-fiction/adults-should-read-adult-books.

2 REWRITING *ROBINSON CRUSOE*: AGE AND THE ISLAND

1. Jean-Jacques Rousseau, *Emile: Or, On Education* (New York: Basic Books, 1979), 184. All quotations in this chapter are from this edition, with page references noted parenthetically in the text.
2. Leslie Stephen, *Hours in a Library*, new edn., with additions (New York: Johnson Reprint Corp., 1968).
3. *The Family Instructor. In Three Parts. With a Recommendatory Letter by the Reverend Mr. S. Wright* (London, 1715). Page references to this edition throughout this chapter will be noted parenthetically in the text.
4. C. John Sommerville, *The Discovery of Childhood in Puritan England* (Athens: University of Georgia Press, 1992).
5. James Janeway, *A Token for Children. Being an Exact Account of the Conversion, Holy and Exemplary Lives and Joyful Deaths of Several Young Children. By James Janeway Minister of the Gospel. To Which Is Added, A Token for the Children of New-England. Or, Some Examples of Children, in Whom the Fear of God Was Remarkably Budding before They Dyed; in Several Parts of New-England. Preserved and Published for the Encouragement of Piety in Other Children. With New Additions* (Boston in New-England, 1728), 2.
6. John Bunyan, *A Book for Boys and Girls: Or Temporal Things Spiritualized. By John Bunyan. Licensend and Entred According to Order* [1686] (London, 1701).
7. Charles Gildon and Miscellaneous Pamphlet Collection (Library of Congress), *The Life and Strange Surprizing Adventures of Mr. D— De F–, of London, Hosier: Who Has Liv'd Above Fifty Yeares by Himself in the Kingdoms of North and South Britain . . . : In a Dialogue Between Him, Robinson Crusoe, and His Man Friday, with Remarks Serious and Comical Upon the Life of Crusoe* (London: Printed for J. Roberts, 1719), 71.
8. On the relative unimportance of puberty to early modern developmental schemes, see Ben-Amos, *Adolescence and Youth in Early Modern England*, and my Introduction.
9. See also Kristina Straub, *Domestic Affairs: Intimacy, Eroticism, and Violence Between Servants and Masters in Eighteenth-Century Britain* (Baltimore: Johns Hopkins University Press, 2009).
10. Daniel Defoe, *Robinson Crusoe*, new edn., Oxford World's Classics (Oxford University Press, 2007), 1. All quotations in this chapter are from this edition unless otherwise noted, and page references are given in parentheses in the text.
11. Pat Rogers, ed., *Daniel Defoe: The Critical Heritage* (London: Routledge, 1995), 87.
12. Rogers, *Daniel Defoe*, Letter from Lamb to Walter Wilson, December 1822.
13. Margaret R. Hunt, *The Middling Sort: Commerce, Gender, and the Family in England, 1680–1780* (Berkeley: University of California Press, 1996), 23; Craig Muldrew, *The Economy of Obligation: The Culture of Credit and Social Relations in Early Modern England* (New York: St. Martin's Press, 1998), 182.
14. Hunt, *The Middling Sort*, 34.
15. Muldrew, *The Economy of Obligation*, 188.

16. Ibid., 306.
17. William Fleetwood, *The Relative Duties of Parents and Children, Husbands and Wives, Masters and Servants, Consider'd in Sixteen Sermons: With Three More Upon the Case of Self-murther. By W. Fleetwood, Rector of St. Augustine's, London, and Chaplain in Ordinary to Her Majesty* (London, 1705), 151.
18. Daniel Defoe, *The Complete English Tradesman: Directing Him in the Several Parts . . .* (London: Printed for J. Rivington, 1745). Further page references will be cited parenthetically in the text.
19. Introduction to Oxford World's Classics edition of *Robinson Crusoe*, xxix.
20. Daniel Defoe, *A Second Volume of the Writings of the Author of the True-Born Englishman* (London: 1705), 267.
21. Karl Marx, *Capital: A Critique of Political Economy* (Moscow: Progress Publishers, 1971), 167.
22. Ian P. Watt, *The Rise of the Novel: Studies in Defoe, Richardson and Fielding*, 2nd American edn. (Berkeley: University of California Press, 2001), 63.
23. Muldrew, *The Economy of Obligation*; on the generally low standard of book-keeping in the eighteenth century, see Basil S. Yamey, *Accounting in England and Scotland, 1543–1800* (New York: Garland, 1982); for an example of accurate book-keeping and the challenges of interpreting account books at this historical remove, see Keith Ian Desmond Maslen, *Masters and Men* (London: Kegan Paul, 1975).
24. Gildon, *The Life and Strange Surprizing Adventures of Mr. D*, 92.
25. Diana Spearman, *The Novel and Society* (New York: Barnes & Noble, 1966), 166.
26. See Muldrew, *The Economy of Obligation*, 328, on the importance of the household rather than the individual to the "economic epistemology" of the mid-sixteenth to early eighteenth centuries.
27. Hunt, *The Middling Sort*, 23, 29; similarly Robert B. Shoemaker, "The Decline of Public Insult in London 1660–1800," *Past and Present* 169 (November 2000): 130, suggests that the significance of personal reputation changed over the late seventeenth and early eighteenth centuries as "an increasingly firm distinction was drawn between the public and the private."
28. Quoted in Muldrew, *The Economy of Obligation*, 319.
29. John Locke, *Locke's Second Treatise of Civil Government: An Essay Concerning the True Original, Extent, and End of Civil Government: A Contemporary Selection* (Grand Rapids: W. B. Eerdmans, 1978), section 15.
30. Wolfram Schmidgen, "Robinson Crusoe, Enumeration, and the Mercantile Fetish," *Eighteenth-Century Studies* 35, no. 1 (2001): 54.
31. Ibid.
32. Andrew O'Malley, "Poaching on Crusoe's Island: Popular Reading and Chapbook Editions of Robinson Crusoe," *Eighteenth-Century Life* 35, no. 2 (2011): 18–38.
33. See Margaret Spufford, *Small Books and Pleasant Histories: Popular Fiction and Its Readership in Seventeenth-Century England* (Athens, Ga.: University

of Georgia Press, 1982); Victor E. Neuburg, *The Penny Histories: A Study of Chapbooks for Young Readers over Two Centuries* (New York: Harcourt, Brace & World, 1969); Roger Davis, *Kendrew of York and His Chapbooks for Children: With a Checklist* (Collingham, UK: Elmete Press, 1988).

34. William St. Clair, *The Reading Nation in the Romantic Period* (Cambridge University Press, 2004), 342, cautions against a nostalgic view of chapbooks as the simple and authentic voice of the non-elite readers who bought them.
35. Ibid., 345–50.
36. Spufford, *Small Books and Pleasant Histories.*
37. Bennett A. Brockman, "Robin Hood and the Invention of Children's Literature," *Children's Literature: Annual of The Modern Language Association Division on Children's Literature and The Children's Literature Association* 10 (1982): 3, 5; see also Robert P. Adams, "Bold Bawdry and Open Manslaughter: The English New Humanist Attack on Medieval Romance," *Huntington Library Quarterly* 23, no. 1 (1959): 33–48.
38. M. O. Grenby, "Chapbooks, Children, and Children's Literature," *The Library: The Transactions of the Bibliographical Society* 8, no. 3 (2007): 280; see also St. Clair, *The Reading Nation in the Romantic Period*, 343; Jan S. Fergus, *Provincial Readers in Eighteenth-Century England* (Oxford University Press, 2006), 161.
39. Gildon, *The Life and Strange Surprizing Adventures of Mr. D*, x.
40. O'Malley, "Poaching on Crusoe's Island," 19.
41. Ibid., 20.
42. Daniel Defoe, *Voyages and Travels: Being the Life and Adventures of Robinson Crusoe, of York, Mariner. Who Lived Eight and Twenty Years All Alone in an Unihabited [sic] Island on the Coast of America... Written by Himselfe.* ([London?], 1750).
43. Rousseau, *Emile*, 206; Franco Moretti, *The Novel* (Princeton University Press, 2006), 373, also notes Rousseau's influential decision to edit *Robinson Crusoe* down to the island episode; see also Pat Rogers, *Literature and Popular Culture in Eighteenth Century England* (Brighton: Harvester Press, 1985).
44. Warner, *Licensing Entertainment*, 139.
45. Ian Frederick Moulton, *Before Pornography: Erotic Writing in Early Modern England* (Oxford University Press, 2000), 6, 12, 13–14.
46. Grenby, "Chapbooks, Children, and Children's Literature," 283.
47. See Moulton, *Before Pornography*, 103, for concern about the effect of certain books and pamphlets on "the simpler and least advised" in general rather than on the numerically young in particular; Debora K. Shuger, *Censorship and Cultural Sensibility: The Regulation of Language in Tudor–Stuart England* (Philadelphia: University of Pennsylvania Press, 2006), 64, discusses censorship through the Stuart era, especially the censorship of secular writing, also without reference to age.
48. Maria Edgeworth, *Practical Education; by Maria Edgeworth, Author Of Letters For Literary Ladies, And The Parent's Assistant; and by Richard Lovell Edgeworth, F.R.S. and M.R.I.A.*, (London, 1798), vol. 1, 177.

49. See, for example, Thomas Day's effort to raise two foundlings according to Rousseau's guidelines, or Richard Lovell Edgeworth's similarly disastrous attempt to raise his oldest son as a second Emile.
50. See, for example, Ronald L. Meek, *Social Science and the Ignoble Savage* (Cambridge University Press, 1976). We will consider this link between ideas of age and conjectural history more fully in Chapter 3.
51. See Deborah A. Redman, *The Rise of Political Economy as a Science* (Cambridge, Mass.: MIT Press, 1997), 140.
52. Quoted in Michael White, "Reading and Rewriting: The Production of an Economic Robinson Crusoe," *Southern Review* 15, no. 2 (1982): 134.
53. Ibid., 136; the "individual and isolated hunter or fisher who forms the starting point with Smith and Ricardo, belongs to the insipid illusions of the eighteenth century. They are Robinsonades ... They are the fiction and only the aesthetic fiction of the small and great Robinsonades." Karl Marx, *A Contribution to the Critique of Political Economy* (Chicago: C. H. Kerr, 1913), 265–66.
54. See, for example, Richardson, *Literature, Education, and Romanticism.*
55. Ian P. Watt, *Myths of Modern Individualism: Faust, Don Quixote, Don Juan, Robinson Crusoe* (Cambridge University Press, 1996), 178.
56. Joachim Heinrich Campe, *The New Robinson Crusoe: An Instructive and Entertaining History, for the Use of Children of Both Sexes* (London: Printed for John Stockdale, 1789); Clarence S. Brigham, *Bibliography of American Editions of Robinson Crusoe to 1830* (Worcester, Mass.: The American Antiquarian Society, 1958), 141; Henry Clinton Hutchins and A. Edward Newton Collection (Library of Congress), *Robinson Crusoe and Its Printing, 1719–1731: A Bibliographical Study* (New York: Columbia University Press, 1925).
57. For more on the role of the father in this kind of middle-class domestic education, see Teresa Michals, "Experiments Before Breakfast," in *The Nineteenth-Century Child and Consumer Culture*, ed. Dennis Denisoff (Aldershot: Ashgate, 2008).
58. Mary Wollstonecraft Shelley, *Frankenstein, or, The Modern Prometheus* (Washington, DC: Orchises, 1988), chapter 2.
59. Daniel Defoe, *The Life and Adventures of Robinson Crusoe* (London: Printed for Tabart & Co., 1805). At the Juvenile and School Library No. 157 New Bond Street.
60. Gary Kelly, "Revolution, Reaction, and the Expropriation of Popular Culture: Hannah More's 'Cheap Repository'," *Man and Nature/L'Homme et la Nature* 6 (1987): 147–59; Andrew O'Malley, *The Making of the Modern Child: Children's Literature and Childhood in the Late Eighteenth Century* (New York: Routledge, 2003).
61. Edgeworth, *Practical Education*, 1, 336.
62. Ibid., 1, 337.
63. James, "The Age of Majority," 6.
64. On the fondness of nineteenth-century economic popularizers such as Harriet Martineau for combining Defoe with Adam Smith, see Willie Henderson,

Evaluating Adam Smith (London: Routledge, 2006); Willie Henderson, *Economics as Literature* (London: Routledge, 1995).

65. Peter Ghosh, "'Robinson Crusoe,' The Isolated Economic Man: Max Weber, Marginal Utility Theory, and the 'Spirit' of Capitalism," *Max Weber Studies* 1 (2006): 73.
66. Robert J. Barro, *Macroeconomics* (Cambridge, Mass.: MIT Press, 1997), 59.
67. White, "Reading and Rewriting," 116.
68. Carl Menger, *Principles of Economics: First, General Part* (Glencoe, Ill., Free Press, 1950), 133–36.
69. White, "Reading and Rewriting," 137. Marginalist texts spread this version of Crusoe "as economic calculator and as isolated individual" in England. See, for example, Gossen's *The Development of the Laws of Human Intercourse and the Consequent Rules of Human Action*, published in Braunschweig in 1854; Carl Menger, *Principles of Economics* (1871) (*Grundsätze der Volkswirtschaftslehre*); and W. S. Jevon's *The Theory of Political Economy* (1871).
70. Quoted in Ghosh, "'Robinson Crusoe,' The Isolated Economic Man," 86.
71. White, "Reading and Rewriting," 136; see also Werner Stark, *The Ideal Foundations of Economic Thought; Three Essays on the Philosophy of Economics* (London: K. Paul, Trench, Trubner & Co. Ltd., 1943), 159.
72. Quoted in White, "Reading and Rewriting," 135.
73. William Stanley Jevons, *The Theory of Political Economy* (London: Macmillan and Co., 1888), 80; see also "The Future of Political Economy," in William Stanley Jevons, *The Principles of Economics: A Fragment of a Treatise on the Industrial Mechanism of Society, and Other Papers*, ed. Henry Higgs (New York: A. M. Kelley, 1965).
74. See Michael White's explanation of how this version of Crusoe helped to defend neo-classical economics from the charge that it was too abstract. White, "Reading and Rewriting," 138.
75. Jevons, *The Theory of Political Economy*, 35.
76. Ibid.
77. John Stuart Mill, *Autobiography* (London: Penguin Books, 1990), 155, 122. On the importance to Mill of altruism rather than an "aggregation" model of pleasure, see Elaine Hadley, *Living Liberalism: Practical Citizenship in Mid-Victorian Britain* (University of Chicago Press, 2010).
78. *The Works of Charles and Mary Lamb*, ed. E. V. Lucas (London: Methuen, 1905), 88.
79. Rogers, *Daniel Defoe*, 88. Similarly, in 1841, Thomas De Quincey could still praise the "double character" not just of Robinson Crusoe, but of all Defoe's tales. Unlike Lamb, De Quincey seems unruffled by the prospect even of little girls reading *Roxana: The Fortunate Mistress* (118).
80. Stephen, *Hours in a Library*.
81. Ibid., 173, 175.
82. Ibid., 174.
83. Ibid., 175.

84. John Forster, *The Life of Charles Dickens*, 3 vols. (Boston: Estes & Lauriat, 1872), vol. III, 113.
85. Mary Poovey, "Discriminating Reading," *Victorian Review* 31, no. 2 (2005): 22; Stephen Arata, "On Not Paying Attention," *Victorian Studies* 46, no. 2 (Winter 2004): 193–205.
86. Rogers, *Daniel Defoe*, 130.
87. Ibid.
88. Ibid., 151.
89. Quoted in John Murray, "Books and Reading," *Quarterly Review* 162, no. 324 (April 1886).
90. John Dennis, *Cornhill Magazine* (March 1871), 310–20; quoted in Rogers, *Daniel Defoe*, 200, 201.
91. Ibid., 304.
92. On the development of literary criticism as a profession, see John Guillory, *Cultural Capital: The Problem of Literary Canon Formation* (University of Chicago Press, 1993).
93. Seth Lerer, *Children's Literature: A Reader's History, from Aesop to Harry Potter* (University of Chicago Press, 2009), sums up this idea of the desert island as the ideal developmental playground in describing "the Robinsonian tradition" (131). Boys' fiction leaves the island only in the late nineteenth century, reflecting a larger shift from exploration to Empire: "Throughout the Victorian age, the boy's imaginative geography was moving from the island to the continent" (152).
94. John Robert Moore, "Defoe, Stevenson, and the Pirates," *ELH* 10, no. 1 (1943): 37, 60.
95. Harry F. Robins, "How Smart Was Robinson Crusoe?," *PMLA* 67, no. 5 (1952): 788.

3 DATING *PAMELA*: MR. B., *GOODY TWO-SHOES*, AND THE AGE OF CONSENT

1. Samuel Richardson, *Pamela, or, Virtue Rewarded*, repr. with chronology and updated further reading (London: Penguin Books, 2003), Preface.
2. Although there is no evidence that Richardson read *Robinson Crusoe*, he did print and possibly help to revise Defoe's *Complete English Tradesman*, a book aimed at a similarly "low" audience as the volume of sample letters that became *Pamela*. See T. C. Duncan Eaves and Ben D. Kimpel, *Samuel Richardson: A Biography* (Oxford: Clarendon Press, 1971), 71, 72, 153, 571, and 584.
3. For a contrary view, see, for example, Raymond F. Hilliard, "*Pamela*: Autonomy, Subordination, and the State of Childhood," *Studies in Philology* 83, no. 2 (1986): 201–17; Stuart Wilson, "Richardson's *Pamela*: An Interpretation," *PMLA* 88, no. 1 (January, 1973): 79–91; Patricia Ann Meyer Spacks, *The Adolescent Idea: Myths of Youth and the Adult Imagination* (New York: Basic Books, 1981); Terry J. Castle, "P/B: Pamela as Sexual Fiction," *Studies in English Literature, 1500–1900* 22, no. 3 (1982): 469–89.

4. Helen Shipton, "'Jane Eyre' and the Older Novel," *The Monthly Packet*, 1 November 1896, n.p.
5. Richardson, *Pamela, or, Virtue Rewarded*, 49, 52. Further page references to this edition will be cited parenthetically in the text.
6. Charlotte Brontë, *Jane Eyre* (London: Penguin Books, 2006), 11.
7. See Brewer, *By Birth or Consent*; Ala A. Alryyes, *Original Subjects: The Child, the Novel, and the Nation* (Cambridge, Mass.: Harvard University Press, 2001).
8. Of course, as I discuss in the previous chapter, we should remember that amusing books for children or adults (with or without product tie-ins) still made up a relatively small proportion of printed material through the long eighteenth century. Fictional works are estimated to be still only 4 percent of the books and pamphlets produced in 1770. Bibles, sermons and other devotional works continued to be the most common works in print. See Christopher Flint, *Family Fictions: Narrative and Domestic Relations in Britain, 1688–1798* (Stanford University Press, 1998), 344, 348.
9. Julian Roberts, "The 1765 Edition of 'Goody Two-Shoes'," *The British Museum Quarterly* 29, no. 3/4 (1965): 67–70.
10. On the complex relationship between chapbooks and the new eighteenth-century market in children's books, see Chapter 1 and Grenby, "Chapbooks, Children, and Children's Literature."
11. See, for example, Fergus, *Provincial Readers in Eighteenth-Century England.*
12. Ibid., 164; see also M. O. Grenby, "Adults Only? Children and Children's Books in British Circulating Libraries, 1748–1848," *Book History* 5 (2002): 19–38.
13. John Newbery, *A Little Pretty Pocket-book, Intended for the Instruction and Amusement of Little Master Tommy, and Pretty Miss Polly: With Two Letters from Jack the Giant-Killer; as Also a Ball and Pincushion; The Use of Which Will Infallibly Make Tommy a Good Boy, and Polly a Good Girl. The Tenth Edition. To Which Is Added, a Little Song-book, Being a New Attempt to Teach Children the Use of the English Alphabet, by Way of Diversion* (London, 1760), 66. Further page references to this edition will be cited parenthetically in the text.
14. John W. Yolton, "Locke's Man," *Journal of the History of Ideas* 62, no. 4 (2001): 665.
15. John Locke, *Some Thoughts Concerning Education: And, Of the Conduct of the Understanding*, ed. Ruth Weissbourd Grant and Nathan Tarcov (Indianapolis: Hackett, 1996), 25. Further page references will be cited parenthetically in the text.
16. On the history of children's literature in England, see, for example, F. J. Harvey Darton, *Children's Books in England: Five Centuries of Social Life*, 3rd edn. (Cambridge University Press, 1982); Patricia Demers, *From Instruction to Delight: An Anthology of Children's Literature to 1850* (Oxford University Press, 2008); Mary V. Jackson, *Engines of Instruction, Mischief, and Magic: Children's Literature in England from its Beginnings to 1839* (Aldershot: Scolar Press, 1989); Mary Hilton, Morag Styles, and Victor Watson, *Opening the*

Nursery Door (London: Routledge, 1997). Lerer, *Children's Literature: A Reader's History* stresses pre-eighteenth-century works, especially the creativity involved in editing medieval and early modern school texts.

17. See especially Brewer, *By Birth or Consent.*
18. Locke, *Locke's Second Treatise of Civil Government*, 61.
19. John Locke, *Locke: Political Essays*, ed. Mark Goldie (Cambridge University Press, 1997), 190.
20. Quoted in Brewer, *By Birth or Consent*, 122.
21. Samuel Taylor Coleridge, *The Stateman's Manual* (London: Printed for Gale and Fenner, 1816), 49.
22. Letitia Barbauld, *Lessons for Children. Part III. Being the Second for Children of Three Years Old* (London: J. Johnson, 1795), 6–7.
23. Grenby, *The Child Reader, 1700–1840*, 137.
24. This dedication alludes to Newbery's 1757 *A Collection of Pretty Poems for the Amusement of Children Six Feet High*, a political satire printed in a format identical to his children's books, the title adapted from his earlier *A Collection of Pretty Poems for the Amusement of Children Three Feet High. A Collection . . . for Children Six Feet High* itself points to its mock-status as a children's book as a mock-defense against political libel: as "these poems are professedly published for the use of children six feet high, none else have any business to buy them . . . which consideration alone will prevent any application being made to those of a more elevated rank and situation" (London: J. Newbery, 1757), iv; also quoted in Marcus Wood, *Radical Satire and Print Culture, 1790–1822* (Oxford University Press, 1994). Similarly, Thomas Spence argued for land reform and attacked his political enemies in a series of chapbooks, including *A Supplement to The History of Robinson Crusoe* (1782), "Published for the agreeable perusal of Robinson Crusoe's friends of all sizes"; Wood, *Radical Satire*, 219.
25. Overall, the "Introduction" so closely echoes Oliver Goldsmith's "The Deserted Village," that Goldsmith is often cited as the author (Newbery was also paying Goldsmith's rent at the time the book was published). See Ronald Paulson, "*The History of Little Goody Two-Shoes* as a Children's Book," in *Literary Theory and Criticism: Festschrift Presented to René Wellek in Honor of His Eightieth Birthday* (New York: P. Lang, 1984); and Patricia Crain, "Spectral Literacy: The Case of Goody Two-Shoes," in *Childhood and Children's Books in Early Modern Europe, 1550–1800*, ed. Immel and Witmore, pp. 213–42.
26. On the double address of *Goody Two-Shoes*, see Adrienne E. Kertzer, "Inventing the Child Reader: How We Read Children's Books," *Children's Literature in Education*, 15, no. 1 (1984): 12–21.
27. *The History of Little Goody Two-Shoes: Otherwise Called Mrs. Margery Two-Shoes*, the third edition (London: Printed for J. Newbery, at the Bible and Sun in St. Paul's Church-Yard, 1766), 11. Further references to *Goody Two-Shoes* are to this edition and page references are cited parenthetically in the text.
28. See Alan Richardson, *Literature, Education and Romanticism*, 144.

29. On the prominent place of collections of Aesop's fables in the history of printing, see Lerer, *Children's Literature: A Reader's History*; on Richardson's edition of Aesop, see David Whitley, "Samuel Richardson's Aesop," in *Opening the Nursery Door*, ed. Hilton, Styles, and Watson, 65–79.
30. Letters to Johannes Stinstra, 2 June 1753 and 20 March 1754, respectively, in Samuel Richardson, *The Richardson–Stinstra Correspondence, and Stinstra's Prefaces to Clarissa*, ed. William C. Slattery (Carbondale: Southern Illinois University Press, 1969), 30, 71.
31. For more on the difference between "youth" and "adolescence," see my Introduction and Chapter 1.
32. Alryyes, *Original Subjects*, 125.
33. Samuel Richardson, *A Collection of the Moral and Instructive Sentiments, Maxims, Cautions, and Reflexions, Contained in the Histories of Pamela, Clarissa, and Sir Charles Grandison: Digested Under Proper Heads, with References to the Volume, and Page, Both in Octavo and Twelves, in the Respective Histories; to Which Are Subjoined, Two Letters from the Editor of Those Works: The One, in Answer to a Lady Who Was Solicitous for an Additional Volume to the History of Sir Charles Grandison; the Other, in Reply to a Gentleman, Who Had Objected to Sir Charles's Offer'd Compromise in the Article of Religion, Had He Married a Roman Catholic Lady* (London: Printed for S. Richardson; and sold by C. Hitch and L. Hawes, 1755).
34. Pamela's concluding peroration about the novel's relevance to the proud and high-born, those reduced to low estate, upper servants, lower servants, etc., uses similar status categories, and is often included in adaptations, even those explicitly intended for children.
35. Thomas Keymer and Peter Sabor, *"Pamela" in the Marketplace: Literary Controversy and Print Culture in Eighteenth-Century Britain and Ireland* (Cambridge University Press, 2005), 41; Peter Sabor, "Richardson's Index to his Correspondence on Pamela," *Notes and Queries* 26 (1979): 556–60.
36. Samuel Richardson, *Pamela, or, Virtue Rewarded*, ed. Thomas Keymer and Alice Wakely, Oxford World's Classics (Oxford University Press, 2008), 515.
37. Fergus, *Provincial Readers in Eighteenth-Century England*, 121.
38. Samuel Richardson, *The History of Pamela, or, Virtue Rewarded* (London: Printed for F. Newbery, 1769).
39. Keymer and Sabor, *"Pamela" in the Marketplace*, 5.
40. Ibid., 39.
41. Since *Pamela Censured* comes complete with page numbers and is in itself mildly pornographic, and because the fourth edition of *Pamela* was regularly advertised alongside it, critics such as Thomas Keymer and Peter Sabor have suggested it was thinly veiled promotion rather than a serious attempt to get *Pamela* out of the hands of "the youth"; ibid., 34.
42. Ibid., 23.
43. Samuel Richardson and Anna Letitia Barbauld, *The Correspondence: Selected from the Original Manuscripts, Bequeathed by Him to His Family to Which*

Are Prefixed a Biographical Account of That Author and Observations on His Writings: in Six Volumes (London: Phillips, 1804), lix.

44. Keymer and Sabor, *"Pamela" in the Marketplace*, 37.
45. *John Bull* (London, England), Saturday, 13 January 1883; page 25; Issue 3,243.
46. *The Life of Pamela Being a Full and Particular Relation of the Birth and Advancement of That Fortunate and Beautiful Young Damsel* (London: Printed for C. Whitefield, 1741); *The Paths of Virtue Delineated; or, The History in Miniature of the Celebrated Pamela, Clarissa Harlowe, and Sir Charles Grandison* (London: Printed for and sold by the booksellers, 1768), iv.
47. Samuel Richardson and Marian S. Carson Collection (Library of Congress), *The History of Pamela, or, Virtue Rewarded: A Narrative Which Has Its Foundation in Truth, Adapted to Inculcate in the Minds of Both Sexes the Principles of Virtue and Religion*, First American from the last London edition (New York: Published by W. C. Borradaile, 1830).
48. *The Life of Pamela Being a Full and Particular Relation of the Birth and Advancement of That Fortunate and Beautiful Young Damsel*, 73.
49. Richardson and Carson Collection, *The History of Pamela, or, Virtue Rewarded*, 55.
50. *The Paths of Virtue Delineated, or, The History in Miniature of the Celebrated Pamela, Clarissa Harlowe, and Sir Charles Grandison: Familiarised and Adapted to the Capacities of Youth* (London: Printed for R. Baldwin, in Paternoster-Row, 1756), 36; Richardson and Carson Collection, *The History of Pamela, or, Virtue Rewarded*, 55.
51. Richardson, *Pamela, or, Virtue Rewarded*; *The Life of Pamela Being a Full and Particular Relation of the Birth and Advancement of That Fortunate and Beautiful Young Damsel*, 164.
52. Heather Wolfe, Curator of Manuscripts, Folger Shakespeare Library. Personal Conversation.
53. Bonnie Latimer, "Leaving Little to the Imagination: The Mechanics of Didacticism in Two Children's Adaptations of Samuel Richardson's Novels," *The Lion and the Unicorn* 33, no. 2 (2009): 167–88.
54. On the abridger's consistent rejection of Richardson's epistolary format, see Leah Price, *The Anthology and the Rise of the Novel: From Richardson to George Eliot* (Cambridge University Press, 2003), 16–18.
55. *The Life of Pamela Being a Full and Particular Relation of the Birth and Advancement of That Fortunate and Beautiful Young Damsel*, 374.
56. William Blackstone, *Commentaries on the Laws of England in Four Books: With Analysis of the Work* (New York: W. E. Dean, 1844); Daniel J. Boorstin, *The Mysterious Science of the Law: An Essay on Blackstone's Commentaries* (Boston: Beacon Press, 1958).
57. Carolyn Steedman, "Servants and Their Relationship to the Unconscious," *Journal of British Studies* 42, no. 3 (2003): 320; Carolyn Steedman, "A Boiling Copper and Some Arsenic: Servants, Childcare, and Class Consciousness in Late Eighteenth-Century England," *Critical Inquiry* 34, no. 1 (2007): 36–77.

58. Robert J. Steinfeld, *The Invention of Free Labor: The Employment Relation in English and American Law and Culture, 1350–1870* (Chapel Hill: University of North Carolina Press, 1991), 18.
59. Douglas Hay, *Masters, Servants, and Magistrates in Britain and the Empire, 1562–1955*, Studies in Legal History (Chapel Hill: University of North Carolina Press, 2004), 62.
60. Quoted in ibid., 60.
61. Blackstone, *Commentaries on the Laws of England in Four Books*, 1, 171.
62. Ibid.
63. See Chapter 1 and Fox, Griffiths, and Hindle, eds., *The Experience of Authority in Early Modern England.*
64. Brewer, *By Birth or Consent*, 107; see also Brewer's description of most adults as "perpetual children" (2) in relation to their social superiors.
65. Henry Sumner Maine, *Ancient Law: Its Connection with the Early History of Society, and Its Relation to Modern Ideas* (New York: Dorset Press, 1986), 80; see also Brewer, *By Birth or Consent*, 80.
66. Quoted in Brewer, *By Birth or Consent*, 22.
67. Alryyes, *Original Subjects*, 124.
68. Bruce Burgett, "Between Speculation and Population: The Problem of 'Sex' in Our Long Eighteenth Century," *Early American Literature* 37, no. 1 (2002): 119–53; Michel Foucault, *The History of Sexuality, Vol. 1: An Introduction*, trans. Robert Hurley (New York: Vintage, 1990); Thomas Laqueur, *Making Sex: Body and Gender from the Greeks to Freud* (Cambridge, Mass.: Harvard University Press, 1992).
69. Lawrence Stone, *Uncertain Unions: Marriage in England, 1660–1753* (Oxford University Press, 1992), 31.
70. Sir Edward Coke, *The Third Part of the Institutes of the Laws of England: Concerning High Treason, and Other Pleas of the Crown, and Criminal Causes* (London: A. Crooke, 1669), 60.
71. *Old Bailey Proceedings Online* (www.oldbaileyonline.org), April 1747, trial of John Hunter (t17470429–28).
72. Brewer, *By Birth or Consent*, 295.
73. See Stone, *Uncertain Unions*; Alan Macfarlane, *Marriage and Love in England: Modes of Reproduction, 1300–1840* (Oxford: B. Blackwell, 1986).
74. In the 1580s Philip Stubbs invokes a similar sense of age in a tirade against "beggar weddings," which he sees not only as improvident but also as a form of insubordination, a claim to a status to which poor men are not entitled: "You have every saucy boy of ten, fourteen, or twenty years of age to catch up a woman and marry her . . . they live as beggars all their lives." Quoted in John R. Gillis, *For Better, for Worse: British Marriages, 1600 to the Present* (Oxford University Press, 1986), 88. Holly Brewer reminds us that the marriages of ten-year-olds were in fact perfectly legal up to the early eighteenth century, but they generally took place among wealthy families eager to secure their property, not among the poor. There probably were not many ten-year-olds marrying

grown women in the 1580s. But to put presumptuous poor men in their place, it feels right to Stubbs to call them all saucy boys.

75. Judith Lewis, "'Tis a Misfortune to Be a Great Ladie': Maternal Mortality in the British Aristocracy, 1558–1959," *The Journal of British Studies* 37, no. 1 (1998): 26–53; Jeffrey Weeks, *Sex, Politics, and Society: The Regulation of Sexuality Since 1800*, 2nd edn. (London: Longman, 1989).
76. Brewer, *By Birth or Consent*, 295.
77. O'Malley, *The Making of the Modern Child.*
78. Richardson and Barbauld, *The Correspondence*, lxvi.
79. Similarly, Price notes the striking prominence of wills in *Sir Charles Grandison*: "Although Richardson claims in the 'Letter to a Lady' appended to *Grandison* that the 'great and decisive event' of a novel can be either 'a Death or a Marriage' (3.471), the novel concludes not with Harriet becoming one suitor's wife (an event buried in the sixth volume), but with her becoming the administrator of another suitor's charitable bequest, 'a very large Legacy in money and his jewels and plate' (7.61.462)." *The Anthology and the Rise of the Novel*, 42–43.
80. Margery and Tommy finance a victorious legal case against Sir Timothy Gripe, which results directly in his being struck from the rolls of the Justices of the Peace, and indirectly the loss of his estate: "She purchased the Whole, and threw it into different Farms, that the Poor might be no longer under the Dominion of two Over-grown Men." Sir Timothy's and Farmer Graspall's ruin is complete: his family depends for their survival on the very parish poor laws he had once manipulated so ruthlessly. Interestingly, the tyrant's children get special mention as being exempt from the general revenge: "those who had felt the weight of his Iron Hand rejoiced; but Lady Margery desired, that his Children might be treated with Care and Tenderness; for they, says she, are in no way Accountable for the Actions of their Father" (136).
81. Richardson and Barbauld, *The Correspondence*, lxvi.
82. James Ballantyne, *Ballantyne's Novelist's Library* (Hurst, Robinson and Co., 1824), xxiii.
83. Ibid.
84. Richardson, *Pamela, or, Virtue Rewarded*, 107.
85. Arguing against charity schools, for example, Bernard Mandeville sneers at what he sees as the predictable support of printers and stationers for education, claiming "the Company of Stationers would certainly . . . have me buried alive in their Hall under a great heap of Primers and Spelling-books, they would not be able to sell." Bernard Mandeville, *The Fable of the Bees: Or, Private Vices, Public Benefits. With An Essay on Charity and Charity Schools, and a Search Into the Nature of Society* (London: C. Bathurst, 1795), 182.
86. On Locke's general importance to *Pamela*, see Margaret J. M. Ezell, "John Locke's Images of Childhood: Early Eighteenth Century Response to Some Thoughts Concerning Education," *Eighteenth-Century Studies* 17, no. 2 (1983): 139–55; Janet E. Aikins, "Pamela's Use of Locke's Words," *Studies in*

Eighteenth-Century Culture 25, no. 1 (1996): 75–97; Julia Briggs, "'Delightful Task!' Women, Children, and Reading in the Mid-Eighteenth Century," and William McCarthy, "Mother of All Discourses: Anna Barbauld's Lessons for Children," both in *Culturing the Child, 1690–1914: Essays in Memory of Mitzi Myers*, ed. Donelle Ruwe (Lanham, Md: Children's Literature Association and Scarecrow Press, 2005); Lois A. Chaber, "From Moral Man to Godly Man: 'Mr. Locke' and Mr. B in Part 2 of Pamela," *Studies in Eighteenth-Century Culture* 18 (1988): 213–61; Amit Yahav-Brown, "Reasonableness and Domestic Fiction," *ELH* 73, no. 4 (2006): 805–30.

87. See Paula McDowell, "Why Fanny Can't Read: *Joseph Andrews* and the (Ir)relevance of Literacy," in *A Companion to the Eighteenth-Century English Novel and Culture*, ed. Paula R. Backscheider and Catherine Ingrassia (Oxford: Blackwell, 2005). Conversely, Harvey J. Graff has questioned what he calls the "literacy myth," the idea that the ability to read and write in and of itself guarantees progress either for an individual or for a society as a whole; Harvey J. Graff, *The Literacy Myth: Cultural Integration and Social Structure in the Nineteenth Century* (London: Transaction Publishers, 1979).

88. On Pamela's education by Mr. B.'s mother, see, for example, Carolyn Williams, who stresses her acquisition of social graces. Carolyn D. Williams, "Pamela and the Case of the Slandered Duchess," *Studies in English Literature, 1500–1900* 29, no. 3 (1989): 515–33; Erica Harth, "The Virtue of Love: Lord Hardwicke's Marriage Act," *Cultural Critique* no. 9 (Spring 1988): 123–54.

89. John Locke, *Two Treatises on Government*, ed. Peter Laslett (Cambridge University Press, 1988), 287.

90. See my Introduction, p. 4. Watt, "Serious Reflections on *The Rise of the Novel*," 218.

91. Ibid.

92. Brewer, *By Birth or Consent*, 316.

93. Henry Stebbing, *An Inquiry into the Force and Operation of the annulling Clauses of a late Act for the better Preventing of Clandestine Marriages* (London, 1754), 6. See also Harth, "The Virtue of Love."

94. Stebbing, *An Inquiry*, 6. For another discussion of Lord Hardwicke's Marriage Act in the context of *Pamela*, see Harth, "The Virtue of Love": "For those in power in 1753, considerations of love and marriage were embedded in those of money and property" (133).

95. Quoted in Katherine Sobba Green, "The Heroine's Blazon and Hardwicke's Marriage Act: Commodification for a Novel Market," *Tulsa Studies in Women's Literature* 9, no. 2 (1990): 273.

96. Richardson, *The Richardson–Stinstra Correspondence, and Stinstra's Prefaces to Clarissa*, 60. See "Tom Potts," Child number 109.

97. Stone, *Uncertain Unions*, 158–60; quote on 160.

98. More common were marriages between servants and older widowers eager to find a dependable replacement for their wives as household managers. See Bridget Hill, *Servants: English Domestics in the Eighteenth Century* (Oxford: Clarendon Press, 1996).

99. Randolph Trumbach, *The Rise of the Egalitarian Family: Aristocratic Kinship and Domestic Relations in Eighteenth-Century England* (New York: Academic Press, 1978), 102.
100. *A Letter to the Public... for the Better Preventing of Clandestine Marriages* (London: Printed for Charles Marsh, 1753), 33–35; Brewer, *By Birth or Consent*, 318.
101. Benjamin Rush, *A Plan for the Establishment of Public Schools and the Diffusion of Knowledge in Pennsylvania* (1786), 126.
102. Henry Fielding, *Shamela* (Whitefish, Mont.: Kessinger Publishing, 2004), 7.
103. Toni Bowers, *Force or Fraud: British Seduction Stories and the Problem of Resistance, 1660–1760* (Oxford University Press, 2011). This subject also interested ambitious middle-class men trying to rise in a society still largely organized by status based on inherited property.
104. Richardson and Barbauld, *The Correspondence*, lx.
105. Ballantyne, *Ballantyne's Novelist's Library*, xxii.
106. Ibid.
107. Stephen, *Hours in a Library*, 63.
108. Ibid., 49, 63.
109. Ibid., 53, 48.
110. Ibid., 59, 91.
111. Ibid., 61.
112. Ibid., 62.
113. Leslie Stephen, "Jonathan Edwards," *Fraser's Magazine* New Series 8, no. 47 (November 1873): 535–36.
114. Thomas H. Johnson, "Jonathan Edwards and the 'Young Folks' Bible'," *The New England Quarterly* 5, no. 1 (1932): 37–54.
115. Nancy Armstrong, *Desire and Domestic Fiction: A Political History of the Novel* (Oxford University Press, 1987), 26.
116. James Peale, *A Girl Holding a Doll*, oil on canvas, 1804, The Huntington Library, Art Collections, and Botanical Gardens, San Marino, California.

4 RATIONAL MORALISTS, HIGHLAND BARBARIANS, AND THE TASTE FOR ADVENTURES

1. Franco Moretti, *The Way of the World: The Bildungsroman in European Culture*, new edn. (London: Verso, 2000), 185.
2. Leslie A. Fiedler, *Love and Death in the American Novel* (Normal, Ill.: Dalkey Archive Press, 1997), xvii.
3. Mikhail Mikhaĭlovich Bakhtin, *Speech Genres and Other Late Essays*, ed. Michael Holquist and Caryl Emerson, trans. Vern W. McGee (Austin, Tex.: University of Texas Press, 1986), 26, 44.
4. Ibid., 21.
5. Ibid., 53.
6. Moretti, *The Way of the World*, 213, 191.

7. Leonore Davidoff and Catherine Hall, *Family Fortunes: Men and Women of the English Middle Class 1780–1850*, 2nd edn. (London: Routledge, 2003), 454.
8. Dugald Stewart, "Account of the Life and Writings of Adam Smith, LL.D," in *Collected Works of Dugald Stewart*, ed. William Hamilton (Edinburgh: Constable, 1858), vol. x, 1–98, 34.
9. Meek, *Social Science and the Ignoble Savage*, 1.
10. See H. M. Hopfl, "From Savage to Scotsman: Conjectural History in the Scottish Enlightenment," *The Journal of British Studies* 17, no. 2 (1978): 38.
11. William Robertson, *The History of the Discovery and Settlement of America* (New York: Derby and Jackson, 1857), 137.
12. Hopfl, "From Savage to Scotsman," 38.
13. Peter D. Garside, "Scott and the 'Philosophical' Historians," *Journal of the History of Ideas* 36 (1975): 497–512.
14. Edgeworth, *Practical Education*, 1, 364. It should be noted that Edgeworth generally respects Condillac, in particular his interest in the "history of the progress of the human mind, of arts, and sciences" (354–55).
15. See Teresa Michals, "Commerce and Character in Maria Edgeworth," *Nineteenth-Century Literature* 49, no. 1 (1994): 1–20.
16. Smith, *An Inquiry into the Nature and Causes of the Wealth of Nations*, III, 4, 15.
17. See Mitzi Myers, "Of Mice and Mothers: Mrs. Barbauld's 'New Walk' and Gendered Codes in Children's Literature," in *Feminine Principles and Women's Experience in American Composition and Rhetoric*, ed. Louise Wetherbee Phelps and Janet A. Emig (University of Pittsburgh Press, 1995); William McCarthy, *Anna Letitia Barbauld: Voice of the Enlightenment* (Baltimore: Johns Hopkins University Press, 2008).
18. John Aikin and Mrs Barbauld (Anna Letitia), *Miscellaneous Pieces, in Prose: By J. and A. L. Aikin* (printed by James Magee, 1774), 29–30.
19. Ibid., 30.
20. Donelle Rae Ruwe and Mitzi Myers, *Culturing the Child, 1690–1914: Essays in Memory of Mitzi Myers* (Lanham, Md: Scarecrow Press, 2005).
21. Mary Hilton and Pam Hirsch, *Practical Visionaries: Women, Education and Social Progress 1790–1930* (Harlow: Longman, 2000), 21.
22. Maria Edgeworth, *Rosamond: With Other Tales* (New York: Harper and Bros., 1844), 8, 11.
23. Ibid., 17.
24. Maria Edgeworth, *The Absentee* (Oxford University Press, 1988), 202.
25. Henry John Stephen and William Gifford, "Review of Tales of Fashionable Life by Miss Edgeworth (Article 7)," *Quarterly Review* 2, no. 3 (August 1809): 138; for the attribution of the review to Stephen and Gifford see Jonathan Cutmore, *The Quarterly Review Archive* in *Romantic Circles*, www.rc.umd.edu/reference/qr/index/03.html.
26. Quoted in McCarthy, *Anna Letitia Barbauld*, 431.
27. Hopfl, "From Savage to Scotsman," 29. See also Meek, *Social Science and the Ignoble Savage*.

28. David Hume, *Selected Essays* (Oxford University Press, 1988), 56.
29. See John Guillory, "Literary Capital: Gray's 'Elegy,' Anna Laetitia Barbauld, and the Vernacular Canon," in *Early Modern Conceptions of Property*, ed. John Brewer and Susan Staves (London: Routledge, 1996); Claudia L. Johnson, "'Let Me Make the Novels of a Country': Barbauld's 'The British Novelists' (1810/1820)," *NOVEL: A Forum on Fiction* 34, no. 2 (2001): 163–79.
30. McCarthy, "Mother of All Discourses."
31. On this long campaign to separate children's literature from "associations with vulgar popular print culture," see M. O. Grenby, "A Conservative Woman Doing Radical Things: Sarah Trimmer and the Guardian of Education," in *Culturing the Child, 1690–1914*, ed. Ruwe, 137–64.
32. See McCarthy, "Mother of All Discourses," 215–16, on the near-ubiquity of Barbauld's Lessons and Hymns through the nineteenth century wherever English-speaking Protestants were found: not merely Britain, the United States, and Europe, but also Brazil and Calcutta.
33. For Sarah Trimmer's contribution to this process of age-leveling reading for children and young people, see Michelle Levy, "The Radical Education of Evenings at Home," *Eighteenth-Century Fiction* 19, no. 1 (2006): 123–50. Levy perhaps overstates the oppressive nature of this process.
34. Edgeworth, *Practical Education*, 1, 340, 384.
35. We should here note that Letitia Barbauld and Maria Edgeworth have some important differences. Barbauld was the more openly political and the more radical figure, a Rational Dissenter and close friend of Joseph Priestley who began her political career by protesting the Test and Corporation Acts, who supported the French Revolution, and who in the violently reactionary political climate of the Napoleonic wars went down with flying colors by publishing "Eighteen Hundred and Eleven." Unlike the canonical Romantic poets, Barbauld stuck to the liberal principles of her youth and was, predictably, lampooned as unpatriotic in a reactionary era. Edgeworth was born too late for the radical politics of the 1790s. She was also a member of the landed Anglo-Irish gentry who supported the Establishment in church and state. She largely confined her published political remarks to support of the Act of Union between Ireland and England.
36. Continuing the age-leveling trend, Sarah Trimmer's influential periodical *The Guardian of Education* (1802–6) reviewed books under age-leveled headings such as "Books for Children" and "Books for Young Persons," and often specified the exact year for which a particular book would be appropriate.
37. Renée Balibar, "National Language, Education, Literature," in *The Politics of Theory*, ed. Francis Barker et al. (Colchester: University of Essex, 1983), 140, 141.
38. Letitia Barbauld, *Lessons for Children: With Four Original Tales* (New York: Pendleton and Hill, 1831), 3.
39. McCarthy, *Anna Letitia Barbauld*, 217; McCarthy, "Mother of All Discourses," 88.

40. Letitia Barbauld, *Selected Poetry and Prose*, ed. Elizabeth Kraft and William McCarthy (Peterborough, Ont.: Broadview Press, 2002), 407.
41. Quoted in John O. Hayden, ed., *Walter Scott: The Critical Heritage* (London: Routledge, 1995).
42. McCarthy, *Anna Letitia Barbauld*, 184.
43. Barbauld, *Selected Poetry and Prose*, 32, 26.
44. Maria Edgeworth, *Belinda*, ed. Kathryn J. Kirkpatrick (Oxford University Press, 2009).
45. Barbauld, *Selected Poetry and Prose*, 300.
46. Sir Walter Scott, *Waverley Novels: Waverley* (Boston: S. H. Parker, 1830), 9.
47. A slightly modified version from Horace's *Ars Poetica*. Horace stresses the simultaneity of instruction and delight, giving each term equal weight. Newbery's revision gives greater stress to instruction, subordinating delight as a means to this end.
48. Samuel Johnson, *Dr. Johnson's Works* (New York: AMS Press, 1970), vol. IV.
49. Hayden, *Walter Scott*.
50. Ibid. (Introductory Epistle to *The Fortunes of Nigel*), 266.
51. Hayden, *Walter Scott*.
52. Ibid. (Review in the *New Monthly Magazine*, 1823), 277.
53. Ibid., 12.
54. Ibid., 75.
55. Ibid., 78, 75.
56. Ibid., 78, 75, 76.
57. Anne H. Lundin, "Victorian Horizons: The Reception of Children's Books in England and America, 1880–1900," *The Library Quarterly* 64, no. 1 (1994): 30–59.
58. Emily Jenkins, "Trilby: Fads, Photographers, and 'Over-Perfect Feet'," *Book History* 1 (1998): 221–67.
59. Ibid., 228.
60. Hayden, *Walter Scott*, Introduction, *The Fortunes of Nigel*.
61. Barbauld, *Selected Poetry and Prose*, 396.
62. Warner, *Licensing Entertainment*, 19.
63. Michael Sadleir, *XIX Century Fiction: A Bibliographical Record Based on His Own Collection* (Cambridge University Press, 1951), vol. II, 90; see Claudia Johnson's discussion of Sadleir in "Let Me Make the Novels of a Country."
64. Hayden, *Walter Scott* (8 April 1820, letter to Thomas Alsop), 179.
65. John Henry Raleigh, "What Scott Meant to the Victorians," *Victorian Studies* 7, no. 1 (1963): 13.
66. Walter Scott, *Waverley*, ed. Andrew Hook (London: Penguin Classics, 1981), 48, 53.
67. Ibid., 48.
68. Ibid., 520.
69. "Adults Only? Children and Children's Books in British Circulating Libraries," 20.
70. Scott, *Waverley*, 521.

71. Ibid., 523.
72. Walter Scott, *Redgauntlet*, ed. G. A. M. Wood and David Hewitt (London: Penguin Classics, 2001), 47.
73. Scott, *Waverley*, 370.
74. Ibid., 54.
75. Walter Scott, *Ivanhoe*, ed. Graham Tulloch (London: Penguin Classics, 2000), 365.
76. Scott, *Waverley*, 339.
77. Scott, *Ivanhoe*, 392.
78. Scott, *Waverley*, 333.
79. Of course, Scott includes a positive figure of modern military courage in Colonel Talbot. But Talbot does not dominate the novel as does the opposition between Fergus MacIvor and his clan, on the one hand, and the peace of commercial society, on the other. And the novel never suggests that Waverley should emulate Talbot's military career.
80. Scott, *Waverley*, 482, 489.
81. Rosalind Carr, "The Gentleman and the Soldier: Patriotic Masculinities in Eighteenth-Century Scotland," *Journal of Scottish Historical Studies* 28, no. 2 (2008): 102–21.
82. Adam Smith, *The Wealth of Nations* (New York: Bantam Classics, 2003), 418.
83. Aikin and Barbauld, *Miscellaneous Pieces, in Prose*, "Evenings at Home," 62.
84. Maria Edgeworth, *Patronage* (Whitefish, Mont.: Kessinger Publishing, 2010), 279, 11.
85. Elizabeth Goodenough and Andrea Immel, *Under Fire: Childhood in the Shadow of War* (Detroit: Wayne State University Press, 2008), 55.
86. N. A. M. Rodger, *The Command of the Ocean: A Naval History of Britain, 1649–1815* (New York: W.W. Norton, 2005), i.
87. M. O. Grenby, "'Surely There is No British Boy or Girl Who Has not Heard of the Battle of Waterloo!': War and Children's Literature in the Age of Napoleon," in *Under Fire*, ed. Goodenough and Immel, 49, 55–56.
88. Ibid., 51, 52.
89. Edgeworth, *Practical Education*, 1, 336.
90. Ibid.
91. Ibid., 1, 337.
92. Rodger, *The Command of the Ocean*, 386.
93. Brewer, *By Birth or Consent*.
94. See S. A. Cavell, *Midshipmen and Quarterdeck Boys in the British Navy, 1771–1831* (Woodbridge: The Boydell Press, 2012): "According to regulations, young gentlemen were not to enter the [the Royal Navy] before the age of eleven. The rules, however, were often ignored" (8).
95. Ibid., 150.
96. Bernard Coleridge, *The Story of a Devonshire House* (London: T. Fisher Unwin, 1905), 28; Carl Ketcham, ed., *The Letters of John Wordsworth* (Ithaca, NY:

Cornell University Press, 1969), 4, 10; Richard E. Matlak, *Deep Distresses: William Wordsworth, John Wordsworth, Sir George Beaumont, 1800–1808* (University of Delaware Press, 2003); Frank Prentice Rand, *Wordsworth's Mariner Brother* (Amherst, Mass.: Newell Press, 1966).

97. Only 2 or 3 percent of officers attended the Royal Naval Academy (among them Jane Austen's brothers) – those who lacked the patronage of a captain and so were unable to start their career by simply joining a ship. Seen as a second-rate way into the navy, the Academy received students from the ages of twelve to fifteen. See B. C. Southam, *Jane Austen and the Navy* (London: Hambledon, 2000); for Robert Scott, see John Sutherland, *The Life of Walter Scott: A Critical Biography* (Oxford: Wiley-Blackwell, 1998), 37. Sutherland suggests uncertainty about when Robert was born. I am using the date provided by the *ODNB*.
98. Cavell, *Midshipmen and Quarterdeck Boys*, 150.
99. Rodger, *The Command of the Ocean*, 512.
100. Ibid., 386.
101. Cavell, *Midshipmen and Quarterdeck Boys*.
102. Robert Southey, *Robert Southey's Life of Nelson* (London: Longmans, Green, and Company, 1896), 9.
103. Goodenough and Immel, *Under Fire*.
104. Elizabeth Longford, *Wellington: The Years of the Sword* (London: Weidenfeld & Nicolson, 1969).
105. Rodger, *The Command of the Ocean*, 505, 499, 508.
106. Quoted in Mary A. Conley, *From Jack Tar to Union Jack: Representing Naval Manhood in the British Empire, 1870–1918* (Manchester University Press, 2009), 87.
107. Critical attention to William Styron's *Confessions of Nat Turner* and, more recently, Toni Morrison's *Beloved*, has brought into question this equation of the historical novel with the juvenile. *Beloved* had a similar effect on the age-leveling of fantasy.
108. Suzanne Rahn, "An Evolving Past: The Story of Historical Fiction and Nonfiction for Children," *The Lion and the Unicorn* 15, no. 1 (1991): 7. On the boys' adventure story, see Elaine Showalter, *Sexual Anarchy: Gender and Culture at the Fin de Siècle* (New York: Viking, 1990), chapter 5; Don Randall, *Kipling's Imperial Boy: Adolescence and Cultural Hybridity* (Basingstoke: Palgrave, 2000); Joseph Bristow, *Empire Boys: Adventures in a Man's World* (London: Harper Collins Academic, 1991).
109. Avrom Fleishman, *The English Historical Novel: Walter Scott to Virginia Woolf* (Baltimore: Johns Hopkins University Press, 1972), 31, 36.
110. Ibid., 36.
111. For the importance of gender to historical fiction's critical standing, see Ferris, *The Achievement of Literary Authority*.
112. Hayden, *Walter Scott* ("An Essay on Fashionable Literature," 1818), 145.
113. Ibid., 80.
114. Ibid., 134.

115. Ibid., 287.
116. Ibid., 313.
117. Ibid., 86.
118. Arata, "On Not Paying Attention."
119. Hayden, *Walter Scott*, 179, 181.
120. Ibid., 314, 460.
121. Claudia Nelson, *Boys Will Be Girls: The Feminine Ethic and British Children's Fiction, 1857–1917* (New Brunswick, NJ: Rutgers University Press, 1991), 106.
122. G. A. Henty, *By Conduct and Courage: A Story of Nelson's Days* (London: Blackie, 1905), 153, 23.
123. Ibid., 30, 43, 45.
124. Nelson, *Boys Will Be Girls*, 2.
125. See Edward Salmon, "What Girls Read," *Nineteenth Century* 20 (1886): 515–29.
126. Robert Louis Stevenson, "My First Book – 'Treasure Island'," *McClure's Magazine* (September 1894): 283–94. See also Bradley Deane, "Imperial Boyhood: Piracy and the Play Ethic," *Victorian Studies* 53, no. 4 (2011): 689–714.
127. Hayden, *Walter Scott*, 429, 431.
128. Ibid., 395, 394, 395.
129. Ibid., 409.
130. Ibid., 453, 458.
131. Virginia Woolf, *To the Lighthouse*, 1st Harvest edn. (San Diego: Harcourt, Brace & Company, 1989).
132. Dedria Bryfonski and Gerald J. Senick, eds., "J. R. R. Tolkien (1892–1973)," in *Contemporary Literary Criticism* (Detroit, Mich.: Gale Research, 1980), vol. XII, 565.
133. Ibid. Maurice Richardson's adult is heterosexual. To this way of thinking, not only Auden's love for Old Norse sagas, but also his love for Christopher Isherwood and Chester Kallman disqualifies him. See Anna Smol, "'Oh . . . Oh . . . Frodo!': Readings of Male Intimacy in *The Lord of the Rings*," *Modern Fiction Studies* 50, no. 4 (2004): 949–79, who also quotes this comment of Richardson's.
134. Edward Salmon, "Should Children Have a Special Literature?," *Parent's Review* 5 (1890): 337–44, reprinted in Lance Salway, *A Peculiar Gift: Nineteenth Century Writings on Books for Children* (Harmondsworth: Kestrel Books, 1976).
135. Hayden, *Walter Scott*, 468.

5 EDUCATING DICKENS: OLD BOYS, LITTLE MOTHERS, AND SCHOOL TIME

1. Janice Carlisle, *The Sense of an Audience: Dickens, Thackeray, and George Eliot at Mid-Century* (Athens, Ga.: University of Georgia Press, 1981).

2. Michael Patrick Hearn, "Dickens, Charles 1812–1870," in *Writers for Children: Critical Studies of Major Authors Since the Seventeenth Century*, ed. Jane M. Bingham (New York: Charles Scribner's Sons, 1988), 187.
3. Perry Nodelman, *The Hidden Adult: Defining Children's Literature* (Baltimore: Johns Hopkins University Press, 2008).
4. *Our Young Folks*, a children's monthly produced by Dickens's Boston publisher, commissioned *Holiday Romance* in anticipation of Dickens's American reading tour. The novella was simultaneously published in *All the Year Round* from January to May 1868.
5. Charles Dickens, "A Holiday Romance," text, n.d., n.p., http://ebooks.adelaide.edu.au/d/dickens/charles/d54hr/.
6. Hearn, "Dickens, Charles 1812–1870," 188.
7. Ibid., 187.
8. William Makepeace Thackeray, *The English Humourists of the Eighteenth Century and Charity and Humour*, ed. Edgar F. Harden (Ann Arbor: University of Michigan Press, 2007), 204.
9. Forster, *The Life of Charles Dickens*, 1, 9.
10. Ibid. 9–10.
11. Charles Dickens, "Where We Stopped Growing," *Uncollected Writings from Household Words, 1850–1859* (Bloomington: Indiana University Press, 1968), 108.
12. See Barbara Hardy, "*Martin Chuzzlewit*," in John J. Gross, *Dickens and the Twentieth Century* (University of Toronto Press, 1966).
13. G. K. Chesterton, *Charles Dickens: A Critical Study* (Whitefish, Mont.: Kessinger Publishing, 2005), 207.
14. Moretti, *The Way of the World*, 185.
15. Robbins rightly cautions readers looking for historical significance in literary texts to be aware of the long-running comic conventions of the master–servant dialogue, which repeat themselves with striking fidelity all the way back to Menander. Bruce Robbins, "The Butler Did It: On Agency in the Novel," *Representations* no. 6 (Spring 1984): "Response" 219; see also Bruce Robbins, *The Servant's Hand: English Fiction From Below* (New York: Columbia University Press, 1986).
16. For an interesting account of critics' attempts to demonstrate Pickwick's growth, see Philip Rogers, "Mr. Pickwick's Innocence," *Nineteenth-Century Fiction* 27, no. 1 (1972): 21–37. With "The Education of Mr. Pickwick" in 1969 and "Fattening Up on Pickwick" in 1995, James Kincaid weighs in on both sides of this debate; James R. Kincaid, "Fattening up on Pickwick," *NOVEL: A Forum on Fiction* 25, no. 3 (1992): 235–44; James R. Kincaid, "The Education of Mr. Pickwick," *Nineteenth-Century Fiction* 24, no. 2 (1969): 127–41. Alexander Welsh more convincingly reads Pickwick in terms of the kind of national development that fascinated Walter Scott and Maria Edgeworth; Alexander Welsh, "Waverley, Pickwick, and Don Quixote," *Nineteenth-Century Fiction* 22, no. 1 (1967): 19–30.

17. Rogers, "Mr. Pickwick's Innocence," 36.
18. Forster, *The Life of Charles Dickens*, I, 46.
19. Forster, *The Life of Charles Dickens*, I, 17.
20. Philip Collins, ed., *Charles Dickens: The Critical Heritage* (London: Routledge, 1971), 587.
21. Charles Dickens, *Great Expectations*, ed. Graham Law and Adrian J. Pinnington (Peterborough, Ont.: Broadview Press, 1998), 192.
22. Ibid., 487.
23. Nelson, *Precocious Children and Childish Adults*, 180.
24. Charles Dickens, "Where We Stopped Growing," in *The Uncommercial Traveller and Other Papers*, The Dent Uniform Edition of Dickens' Journalism, vol. IV (London: Dent, 2000), 107.
25. Charles Dickens, *Our Mutual Friend*, ed. Adrian Poole (London: Penguin Books, 1998), 68.
26. Charles Dickens, *David Copperfield*, ed. Jeremy Tambling (London: Penguin Books, 1997), 637.
27. "A Flight," in *Gone Astray and Other Papers from Household Words, 1851–59*. The Dent Uniform Edition of Dickens' Journalism, vol. III (Columbus: Ohio State University Press, 1999), 3 (August 1851, Dent vol. III, 33).
28. Charles Dickens, *Bleak House*, ed. Norman Page (London: Penguin Books, 1971), 342.
29. For an interesting discussion of the more general Victorian fascination with old age as "second childhood," see Nelson, *Precocious Children and Childish Adults*, 2.
30. Dickens, *Bleak House*, 341, 344, 342.
31. Nelson, *Precocious Children and Childish Adults*, 58–70.
32. Charles Dickens, *The Old Curiosity Shop*, ed. Norman Page (London: Penguin Books, 2001), 18.
33. Winthrop D. Jordan, "Searching for Adulthood in America," *Daedalus* 105, no. 4 (1976): 6.
34. Chesterton, *Charles Dickens*; see also F. S. Schwarzbach, *Dickens and the City* (London: Athlone Press, 1979).
35. Dickens, *Bleak House*, 351, 262.
36. See, for example, *Bleak House*'s pamphlet-writing, home-neglecting philanthropist, Mrs. Jellyby.
37. Dickens, *David Copperfield*, 651.
38. Ibid., 239, 241.
39. Ibid., 229, 233, 278.
40. Dickens, *Bleak House*, 933.
41. J. M. Barrie, *Peter Pan: The Original Story* (New York: HarperFestival, 2003), chapter 3.
42. Henry James, "'The Limitations of Dickens': 'The Troop of Hunchbacks, Imbeciles, and Precocious Children'," in *Views and Reviews*, ed. Le Roy Phillips (Boston: Ball Publishing, 1908), 156.

43. Dickens, *The Old Curiosity Shop*, 261, 264.
44. Ibid., 549.
45. Ibid.
46. Charles Dickens, *A Christmas Carol and Other Christmas Stories* (New York: Signet Classics, 2008), 107.
47. Dickens, *Bleak House*, 344.
48. See Judith A. Plotz, *Romanticism and the Vocation of Childhood* (New York: Palgrave, 2001); Hugh Cunningham, *The Children of the Poor: Representations of Childhood Since the Seventeenth Century* (Oxford: Blackwell, 1991).
49. Dickens, *Bleak House*, 348.
50. Like Sir Everard Waverley, Boythorn is one of the English novel's many permanent bachelors who move from an early romantic disappointment into a life of general benevolence, but he is more conspicuously boyish than most.
51. Dickens, *David Copperfield*, 262.
52. Dickens, *Bleak House*, 147.
53. Ibid., 118, 244.
54. Ibid., 270, 831.
55. Sarah Norcliffe Cleghorn, *Portraits and Protests* [1917] (Cornell University Library, 2009), 75.
56. On the continuing view of child labor as an "unavoidable and perhaps desirable necessity" after the passage of the Ten Hours Act in 1847, see Cunningham, *The Children of the Poor*, 164, 225, 17.
57. David Post, "Review: Education and the Child Labor Paradox Today," *Comparative Education Review* 45, no. 1 (2001): 133.
58. Dickens, "Gaslight Fairies," in *Gone Astray*, 276.
59. Ibid., 281.
60. Ibid., 276.
61. Carolyn Steedman has described the sexual appeal of the age ambiguity of nineteenth-century theatrical girls and women, the girlishness of the women and the apparent sexual precocity of the "babies." In Dickens's account, from age fourteen to age twenty-three alike, the danger performers face is sexual corruption, not work itself. Carolyn Steedman, *Strange Dislocations: Childhood and the Idea of Human Interiority, 1780–1930* (Cambridge, Mass.: Harvard University Press, 1995), 282.
62. Olga Nieuwenhuys, "The Paradox of Child Labor and Anthropology," *Annual Review of Anthropology* 25 (1996): 238.
63. Patrick Brantlinger, "Dickens and the Factories," *Nineteenth-Century Fiction* 26, no. 3 (1971): 277.
64. 29 December 1838. *The Letters of Charles Dickens*, ed. Madeline House and Graham Storey, 8 vols. (Oxford: Clarendon Press, 1965–1995), 1, 483–84. We should remember that even Frances Trollope writes hoping to "ameliorate the lot of the infant laborer" rather than to stop infants from laboring at all. Frances Trollope, *Life and Adventures of Michael Armstrong, the Factory Boy* (London: Henry Colburn, 1840).

65. Brantlinger, "Dickens and the Factories," 274.
66. Collins, *Charles Dickens*, 78; italics in original, 277.
67. Cunningham, *The Children of the Poor*, 177: summing up the cultural difference traveled, the title of Edith Hogg's 1897 article, "School Children as Wage Earners," assumes that all children really are schoolchildren. The only remaining question is whether schoolchildren may earn wages without harming their primary academic role. And Hogg's answer, unsurprisingly, is No.
68. Ibid., 191.
69. Trollope, *Life and Adventures of Michael Armstrong, the Factory Boy*, 80.
70. Beatrice Webb and Sidney Webb, "Report of the Royal Commission on the Poor Laws and Relief of Distress: Minority Report," in *Social Welfare in Transition: Selected English Documents, 1834–1909*, ed. Roy Lubove (University of Pittsburgh Press, 1966), 288.
71. Plotz, *Romanticism and the Vocation of Childhood.*
72. See, for example, George Orwell: "David escapes from the warehouse, but Mick Walker and Mealy Potatoes and the others are still there, and there is no sign that this troubles Dickens particularly." "Charles Dickens," in George Orwell, *The Collected Essays, Journalism and Letters of George Orwell. Volume 1: 1920–40*, edited by Sonia Orwell and Ian Angus (New York: Harcourt, 1968), 419.
73. Dickens, *David Copperfield*, 166.
74. Forster, *The Life of Charles Dickens*, 47.
75. Dickens, *David Copperfield*, 238.
76. Ibid., 339, 269.
77. Cunningham, *The Children of the Poor*, 231, 229.
78. Harold Silver, *The Concept of Popular Education: A Study of Ideas and Social Movements in the Early Nineteenth Century* (Totowa, NJ: Rowman and Littlefield, 1977).
79. Cunningham, *The Children of the Poor*, 169.
80. Dickens, "The Short-Timers," in *The Uncommercial Traveller and Other Papers*, 265–79.
81. John Lawson and Harold Silver, *A Social History of Education in England* (London: Routledge, 2007), 158. See also Harold Silver, *English Education and the Radicals 1780–1850* (London: Routledge & K. Paul, 1975).
82. E. Nesbit, *The Story of the Treasure Seekers* (San Francisco, Calif.: Chronicle Books, 2006), chapters 7 and 16.
83. Cunningham, *The Children of the Poor*, 197.
84. John Chandos, *Boys Together: English Public Schools, 1800–1864* (New Haven, Conn.: Yale University Press, 1984).
85. Orwell, *The Collected Essays*, 418.
86. Dickens, *Bleak House*, 422, 357.
87. Dickens, *Bleak House*, 419.
88. Ibid., 349.
89. Ibid., 344, 341.

90. Charles Dickens, *Hard Times: An Authoritative Text, Backgrounds, Sources, and Contemporary Reactions, Criticism*, 2nd edn. (New York: Norton, 1990), 51.
91. Ibid., 222.
92. Dickens, *Our Mutual Friend*, 220.
93. Cunningham, *The Children of the Poor*, 231.
94. Ibid., 188.
95. Dickens, *Hard Times*, 46, 47.
96. Charles Dickens, "Frauds on the Fairies," in *Gone Astray*, 168.
97. Dickens, "Frauds on the Fairies," 173.
98. Michael Quinlan, Margaret Gardner, and Peter Akers, "A Failure of Voluntarism: Shop Assistants and the Struggle to Restrict Trading Hours in the Colony of Victoria, 1850–85," *Labour History* 88 (1 May 2005): 1.
99. George Howell, *The Conflicts of Capital and Labour: Historically and Economically Considered. Being a History and Review of the Trade Unions of Great Britain, Showing Their Origin, Progress, Constitution, and Objects, in Their Varied Political, Social, Economical, and Industrial Aspects* (London: Macmillan, 1890), 269.
100. Hadley, *Living Liberalism*, 25.
101. Dickens, *Our Mutual Friend*, 28.
102. Dickens, *Bleak House*, 42.
103. William Makepeace Thackeray, *The Letters and Private Papers of William Makepeace Thackeray*, ed. Gordon Norton Ray (Cambridge, Mass.: Harvard University Press, 1945), 1 November 1859.
104. Collins, *Charles Dickens*, 81. When unsoftened by the eulogistic impulse, Dickens's later reviewers can still criticize him for the same lack of rational self-control that marks his readers. See 490, 474–75.
105. Ibid., 64.
106. Ibid., 36.
107. George H. Ford, *Dickens and His Readers* (New York: Gordian Press, 1974), 12, 79.
108. Collins, *Charles Dickens*, 86.
109. Ibid., 95, 513.
110. Collins, *Charles Dickens*, 149.
111. Thackeray, *The English Humourists of the Eighteenth Century*, 275.
112. George H. Ford, *The Dickens Critics* (Westport, Conn.: Greenwood Press, 1972).
113. Deborah Epstein Nord, "The Making of Dickens Criticism," in *Contemporary Dickens*, ed. Eileen Gillooly and Deirdre David (Columbus: Ohio State University Press, 2009), 264–87.
114. Collins, *Charles Dickens*, 494.
115. Ibid., 556.
116. See also Ben Winyard and Holly Furneaux, "Introduction: Dickens, Science and the Victorian Literary Imagination," *19: Interdisciplinary Studies in the Long Nineteenth Century* 10 (2010); George Levine, *Darwin and the Novelists:*

Patterns of Science in Victorian Fiction (University of Chicago Press, 1992), 151.

117. See "The Study of Psychology," one volume of Lewes's series, Problems of Life and Mind (1874–79), which was included in Significant Contributions to the History of Psychology. F. Froebel and J. F. Herbart, *Significant Contributions to the History of Psychology, 1750–1920: Series B: Psychometrics and Educational Psychology* (Washington, DC: University Publications of America, 1977); On Lewes's place in the history of psychology, see Daniel N. Robinson, *An Intellectual History of Psychology* (New York: Macmillan, 1981).
118. Collins, *Charles Dickens*, 576.
119. Ibid.
120. Ford, *The Dickens Critics*, 223, 229.
121. "Dickens in Relation to Criticism," *Fortnightly Review*, 11, New Series; 1 January to 1 June 1872 (Vol. 17, Old Series).
122. Collins, *Charles Dickens*, 576. Subsequent page references to this essay are noted in parentheses in the text.
123. See also Nelson, *Precocious Children and Childish Adults*, 163.
124. Virginia Woolf, *The Common Reader: First and Second Series* (New York: Harcourt, Brace, 1948), 175.
125. Ford, *Dickens and His Readers*, 198.
126. Collins, *Charles Dickens*, 313, 318.
127. Ford, *Dickens and His Readers*, 154.
128. Steedman, *Strange Dislocations*, 144.
129. Ibid.

6 "THE TIME OF REAL AMUSEMENT": HENRY JAMES AND THE CULT OF ADULTHOOD

1. Henry James, *The Art of the Novel: Critical Prefaces*, ed. R. P. Blackmur (New York: Scribner, 1962), 153.
2. See, for example, Huyssen's influential formulation of this point: "The political, psychological, and aesthetic discourse around the turn of the century consistently and obsessively genders mass culture and the masses as feminine, while high culture, whether traditional or modern, clearly remains the privileged realm of male activities." Andreas Huyssen, *After the Great Divide: Modernism, Mass Culture, Postmodernism* (Bloomington: Indiana University Press, 1986), 47. While they remain crucial to understanding it, I do not believe the elitist and misogynist elements of James's notion of the adult exhaust its meaning. On James and the art novel, see Mark McGurl, *The Novel Art: Elevations of American Fiction After Henry James* (Princeton University Press, 2001); Jonathan L. Freedman, *Professions of Taste: Henry James, British Aestheticism and Commodity Culture* (Stanford University Press, 1990); Maria DiBattista and Lucy McDiarmid, eds., *High and Low Moderns: Literature and Culture, 1889–1939* (Oxford University Press, 1996); Clark, *Kiddie Lit*. In considering James in

relation to family reading, I share these critics' interest in investigating how modernism is in dialogue with kinds of writing that it also devalues.

3. See Freedman, *Professions of Taste*.
4. A portion of this chapter appeared in *NOVEL* and is reprinted with the permission of the present publisher, Duke University Press. Teresa Michals, "Henry James and the Invention of Adulthood," *NOVEL: A Forum on Fiction* 44, no. 2 (2011): 229–48.
5. Henry James, "Future of the Novel," 243.
6. Henry James, *The Future of the Novel*, ed. Leon Edel (New York: Vintage Books, 1956), Introduction.
7. On differences between the French and English novelistic traditions with regard to the "young person" and sexual knowledge in particular, see Ruth Bernard Yeazell, "Podsnappery, Sexuality, and the English Novel," *Critical Inquiry* 9, no. 2 (1982): 339–57.
8. James, *Literary Criticism*, ed. Leon Edel, 2 vols. (New York: Library of America, 1984) II, 290; the poetic justice defense was also used at the 1857 trial of Madame Bovary for obscenity; see Dominick LaCapra, *Madame Bovary on Trial* (Ithaca, NY: Cornell University Press, 1982); Elisabeth Ladenson, *Dirt for Art's Sake: Books on Trial from Madame Bovary to Lolita* (Ithaca: Cornell University Press, 2007).
9. See Hughes, "Children's Literature," 544: "novelists in a bid for critical respectability, tried to dissociate the novel from its family readership and redirect it toward what was seen as art's traditional elite audience of educated adult males outside the home, at court, the coffee house, or the club. The 'serious novel' would have to earn its laurels, or win its spurs, at the cost of being unsuitable for women and children."
10. James, "Future of the Novel: An Analysis and a Forecast," 243.
11. On the figure of the novelist as children's storyteller, see, for example, Armstrong's reading of Sir Joshua Reynolds's portrait of young Master Bunbury supposedly listening to a story, in the introduction to *How Novels Think: The Limits of British Individualism from 1719–1900* (New York: Columbia University Press, 2005), 2–3. See as well my Chapter 3 for James's description of Walter Scott as a storyteller holding enthralled a flock of children as dusk falls.
12. James, *The Art of the Novel*, 106. For a wonderful account of the complexities of the metaphor of reading as eating in James, see Jennifer L. Fleissner, "Henry James's Art of Eating," *ELH* 75, no. 1 (2008): 27–62.
13. Henry James, *Letters, Fictions, Lives: Henry James and William Dean Howells*, ed. Michael Anesko (Oxford University Press, 1997), 379–80.
14. Henry James, *The Letters of Henry James* (New York: Octagon Books, 1970), 209–10.
15. James, *The Art of the Novel*, viii.
16. For an account of the "most curious split between Tom Sawyer and Huckleberry Finn, both considered to be for the young and old in the nineteenth century," see Clark, *Kiddie Lit*, 33–34, 77.

17. Marcia Ann Jacobson, *Henry James and the Mass Market* (University of Alabama Press, 1983), 14.
18. Hayden, *Walter Scott*, 75.
19. Clark, *Kiddie Lit*, 42.
20. Eric L. Haralson, *Henry James and Queer Modernity* (Cambridge University Press, 2003); Eve Kosofsky Sedgwick, *Epistemology of the Closet* (Berkeley: University of California Press, 1990).
21. Holly Brewer sums up the importance of status, and the relative unimportance of adulthood, in this older world: well into the eighteenth century, she writes, "rank outweighed age in allocating power." Brewer, *By Birth or Consent*, 341. See also my Introduction.
22. Côté, *Arrested Adulthood*, 31.
23. Steven Mintz, "Reflections on Age as a Category of Historical Analysis." That is, rather than the fact of achieving a new legal status moving one from one age category to another, under this new system age in and of itself changes legal status – for example, licensing one to drink, vote, or drive a car.
24. Côté, *Arrested Adulthood*, 28.
25. On modernism and pornography, see, respectively, Allison Pease, *Modernism, Mass Culture, and the Aesthetics of Obscenity* (Cambridge University Press, 2000) and Adam Parkes, *Modernism and the Theater of Censorship* (Oxford University Press, 1996). On pornography and the novel more generally, see Frances Ferguson, *Pornography, the Theory: What Utilitarianism Did to Action* (University of Chicago Press, 2004). On the rise in the United Kingdom of legal protection for pornography itself on the condition that it target adults only, see Geoffrey Robertson, *Obscenity: An Account of Censorship Laws and Their Enforcement in England and Wales* (London: Weidenfeld & Nicolson, 1979).
26. James, *The Art of the Novel*, 102.
27. For the earlier history of the paired figures of the domestic woman and the society lady, see Armstrong, *Desire and Domestic Fiction*; Teresa Michals, "'Like a Spoiled Actress Off the Stage': Anti-Theatricality, Nature, and the Novel," *Studies in Eighteenth-Century Culture* 39, no. 1 (2010): 191–214.
28. James, *Literary Criticism*, II, 957.
29. F. O. Matthiessen, *The James Family: Including Selections from the Writings of Henry James, Senior, William, Henry and Alice James* (New York: Knopf, 1961), 500.
30. Henry James, *Autobiography* (Princeton University Press, 1983), 547.
31. Plotz, *Romanticism and the Vocation of Childhood*; Barbara Garlitz, "The Immortality Ode: Its Cultural Progeny," *Studies in English Literature, 1500–1900* 6, no. 4 (1966): 639–49.
32. James, *The Art of the Novel*, 156.
33. James, *Autobiography*, 40.
34. Ibid., 44.

35. Muriel G. Shine, *The Fictional Children of Henry James* (Chapel Hill: University of North Carolina Press, 1969).
36. James, *The Art of the Novel*, 153–54.
37. John Felstiner, "Max Beerbohm and the Wings of Henry James," *The Kenyon Review* 29, no. 4 (1967): 464.
38. Sir Max Beerbohm, *A Christmas Garland* (New York: E. P. Dutton & Company, 1922), 9.
39. Henry James, *The Novels and Tales of Henry James*, 26 vols., Scribner Reprint Editions (Fairfield, NJ: A. M. Kelley, 1976), XI, 552.
40. Ibid., Preface, xv.
41. Elliot M. Schrero, "Exposure in *The Turn of the Screw*," *Modern Philology* 78, no. 3 (1981): 261–74. Although at first glance the governess cannot tell whether Quint is dead or alive, she can see that he is no gentleman. He does, however, imitate the only gentleman in the story, borrowing not only the Master's clothes but also his opportunism, his irresponsibility, and his sexual allure.
42. James, *The Novels and Tales of Henry James*, XII, 200.
43. Ibid., XII, 236, 237.
44. Jacobson, *Henry James and the Mass Market*, 110; E. Nesbit's *The Treasure-Seekers* (1898) is another especially interesting example of the "child novel" genre. It is now valued as a children's classic but was originally published serially in *The Strand* for a mixed-age audience. Much of the humor of this book comes from its child narrator's misinterpretations of adult matters, especially financial ones, and is aimed at an adult reader. Although Nesbit admired James, she does not share his project of elevating adulthood and adult readers: her children spend most of their time away from adults, planning and enjoying their own adventures. See Julia Briggs, "E. Nesbit, the Bastables, and The Red House: A Response," *Children's Literature* 25, no. 1 (1997): 71–85.
45. Jacobson, *Henry James and the Mass Market*, 106.
46. Roger Gard, *Henry James: The Critical Heritage* (London: Routledge & K. Paul, 1968), 223.
47. Clark, *Kiddie Lit*, 47; on the place of the "genteel tradition" in American literature, see also F. Brett Cox, "'What Need, Then, for Poetry?': The Genteel Tradition and the Continuity of American Literature," *The New England Quarterly* 67, no. 2 (1994): 212–33.
48. Clark, *Kiddie Lit*, 23.
49. Burnett also uses distance as a metaphor for age, describing growing up as emigration: "The Small Person is gone to that undiscoverable far-away land where other Small Persons have emigrated." Frances Hodgson Burnett, *The One I Knew Best of All: A Memory of the Mind of a Child* (New York: C. Scribner's Sons, 1893), viii.
50. James, *The Letters of Henry James*, 335.
51. Ibid., 244.
52. James was in good company among nineteenth-century Americans in his habit of seeing in England a paradoxical ability to stand for both sameness and difference, and in his hope of finding something distinctively aesthetic

in the experience of thinking about it. Elisa Tamarkin sees the phenomenon of nineteenth-century American Anglophilia as, in part, the experience of a specifically aesthetic distance: "a devotion to a mythology of British sovereign power that sees it grow in strength the more that it recedes." She points out that, in Walter Benjamin's terms, American Anglophilia gives England the aura of an aesthetic object: "the unique phenomenon of a distance, however close it may be." Elisa Tamarkin, *Anglophilia: Deference, Devotion, and Antebellum America* (University of Chicago Press, 2008), xxv.

53. James, *The Novels and Tales of Henry James*, xv, 4, 18.
54. Frances Hodgson Burnett, *A Little Princess* (New York: Penguin Books, 2002), 187.
55. Matthiessen, *The James Family*, 316–17.
56. On James and vulgarity, see, for example, Andrew Cutting, "Henry James and 'Vulgarity'," *English: The Journal of the English Association* 41 (1992): 113–25.
57. Burnett, *The One I Knew Best of All*, 3–4.
58. Ibid., vii, 8.
59. James, *The Novels and Tales of Henry James*, xi, 204.
60. Ibid.
61. Burnett, *The One I Knew Best of All*, 2.
62. James, *The Novels and Tales of Henry James*, xi, 55, 68, 34.
63. Ibid., xi, 75, 70, 68.
64. Thomas Hardy, *Jude the Obscure*, ed. Dennis Taylor (London: Penguin Books, 1998), 3.
65. Woolf, *The Common Reader: First and Second Series*, 237.
66. Hardy, *Jude the Obscure*, 466.
67. Norman Hapgood, *Literary Statesmen and Others* (New York: Herbert Stone & Co., 1897), 194.
68. Henry James, *Literary Criticism*, I, 676.
69. James, *The Novels and Tales of Henry James*, xvi, 42.
70. Henry James, "The Future of the Novel," 247. For the "obligation" to be "interesting" see "The Art of Fiction," in *The Art of Criticism: Henry James on the Theory and the Practice of Fiction*, ed. William R. Veeder and Susan M. Griffin (University of Chicago Press, 1986), 170.
71. Quoted in McGurl, *The Novel Art*, 119. On the history of intelligence testing, see Stephen Jay Gould, *The Mismeasure of Man*, rev. edition (New York: Norton, 1996).
72. James, "The Art of Fiction," 181.
73. Henry James, *The House of Fiction; Essays on the Novel* (Westport, Conn.: Greenwood Press, 1973).
74. Tessa Hadley, *Henry James and the Imagination of Pleasure* (Cambridge University Press, 2002), 4.
75. Peter Brooks, "Henry James and Dirty French Novels," *The Henry James Review* 28, no. 3 (2007): 205. "Qu'en savons-nous du reste et comment peut-on parler, dans toute cette matière, pour un autre que pour soi? C'est pourquoi il vaut mieux en parler le moins possible." "What do we know about it moreover and

how can one speak, in this whole business, for anyone other than oneself? That is why one should speak of it as little as possible" (quoted in Brooks; Brooks's translation).

76. Michael Moon, *A Small Boy and Others: Imitation and Initiation in American Culture from Henry James to Andy Warhol* (Durham, NC: Duke University Press, 1998), 190. See also Michael Moon, "Review: Burn Me at the Stake Always," *The New England Quarterly* 78, no. 4 (2005): 631–42.
77. James, "Future of the Novel: An Analysis and a Forecast."
78. See Kevin Ohi, "'The Author of "Beltraffio"': The Exquisite Boy and Henry James's Equivocal Aestheticism," *ELH* 72, no. 3 (2005): 747–67.
79. Henry James, *Novels, 1871–1880* (New York, NY: Literary Classics of the United States, 1983), 25
80. Alfred Habegger, "Precocious Incest: First Novels by Louisa May Alcott and Henry James," *The Massachusetts Review* 26, no. 2/3 (1985): 257.
81. Gard, *Henry James*, 284.
82. James, *Literary Criticism*, 1, 276.
83. Katharine Susan Anthony, *Louisa May Alcott* (New York: A. A. Knopf, 1938).
84. James, *Novels, 1871–1880*, 55, 54, 54.
85. Jemima Montgomery, Baroness Tautphoeus, *The Initials: A Novel*, New Edition (London: R. Bentley, 1858), 266.
86. Ibid., 267.
87. James, *The Novels and Tales of Henry James*, 251.
88. James, *Autobiography*, 44.
89. Henry James, *A Small Boy and Others* (New York: C. Scribner's Sons, 1913), 46, 45.
90. Gerald Martin Bordman and Thomas S. Hischak, "Hot Corn: Life Scenes in New York Illustrated," *The Oxford Companion to American Theatre* (Oxford University Press, 1984).
91. Solon Robinson, *Hot Corn: Life Scenes in New York Illustrated. Including the Story of Little Katy, Madalina, the Rag-picker's Daughter, Wild Maggie, &c. With Original Designs, Engraved by N. Orr* (New York: De Witt and Davenport Publishers, 1854), 14.
92. Judith N. McArthur, "Demon Rum on the Boards: Temperance Melodrama and the Tradition of Antebellum Reform," *Journal of the Early Republic* 9, no. 4 (Winter 1989): 524; Barnum is quoted on p. 535.
93. Robinson, *Hot Corn*, Introduction, v.
94. Judith R. Walkowitz, *City of Dreadful Delight: Narratives of Sexual Danger in Late-Victorian London* (University of Chicago Press, 1992). See also Jacobson, *Henry James and the Mass Market*, 162.
95. Robinson, *Hot Corn*, 65, 79.
96. Ibid., "New York Evangelist," front cover, Author's Preface vii.
97. James, *A Small Boy and Others*, 78.
98. Maria Susanna Cummins, *The Lamplighter*, ed. Nina Baym (New Brunswick, NJ: Rutgers University Press, 1988), 1.

99. James, *A Small Boy and Others.*
100. Ibid., 78.
101. Tautphoeus, *The Initials: A Novel*, 13.
102. Judith Plotz, "Secret Garden II: Or, Lady Chatterley's Lover as Palimpsest," *Children's Literature Association Quarterly* 19, no. 1 (1994): 15.

Bibliography

Adams, Robert P. "Bold Bawdry and Open Manslaughter: The English New Humanist Attack on Medieval Romance." *Huntington Library Quarterly* 23, no. 1 (November 1, 1959): 33–48.

Aikin, John, and Mrs Barbauld (Anna Letitia). *Miscellaneous Pieces, in Prose: By J. and A. L. Aikin*. Belfast: printed by James Magee, 1774.

Aikins, Janet E. "Pamela's Use of Locke's Words." *Studies in Eighteenth-Century Culture* 25, no. 1 (1996): 75–97.

Alryyes, Ala A. *Original Subjects: The Child, the Novel, and the Nation*. Cambridge, Mass.: Harvard University Press, 2001.

Anthony, Katharine Susan. *Louisa May Alcott*. New York: Knopf, 1938.

Arata, Stephen. "On Not Paying Attention." *Victorian Studies* 46, no. 2 (Winter 2004): 193–205.

Ariès, Philippe. *Centuries of Childhood: A Social History of Family Life*. New York: Vintage Books, 1965.

Armstrong, Nancy. *Desire and Domestic Fiction: A Political History of the Novel*. Oxford University Press, 1987.

How Novels Think: The Limits of British Individualism from 1719–1900. New York: Columbia University Press, 2005.

Arnett, Jeffrey Jensen. "Emerging Adulthood(s): The Cultural Psychology of a New Life Stage." In *Bridging Cultural and Developmental Approaches to Psychology: New Syntheses in Theory, Research, and Policy*, edited by Lene Arnett Jensen, 255–75. Oxford University Press, 2011.

Arnett, Jeffrey Jensen, and Susan Taber. "Adolescence Terminable and Interminable: When Does Adolescence End?" *Journal of Youth and Adolescence* 23, no. 5 (1994): 517–37.

Atwood, Joan D., and Corinne Scholtz. "The Quarter-life Time Period: An Age of Indulgence, Crisis or Both?" *Contemporary Family Therapy: An International Journal* 30, no. 4 (2008): 233–50.

Backscheider, Paula R., and Catherine Ingrassia. *A Companion to the Eighteenth-century English Novel and Culture*. Oxford: Blackwell, 2005.

Bakhtin, Mikhail Mikhaĭlovich. *Speech Genres and Other Late Essays*. Edited by Michael Holquist and Caryl Emerson. Translated by Vern W. McGee. Austin, Tex.: University of Texas Press, 1986.

Balibar, Renée. "National Language, Education, Literature." In *The Politics of Theory*, edited by Francis Barker, Peter Hulme, Margaret Iverson, and Dianna Loxley, 134–47. Colchester: University of Essex, 1983.

Ballantyne, James. *Ballantyne's Novelist's Library*. London: Hurst, Robinson and Co., 1824.

Barbauld, Letitia. *Lessons for Children. Part III. Being the Second for Children of Three Years Old*. London: J. Johnson, 1795.

Lessons for Children: With Four Original Tales. New York: Pendleton and Hill, 1831.

Barbauld, Letitia, *Selected Poetry and Prose*. Edited by Elizabeth Kraft and William McCarthy. Peterborough, Ont.: Broadview Press, 2002.

Barrie, J. M. *Peter Pan: The Original Story*. HarperFestival, 2003.

Barro, Robert J. *Macroeconomics*. Cambridge, Mass.: MIT Press, 1997.

Beerbohm, Sir Max. *A Christmas Garland*. New York: E. P. Dutton & Company, 1922.

Ben-Amos, Ilana Krausman. *Adolescence and Youth in Early Modern England*. New Haven: Yale University Press, 1994.

Blackstone, William. *Commentaries on the Laws of England in Four Books: With Analysis of the Work*. New York: W. E. Dean, 1844.

Boorstin, Daniel J. *The Mysterious Science of the Law: An Essay on Blackstone's Commentaries*. Boston: Beacon Press, 1958.

Bordman, Gerald Martin, and Thomas S. Hischak. "Hot Corn: Life Scenes in New York Illustrated." *The Oxford Companion to American Theatre*. New York: Oxford University Press, 1984.

Boucé, Paul-Gabriel. *Sexuality in Eighteenth-Century Britain*. Manchester University Press, 1982.

Bowers, Toni. *Force or Fraud: British Seduction Stories and the Problem of Resistance, 1660–1760*. Oxford University Press, 2011.

Brantlinger, Patrick. "Dickens and the Factories." *Nineteenth-Century Fiction* 26, no. 3 (December 1971): 270–85.

Brewer, Holly. *By Birth or Consent: Children, Law, and the Anglo-American Revolution in Authority*. Chapel Hill: Published for the Omohundro Institute of Early American History and Culture, Williamsburg, Virginia, by the University of North Carolina Press, 2005.

Briggs, Julia. "E. Nesbit, the Bastables, and The Red House: A Response." *Children's Literature* 25, no. 1 (1997): 71–85.

Brigham, Clarence S. *Bibliography of American Editions of "Robinson Crusoe" to 1830*. Worcester, Mass.: The American Antiquarian Society, 1958.

Bristow, Joseph. *Empire Boys: Adventures in a Man's World*. London: Harper Collins Academic, 1991.

Brockman, Bennett A. "Robin Hood and the Invention of Children's Literature." *Children's Literature: Annual of The Modern Language Association Division on Children's Literature and The Children's Literature Association* 10 (1982): 1–17.

Brontë, Charlotte. *Jane Eyre*. London: Penguin Books, 2006.

Brooks, Peter. "Henry James and Dirty French Novels." *The Henry James Review* 28, no. 3 (2007): 202–12.

Bryfonski, Dedria, and Gerald J. Senick, eds. "J. R. R. Tolkien (1892–1973)." In *Contemporary Literary Criticism* 12: 563–87. Detroit, Mich.: Gale Research, 1980.

Bunyan, John. *A Book for Boys and Girls: Or Temporal Things Spiritualized. By John Bunyan. Licensend and Entred According to Order*. London, 1701.

Burgett, Bruce. "Between Speculation and Population: The Problem of 'Sex' in Our Long Eighteenth Century." *Early American Literature* 37, no. 1 (1 January 2002): 119–53.

Burnett, Frances Hodgson. *A Little Princess*. New York: Penguin Books, 2002.

The One I Knew Best of All: A Memory of the Mind of a Child. New York: C. Scribner's Sons, 1893.

Carlisle, Janice. *The Sense of an Audience: Dickens, Thackeray, and George Eliot at Mid-Century*. Athens: University of Georgia Press, 1981.

Carr, Rosalind. "The Gentleman and the Soldier: Patriotic Masculinities in Eighteenth-Century Scotland." *Journal of Scottish Historical Studies* 28, no. 2 (December 2008): 102–21.

Castle, Terry J. "P/B: Pamela as Sexual Fiction." *Studies in English Literature, 1500–1900* 22, no. 3 (1982): 469–89.

Cavell, S. A. *Midshipmen and Quarterdeck Boys in the British Navy, 1771–1831*. Woodbridge: The Boydell Press, 2012.

Chaber, Lois A. "From Moral Man to Godly Man: 'Mr. Locke' and Mr. B. in Part 2 of Pamela." *Studies in Eighteenth-Century Culture* 18 (1988): 213–61.

Chandos, John. *Boys Together: English Public Schools, 1800–1864*. New Haven, Conn.: Yale University Press, 1984.

Chesterton, G. K. *Charles Dickens: A Critical Study*. Whitefish, Mo.: Kessinger Publishing, 2005.

Clark, Beverly Lyon. *Kiddie Lit: The Cultural Construction of Children's Literature in America*. Baltimore: Johns Hopkins University Press, 2003.

Cleghorn, Sarah Norcliffe. *Portraits and Protests* [1917]. Cornell University Library, 2009.

Coke, Sir Edward. *The Third Part of the Institutes of the Laws of England: Concerning High Treason, and Other Pleas of the Crown, and Criminal Causes*. A. Crooke, 1669.

Coleridge, Bernard. *The Story of a Devonshire House*. London: T. Fisher Unwin, 1905.

Coleridge, Samuel Taylor. *The Stateman's Manual*. London: Printed for Gale and Fenner, 1816.

Collins, Philip, ed. *Charles Dickens: The Critical Heritage*. London: Routledge, 1971.

Conley, Mary A. *From Jack Tar to Union Jack: Representing Naval Manhood in the British Empire, 1870–1918*. Manchester University Press, 2009.

Côté, James E. *Arrested Adulthood: The Changing Nature of Maturity and Identity*. New York University Press, 2000.

Cox, F. Brett. "'What Need, Then, for Poetry?': The Genteel Tradition and the Continuity of American Literature." *The New England Quarterly* 67, no. 2 (June 1994): 212–33.

Cummins, Maria Susanna. *The Lamplighter*. Edited by Nina Baym. New Brunswick, NJ: Rutgers University Press, 1988.

Cunningham, Hugh. *The Children of the Poor: Representations of Childhood Since the Seventeenth Century*. Oxford: Blackwell, 1991.

Cutmore, Jonathan. *The Quarterly Review Archive. Romantic Circles*. www.rc.und./reference/qr/.

Cutting, Andrew. "Henry James and 'Vulgarity'." *English: The Journal of the English Association* 41 (1992): 113–25.

Darton, F. J. Harvey. *Children's Books in England: Five Centuries of Social Life*. 3rd edn. Cambridge University Press, 1982.

Davidoff, Leonore, and Catherine Hall. *Family Fortunes: Men and Women of the English Middle Class 1780–1850*. 2nd edn. London: Routledge, 2003.

Davis, Roger. *Kendrew of York and His Chapbooks for Children: With a Checklist*. Collingham, UK: Elmete Press, 1988.

Deane, Bradley. "Imperial Boyhood: Piracy and the Play Ethic." *Victorian Studies* 53, no. 4 (2011): 689–714.

Defoe, Daniel. *The Complete English Tradesman*. London: Printed for J. Rivington, 1745.

The Family Instructor. In Three Parts. With a Recommendatory Letter by the Reverend Mr. S. Wright. London, 1715.

The Life and Adventures of Robinson Crusoe. London: Printed for Tabart & Co., 1805.

Robinson Crusoe. New edn. Oxford World's Classics. Oxford University Press, 2007.

Voyages and Travels: Being the Life and Adventures of Robinson Crusoe, of York, Mariner. Who Lived Eight and Twenty Years All Alone in an Unihabited [sic] Island on the Coast of America, . . . Written by Himselfe. [London?], 1750.

Demers, Patricia. *From Instruction to Delight: An Anthology of Children's Literature to 1850*. Oxford University Press, 2008.

DiBattista, Maria, and Lucy McDiarmid, eds. *High and Low Moderns: Literature and Culture, 1889–1939*. Oxford University Press, 1996.

Dickens, Charles. *Bleak House*. Edited by Norman Page. London: Penguin Books, 1971.

A Christmas Carol and Other Christmas Stories. New York: Signet Classics, 2008.

David Copperfield. Edited by Jeremy Tambling. London: Penguin Books, 1996.

"A Holiday Romance." Text, n.d. http://ebooks.adelaide.edu.au/d/dickens/charles/d54hr/.

Gone Astray and Other Papers from Household Words, 1851–59. The Dent Uniform Edition of Dickens' Journalism, Volume III. Columbus: Ohio State University Press, 1999.

Great Expectations. Edited by Graham Law and Adrian Pinnington. Peterborough, Ont.: Broadview Press, 1998.

Hard Times: An Authoritative Text, Backgrounds, Sources, and Contemporary Reactions, Criticism. 2nd edn. New York: Norton, 1990.

The Letters of Charles Dickens. Edited by Madeline House and Graham Storey. 8 vols. Oxford: Clarendon Press, 1965–95.

The Old Curiosity Shop. Edited by Norman Page. London: Penguin Books, 2001.

Our Mutual Friend. Edited by Adrian Poole. London: Penguin Books, 1998.

The Uncommercial Traveller and Other Papers. The Dent Uniform Edition of Dickens' Journalism, Volume IV. London: Dent, 2000.

Uncollected Writings from Household Words, 1850–1859. Bloomington: Indiana University Press, 1968.

Eaves, T. C. and Ben D. Kimpel. *Samuel Richardson: A Biography*. Oxford: Clarendon Press, 1971.

Edgeworth, Maria. *The Absentee*. Oxford University Press, 1988.

Belinda. Edited by Kathryn J. Kirkpatrick. Oxford University Press, 2009.

Patronage. Whitefish, Mont.: Kessinger Publishing, 2010.

Practical Education; by Maria Edgeworth, Author Of Letters For Literary Ladies, And The Parent's Assistant; and by Richard Lovell Edgeworth, F.R.S. and M.R.I.A. ... Volume I. London, 1798.

Rosamond: With Other Tales, 1844.

Ezell, Margaret J. M. "John Locke's Images of Childhood: Early Eighteenth Century Response to Some Thoughts Concerning Education." *Eighteenth-Century Studies* 17, no. 2 (1983): 139–55.

Felstiner, John. "Max Beerbohm and the Wings of Henry James." *The Kenyon Review* 29, no. 4 (1967): 449–71.

Fergus, Jan S. *Provincial Readers in Eighteenth-Century England*. Oxford University Press, 2006.

Ferguson, Frances. "The Afterlife of the Romantic Child: Rousseau and Kant Meet Deleuze and Guattari." *The South Atlantic Quarterly* 102, no. 1 (2003): 215–34.

Pornography, the Theory: What Utilitarianism Did to Action. University of Chicago Press, 2004.

Ferris, Ina. *The Achievement of Literary Authority: Gender, History, and the Waverley Novels*. Ithaca, NY: Cornell University Press, 1991.

Fiedler, Leslie A. *Love and Death in the American Novel*. Normal, Ill.: Dalkey Archive Press, 1997.

Fielding, Henry. *Shamela*. Whitefish, Mont.: Kessinger Publishing, 2004.

Fleetwood, William. *The Relative Duties of Parents and Children, Husbands and Wives, Masters and Servants, Consider'd in Sixteen Sermons: With Three More Upon the Case of Self-murther. By W. Fleetwood, Rector of St. Augustine's, London, and Chaplain in Ordinary to Her Majesty*. London, 1705.

Fleishman, Avrom. *The English Historical Novel: Walter Scott to Virginia Woolf*. Baltimore: Johns Hopkins University Press, 1972.

Fleissner, Jennifer L. "Henry James's Art of Eating." *ELH* 75, no. 1 (2008): 27–62.

Flint, Christopher. *Family Fictions: Narrative and Domestic Relations in Britain, 1688–1798*. Stanford University Press, 1998.

Ford, George H. *Dickens and His Readers*. New York: Gordian Press, 1974.

The Dickens Critics. Westport, Conn.: Greenwood Press, 1972.

Forster, John. *The Life of Charles Dickens*. 3 vols. Boston: Estes & Lauriat, 1872.

Foucault, Michel. *The History of Sexuality, Volume I: An Introduction*. Translated by Robert Hurley. New York: Vintage, 1990.

Fox, Adam, Paul Griffiths, and Steve Hindle, eds. *The Experience of Authority in Early Modern England*. New York: St. Martin's Press, 1996.

Freedman, Jonathan L. *Professions of Taste: Henry James, British Aestheticism and Commodity Culture*. Stanford University Press, 1990.

Froebel, F., and J. F. Herbart. *Significant Contributions to the History of Psychology, 1750–1920: Series B: Psychometrics and Educational Psychology*. University Publications of America, 1977.

Gard, Roger. *Henry James: The Critical Heritage*. London: Routledge & K. Paul, 1968.

Garlitz, Barbara. "The Immortality Ode: Its Cultural Progeny." *Studies in English Literature, 1500–1900* 6, no. 4 (Autumn 1966): 639–49.

Garside, Peter D. "Scott and the 'Philosophical' Historians." *Journal of the History of Ideas* 36 (1975): 497–512.

Ghosh, Peter. "'Robinson Crusoe,' The Isolated Economic Man: Max Weber, Marginal Utility Theory, and the 'Spirit' of Capitalism." *Max Weber Studies* 1 (2006): 71–99.

Gildon, Charles, and Miscellaneous Pamphlet Collection (Library of Congress). *The Life and Strange Surprizing Adventures of Mr. D—De F–, of London, Hosier: Who Has Liv'd Above Fifty Yeares by Himself in the Kingdoms of North and South Britain . . . :In a Dialogue Between Him, Robinson Crusoe, and His Man Friday, with Remarks Serious and Comical Upon the Life of Crusoe*. London: Printed for J. Roberts, 1719.

Gillis, John R. *For Better, for Worse: British Marriages, 1600 to the Present*. Oxford University Press, 1986.

Goldstein, Joseph. "On Being Adult and Being an Adult in Secular Law." *Daedalus* 105, no. 4 (Fall 1976): 69–87.

Goodenough, Elizabeth, and Andrea Immel, eds. *Under Fire: Childhood in the Shadow of War*. Detroit: Wayne State University Press, 2008.

Gould, Stephen Jay. *The Mismeasure of Man*. Rev. edn. New York: Norton, 1996.

Graff, Harvey J. *The Literacy Myth: Cultural Integration and Social Structure in the Nineteenth Century*. New Brunswick, NJ: Transaction Publishers, 1979.

Green, Katherine Sobba. "The Heroine's Blazon and Hardwicke's Marriage Act: Commodification for a Novel Market." *Tulsa Studies in Women's Literature* 9, no. 2 (1990): 273–90.

Grenby, M. O. "Adults Only? Children and Children's Books in British Circulating Libraries, 1748–1848." *Book History* 5 (2002): 19–38.

"Chapbooks, Children, and Children's Literature." *The Library: The Transactions of the Bibliographical Society* 8, no. 3 (2007): 277–303.

The Child Reader, 1700–1840. Cambridge University Press, 2011.
"Surely There is No British Boy or Girl Who Has Not Heard of the Battle of Waterloo!" In *Under Fire*, edited by Goodenough and Immel.
Gross, John J. *Dickens and the Twentieth Century*. University of Toronto Press, 1966.
Guillory, John. *Cultural Capital: The Problem of Literary Canon Formation*. University of Chicago Press, 1993.
"Literary Capital: Gray's 'Elegy,' Anna Laetitia Barbauld, and the Vernacular Canon." In *Early Modern Conceptions of Property*, edited by John Brewer and Susan Staves. London: Routledge, 1996.
Habegger, Alfred. "Precocious Incest: First Novels by Louisa May Alcott and Henry James." *The Massachusetts Review* 26, no. 2/3 (1985): 233–62.
Hadley, Elaine. *Living Liberalism: Practical Citizenship in Mid-Victorian Britain*. University of Chicago Press, 2010.
Hadley, Tessa. *Henry James and the Imagination of Pleasure*. Cambridge University Press, 2002.
Hall, G. Stanley. *Adolescence: Its Psychology and Its Relations to Physiology, Anthropology, Sociology, Sex, Crime, Religion and Education*. New York: D. Appleton and Company, 1904.
Haralson, Eric L. *Henry James and Queer Modernity*. Cambridge University Press, 2003.
Hardy, Thomas. *Jude the Obscure*. Edited by Dennis Taylor. London: Penguin Books, 1998.
Harth, Erica. "The Virtue of Love: Lord Hardwicke's Marriage Act." *Cultural Critique* no. 9 (Spring 1988): 123–54.
Hayden, John O., ed. *Walter Scott: The Critical Heritage*. London: Routledge, 1995.
Hearn, Michael Patrick. "Dickens, Charles 1812–1870." In *Writers for Children: Critical Studies of Major Authors Since the Seventeenth Century*, edited by Jane M. Bingham, 181–91. New York: Charles Scribner's Sons, 1988.
Henderson, Willie. *Economics as Literature*. London: Routledge, 1995.
Evaluating Adam Smith. London: Routledge, 2006.
Henty, G. A. *By Conduct and Courage; a Story of Nelson's Days*. New York, 1904.
Hill, Bridget. *Servants: English Domestics in the Eighteenth Century*. Oxford: Clarendon Press, 1996.
Hilliard, Raymond F. "*Pamela*: Autonomy, Subordination, and the State of Childhood." *Studies in Philology* 83, no. 2 (Spring 1986): 201–17.
Hilton, Mary, and Pam Hirsch. *Practical Visionaries: Women, Education and Social Progress 1790–1930*. Harlow: Longman, 2000.
Hilton, Mary, Morag Styles, and Victor Watson. *Opening the Nursery Door*. London: Routledge, 1997.
Hopfl, H. M. "From Savage to Scotsman: Conjectural History in the Scottish Enlightenment." *The Journal of British Studies* 17, no. 2 (Spring 1978): 19–40.
Howell, George. *The Conflicts of Capital and Labour: Historically and Economically Considered. Being a History and Review of the Trade Unions of Great Britain,*

Showing Their Origin, Progress, Constitution, and Objects, in Their Varied Political, Social, Economical, and Industrial Aspects. London: Macmillan, 1890.

Hughes, Felicity A. "Children's Literature: Theory and Practice." *ELH* 45, no. 3 (Autumn 1978): 542–61.

Hume, David. *Selected Essays.* Oxford University Press, 1998.

Hunt, Margaret R. *The Middling Sort: Commerce, Gender, and the Family in England, 1680–1780.* Berkeley: University of California Press, 1996.

Hutchins, Henry Clinton, and A. Edward Newton Collection (Library of Congress). *Robinson Crusoe and Its Printing, 1719–1731; a Bibliographical Study.* New York: Columbia University Press, 1925.

Huyssen, Andreas. *After the Great Divide: Modernism, Mass Culture, Postmodernism.* Bloomington: Indiana University Press, 1986.

Immel, Andrea, and Michael Witmore, eds., *Childhood and Children's Books in Early Modern Europe, 1550–1800.* New York: Routledge, 2006.

Jackson, Mary V. *Engines of Instruction, Mischief, and Magic: Children's Literature in England from Its Beginnings to 1839.* Aldershot: Scolar Press, 1989.

Jacobs, Edward H. "Eighteenth-Century British Circulating Libraries and Cultural Book History." *Book History* 6, no. 1 (2003): 1–22.

Jacobson, Marcia Ann. *Henry James and the Mass Market.* University of Alabama Press, 1983.

James, Henry. "The Art of Fiction." In *The Art of Criticism*, edited by Veeder and Griffin.

The Art of the Novel: Critical Prefaces. Edited by R. P. Blackmur. New York: Scribner, 1962.

Autobiography. Princeton University Press, 1983.

"Future of the Novel: An Analysis and a Forecast." In *The Art of Criticism*, edited by Veeder and Griffin.

The Future of the Novel: Essays on the Art of Fiction. Edited by Leon Edel. New York: Vintage, 1956.

The House of Fiction; Essays on the Novel. Westport, Conn.: Greenwood Press, 1973.

Letters, Fictions, Lives: Henry James and William Dean Howells. Edited by Michael Anesko. Oxford University Press, 1997.

The Letters of Henry James. New York: Octagon Books, 1970.

"'The Limitations of Dickens': 'The Troop of Hunchbacks, Imbeciles, and Precocious Children'." In *Views and Reviews*, edited by Le Roy Phillips, 156. Boston: Ball Publishing, 1908.

Literary Criticism. 2 vols. Edited by Leon Edel. New York: Library of America, 1984.

Novels, 1871–1880. New York: Literary Classics of the United States, 1983.

The Novels and Tales of Henry James. 26 vols. Scribner Reprint Editions. Fairfield, NJ: A. M. Kelley, 1976.

A Small Boy and Others. New York: C. Scribner's Sons, 1913.

James, T. E. "The Age of Majority." *The American Journal of Legal History* 4, no. 1 (January 1960): 22–33.

Janeway, James. *A Token for Children. Being an Exact Account of the Conversion, Holy and Exemplary Lives and Joyful Deaths of Several Young Children.* Boston in New-England, 1728.

Jenkins, Emily. "Trilby: Fads, Photographers, and 'Over-Perfect Feet'." *Book History* 1 (1998): 221–67.

Jevons, William Stanley. *The Principles of Economics: A Fragment of a Treatise on the Industrial Mechanism of Society, and Other Papers.* Edited by Henry Higgs. New York, A. M. Kelley, 1965.

The Theory of Political Economy. London: Macmillan and Co., 1888.

"John Bull (London, England), Saturday, 13 January 1883; page 25; Issue 3,243."

Johnson, Claudia L. "'Let Me Make the Novels of a Country': Barbauld's 'The British Novelists' (1810/1820)." *NOVEL: A Forum on Fiction* 34, no. 2 (Spring 2001): 163–79.

Johnson, Samuel. *Dr. Johnson's Works.* Oxford English Classics. New York: AMS Press, 1970.

Johnson, Thomas H. "Jonathan Edwards and the 'Young Folks' Bible'." *The New England Quarterly* 5, no. 1 (January 1, 1932): 37–54.

Jordan, Winthrop D. "Searching for Adulthood in America." *Daedalus* 105, no. 4 (Fall 1976): 1–11.

Kertzer, Adrienne. "Inventing the Child Reader: How We Read Children's Books." In *Children's Literature in Education*, 15, no. 1 (1984), 12–21.

Ketcham, Carl, ed. *The Letters of John Wordsworth.* Ithaca, NY: Cornell University Press, 1969.

Keymer, Thomas, and Peter Sabor. *"Pamela" in the Marketplace: Literary Controversy and Print Culture in Eighteenth-Century Britain and Ireland.* Cambridge University Press, 2005.

Kincaid, James R. "The Education of Mr. Pickwick." *Nineteenth-Century Fiction* 24, no. 2 (September 1969): 127–141.

"Fattening up on Pickwick." *NOVEL: A Forum on Fiction* 25, no. 3 (Spring 1992): 235–44.

King, Thomas Alan. *The Gendering of Men, 1600–1750.* Madison: University of Wisconsin Press, 2004.

LaCapra, Dominick. *Madame Bovary on Trial.* Ithaca, NY: Cornell University Press, 1982.

Ladenson, Elisabeth. *Dirt for Art's Sake: Books on Trial from Madame Bovary to Lolita.* Ithaca, NY: Cornell University Press, 2007.

Laqueur, Thomas. *Making Sex: Body and Gender from the Greeks to Freud.* Cambridge, Mass.: Harvard University Press, 1992.

Latimer, Bonnie. "Leaving Little to the Imagination: The Mechanics of Didacticism in Two Children's Adaptations of Samuel Richardson's Novels." *The Lion and the Unicorn* 33, no. 2 (2009): 167–88.

Lawson, John, and Harold Silver. *A Social History of Education in England.* London: Routledge, 2007.

Lerer, Seth. *Children's Literature A Reader's History from Aesop to Harry Potter.* University of Chicago Press, 2009.

Levy, Michelle. "The Radical Education of Evenings at Home." *Eighteenth Century Fiction* 19, no. 1 (2006): 123–50.

Lewis, Judith. "'Tis a Misfortune to Be a Great Ladie': Maternal Mortality in the British Aristocracy, 1558–1959." *The Journal of British Studies* 37, no. 1 (January 1, 1998): 26–53.

Locke, John. *Locke: Political Essays.* Edited by Mark Goldie. Cambridge University Press, 1997.

Locke's Second Treatise of Civil Government: An Essay Concerning the True Original, Extent, and End of Civil Government: A Contemporary Selection. Grand Rapids: W. B. Eerdmans, 1978.

Some Thoughts Concerning Education: And, Of the Conduct of the Understanding. Edited by Ruth Weissbourd Grant and Nathan Tarcov. Indianapolis: Hackett, 1996.

Longford, Elizabeth. *Wellington: The Years of the Sword.* London: Weidenfeld & Nicolson, 1969.

Lundin, Anne H. "Victorian Horizons: The Reception of Children's Books in England and America, 1880–1900." *The Library Quarterly* 64, no. 1 (January 1994): 30–59.

Macfarlane, Alan. *Marriage and Love in England: Modes of Reproduction, 1300–1840.* Oxford: B. Blackwell, 1986.

Maine, Henry Sumner. *Ancient Law: Its Connection with the Early History of Society, and Its Relation to Modern Ideas.* New York: Dorset Press, 1986.

Mandeville, Bernard. *The Fable of the Bees: Or, Private Vices, Public Benefits. With An Essay on Charity and Charity Schools, and a Search Into the Nature of Society.* London: C. Bathurst, 1795.

Marx, Karl. *Capital: A Critique of Political Economy.* Moscow: Progress Publishers, 1971.

A Contribution to the Critique of Political Economy. Chicago: C. H. Kerr, 1913.

Maslen, Keith Ian Desmond. *Masters and Men.* London: Kegan Paul, 1975.

Matlak, Richard E. *Deep Distresses: William Wordsworth, John Wordsworth, Sir George Beaumont, 1800–1808.* University of Delaware Press, 2003.

Matthiessen, F. O. *The James Family: Including Selections from the Writings of Henry James, Senior, William, Henry and Alice James.* New York: Knopf, 1961.

McArthur, Judith N. "Demon Rum on the Boards: Temperance Melodrama and the Tradition of Antebellum Reform." *Journal of the Early Republic* 9, no. 4 (Winter 1989): 517–40.

McCarthy, William. *Anna Letitia Barbauld: Voice of the Enlightenment.* Baltimore: Johns Hopkins University Press, 2008.

"Mother of All Discourses: Anna Barbauld's Lessons for Children." In *Culturing the Child, 1690–1914: Essays in Memory of Mitzi Myers*, edited by Donelle Ruwe. Lanham, Md.: Children's Literature Association and Scarecrow Press, 2005.

McGurl, Mark. *The Novel Art: Elevations of American Fiction After Henry James.* Princeton University Press, 2001.

Meek, Ronald L. *Social Science and the Ignoble Savage.* Cambridge University Press, 1976.

Menger, Carl. *Principles of Economics: First, General Part.* Glencoe, Ill., Free Press, 1950.

Michals, Teresa. "Commerce and Character in Maria Edgeworth." *Nineteenth-Century Literature* 49, no. 1 (June 1994): 1–20.

"Experiments Before Breakfast." In *The Nineteenth-Century Child and Consumer Culture*, edited by Dennis Denisoff. Aldershot: Ashgate, 2008.

"Henry James and the Invention of Adulthood." *NOVEL: A Forum on Fiction* 44, no. 2 (July 1, 2011): 229–48.

"'Like a Spoiled Actress Off the Stage': Anti-Theatricality, Nature, and the Novel." *Studies in Eighteenth-Century Culture* 39, no. 1 (2010): 191–214.

Mill, John Stuart. *Autobiography.* London: Penguin Books, 1990.

Mintz, Steven. "Reflections on Age as a Category of Historical Analysis." *The Journal of the History of Childhood and Youth* 1, no. 1 (2008): 91–94.

Moon, Michael. "Review: Burn Me at the Stake Always." *The New England Quarterly* 78, no. 4 (2005): 631–42.

A Small Boy and Others: Imitation and Initiation in American Culture from Henry James to Andy Warhol. Duke University Press, 1998.

Moore, John Robert. "Defoe, Stevenson, and the Pirates." *ELH* 10, no. 1 (1943): 35–60.

Moretti, Franco. *The Novel.* Princeton University Press, 2006.

The Way of the World: The Bildungsroman in European Culture. New edn. London: Verso, 2000.

Moulton, Ian Frederick. *Before Pornography: Erotic Writing in Early Modern England.* Oxford University Press, 2000.

Muldrew, Craig. *The Economy of Obligation: The Culture of Credit and Social Relations in Early Modern England.* New York: St. Martin's Press, 1998.

Murray, John. "Books and Reading." *The Quarterly Review* 162, no. 324 (April 1886).

Myers, Mitzi. "The Erotics of Pedagogy: Historical Intervention, Literary Representation, the 'Gift of Education,' and the Agency of Children." *Children's Literature* 23 (1995): 1–30.

"Of Mice and Mothers : Mrs. Barbauld's 'New Walk' and Gendered Codes in Children's Literature." In *Feminine Principles and Women's Experience in American Composition and Rhetoric*, edited by Louise Wetherbee Phelps and Janet A. Emig. University of Pittsburgh Press, 1995.

"Moral Majorities?: Reconceiving the Literary World We Have Lost." *The Lion and the Unicorn* 19, no. 1 (1995): 134–44.

Nelson, Claudia. *Boys Will Be Girls: The Feminine Ethic and British Children's Fiction, 1857–1917.* New Brunswick, NJ: Rutgers University Press, 1991.

Precocious Children and Childish Adults: Age Inversion in Victorian Literature. Baltimore: Johns Hopkins University Press, 2012.
Nesbit, E. *The Story of the Treasure Seekers.* San Francisco, Calif.: Chronicle Books, 2006.
Neuburg, Victor E. *The Penny Histories: A Study of Chapbooks for Young Readers over Two Centuries.* New York: Harcourt, Brace & World, 1969.
Newbery, John. *A Little Pretty Pocket-book, Intended for the Instruction and Amusement of Little Master Tommy, and Pretty Miss Polly: With Two Letters from Jack the Giant-Killer; as Also a Ball and Pincushion; The Use of Which Will Infallibly Make Tommy a Good Boy, and Polly a Good Girl. The Tenth Edition. To Which Is Added, a Little Song-book, Being a New Attempt to Teach Children the Use of the English Alphabet, by Way of Diversion.* London, 1760.
Nieuwenhuys, Olga. "The Paradox of Child Labor and Anthropology." *Annual Review of Anthropology* 25 (January 1, 1996): 237–51.
Nodelman, Perry. *The Hidden Adult: Defining Children's Literature.* Baltimore: Johns Hopkins University Press, 2008.
Nord, Deborah Epstein. "The Making of Dickens Criticism." In *Contemporary Dickens*, edited by Eileen Gillooly and Deirdre David, 264–87. Columbus: Ohio State University Press, 2009.
Ohi, Kevin. "'The Author of "Beltraffio"': The Exquisite Boy and Henry James's Equivocal Aestheticism." *ELH* 72, no. 3 (2005): 747–67.
O'Malley, Andrew. *The Making of the Modern Child: Children's Literature and Childhood in the Late Eighteenth Century.* New York: Routledge, 2003.
"Poaching on Crusoe's Island: Popular Reading and Chapbook Editions of Robinson Crusoe." *Eighteenth-Century Life* 35, no. 2 (2011): 18–38.
Orwell, George. *Inside the Whale, and Other Essays.* Harmondsworth: Penguin, in association with Secker & Warburg, 1962.
Paris, Leslie. "Through the Looking Glass: Age, Stages, and Historical Analysis." *The Journal of the History of Childhood and Youth* 1, no. 1 (2008): 111.
Parkes, Adam. *Modernism and the Theater of Censorship.* New York: Oxford University Press, 1996.
Paulson, Ronald. "*The History of Little Goody Two-Shoes* as a Children's Book." In *Literary Theory and Criticism: Festschrift Presented to René Wellek in Honor of His Eightieth Birthday.* New York: P. Lang, 1984.
Pease, Allison. *Modernism, Mass Culture, and the Aesthetics of Obscenity.* Cambridge University Press, 2000.
Plotz, Judith A. *Romanticism and the Vocation of Childhood.* New York: Palgrave, 2001.
"Secret Garden II: Or, Lady Chatterley's Lover as Palimpsest." *Children's Literature Association Quarterly* 19, no. 1 (1994): 15–19.
Poovey, Mary. "Discriminating Reading." *Victorian Review* 31, no. 2 (2005): 10–35.
Post, David. "Review: Education and the Child Labor Paradox Today." *Comparative Education Review* 45, no. 1 (2001): 127–39.
Price, Leah. *The Anthology and the Rise of the Novel: From Richardson to George Eliot.* Cambridge University Press, 2003.

Quinlan, Michael, Margaret Gardner, and Peter Akers. "A Failure of Voluntarism: Shop Assistants and the Struggle to Restrict Trading Hours in the Colony of Victoria, 1850–85." *Labour History* no. 88 (2005): 165–82.

Rahn, Suzanne. "An Evolving Past: The Story of Historical Fiction and Nonfiction for Children." *The Lion and the Unicorn* 15, no. 1 (1991): 1–26.

Raleigh, John Henry. "What Scott Meant to the Victorians." *Victorian Studies* 7, no. 1 (1963): 7–34.

Rand, Frank Prentice. *Wordsworth's Mariner Brother*. Amherst, Mass.: Newell Press, 1966.

Randall, Don. *Kipling's Imperial Boy: Adolescence and Cultural Hybridity*. Houndmills, Basingstoke: Palgrave, 2000.

Redman, Deborah A. *The Rise of Political Economy as a Science*. Cambridge, Mass.: MIT Press, 1997.

Richardson, Alan. *Literature, Education, and Romanticism: Reading as Social Practice, 1780–1832*. Cambridge University Press, 1994.

Richardson, Samuel. *A Collection of the Moral and Instructive Sentiments, Maxims, Cautions, and Reflexions, Contained in the Histories of Pamela, Clarissa, and Sir Charles Grandison*. London: Printed for S. Richardson; and sold by C. Hitch and L. Hawes, 1755.

The History of Pamela, or, Virtue Rewarded. London: Printed for F. Newbery, 1769.

Pamela, or, Virtue Rewarded. Repr. with chronology and updated further reading. London: Penguin Books, 2003.

Pamela, or, Virtue Rewarded. Edited by Thomas Keymer and Alice Wakely. Oxford World's Classics. Oxford University Press, 2008.

The Richardson–Stinstra Correspondence, and Stinstra's Prefaces to Clarissa. Edited by William C. Slattery. Carbondale: Southern Illinois University Press, 1969.

Richardson, Samuel, and Anna Letitia Barbauld. *The Correspondence: Selected from the Original Manuscripts, Bequeated by Him to His Family to Which Are Prefixed a Biographical Account of That Author and Observations on His Writings: in Six Volumes*. London: Phillips, 1804.

Richardson, Samuel, and Marian S. Carson Collection (Library of Congress). *The History of Pamela, or, Virtue Rewarded: A Narrative Which Has Its Foundation in Truth, Adapted to Inculcate in the Minds of Both Sexes the Principles of Virtue and Religion*. First American from the last London edition. New York: W. C. Borradaile, 1830.

Robbins, Bruce. "The Butler Did It: On Agency in the Novel." *Representations* no. 6 (Spring 1984): 85–97.

The Servant's Hand: English Fiction From Below. New York: Columbia University Press, 1986.

Roberts, Julian. "The 1765 Edition of 'Goody Two-Shoes'." *The British Museum Quarterly* 29, no. 3/4 (Summer 1965): 67–70.

Robertson, Geoffrey. *Obscenity: An Account of Censorship Laws and Their Enforcement in England and Wales*. London: Weidenfeld & Nicolson, 1979.

Robertson, William. *The History of the Discovery and Settlement of America*. New York: Derby and Jackson, 1857.

Robins, Harry F. "How Smart Was Robinson Crusoe?" *PMLA* 67, no. 5 (1952): 782–89.

Robinson, Daniel N. *An Intellectual History of Psychology*. New York: Macmillan, 1981.

Robinson, Solon. *Hot Corn: Life Scenes in New York Illustrated. Including the Story of Little Katy, Madalina, the Rag-picker's Daughter, Wild Maggie, &c. With Original Designs, Engraved by N. Orr*. New York: De Witt and Davenport, Publishers, 1854.

Rodger, N. A. M. *The Command of the Ocean: A Naval History of Britain, 1649–1815*. New York: W. W. Norton, 2005.

Rogers, Pat, ed. *Daniel Defoe: The Critical Heritage*. London: Routledge, 1995.

Literature and Popular Culture in Eighteenth Century England. Brighton: Harvester Press, 1985.

Rogers, Philip. "Mr. Pickwick's Innocence." *Nineteenth-Century Fiction* 27, no. 1 (June 1972): 21–37.

Rolph, C. H., ed. *The Trial of Lady Chatterley: Regina V. Penguin Books Limited*. Baltimore: Penguin Books, 1961.

Rousseau, Jean-Jacques. *Emile: Or, On Education*. New York: Basic Books, 1979.

Ruwe, Donelle Rae, and Mitzi Myers. *Culturing the Child, 1690–1914: Essays in Memory of Mitzi Myers*. Lanham, Md: Scarecrow Press, 2005.

Sabor, Peter. "Richardson's Index to His Correspondence on Pamela." *Notes and Queries* 26 (1979): 556–60.

Sadleir, Michael. *XIX Century Fiction: A Bibliographical Record Based on His Own Collection, by Michael Sadleir. In 2 Volumes*... Cambridge University Press, 1951.

Safire, William. "Besotted With Potter." *New York Times*, 27 January 2000.

Salway, Lance. *A Peculiar Gift: Nineteenth Century Writings on Books for Children*. Harmondsworth: Kestrel Books, 1976.

Schmidgen, Wolfram. "Robinson Crusoe, Enumeration, and the Mercantile Fetish." *Eighteenth-Century Studies* 35, no. 1 (2001): 19–39.

Schochet, Gordon J. *The Authoritarian Family and Political Attitudes in Seventeenth-Century England: Patriarchalism in Political Thought*. New Brunswick, NJ: Transaction Books, 1988.

Schrero, Elliot M. "Exposure in *The Turn of the Screw*." *Modern Philology* 78, no. 3 (February 1981): 261–74.

Schwarzbach, F. S. *Dickens and the City*. London: Athlone Press, 1979.

Scott, Walter. *Ivanhoe*. Edited by Graham Tulloch. London: Penguin Books, 2000.

Redgauntlet. Edited by G. A. M. Wood and David Hewitt. London: Penguin Books, 2001.

Waverley. Edited by Andrew Hook. London: Penguin Books, 1981.

Waverley Novels: Waverley. Boston: S. H. Parker, 1830.

Sedgwick, Eve Kosofsky. *Epistemology of the Closet*. Berkeley: University of California Press, 1990.

Shelley, Mary Wollstonecraft. *Frankenstein, or, The Modern Prometheus*. Washington, DC: Orchises, 1988.

Shine, Muriel G. *The Fictional Children of Henry James*. Chapel Hill: University of North Carolina Press, 1969.

Shipton, Helen. "'Jane Eyre' and the Older Novel." *The Monthly Packet*, November 1896.

Shoemaker, Robert B. "The Decline of Public Insult in London 1660–1800." *Past and Present* 169 (2000): 97–131.

Showalter, Elaine. *Sexual Anarchy: Gender and Culture at the Fin de Siècle*. New York: Viking, 1990.

Shuger, Debora K. *Censorship and Cultural Sensibility: The Regulation of Language in Tudor-Stuart England*. Philadelphia: University of Pennsylvania Press, 2006.

Silver, Harold. *The Concept of Popular Education: A Study of Ideas and Social Movements in the Early Nineteenth Century*. Totowa, NJ: Rowman and Littlefield, 1977.

Smith, Adam. *An Inquiry into the Nature and Causes of the Wealth of Nations*. Oxford: Clarendon Press, 1976.

The Wealth of Nations. Bantam Classics, 2003.

Smol, Anna. "'Oh . . . Oh . . . Frodo!': Readings of Male Intimacy in The Lord of the Rings." *MFS: Modern Fiction Studies* 50, no. 4 (2004): 949–79.

Sommerville, C. John. *The Discovery of Childhood in Puritan England*. Athens: University of Georgia Press, 1992.

Southam, B. C. *Jane Austen and the Navy*. London: Hambledon and London, 2000.

Southey, Robert. *Robert Southey's Life of Nelson*. London: Longmans, Green, and Company, 1896.

Spacks, Patricia Ann Meyer. *The Adolescent Idea: Myths of Youth and the Adult Imagination*. New York: Basic Books, 1981.

Spearman, Diana. *The Novel and Society*. New York: Barnes & Noble, 1966.

Spufford, Margaret. *Small Books and Pleasant Histories: Popular Fiction and Its Readership in Seventeenth Century England*. Athens: University of Georgia Press, 1982.

St. Clair, William. *The Reading Nation in the Romantic Period*. Cambridge University Press, 2004.

Stark, Werner. *The Ideal Foundations of Economic Thought; Three Essays on the Philosophy of Economics*. London: K. Paul, Trench, Trubner & Co. Ltd, 1943.

Steedman, Carolyn. "A Boiling Copper and Some Arsenic: Servants, Childcare, and Class Consciousness in Late Eighteenth-Century England." *Critical Inquiry* 34, no. 1 (2007): 36–77.

"Servants and Their Relationship to the Unconscious." *Journal of British Studies* 42, no. 3 (July 2003): 316–50.

Strange Dislocations: Childhood and the Idea of Human Interiority, 1780–1930. Cambridge, Mass.: Harvard University Press, 1995.

Stein, Joel. "Adults Should Read Adult Books." *The New York Times – Room for Debate*, 28 March 2012. www.nytimes.com/roomfordebate/2012/03/28/the-power-of-young-adult-fiction/adults-should-read-adult-books.

Steinfeld, Robert J. *The Invention of Free Labor: The Employment Relation in English and American Law and Culture, 1350–1870*. Chapel Hill: University of North Carolina Press, 1991.

Stephen, Henry John, and William Gifford. "Review of Tales of Fashionable Life by Miss Edgeworth (Article 7)." *Quarterly Review* 2, no. 3 (1809): 135–44.

Stephen, Leslie. *Hours in a Library*. New edn., with additions. New York: Johnson Reprint Corp, 1968.

"Jonathan Edwards." *Fraser's Magazine* New Series 8, no. 47 (November 1873): 529–51.

Stevenson, Robert Louis. "My First Book – 'Treasure Island'." *McClure's Magazine* (September 1894): 283–94.

Stone, Lawrence. *Uncertain Unions: Marriage in England, 1660–1753*. Oxford University Press, 1992.

Straub, Kristina. *Domestic Affairs: Intimacy, Eroticism, and Violence Between Servants and Masters in Eighteenth-Century Britain*. Baltimore: Johns Hopkins University Press, 2009.

Sutherland, John. *The Life of Walter Scott: A Critical Biography*. Oxford: Wiley-Blackwell, 1998.

Tamarkin, Elisa. *Anglophilia: Deference, Devotion, and Antebellum America*. University of Chicago Press, 2008.

Tatar, Maria. "No More Adventures in Wonderland." *The New York Times*, 10 October 2011.

Tautphoeus, Jemima Montgomery, Baroness. *The Initials: A Novel*. New edition. London: R. Bentley, 1858.

Thackeray, William Makepeace. *The English Humourists of the Eighteenth Century and Charity and Humour*. Edited by Edgar F. Harden. Ann Arbor: University of Michigan Press, 2007.

The History of Little Goody Two-Shoes: Otherwise Called Mrs. Margery Two-Shoes. Third edition. London: Printed for J. Newbery, at the Bible and Sun in St. Paul's Church-Yard, 1766.

The Letters and Private Papers of William Makepeace Thackeray. Edited by Gordon Norton Ray. Cambridge, Mass.: Harvard University Press, 1945.

The Life of Pamela Being a Full and Particular Relation of the Birth and Advancement of That Fortunate and Beautiful Young Damsel. London: Printed for C. Whitefield, 1741.

The Paths of Virtue Delineated, or, The History in Miniature of the Celebrated Pamela, Clarissa Harlowe, and Sir Charles Grandison: Familiarised and Adapted to the Capacities of Youth. London: Printed for R. Baldwin, in Paternoster-Row, 1756.

The Paths of Virtue Delineated; or, The History in Miniature of the Celebrated Pamela, Clarissa Harlowe, and Sir Charles Grandison. London: Printed for and sold by the booksellers, 1768.

Thomas, Keith. *Age and Authority in Early Modern England.* Oxford University Press, 1976.

Trollope, Frances. *Life and Adventures of Michael Armstrong, the Factory Boy.* London: Henry Colburn, 1840.

Trumbach, Randolph. *The Rise of the Egalitarian Family: Aristocratic Kinship and Domestic Relations in Eighteenth-Century England.* New York: Academic Press, 1978.

Veeder, William R. and Susan M. Griffin, eds. *The Art of Criticism: Henry James on the Theory and Practice of Fiction.* University of Chicago Press, 1986.

Walkowitz, Judith R. *City of Dreadful Delight: Narratives of Sexual Danger in Late-Victorian London.* University of Chicago Press, 1992.

Warner, William Beatty. *Licensing Entertainment: The Elevation of Novel Reading in Britain, 1684–1750.* Berkeley: University of California Press, 1998.

Watt, Ian P. *Myths of Modern Individualism: Faust, Don Quixote, Don Juan, Robinson Crusoe.* Cambridge University Press, 1996.

The Rise of the Novel: Studies in Defoe, Richardson and Fielding. 2nd American edn. Berkeley: University of California Press, 2001.

"Serious Reflections on *The Rise of the Novel.*" *Novel: A Forum on Fiction* 1, no. 3 (1968): 205–18.

Webb, Beatrice, and Sidney Webb. "Report of the Royal Commission on the Poor Laws and Relief of Distress: Minority Report." In *Social Welfare in Transition: Selected English Documents, 1834–1909*, edited by Roy Lubove. University of Pittsburgh Press, 1966.

Weeks, Jeffrey. *Sex, Politics, and Society: The Regulation of Sexuality Since 1800.* 2nd edn. London: Longman, 1989.

Welsh, Alexander. "Waverley, Pickwick, and Don Quixote." *Nineteenth-Century Fiction* 22, no. 1 (June 1967): 19–30.

White, Michael. "Reading and Rewriting: The Production of an Economic Robinson Crusoe." *Southern Review* 15, no. 2 (1982): 115–42.

Williams, Carolyn D. "Pamela and the Case of the Slandered Duchess." *Studies in English Literature, 1500–1900* 29, no. 3 (1989): 515–33.

Wilson, Stuart. "Richardson's Pamela: An Interpretation." *PMLA* 88, no. 1 (1973): 79–91.

Winyard, Ben, and Holly Furneaux. "Introduction: Dickens, Science and the Victorian Literary Imagination." *19: Interdisciplinary Studies in the Long Nineteenth Century* no. 10 (2010).

Wood, Marcus. *Radical Satire and Print Culture, 1790–1822.* Oxford University Press, 1994.

Woolf, Virginia. *The Common Reader: First and Second Series.* New York: Harcourt, Brace, 1948.

To the Lighthouse. San Diego: Harcourt, Brace & Company, 1989.

Yahav-Brown, Amit. "Reasonableness and Domestic Fiction." *ELH* 73, no. 4 (2006): 805–30.

Yamey, Basil S. *Accounting in England and Scotland, 1543–1800*. New York: Garland, 1982.
Yeazell, Ruth Bernard. "Podsnappery, Sexuality, and the English Novel." *Critical Inquiry* 9, no. 2 (December 1982): 339–357.
Yolton, John W. "Locke's Man." *Journal of the History of Ideas* 62, no. 4 (2001): 665–83.

Index

Lightning Source UK Ltd.
Milton Keynes UK
UKHW021959201019
351986UK00013B/109/P

9 781107 649262